The Selected Poetry of Pier Paolo Pasolini

The Selected Poetry of Pier Paolo Pasolini

A BILINGUAL EDITION

Edited and Translated by Stephen Sartarelli
With a Foreword by James Ivory

THE UNIVERSITY OF CHICAGO PRESS   *Chicago and London*

The University of Chicago Press, Chicago 60637
The University of Chicago Press, Ltd., London
© 2014 by The University of Chicago
Italian poems © The Estate of Pier Paolo Pasolini, unless otherwise noted (see page 491)
All rights reserved. Published 2014.
Paperback edition 2015
Printed in the United States of America

33 32 31 30 29 28 27 26 25 24   3 4 5 6 7

ISBN-13: 978-0-226-64844-6 (cloth)
ISBN-13: 978-0-226-32544-6 (paper)
ISBN-13: 978-0-226-12116-1 (e-book)
DOI: https://doi.org/10.7208/chicago/9780226121161.001.0001

Published by arrangement with Garzanti S.r.l., Milano. Gruppo editoriale Mauri Spagnol.

The University of Chicago Press gratefully acknowledges the generous support of
James Ivory and the Merchant and Ivory Foundation toward the publication of this book.

All the images in this volume have been reproduced by permission of the Gabinetto
Scientifico Letterario G.P. Vieusseux, of Florence, Italy. No further reproduction or
duplication thereof can be made without the express written permission of the Gabinetto
Vieusseux.

Library of Congress Cataloging-in-Publication Data
Pasolini, Pier Paolo, 1922–1975, author.
The selected poetry of Pier Paolo Pasolini / edited and translated by Stephen Sartarelli ;
with a foreword by James Ivory. — Bilingual edition.
pages : illustrations ; cm
Includes bibliographical references and index.
ISBN 978-0-226-64844-6 (cloth : alk. paper) —
ISBN 978-0-226-12116-1 (e-book)
I. Ivory, James, writer of preface. II. Sartarelli, Stephen, 1954– translator, editor.
III. Pasolini, Pier Paolo, 1922–1975. Poems. Selections. English. IV. Pasolini, Pier Paolo,
1922–1975. Poems. Selections. Italian. V. Title.
PQ4835.A48A2 2014
851′.914—dc23

2014007478

♾ This paper meets the requirements of ANSI/NISO Z39.48-1992 (Permanence of Paper).

CONTENTS

*   *   *   *   *   *   *   *   *   *   *   *   *   *   *

I. Da *La meglio gioventù* (1954) / From *The Best of Youth* (The Friulian Poems)

II. Da *L'usignolo della Chiesa Cattolica* (1958) / From *The Nightingale of the Catholic Church*

III. Da *I diari* (1950) /
From *The Diaries*

IV. Da *Le ceneri di Gramsci* (1957) /
From *Gramsci's Ashes*

V. Da *La religione del mio tempo* (1961) /
From *The Religion of My Time*

VIII. *Last Poems*

*   *   *   *   *   *   *   *   *   *   *   *   *   *   *   *   *   *   *   *

ILLUSTRATIONS

FOREWORD

There may be people who ask why the Merchant and Ivory Foundation is interested in helping to publish these English translations of seventy-six poems by Pier Paolo Pasolini. Merchant Ivory and Pasolini, together in the same sentence, almost the same breath, in some kind of artistic or literary collaboration? Such a seeming misalliance could not be imagined. To put it simply, Pasolini's films were everything ours were not: "punchy," iconoclastic, coolly fashioned by a graceful and highly cultured Communist who was eventually expelled by the party because of his supposed immorality. Pasolini was a filmmaker from the rebellious Sixties who, on the one hand, was celebrated for fiercely shaking things up, for striking out at his countrymen's acceptance of the most ingrained Italian values via starkly brutal images of family life, caste and class, religion, commerce, art, literature, and even history itself being blown apart. And we, on the other hand, were a pair of filmmakers from the comfortable Eighties who gained our reputation by seeming to exalt in our films what Pasolini chose to obliterate in his, via optimistic stories about seeking connection, seeking completeness, seeking beauty even, in imperfect worlds from which there is little chance of escape and little chance of change for the better. It is true that in our own way, from time to time, we also came out against the order of things, but our slyer protests were far more decorous than Pasolini's could ever be.

Do I have delayed feelings of remorse because in my forties I did not feel compelled to watch Pasolini's films with the same avidity that I had for Fellini's more jovial and brightly hued ones? Now that I am in my eighties, am I making up for my passive neglect of this terrific artist by hastening to underwrite translations of his poetry, mostly unknown in the United States as well as unknown to me? There may be some truth in that; but what I like is the notion of our foundation's putting 7,544 lines of this auteur's finest poetry before a public that may not remember him now, probably has not seen any of his films in a commercial theater in decades, and may not have read a single word of Italian or English from his very large body of work.

The lives of twentieth-century auteur filmmakers can seem awfully brief. The unstable nature of both black-and-white and color film can, within four or five decades, doom their finest images, making them resemble so many faded flowers pressed between the pages of a book. The visually dynamic sequences that thousands of a director's fans watched in cinemas on both sides of the Atlantic and in Japan are now viewed on DVDs by film scholars via their computers. These DVDs are often labeled "restorations." The 35mm and 70mm prints that cast their thrilling images on immense theater screens are now mostly dust, or have been recycled. (In India, old films are sometimes made into women's bangles; when a film is a flop, it's said to have gone "to the bangle factory.") Prints that have survived are prone to "vinegar disease," are too fragile to project, and may be in quarantine. Color films go all pink. If, by chance, prints remain uncontaminated, they can only be projected at a film archive, where they are displayed to respectful viewers like relics and are handled by curators wearing white gloves. After viewing, they are returned to their ever-chilled underground chambers.

In 2012 the Museum of Modern Art in New York screened all of Pasolini's features, shorts, and unfinished films. Wounded and hospitalized original prints from their own and other archives were no doubt collected in order to create such an extensive program. A mostly aging audience, who had grown up on Pasolini's subtitled films, watched favorites like *Accatone*, *The Gospel According to Matthew*, *La ricotta*, *Teorema*, and *Hawks and Sparrows*. One misses the work of the old European auteur filmmakers, as one misses friends from one's youth who have died. (I miss François Truffaut.) You miss their tone of voice, their presence, their beauty, their uniqueness, even their sometimes tiresome preoccupations.

A poet of the cinema, Pasolini has left a trove of words on paper that can live on as the fast-deteriorating images he created on celluloid cannot. In the cinema, as in the other visual arts, great images are rarely produced alongside comparable and separate written images in the work of a single artist. There are few William Blakes and as yet no Michelangelos of the cinema. Almost entirely a visual medium, films must be seen and can be heard; their greatest words come only with perishable images. Of all the twentieth-century arts, cinema is probably the most ephemeral, on a par with choreography. Great choreography lives best through great dancers, but dancers are mortal. We can think of them as large, gorgeous, fluttering insects, doomed at the end of their season. So, too, are the last century's most renowned film directors, whose works began fading even before the end of their brilliant seasons.

Pier Paolo Pasolini was a true modernist working in an age of cinematic reinvention. How fortunate then that some of his greatest written images, gathered here, can live on, can gain strength with time, and can find a new audience in the new century. Merchant Ivory is proud to have helped this volume's subtle translator, Stephen Sartarelli—himself a poet—and the University of Chicago Press in bringing out a fascinating and charismatic director's saved other words, other images, other tones of voice—works that do not share the inevitable destiny of celluloid, cannot be contaminated, and need not be handled with white gloves.

James Ivory
New York
July 2013

ACKNOWLEDGMENTS

The idea for this book—or, more precisely, the will and the wherewithal to make this book a reality—dates from 2004. My wife, Sophie Hawkes, and I, in New York for a visit from our new home in France, were taking tea one afternoon on the Upper East Side of Manhattan at the apartment of our friends Ruth Prawer Jhabvala and her husband, Cyrus "Jhab" Jhabvala, in the company of James Ivory, the film director, also a personal friend. In the course of the conversation, jumping from one topic to another, we lighted upon the subject of Pier Paolo Pasolini's films. Long a fervent admirer of Pasolini's cinematic efforts, I asked the present company whether they knew that he had also been a leading poet of his age, and the answer was a unanimous no. I commented that this response was not unusual, and that despite the existence of three slim bilingual editions of Pasolini's verse in English, his role as a prolific, influential Italian poet—indeed, the simple fact that he was a poet first and foremost—was unknown to a great many otherwise cultured readers of English.

I attributed this general unawareness in part to the fact that the existing translations of Pasolini's vast poetic output were limited in scope and usually not integrated into our common portrait of the man, and I added that I had long thought that a more thorough presentation of Pasolini's verse was needed in English. Without missing a beat, Mr. Ivory, in that thoughtful, understated way of his, immediately said: "I think that would be a good project for the foundation." He was referring, of course, to the Merchant and Ivory Foundation, a not-for-profit endowment that since 1991 has provided grants for visual artists and aspiring young filmmakers, and whose first and most famous project was the restoration, in collaboration with the Academy of Motion Picture Arts and Sciences, of the films of the great Indian cineast Satyajit Ray. He needed only to ask Ismail Merchant whether he liked the idea, after which I could get on with the business of submitting a proposal to the foundation and finding a publisher.

Needless to say, it all passed muster, and so my first and most heartfelt thanks go to James Ivory, the late Ismail Merchant, and the supporters of their foundation, without whose generous assistance and encouragement this project would never have got off the ground. For their incalculable moral support, I extend my gratitude as well to the members and players of the vibrant Merchant and Ivory "family," including the late Ruth Prawer Jhabvala, "Jhab" Jhabvala, the late Richard Robbins, Michael Schell, John Allen, Seth Rubin, and Marilyn Reynolds, among many others.

For her invaluable philological, technical, and legal assistance and her generosity and warmth, I could never overstate my indebtedness and gratitude to Graziella Chiarcossi, the first cousin of Pier Paolo Pasolini and executor of his literary and artistic estate. Without her firm confidence in me during the many delays in this project, and her always ready availability, I daresay I might never have seen things through to the end.

And for initially putting me in touch with Ms. Chiarcossi and engaging me in lively discussion about Pasolini, I thank French author, publisher, translator, and Pasolinian scholar René de Ceccaty.

For his critical insights, encouragement, and occasional research assistance, I am, as always, grateful to my very good friend Thomas Epstein of Boston College, editor-in-chief of the online journal *New Arcadia Review*, which published my translation of Pasolini's poem "Persecution" (p. 316 in this volume), in their volume 4 (2011) edition.

For their prompt assistance in making available to me the images featured in this book, I thank Gloria Manghetti and Ilaria Spadolini of the Archivio Bonsanti of the Gabinetto Vieusseux of Florence—curators, among other things, of the Pasolini Archive of paintings, drawings, photographs, and autograph manuscripts by the poet.

For his indispensible help in interpreting some of the thornier passages of Pasolini's verse, I thank my old friend Nicola Greco, president of RivaReno Gelati and probably the most cultured ice cream executive in Italy. For similar assistance in the comprehension of references, passages, and other elusive aspects of these poems, I thank the indispensable Walter Siti, prolific editor, scholar and author; Rosanna Camerlingo of the Università di Perugia, Italy; Armando Maggi of the University of Chicago; and my cousin Barbara Lazotti, a retired soprano and presently a *maestra di canto* and musicologist at the Conservatorio di Frosinone, Italy.

To filmmaker and screenwriter Chris Terrio go my thanks for lending his voice to some of these poems at a public reading in late November 2007 at the Italian Cultural Institute of New York, part of a Pasolini festival in New York entitled "Poet of Ashes," which I was unable to attend.

I likewise thank Jytte Jensen, curator of the Department of Film at the Museum of Modern Art, New York, as well as Cecilia Cormanni of the Istituto Luce Cinecettà, for featuring many of these translations in "Recital: An Evening Dedicated to Pier Paolo Pasolini the Poet," on December 14, 2012, as part of the recent film exhibition retrospective of Pasolini held at MOMA from December 13, 2012, to January 5, 2013.

For putting me in touch with Randolph Petilos and the University of Chicago Press at the very start of this project, I thank Lawrence Venuti of Temple University.

For their editorial assistance and infinite patience in the seemingly endless phases of this project, I am indebted and grateful to Randolph Petilos, Renaldo Migaldi, and their colleagues at the University of Chicago Press.

And for her tireless support, help, and love over the many years and vicissitudes of this undertaking, I thank my dear wife, Sophie Hawkes, always the first reader, editor, and critic of anything I write or translate.

Sections I and IV of my translation of "Gramsci's Ashes" (this volume, pp. 166 and 174, respectively) were published in *The FSG Book of Twentieth-Century Italian Poetry* (2012), edited by Geoffrey Brock, to whom I express due thanks.

Stephen Sartarelli
St.-Martial d'Albarède
France
April 2013

El nini muart

Sere imbarlumide, 'tel fosàl
a cres l'aghe, 'na femine plene
a ciamine 'tel ciamp.

Iò ti ricuàrdi, Narcìs, tu ~~aveni~~ vevis el colôr
de le sère, ~~quant~~ les ciampànis
a sùnin a muàrt.

PIER PAOLO PASOLINI:
A LIFE IN POETRY

There are [certain] destinies in literary history, true damnations—men who wear the word *doom* written in mysterious characters in the sinuous furrows of their brows. The blind Angel of atonement has seized hold of them and thrashes them with all his might for the edification of others. Never mind that all their lives they display their talents, virtues, and grace; Society reserves a special anathema for them and accuses them of the very infirmities its persecution has caused them. [. . .] Is there thus a diabolical Providence that prepares unhappiness from the cradle—that, with *premeditation*, hurls spiritual, angelic natures into hostile circumstances like martyrs into arenas? Are there thus *sacred* souls that are destined for the altar, condemned to march to death and glory through their own ruins? · CHARLES BAUDELAIRE, "Edgar Poe, His Life, and Works"

[The new poet] sings of ideas, systems of knowledge, and State theories just as his predecessors sang of nightingales and roses. · OSIP MANDELSTAM, "The Word and Culture"[1]

We have lost above all a poet, and there aren't very many poets in the world—only three or four are born every century! [. . .] When this century is over, Pasolini will be one of the very few, as a poet, who will matter. The poet should be sacred! · ALBERTO MORAVIA, funeral oration for Pier Paolo Pasolini, November 5, 1975

*   *

1. Quoted from the 1921 essay "The Word and Culture," in Osip Mandelstam, *The Complete Critical Prose*, ed. J. G. Harris, trans. J. G. Harris and Constance Link (Ann Arbor: Ardis, 1997), 72. Cited in Gianni d'Elia, *L'eresia di Pasolini* (Milan: Effigie, 2005), 110.

I

"Few writers have been as poorly understood as Pasolini," Alberto Mora-
via wrote in a lecture given shortly after the poet's violent, untimely death.
He was speaking above all of Italian writers, of course, but one could ex-
tend the statement universally. The reasons for such misunderstanding are
manifold. Not least among them is the extreme complexity of this artist
and intellectual who sought to express himself in as many mediums as pos-
sible, from poetry, fiction, and literary and social commentary to various
genres of cinema and even painting. In the English-speaking world, Paso-
lini is known primarily as a filmmaker, secondarily as an essayist—a form
at which he excelled—and hardly at all as a poet. This is, at least in part,
quite understandable, given that the language of cinema is transnational
and has no inherent grammar—the primary reason Pasolini chose to em-
ploy it[2]—and that poetry, unlike prose, has difficulty fully surviving trans-
lation. And, as we all know, poetry, with its general lack of commercial
potential, has become one of the most marginalized of the arts.

   Yet at no time during his intense, multifaceted career was there any
question in Pasolini's own mind as to the wellspring that fed all his cre-
ative efforts: lyric poetry, his first form of artistic expression and the sole
medium he never really ceased using at any stage of his life, not even dur-
ing the relative dry spell that immediately followed the 1964 publication of
Poesia in forma di rosa, when his fame as a filmmaker began to make increas-
ing demands on his time and energy.[3] Of course, any assessment of the
entire oeuvre of Pier Paolo Pasolini must take into account the full range
of mediums to which he applied his ever inquisitive spirit, and clearly he
must, in the end, be judged aesthetically and intellectually on the global re-

2. He called cinema the "written language of reality," and therefore universal.
3. Pasolini's own claims to have "stopped writing poetry" during this period must
be taken with a grain of salt. While his rate of publication of verse certainly de-
creased and his papers for this period show a considerably diminished rate of
poetic production for a man who was an extraordinarily prolific writer, he never-
theless continued to write poetry, especially in the form of plays in verse. In "To
the New Reader," the introduction to his self-edited 1970 Garzanti volume of
selected poems, he even says, contradicting earlier claims, that "only for a year or
two did I fall completely silent as a 'poet in verse' (while still writing things that re-
mained unpublished and unfinished)." On the other hand, he did for the most part
stop writing fiction, or new fiction, after he began making films, as for a time this
seemed to fulfill his need to express himself in a narrative mode—but only until he
began work on the most ambitious work of fiction of his career, the novel *Petrolio*,
left unfinished at the time of his death.

sult, since the singularity and importance of his artistry lies largely in the protean, multimedial quality of his vision. But as Fernando Bandini states in his introduction to the definitive two-volume, nearly three-thousand-page edition of the complete poetry (*Tutte le poesie*, "I Meridiani" Mondadori, 2003), "The one thing that remains always the same is the manner in which, in theory and in practice, Pasolini conceives of poetry writing as the privileged form of writing, the locus of the absolute, where every assertion becomes truth and the personal can present itself as universal. All his other modes of writing, including film, must be traced back to this perennial impulse to poetry."[4]

A brief glance at some of Pasolini's work outside the strictly defined genre of lyric poetry immediately confirms this assertion. A great majority of the critical prose of the first half of his professional career is about poetry, past and present. His first published novel, *Ragazzi di vita* (1955), translated as *The Ragazzi*, is episodic and rhapsodic in form—that is, predominantly nonnarrative and essentially structured around the sonorities of the Roman dialect. The second Roman novel (1959), *Una vita violenta* (A Violent Life)—itself centered around a well-defined plot—he began to transcribe into verse after publication. *Teorema*, the 1968 novel published simultaneously with the eponymous film, contains many passages in verse. Nearly all of his theater is written in verse. He considered *Petrolio*, the vast, transgeneric mythopolitical novel left unfinished at the time of his death, a "poem in prose." His 1975 collection of sociocultural essays, *Lutheran Letters*, ends with a "codicil in verse"—sonnets, to be precise. One could almost say his creative impulse arises entirely from what Mallarmé, speaking of Victor Hugo, called the "majestic idea . . . that the form called 'verse' is simply literature itself."[5]

Of course, Pasolini's verse goes well beyond "literature," strictly speaking. Many of his film treatments, for example, are written in free verse, and some, like *Medea*, inspired ancillary poems. He even wrote, though never quite finished, a screenplay in verse, entitled *Bestemmia* (Blasphemy), effectively inventing a new genre—which he also did in making *La Rabbia* (Rage), a fifty-minute synthesis of newsreel footage of world events set to a background of music and his own poetry, much of it written for the

4. F. Bandini, "Il 'Sogno di una cosa' chiamata poesia," introductory essay to P. P. Pasolini, *Tutte le poesie*, vol. I, ed. W. Siti, xv. All translations of quoted Italian and French texts are my own unless otherwise indicated.
5. Mallarmé, "Crise de vers" (1886–96), in *Igitur.Divagations.Un coup de dès* (Paris: Gallimard, 1976, p. 240); also in *Oeuvres complètes* (Paris: Gallimard, Bibliothèque de la Pléiade, 1945, p. 361).

occasion.[6] In a famous essay of the same name, he defined what he called a "cinema of poetry," and he later claimed that he shot all his films, from *The Gospel According to Matthew* to *Hawks and Sparrows, Oedipus Rex, Teorema, Pigsty,* and *Medea,* "as a poet"—adding, in a footnote, that he meant the term "in a strictly 'technical' sense."[7] That is, he might well be a "poetic" filmmaker, but he was also, quite literally, a poet who happened to make films.

Even at his moment of greatest notoriety in world cinema, then, he was keen to reassert the centrality of poetry to his entire artistic project. But, as is often the case with Pasolini, the question of artistic expression is complex and paradoxical. Within the gesture of expression lies, at once, the lyric impulse and the urge to reach beyond it, into reality. His early dialect poetry, for example, which features a solitary, inward lyricism, was complemented by the founding of a school to teach poetry and the Friulian dialect. The impulse to write embodied a desire to be part of the world, but also to change that world, even as it changed him. Later in his career, his pedagogical vocation would find another outlet in editorial journalism, even as he continued to plumb the depths of his soul in highly personal poetry and increasingly mythological, esoteric films. In all his work, the outward, social gesture is inseparable from the inward-looking, compulsive lyric urge. It is, so to speak, its other side.

For his contemporary and fellow poet, Andrea Zanzotto, Pasolini's was an "idea of poetry as alarming difference, excess, emergency, yet [. . .] always compelled, no matter the cost, to be the center of society, indeed the culmination of a reinstatement of the social."[8] Pasolini took Rimbaud's and the Surrealists' exhortation to *changer la vie* quite literally, bringing his work and his person physically to bear on the reality around him. This allowed him, among other things, to be at once the most narcissistic of poets and yet the most willing of his generation to give voice to the *demos*—to

6. See endnote to the poem "Marilyn," page 472 below.

7. He continues: "It cannot be denied that *a certain way of feeling something* occurs *identically* when faced with some of my lines of poetry and some of my camera shots." Quoted from "Al lettore nuovo" (To the New Reader), Pasolini's preface to the self-selected collection of his own poems, *Poesie* (Milan: Garzanti, 1970). An English translation of the essay is available in the appendix to N. MacAfee and L. Martinengo's translation, *Selected Poems* (New York: Random House, 1982; reprinted, New York: Farrar, Straus & Giroux, 1996).

8. "Pasolini poeta," a 1980 essay included in Andrea Zanzotto's *Aure e disincanti del Novecento letterario* (Milan: Mondadori, 1994). The essay was also published as a postface to *Poesie e pagine ritrovate,* ed. A. Zanzotto and N. Naldini, (Rome: Lato Side editori, 1980), 205.

become, at least for a while, a "civic" poet (*poeta civile*, as Moravia called him), perhaps the last in an Italian tradition stretching all the way back to Dante and Petrarch, even as his "public spirit" was entirely opposed to the established order, including that of the official opposition.

What most distinguishes Pasolini in this regard, however, is that he takes the poet's "public" role so far as to consider acts themselves as part of the poetic oeuvre. In the long, unfinished autobiographical poem, *Poeta delle ceneri* ("Poet of Ashes"), from 1966,[9] he writes:

> . . . there is no poetry other than real action
> (you tremble only when you find it
> in verse, or in pages of prose,
> when the evocation is perfect).

Ideally, then, the life and the poetry inseparably merge. But just as life itself, and one's actions within it, are thus a form of poetry, conversely, and more importantly, poetry is a form of action within life. For this reason it would be a mistake to liken Pasolini's poetic philosophy to certain apparently similar positions of contemporary intellectual vanguards such as the International Situationists, some of whom believed that intervention into social reality was the *only* valid creative act possible in our times. For Pasolini's "activism" is inspired as much by a deep humanistic background — ranging from classical antiquity and the Bible to Freud and Marx by way of the Italian Middle Ages, the Renaissance, and Mannerism, Romanticism, and Symbolism — as it is by an equally thorough acquaintance with the modern and postwar avant-gardes in the arts. His notion of the poet's need to impinge upon reality owes as much to the examples of Dante, and even Christ, as it does to Dada, Surrealism, Marxism, or Neorealism.

Indeed, Pasolini was — in Zanzotto's words — a poet "in the most awkward, 'untimely,' even obsolete meaning of the term." In him "all the different features the poet had managed to assume across the ages — as active, even oppositional consciousness fully within the tradition/institution, and witness to lyric separateness as the optimal, maximal elevation (regression) to a shamanistic if not downright pontifical (or, less meaningfully, counterpontifical) role — became superimposed [. . .] canceling each other out." He felt at once a need "to restore the full significance of 'the figure of the poet' and an ever-renewed awareness of its irrelevance"[10] in the contemporary cultural and historical context.

9. In other words, from the period when Pasolini had supposedly "stopped" writing poetry.
10. Zanzotto, *Aure e disincanti*, 203.

The prior generation of Italian poets, or at least the specific formation still dominant when Pasolini came of age, known broadly under the term "Hermeticism," had withdrawn into a fully private, purely "poetic" language in their forcibly silent opposition to Fascist society and culture. For Pasolini, the expressive freedom afforded by such withdrawal was only "illusory," as it restricted the poet's aesthetic options and had no immediate bearing on reality. The experience of twenty years of Fascism, and the horrors of the war that ensued, demanded more direct forms of representing and communicating reality. Such was the impetus that, among other things, gave rise to the great Neorealist school of Italian literature and cinema from the last years of World War II through the 1950s. But even Neorealism was not quite sufficient for Pasolini. For him, in a curious anticipation of much later postmodern trends, *no* option, stylistic, formal, or rhetorical, could be excluded a priori—not even the much-maligned "eloquence" whose "neck" Eugenio Montale, unofficial *chef d'école* of the Hermetics, had said must be "wrung." The poet *must* be relevant to society, even if this meant a return to closed forms or to rhetorical flourish, a descent into the political arena, or the adoption of mediums other than poetry and prose.

Thus, despite its great novelty within the immediate cultural context, and despite his later penchant for radical formal experiment, Pasolini's poetry and his creative project in general were as *recuperative* as they were innovative and social. There is a direct line of continuity, for example, between his first idea for a literary magazine founded with university friends Francesco Leonetti, Roberto Roversi, and Luciano Serra, to be called *Eredi* (Heirs),[11] which was to feature what he called *arcaismo eredistico* (traditionalist archaism), and his revival in cinema, much later, of such ancient mythological subjects as *Oedipus Rex* and *Medea* as allegories of modern conditions. Even Pasolini's most formally radical poems, such as "A Desperate Vitality," contain a characteristic appeal to tradition.

But Pasolini's relationship to institution and tradition always had a double edge. From the start he excelled at playing by the rules while simultaneously breaking them. He had an uncanny ability to use existing institutions—public, private, literary, stylistic, and so on—to successful ends while undermining them from within and without. He called this his "end-

11. The magazine was never realized under this name, but some fifteen years later the same group of poets founded *Officina*, which had similar goals and quickly became an influential forum for contemporary writing and criticism.

less capacity for obedience" and "endless capacity for rebellion."[12] It was also what he called, taking his cue from art historian Roberto Longhi, his "mannerism." Given this penchant, no system of knowledge, no artistic form or style, no medium could be excluded from the sphere of his cognition and use. He would use Christian imagery to explore his homosexuality, Dantean form to mull the contradictions of the socialist ideal, realism to embody myth. Contradiction, paradox, oxymoron — or *syneciosis*, a favorite term of his — were his stock in trade. No other Italian poet of his generation combined so ferocious a will to preserve tradition with so keen an imperative to experimentation; no other writer or artist of his time so assiduously laid claim to the dictums of high art while so flagrantly flouting the dictates of good form and common sense; and certainly none was able to do so in so many different mediums, and in a manner so personal and at the same time so public.

Little wonder, then, that much of the general public — whom he had yet managed to reach, in spite of everything, even before venturing into film — and more than a few literati tended to misunderstand him. Was he a poet or a filmmaker? Traditional formalist or radical experimentalist? Marxist or Catholic? Elitist aesthete or populist anarchist? Public figure or exhibitionist? Artist or one-man political movement? Pasolini himself would probably say he was all of the above, however unlikely that might seem in this age of hyperspecialization. His manner of knowledge (*conoscere*), he said, was "not dialectical"; it lay "in the eternal coexistence of opposites."[13]

Only in poetry, and not in rational discourse, can such things stand side by side. In this respect, all of Pasolini's creations, in all mediums — including "rationalist" social criticism — are, as Bandini implies, ramifications of his poetry. Like the shaky, hand-held camera in the "cinema of poetry," they are all expressions of a lyric subjectivity.[14] By "broadening the area of poetry beyond its specific connection to the linguistic event, [Pasolini] aimed [. . .] at a 'total poetry,' [. . .] a transcendence of the consolidated partitions of the field of art into a higher unity, a 'suprapoetic' unity"

12. Quoted from "A Desperate Vitality" (see page 353 below).
13. "Pasolini recensisce Pasolini," originally published in the daily *Il Giorno*, June 3, 1971; now in P. P. Pasolini, *Saggi sulla letteratura e sull'arte*, vol. II, ed. W. Siti and S. De Laude (Milan: Mondadori, 1999), 2575–80.
14. Cf. "Il 'cinema di poesia,'" in P. P. Pasolini, *Saggi sulla letteratura e sull'arte*, vol. I, ed. W. Siti and S. De Laude (Milan: "Meridiani" Mondadori, 1999), 1461. The essay was originally published in *Marcatré* nos. 19-20-21-22 (quadruple issue), April 1966, then included in *Empirismo eretico* (Milan: Garzanti, 1972).

(Zanzotto). But any such creation, for Pasolini, any such poetry, was valid *only* if true to life.

Of Pasolini's enigmatic 1969 film, *Teorema*—in which a stranger comes into an upper middle-class home and spiritually transforms every member of the household by having sexual relations with them—the great Jean Renoir wrote: "In every image, in every frame, one feels the agitation Pasolini brings to the screen by involving the spectator's conscience. What scandalizes people is not the obscenity, of which there is none. The scandal lies in the sincerity."[15] Pasolini brought this same sincerity to his every work, his every act. It is this consistency, this faithfulness to life—to his life and to the world around him—that makes his oeuvre, regardless of medium, all of a piece, all part of the poetry at its heart.

> . . . nothing is worth as much as life.
> That's why I want only to live
> even while being a poet
> because life can express itself alone, too, with itself.
> I would like to express myself through examples.
> To throw my body into the struggle.
> —from "Poet of Ashes"

II

Born in 1922, the year Mussolini and the Fascists came to power, Pasolini discovered his poetic vocation in early childhood, at the age of seven.

Pasolini's mother, Susanna, had long cherished a desire to write poetry, and it was she who first prompted the young Pier Paolo to write, "mysteriously" presenting him one day with a sonnet expressing her love for her son. "The following day," writes Pasolini, "I wrote my first lines of verse." By age thirteen Pasolini was already demonstrating the tremendous stores of energy that would stoke his prolific output in adulthood, writing "whole collections of verse," including "epic." And while Pasolini's father, Carlo Alberto, a career military man, was not averse to his son's precocious literary vocation (and much later even served as his secretary), his mother always remained his prime source of encouragement—even, sometimes, his muse. Indeed, the poems to his mother stand as some of the finest and most moving in his entire oeuvre.

Pasolini's mother also indirectly inspired the choice of language for

15. Quoted in N. Naldini, *Pasolini, Una vita* (Turin: Einaudi, 1989), 325. All subsequent quotes from this text will be abbreviated to Naldini, *VP*, and page number.

his first poems of literary significance. It was during the family's summer vacations to her native village of Casarsa della Delizia in the northeastern Italian province of Friuli (usually without Carlo Alberto, away on military assignments) that Pier Paolo learned the dialect he would later privilege as the primary vehicle of his literary expression in late adolescence and early adulthood. Listening to conversations among his mother's family members at their ancestral farmhouse or among local peasants, the adolescent Pasolini was struck by the language's freshness and spontaneity, qualities that persuaded him to choose it as a vehicle for poetry.

In a later essay, Pasolini described the epiphany that inspired his adoption of Friulian as a vehicle of expression:

> One summer morning in 1941 I was on the wooden balcony of my mother's house. [. . .] [I] was either drawing (with green ink or a little ochre tube of oil paint on cellophane) or writing verse, when I heard the sound of the word *rosada*.
>
> It was Livio, the son of the neighbors from across the road, the Socolari, who had spoken. [. . .] Uttered on that sunlit morning, the word *rosada* was but one expressive moment of the boy's lively speech.
>
> Certainly that word, the way it is used in the part of Friuli that extends on this side of the Tagliamento, *had never been written down*. It had always been only a *sound*.
>
> Whatever I may have been doing that morning—sketching or writing—I immediately stopped. . . . And I immediately wrote some lines of verse, in the Friulian speech of the right bank of the Tagliamento, which until that moment had only been a *combination of sounds*: I began, before anything else, by making the word *rosada* graphic."[16]

Pasolini, of course, had been hearing Friulian all his life, above all the Friulian spoken in Susanna's family. But that Friulian was, so to speak, the

16. Pasolini, "Dal laboratorio," in *Empirismo eretico* (1972), now in *Saggi sulla letteratura e sull'arte*, vol. I, 1317–18. *Rosada* means "dew"; in standard Italian the word would be *rugiada*. Pasolini's cousin, the writer Nico Naldini, in his excellent sixty-five-page fine-print *Cronologia* accompanying the various "Meridiani" volumes of Pasolini's collected writings, gives a somewhat more prosaic description of Pier Paolo's discovery of Friulian as a vehicle for poetry: "Despite the fact that a page of *Empirismo eretico* attributes the use of Friulian to a sort of linguistic fulmination, the path that brought [Pasolini to the dialect] was more complex and based on a series of attempts and experiments, even though these were carried out over a very brief space of time." (Naldini, *Cronologia*, in *Tutte le poesie*, vol. II, ed. W. Siti, lxii; all subsequent references to this text will be abbreviated as Naldini, *Crono*, and page number.)

more "urbane" version, which contained elements of the "nobler" Venetian dialect and whose center was the provincial capital of Udine. And this Friulian had in fact had some literary antecedents, however minor. The dialect that struck Pasolini as so virginal was the one spoken *di cà da l'aga*—as he said, "on this side of the water," the Tagliamento torrent mentioned above. This was the tongue spoken by the simple peasants who had so charmed him in adolescence and who seemed to be living the same agrarian life they had been doing for centuries. The decision to write in this language, he later wrote, was a "sort of mystical act of love"[17]—for his mother, but also, and perhaps above all, for an apparently timeless world untainted by the corruptions of modern society.

Yet it was also, by its very nature, an act of rebellion—first and foremost against his father, who, as a descendant of the fallen noble line of the Pasolini dell'Onda of Ravenna, scorned the use of any dialect over the elegance of Tuscan Italian, in which the nation's great classics had been written. The Friulian of Casarsa was "the dialect of a small world / he could not help but disdain."[18] Secondly, writing in dialect was an act of open revolt against the Fascist regime, which frowned upon its use when it did not actually suppress it. Dialect, for example, was officially forbidden in the armed forces—if unofficially tolerated, in the Italian fashion, since many of the simpler folk couldn't speak Italian. It was thus no accident that the first review of Pasolini's first chapbook of poems—*Poesie a Casarsa*, published in 1942 by the Libreria Antiquaria Mario Landa at the poet's own expense—appeared outside of Italy, in the *Corriere di Lugano* in the Ticino canton of Switzerland, penned by none other than the foremost Italian literary philologist of the twentieth century, Gianfranco Contini, who had a passion for dialects. This was to be, the poet later wrote, "the greatest literary joy of my life."[19]

Pasolini was convinced that the Friulian *di cà da l'aga*, like Catalan and Occitan was a minor Romance language in its own right which, for historical reasons—mostly Venetian and Italian domination—had never found literary expression. He, along with his colleagues at the *Academiuta di lenga furlana*—"Little Academy of the Friulian Language" founded by Pasolini himself in 1945—would be the first to fulfill this task.

We too are working, with our little language, towards our own little eternity; and, at least for a few people, we should like to see the sounds

17. Naldini, VP, 31.
18. From "Poeta delle ceneri," *Tutte le poesie*, vol. II, ed. W. Siti, 1261–88.
19. Ibid.

of certain nouns so humbly specific (*mari, país, çamp . . .*) reassigned those universal, absolute images that man, from his native conditions and throughout his unresolved history, has never lost sight of.[20]

Indeed, in this founding statement of the Academiuta, Pasolini goes so far as to reapply, on a humbler level, the very arguments made by Dante in *De vulgari eloquentia* to justify the use of the Italian (specifically Tuscan) vernacular as a viable literary vehicle alternative to Latin. But unlike Dante, who had at least one generation of poets before him, the *stilnovisti*,[21] to cite as proof of his argument, Pasolini and his cohorts were starting ex nihilo, like the first poets to set down an ancient oral tradition. Looking back on that time, Pasolini would later write:

> Taken as it is, the Friulian of Casarsa quietly lent itself to being transmuted into a poetic language, utterly uprooted from the start from any custom of writing in dialect out of linguistic or folkloric interest [. . .] . For me it was simply a very ancient language that was nevertheless entirely virgin, where words such as *còur, fueja, blanc* could evoke primordial imagery.[22]

But Pasolini did not look to preceding models of dialect poetry, either in Udinese Friulian or in other Italian dialects, for guidance in the sort of verse he chose to write. Despite his evocations of the agrarian world, Pasolini was not interested in writing "folk" poetry. In fact, his formal and stylistic approach to dialect poetry sprang from a very broad, erudite sphere of influence. This included, as mentioned, his university studies in Romance philology, specifically the troubadours — indeed, more than a few of his Friulian compositions are based in form on troubadour models[23] — and, perhaps more importantly, at least as far as his approach to language and style was concerned, his already broad background of reading in Symbolist, post-Symbolist, modernist (in all its forms) and Italian "Hermetic" poetry.

The Friulian of Pasolini's poetry is, by the poet's own admission, an artificial language, at least in its first, seminal phase, which lasted roughly until 1947. In a 1945 letter to the poet Franco De Gironcoli, from nearby Gorizia, Pasolini even goes so far as to say:

20. Quoted in Giacomo Jori, *Pasolini* (Turin: Einaudi, 2001), 12.
21. That is, Guido Cavalcanti, Guido Guinizzelli, et al., not to mention the prior generation of Guittone d'Arezzo, to whom the *stilnovisti* were reacting.
22. Quoted in Jori, *Pasolini*, 24.
23. See endnotes to "Dansa di Narcis," "Pastorela di Narcis," "Il dì de la mi muàrt," and "Conzeit," p. 452 below.

I think it is of an inferior order of consideration to relate us to the *félibrige*, the *trobar clus*, or the *laudi* of Jacopone; just as it is of inferior concern to consider Friulian as some sort of Greek or Christian dialect close to the moment when Adam uttered his first words [. . .]. For me, at this point, writing in Friulian is the means I have found to capture what the Symbolists and musicians of the nineteenth century (and our own Pascoli as well, however poorly) tried so hard to find: namely, an "infinite melody" . . .[24]

Of course, Pasolini *did* look to the *trobar* and the *laudi* in his poetry,[25] and founded his own little "felibrist" movement. But these were only means to an end, not ends in themselves. Like Pound with the troubadours, Cavalcanti, and the Chinese, Pasolini used his models—Occitan, early Italian, late Romantic—as well as the dialect to forge something new, something that did not exist before him. In its beauty and strangeness, Friulian proved the ideal vehicle for a "pure poetry," the elusive goal of Symbolists and post-Symbolists up to and including the Italian Hermetics.

Something like a mystical passion [. . .] drove me to master this ancient peasant language [. . .] . I was writing my first Friulian poems when Hermeticism, whose master was Ungaretti, was in full vogue. [. . .] All the Hermetic poets lived for the idea that the language of poetry should be an absolute language.[26]

Pasolini had found his "absolute language"; but the aesthetic idyll was not to last, for a variety of reasons. For one thing, the better he got to know the world that spoke the language he had borrowed, the more authentic, less invented, his use of Friulian became. This was a positive development insofar as it spurred his subsequent evolution, and it also brought him closer to the Neorealist currents then in embryo in the rest of the country. "As soon as I began to use [the dialect]," he wrote, "I realized I had touched upon something alive and real, and it reacted like a boomerang. It was through the use of Friulian that I was able to understand the real peasant world a little."[27] And as the language became more based in reality, so did his subject matter.

Not long after the initial, "Symbolist" phase of dialect composition, Pasolini resumed writing verse in Italian as well, creating a parallel body of work that in some ways mirrored and in other ways diverged from the

24. Quoted in Naldini, *VP*, 89.
25. See, in particular, the endnote to "La domenìa uliva," pp. 450–51 below.
26. Quoted in Jori, *Pasolini*, 23.
27. Quoted in Naldini, *VP*, 32.

Friulian poetry. None of this work, however, escaped the influence of the poet's prior and ongoing experience of writing in dialect.

> I continued writing poems in Friulian, but also began writing analogous ones in Italian. The Friulian of the poetry had become the exact language spoken in Casarsa (and not a Friulian invented from the Pirona [a Friulian dictionary]); while the Italian, being cast from the dialect, had acquired a naïve, Romance quality . . .[28]

Around this time, Pasolini had begun keeping a little notebook of "religious meditations" that would form the basis of the Italian sequence known as *L'usignolo della Chiesa Cattolica* (The Nightingale of the Catholic Church, 1943), the title he would also give to the collection that in 1958 brought together all of the Italian poetry he had written from 1943 to 1949. As one might expect, his early work in Italian displays sources of influence similar to those of the writing in dialect: Symbolism, post-Symbolism, Giovanni Pascoli, and medieval vernacular poetry, among others. But it is curious to note how the linguistic medium itself seems to dictate a different approach to subject matter, form, and poetics. For example, where the Friulian verse draws from the more rarefied Mallarméan trends of Symbolism in its quest for a "pure" poetic language, the Italian work looks more to the "decadent" vein issuing from Baudelaire and running through Rimbaud, Lautréamont, D'Annunzio, and the *poeti crepuscolari* ("twilight poets"). The writing is more direct, less suggestive and oblique than in the dialect verse, and where the Friulian poems tend to treat autobiographical material suggestively and symbolically, the Italian work is at times explicitly confessional, even aggressively so. This personal openness brings to the fore such key subjects as the poet's crisis of faith, his obsession with death, and his deep ambivalence towards Italian cultural institutions.

An article Pasolini published in a left-wing daily in 1946, titled "On the Margins of Existentialism," sheds considerable light on the poems of this period and their sources. Finding the ultimate precursor of modern man's dilemma in Giacomo Leopardi, who displayed "the defenseless nakedness of a spirit without limits or illusions, forever conscious of nothingness, death, and the unreasonability of his own presence,"[29] Pasolini reasserts the relevance of the great spiritual crises of the nineteenth century to literature in a post-Fascist world that generally would have preferred

28. Quoted in Naldini, *VP*, 69.

29. "In margine all'esistenzialismo," in P. P. Pasolini, *Saggi sulla politica e sulla società*, ed. W. Siti and S. De Laude (Milan: Mondadori, 1999), 29, originally published in *Libertà*, June 30, 1946. See also Jori's discussion of this essay (*Pasolini*, 38–40).

to relegate such problems to the past. The experience of nothingness, of "open-minded endurance of the ruin wrought within oneself," which in Baudelaire (and in later Symbolists and "decadents") finds solace only in the perfection of art, is for Pasolini not a "decadence" but rather a "renewal . . . of that human dignity which in the Renaissance found validity in redeeming man from his inferiority complex with regard to the other life." He continues:

> The long crisis that begins with Symbolism and leads to Surrealism and Existentialism, is, from our perspective, an ascent, not a descent, where, one after the other, Baudelaire's *spleen* (and Leopardi's *ennui*), Rimbaud's hell, and Mallarmé's purism—as well as Kirkegaard's angst and Freud's unconscious—become the summits [. . .] of this new, all-too-conscious, desperate civilization that is nevertheless able to suggest a new meaning of human dignity.

Pasolini thus posits the literary culture generally viewed as expressing a crisis of humanism, or its last great flowering, as the reaffirmation of humanism in the face of a spiritual crisis that he sees extending into the present day. For him, the suffering of the existentialist, of "man abandoned entirely to his existence, to this concrete, anguishing fact and nothing else," is that of "a mystic not awaiting grace." Indeed, he calls existentialism nothing less than "atheist mysticism," a formulation that also aptly describes himself. The interpretation brings him closer to Camus than to Sartre, perhaps, but more importantly, it is Pasolini's first explicit assertion of the spiritual crisis of modern man as the central issue of art in our time. It is a concern he shares with the Hermetics, but which he uses far different means to express.

This spiritual anguish will run throughout Pasolini's work, and in the early poetry it takes a number of forms. One is his idiosyncratic, quasi-schizophrenic treatment of the Narcissus theme, which the Italian verse shares equally with the Friulian. Another is his transformation of Pascolian themes, particularly the so-called poetics of the *fanciullino*, or "little boy." Set forth in a work of the same name (*Il Fanciullino*), this was, in brief, Giovanni Pascoli's late-Romantic belief that the wonderment experienced by the small child in face of even the most banal events or the most insignificant objects was fundamental to the poetic sensibility. It was a trope that would have a fertile afterlife in Italian poetry, particularly among the *crepuscolari* around the turn of the century, who added further colorings of melancholy to Pascoli's notion. For Pasolini, it became a fundamental theme of all his poetry to the end of his days. But, as he did with so many other borrowed tropes, Pasolini was to make it entirely his own, to the point of rendering Pascoli's original notion almost unrecognizable. For Pasolini, it became inextricably entwined with his cult of innocence (and its loss), and it was part and parcel of his mystical view of nature, of what one might call his animist mysticism.[30] The death, moreover, of his younger brother Guido at the hands of fellow Partisans in early 1945, in the waning days of World War II,[31] further colored his view of youth and innocence as images of purity destined for sacrifice on the altars of society and history.

In much of the early poetry, both Friulian and Italian, the speaking voice is, in fact, that of a "boy": the words he uses are variously *nini, donzel, fì, fantàt, fantassut, frut, zovin* in Friulian; *fanciullo, fanciulletto, giovinetto, ragazzo* in Italian. And while it's true that Pasolini was rather young when he wrote these poems, his subject is deliberately construed as much younger. It was an image of himself he would never fully relinquish. Not too much later, in 1950, he wrote, as a sort of Peter Pan by way of Pascoli:

> Adult? Never, never — like life itself,
> which never matures, forever green
> from splendid day to splendid day,
> I cannot help but remain true
> to the wondrous monotony of mystery.

And in "Poet of Ashes," composed when he was forty-four, he writes: "Just yesterday two or three soldiers, in a thicket of whores, / thought I was twenty-four — poor boys / who took a small child [*bambino*] for someone their own age."

Compared to the young voice of the Friulian poems, however, the *fanciullo* of the early Italian poems lives under a shadow. Where the slight distance afforded by the dialect apparently allowed the poet to treat such

30. See, inter alia, *Pasolini su Pasolini* (originally published in 1969), where he says: "My way of looking at the world is perhaps too respectful, too reverential, too childish; I look at everything there is in the world, objects no less than people and nature, with a certain sacred veneration." (Now in P. P. Pasolini, *Saggi sulla politica e sulla società*, 1288.)

31. Guido Pasolini, a World War II resistance fighter, was killed late in the war, along with other north Italian compatriots of the Catholic Partito d'Azione, by Titoist communist partisans at whose side they had been fighting the Nazis and Fascists. The Yugoslavians were hoping to annex the bordering Friuli region in the postwar settlements, and the Italian communist partisans fighting at their side were complicit in the massacre. For more on Guido's death and its effect on Pier Paolo, see, in particular, N. Naldini, *VP* and B. D. Schwartz, *Pasolini Requiem* (New York: Pantheon, 1992).

charged subjects as his own narcissism, budding homosexuality, doubled persona, morbid obsessions, and religious ambivalence with a relatively light touch, these same themes become more complicated and fraught with anxiety when developed in the graver, more history-laden Italian tongue. It is as if the language brings with itself the institutions that might pass judgment on the speaking subject, who for this reason feels impelled to struggle against it even as he speaks it. The speaker in the *Nightingale of the Catholic Church* thus appears at once innocent and doomed, at once *fanciullino* and *poète maudit*. And it is paradoxically his very innocence, real or feigned, that dooms him as it pits him against the worldly, "adult" Institution.

On the other hand, the institutions ingrained in the Italian language also enable the poet to address a broader collectivity, the Church and, eventually, the nation, with all the ambivalence this may entail. The difference in religious perspective, for example, and its poetic treatment in the Italian as opposed to the Friulian verse become immediately palpable in the *Nightingale* sequence. Where the dialect poems evoke primarily the simple, almost pagan Christianity that Pasolini was so pleased to find still intact among the Friulian peasantry, in Italian he immediately confronts the instituted Church head-on, flirting with sacrilege ("ah, blasphemies, heresies, sole sweet memory of Christ") and even going so far, in "The Passion," as to evoke not only a sort of voyeuristic eroticism in Christ's agony ("They hammer the nails / and the cloth upon / Thy belly trembles") but a subliminal homosexuality between the Roman soldiers ("two strapping / lads with shoulders / red and eyes / a heavenly blue") and Christ himself, whose voice the poet makes so bold as to assume:

Ah, how wretched
to sully your bodies
the color of dawn
with my hot blood!
You were once boys
and now to kill me
oh! all those days
of cheerful games
and innocence.

But let us make no mistake: however *outré* these artistic gestures, and however specific they may be to his poetics, Pasolini is nevertheless drawing from an "instituted" source—that is, the richly ambiguous Italian iconographic tradition, particularly as represented by such Mannerist painters as Pontormo and Rosso Fiorentino, whose depictions of Christ often smolder with erotic suggestions.[32] They are yet further instances of the poet's "endless capacity for obedience" and "rebellion," for the images derive in large part from his study of iconography at the University of Bologna under Roberto Longhi, the most authoritative Italian art historian of the century, who—like Gianfranco Contini, the other great "authority" in Pasolini's early intellectual formation—would leave a lasting impression on Pasolini's creative methodologies. Not only would Longhi's notion of Mannerism prove definitive in contributing to Pasolini's own self-image as a modern "mannerist," but the poet's experience of Italian painting would actually inform a certain "painterly" technique in his rendering of poetic imagery. We see this even in early work like "The Passion," where such descriptions as we find in the closing image—"Behind Christ / the sky flees / over dead mountains. / It is a blind river."—evoke, with haikuesque economy, miniature landscapes of the sort we find in the backgrounds of the great religiously themed paintings of the early Italian tradition.

It is this ability and tendency to absorb preexisting forms, mediums, styles, and subjects, only to subvert them from within to fit highly personal and individual concerns, that perhaps best characterizes Pasolini's own "mannerism." And clearly, in this respect the Italian language and its associated traditions provided a much richer lode for mining than the limited semantic field of a provincial dialect ever could. Nevertheless, for the adult Pasolini, who had spent his formative years in the Fascist educational system, those same traditions were charged with negative associations, since they were celebrated, for the most part, by the ruling regime and thus came to represent power and authority for the young poet. Not surprisingly, then, the decision to write in Italian—and in the forms that belong to that language's tradition—was fraught with conflict. Perhaps no other

32. On the other hand, this eroticization of Christ also derives from Pasolini's own personal experience of the Crucifixion in preadolescence and adolescence. In one of his diaries (quoted in Naldini, VP, 13), he writes: "That naked body barely covered by a strange band over the loins (which I assumed to be a discreet convention) would provoke illicit thoughts in me, though not openly so, and however often I looked at that strip of silk as a kind of veil spread over a disturbing abyss [. . .], I would immediately turn those feelings into piety and prayer. Later the express desire to imitate Jesus in his sacrifice to mankind of being condemned and killed even while being totally innocent surfaced explicitly in my fantasies. I saw myself hanging, nailed to the cross. My loins were scantily wrapped by that light rag and a vast crowd was watching me. My public martyrdom ended up becoming a voluptuous image and, little by little, I was nailed with my body completely naked."

poem of this period better expresses the ambivalence Pasolini felt about his course of action than the one entitled, appropriately, "Lingua" (where the term is intended primarily to designate the *Italian* language *as opposed to* dialect, and only secondly as "language" as the power of speech).

In the poem, the language and the culture implied within it assume the allegorical form of a "museum," one which is, moreover, "*vigilato dagli Adulti*" — that is, "watched over" or "supervised" by "Adults." The poet enters the museum, as we might expect, as a "boy" — but at this point of growing self-consciousness, he is a "perverse" boy, though virginal, bearing the future of Europe "unsullied" in his "sex." And he is, moreover, an "*eterno fanciulletto*," a boy eternally young, presumably never to attain a maturity that would grant him equal footing with the museum's authorities. He is nonetheless attracted by the formal purity he finds there; all his love is "for the nudest statue." And he has given his "true and formless passions" to the (Platonic) "preexistent Form" in which it is held. Yet despite his love, the statue remains impassive; it is "dreadful" (*orribile*); it is "the death / in my past." He would rather have his own "naked silence," the silence of barbarous innocence:

> the silence of the boy whom a statueless
> Europe set aflame with the dawn,
> the boy who flies in dialect
> over his unworldly, virgin heart.

Without the language's "alabaster threat," the poet says, "I shall relive my passions for my mother, / my subjection to my groin." History and culture, as instituted in the language, impose an "adult" purity of rigor that will not admit the Oedipal infantilism to which the poet clings. Without the language, he says:

> I shall be the Narcissus flower reflected
> as a loveless lover, ear distracted
> by the voices that a wordless love
> invents for the flower.[33]

He would dwell, that is, in a perfectly self-mirroring universe, where names do not exist but are only "voices" — that is, *sounds*, as in the "infinite melody" of his invented Friulian poetry. In this universe he can plumb the innocence of his past and the guilt of his neurotic present, whereas the

33. The flower, moreover, is an image of virginity for Pasolini's Narcissus; see "Narcissus Dancing" (p. 77 below), where he writes: "intact as a flower, / I yearn without desire."

"ivory hendecasyllable,"[34] the "statue of poetics . . . / eternally adult," loves "only joy . . . and purity," and wants nothing to do with "the sins or tears of children." It is classical serenity itself. Yet by his very choice of medium (the Italian language), the poet, though "unique" and "branded"—as homosexual, presumably, but also as cultural and religious "heretic"—has nevertheless opted to enter this classical world, this museum with its "enamels and waters / of Arcadia"; and for this, he says, "I shall be guilty of having loved you, / O Authority." And, having entered, he wants, again with his "infinite capacity for rebellion," to make the placid statue wear "the impish trousers wrapping / my naïve loins"—he wants, that is, to become the statue himself: "I too shall become ivory." He will, in fact, become Art—but on his own terms.

With its tortured discourse, its blend of cryptic allusion, confessional self-reference, and overt Freudianism ("I have murdered my father with silence"), "Lingua" is something of a watershed in Pasolini's early poetry in Italian. It treats a philological dilemma in personal, allusive, and psychological terms, marking at once a definitive break from contemporary Hermetic poetry—which shunned psychology and explicit subjectivism—and a violation of the very tradition Pasolini hopes to become part of. For the first time, he proffers his sexuality defiantly, *against* the world of instituted cultural Authority: "I love my guilt"—which, the poet says, is "the fold in my trousers." But his guilt is also, as we have seen, his love of the language (Authority). Thus is his sex "folded into" the Institution. The poet will enter the language's "museum" at all costs, and he will do so by breaking the rules, charging his own hendecasyllables with a vocabulary the likes of which the form has never seen. What we see in this poem are, in fact, the first instances of Pasolini's "contamination" of traditional verse forms and poetic language with unprecedented modes of discourse and subjects, a process that will reach perhaps its most balanced point of tension in the *terza rima* poems of *Le Ceneri di Gramsci* (Gramsci's Ashes). At the same time there is also a rejection of modernist poetics in the very use, however unorthodox, of rhymed hendecasyllables.

The problem of Pasolini's conflict vis-à-vis the language will, however, remain unresolved in the poem itself and in his artistic practice in general. At poem's end he says to the language, "you disdain / what I love in you,

34. The hendecasyllable is an eleven-syllable line (though often varying to twelve, thirteen, and more syllables, or sometimes less) with fixed stresses on the fourth or sixth and tenth syllables and varying stresses on the others. It is the preferred line of "classic" Italian verse, a sort of parallel to iambic pentameter in English, though less regular.

and leave me unchanged." Nor will the question ever really be put to rest. Indeed, the very same conflict will ultimately lead to the poet's embrace of cinema as a "universal language" unencumbered by the history of associations and prejudices, as well as the glories, of Italian. And even then he won't give up poetry or his native tongue.

For now, however, Pasolini's struggle with the language and what it represents is but one of the many splits in his poetic persona. Torn between Friulian and Italian, youth and maturity, religion and blasphemy, pedagogy and solipsism, repression and desire, innocence and guilt, self and self (Narcissus), he dons a series of overlapping masks throughout the poems of *L'Usignolo* and in the dialect verse of *La meglio gioventù* ("The Best of Youth"). The masks start to fall, however, and the process of self-revelation begins in earnest with the poems written in 1948 and 1949, which coincide with his "discovery" of Marx and, perhaps more importantly, of Antonio Gramsci.

Two poems in particular embody this new, more unified voice. The first is "Memorie" ("Memories") a profession of love to his mother and an exploration of their complex bond and of the poet's passion for the young men he sees as reflections of himself. It is the model for all the subsequent love poems to his mother and certainly one of the finest. Composed in clear, almost prosaic Italian set in somewhat irregular, mostly unrhymed *settenari* (seven-syllable lines) whose form remains nearly invisible, it is also an early example in Italian of the "humbler" style that would remain one of Pasolini's principal manners thereafter. The second is a longer sequence entitled "L'Italia," in which Pasolini's embrace of the Italian language harmonizes with his expressed love of the country, and where a broad overview of the "*saggia nazione*" ("wise nation") coincides with a revisiting of the places of the poet's youth. It is Pasolini's first explicit attempt, outside of his essay writing and journalism—which by the time of this poem (1949) was already rather abundant in the fields of both culture and politics— to wed his nascent "civic" voice with an embrace of the language, in full awareness of the cultural and political conflicts still implicit in this choice:

> Your health, o Italy born with the sun,
> loves only the children who love you not,
> closed in their bodies of violets that won't
> let us glimpse if their Language is only a dream . . .
> who trample you with selfish step,
> who think you their possession
> or a possession of their families . . .

Also foreshadowing his "mature" manner, the poem situates the poet's self, and his gradual evolution, within the temporal and geographical situation of the nation:

In a village of Friuli his soul was born
confused with a damp wall
and a patch of grass black with water

With its harmonized tension between subjective expression and a broad vision of the historical, cultural, and linguistic collective, "L'Italia" is something like an early version of what would be one of the masterpieces of the *Ceneri di Gramsci* collection, the 1951 *poemetto*[35] "L'Appennino" ("The Apennines").

At the same time as he was writing "L'Italia," however, Pasolini was revisiting the schisms in his poetic persona in "L'ex-vita" (here translated as "My Former Life"), one of the many poems written throughout his career in which he contemplates his own death. What dies in the poem, however, is only the unconscious, uncontrollable side of his personality,[36] which in any case would resurrect before long. A further, similar break informs "Ballata del delirio" ("The Ballad of Delirium"), in which the mirror of Narcissus shatters, the voices of the two selves become confused and merge, and in the end the poet is confronted with only his Nothingness. In the process, he finally relinquishes innocence and discovers what will become the ironic, disillusioned voice of his later poems. In this respect, "La ballata del delirio," which in all its frenzy displays a paradoxical clarity, represents the last rite of passage through the irrational darkness before the poet's emergence into the light of reason in "La scoperta di Marx" ("Discovering Marx").

"Marx," for its part, gives a foretaste of what would become the manner of Pasolini's most celebrated poems, the "civic" *poemetti* of *Le ceneri di Gramsci*. While not composed in quite the sweeping register of those works' *terza rima*, its finely chiseled tercets certainly anticipate that vein. Here, the

35. *Poemetto* is the Italian diminutive of *poema*, a term that specifically designates a long narrative composition such as a *poema epico* or a *poema cavalleresco*. A short lyric composition, on the other hand, is called a *poesia*. A *poemetto* is thus something shorter than an epic or a romance, but longer than a *poesia*, and usually employs the *endecasillabo*, the "noblest" verse line in Italian. The notion of *poemetto* used by Pasolini as a midlength form of meditative poem derives directly from Giovanni Pascoli, who wrote a great many of them.
36. See the endnote to "L'ex-vita" (p. 455 below), where Pasolini speaks in a letter of "killing" the naive side of his character.

poet, having fallen "into a world of prose," accepts his lot, his "burdensome body"; and, perhaps inspired by the Gramscian notion of a "national-folk" culture,[37] he embraces the Italian language, which he now calls a "high Romance tongue." The yearning for the timeless world expressed in dialect, which the poet "sought / to unearth at its source," persists, but the tables have been turned: this world, "whose blind, enamored son I am," is, the poet discovers,

> . . . not some joyous
>
> possession of mine
> full of sweet dreams
> laden with goodness,
>
> but an ancient land
> belonging to others, where
> life has the anguish of exile[.]

The "perfect outsider" since birth, as he calls himself, is now an exile in the world of eternal youth. Like Christ, he has entered the world of time and mortality: "Out of time the son / is born, and in it he dies." He has, in fact, crossed the threshold of maturity:

> Now each day I plunge
> into the world of reason,
> that ruthless institution
>
> of adults [. . .]

Yet he enters this world not for the "adult" power of church and state, but rather for the "marvelous gift / that Reason has henceforth become"— that is, the promise of a better future, but also the tool that serves the poet in his pedagogical purpose as teacher and emergent "civic" voice. "Language" (Italian) and "time" (the eventuality of death), "the two walls / between which I entered the world," are simply a matter of fate.

> But in life there is more
> than mere love
> of one's destiny.

There is the transcendent purpose of collective destiny:

> Our history! vice-grip
> of pure love, force
> of reason and divinity.

37. Gramsci's term is *nazional-popolare*.

Scarcely orthodox in his newfound Marxism, Pasolini has, for the moment, apparently reconciled many of the opposing forces of his emotional and intellectual life in a historical vision that manages to recuperate the principal concerns of much of his poetry up to this point: language, spirituality, youth/adulthood, death, sex, and even his mother (the principal inspiration of this poem),[38] who, "through the mystery of sex / . . . brought me to life / in a logical Universe." The result achieved, however, is not so much a synthesis of antithetical forces as a moment of equipoise between them. Even the reconciliation with the Italian language is not definitive; indeed, Pasolini would continue to write in Friulian for some four more years before resuming near the end of his life, and he would continue to view Italian and, more specifically, "literary" Italian, with ambivalence for the rest of his days.

What led Pasolini ultimately to choose Italian as his privileged medium of poetic expression were not, in fact, any conscious philosophical or aesthetic considerations, although it is arguable that, since the poetry seems to have been moving in this direction, and since by the second half of the 1940s he was writing a great deal of journalistic, diaristic, and fictional prose in Italian,[39] he probably would have come to such a decision sooner or later. Rather, the single most determinant factor in the linguistic path his poetic oeuvre would take was a charge for sexual misconduct with minors on the occasion of a country fair in the village of Ramuscello near Casarsa in 1949.[40] He had been seen walking off one evening with three boys, two of them minors, and the following day a man from the village had heard the boys arguing over the matter and denounced Pasolini to the Carabinieri. When the would-be plaintiffs declined to press charges, the local authorities—spurred on by right-wing Christian Democrats and ex-Fascists who had been itching for some time to silence Pasolini, whose pro-Communist political writings bore a great deal of weight within the local

38. An early, longer version of the poem was titled "La ricerca di mia madre" ("The Search for My Mother").

39. The fictional material, much of it drawn from personal experience, included *Il sogno di una cosa*, the novel he continued to work on for a long time thereafter (and whose originally projected title had been *La meglio gioventù*, the one he eventually gave to the 1954 edition of the collected Friulian poems) and published in 1962, as well as the two shorter, and more explicitly homosexual novels, *Atti impuri* ("Impure Acts") and *Amado mio* ("My Beloved"), which were published posthumously.

40. The most thorough discussions of this life-defining event can be found in N. Naldini, VP, and in B. D. Schwartz's biography, *Pasolini Requiem*. See also Enzo Siciliano, *Vita di Pasolini* (Milan: Mondadori, 2005).

agricultural communities—decided to charge the poet with corruption of minors and obscene acts in public, effectively shattering the personal and professional life Pasolini had created for himself in that corner of Italy.[41] Pasolini would ultimately be acquitted of all charges, but not until 1953, after four years of anguish and legal headaches. Meanwhile, the damage had been done and the tone had been set. For this would prove to be the first of no less than thirty-three trials to which Pasolini was subjected over the rest of his life, all resulting in acquittals, and all brought against him not for anything he had done but for what he was; what he thought, said, and represented; and what he created in his art.

In the years immediately after World War II, Pasolini had followed his pedagogical successes at the Academiuta with a stable position teaching literature to entry-level *scuola media* pupils at a public school in the nearby town of Valvasone. His brilliance as a teacher and as an inspiration to students had been noted for many miles around by educational administrators;[42] he had singlehandedly fostered a literary revival of the Friulian dialect, headed a local poetry movement that ennobled this tongue with the poetic art, had a respected reputation across the entire region as a poet and intellectual, and was beginning to make a modest name for himself even nationally;[43] and, aside from his already prolific output of literary journalism, published in his own and other magazines, he had attracted attention with his political journalism as well, which, though written under the aegis of the Communist Party, was undogmatic, personalized, and never hesitant to criticize Party positions. If not for the Ramuscello scandal, he was looking ahead to a respectable, economically comfortable career as a teacher as a way of supporting his writing endeavors. But the trial, and the scandal it caused in what was, after all, a community of rather simple people, changed all that. No sooner had the news spread than he lost his job. He was expelled from the Communist Party, never to rejoin. His home life became unbearable, especially as his father,

41. According to Naldini (in *VP* and in *Crono*), the state charges brought against Pasolini were a thinly veiled attempt at blackmail, warning him to discontinue his political activity or else face the consequences of his "moral conduct"—that is, his homosexuality.

42. News of Pasolini's pedagogical talents even reached the ears of Andrea Zanzotto, Pasolini's contemporary, who lived not far away and was himself teaching at the time.

43. Among other things, shortly before the "events of Ramuscello," in 1949, poet Vittorio Sereni had invited him to contribute work to the Milanese review *La Rassegna d'Italia*.

having returned from war a shattered man after two years as a prisoner of war in Africa and the loss of his younger son, fell prey to depression and alcoholism. Life outside the home, in Casarsa, was perhaps even worse. As Paolo Volponi, a friend and collaborator, later wrote of Pasolini's situation: "He had been beloved of the whole town, considered nothing less than a little prophet. But what would turn out to be the drama of his life suddenly exploded, and the whole town, which had loved him very much, rose up against him, furious and devastated."[44]

In such conditions, Pasolini soon found he had no choice but to leave. And so, one night in late January 1950, he furtively escaped to Rome with his mother. As he later recounts in "Poet of Ashes":

> I fled with my mother and a suitcase and some jewelry that turned out
>   to be fake
> on a train as slow as a freight train
> across a Friulian plain covered by a light, hard layer of snow.
> We were heading to Rome.
> We had abandoned my father
> next to a wretched wood-burning stove
> in his old army greatcoat,
> raving wildly, sick with cirrhosis and paranoia.
> I was living
> a page in a novel, the only time in my life:
> the rest of the time I lived in a lyric
> —what else?—like all lunatics.

The scenery was changing, but the questions posed in the poetry remained the same and would continue to influence his subsequent production. The work in both languages had laid the groundwork for what would be, in fact, the concerns of a lifetime, however different and changeable the forms and even the ways in which he treated them. Pasolini's lifelong preoccupation with realism, authenticity, and primitive spiritualism, his quest for a human and cultural purity untouched by industrialized mass society originate, in somewhat inchoate form, in his Friulian poetry and his love of that world. And his confrontational, love-hate relationships with civil society and its institutions, including the Church, as well as his will to mold the very forces of history into the lines of his verse, are already present in the Italian poetry he wrote before leaving his beloved Friuli. Most importantly, perhaps, he had already given ample evidence of his tendency to use traditional literary forms and languages to entirely un-

44. Quoted in Naldini, VP, 136.

precedented ends. The strange new world of Rome would, of course, provide him with a far broader stage on which to project these concerns. And, always sensitive to his surroundings, Pasolini would be affected to the core of his being by the "city of God" (as he called it), its landscape, and its people.

III

Moving into in a small rented studio in the historic Jewish ghetto of Rome after his mother had found work as a live-in housekeeper, Pasolini continued writing Italian poems in the diaristic vein he had long been exploring in Friuli—brief, often unrhymed, but metrically regular meditations on solitude and his immediate surroundings. His Friulian compositions included longer, unfinished projects, such as a series of historical poems, as well as some short lyrics drawn from autobiographical material in his diaries. And, while working at odd jobs and remaining in a state of considerable penury, he continued writing the autobiographical fiction, in Italian, that he had begun before leaving.

Still smarting from the humiliation that had sent him into exile, he was reticent at first about making literary contacts, though he quickly found Sandro Penna, a somewhat older poet and one of Italy's finest, with whom he soon became inseparable. Penna became his guide to Rome. Among other things, Penna introduced him to the nocturnal demimonde along the Tiber's banks below the massive retaining walls, and shared with him a passion for endless walks around the great city. It was, however, Pasolini's own peculiar passion for the conjunction of language and life that led him almost immediately to the *borgate* of Rome (since made famous by Pasolini himself), those impoverished suburbs which at the time still housed a concentration of lumpen *romani de Roma*[45] who had been forced out of some of the most ancient parts of the city—particularly the quarters around the Vatican—when these were demolished by the Fascist government in the plan to build a new imperial Rome. Drawn at once by the colorful dialect and pagan sensuality of the *borgatari*,[46] Pasolini wrote that the attraction "was not a choice on my part, but a kind of coercion of destiny; and since everyone bears witness to what he knows, I couldn't help but bear witness to the Roman *borgata*."[47]

45. That is, native Romans of ancient date, not originally from other parts of Italy.
46. That is, the inhabitants of the *borgate*.
47. Quoted in Naldini, *Crono*, xci.

Here, in the *borgate*, Pasolini found a population at once ancient in its customs and modern in its alienation. And mixed in with the displaced Roman underclass was a more recent influx of immigrants from the rural south of Italy who had settled outside the capital after the war, in search of a better life. Pasolini found the resultant cultural and linguistic brew rather heady, and immediately began to feel its effects. Eager to incorporate his new experiences and this strange new language into his work, he would go around with a little notebook and pen, jotting down the different idioms and expressions he heard and the modes of behavior he observed, becoming, as he put it, "a tape recorder."[48]

The new dialect of privilege was not, however, finding its way into Pasolini's poetry. Nor would it ever, really, except in occasional inflections and word choices. And this was perhaps because, unlike Friulian, the Roman tongue remained for him a phenomenon somewhat outside of himself. Aside from a few later, minor compositions inspired by the great nineteenth-century *romanesco* poet Giuseppe Gioacchino Belli, Pasolini's use of the dialect would remain restricted to his Roman short stories, two Roman novels, and his first two films. In the novels in particular, *il romanesco* became the vehicle for dialogue and, perhaps more importantly, for the *discorso libero indiretto*—that is, the Flaubertian *style indirect libre* in which the narrator mimics, in the third person, the thought processes of a character. Pasolini thus used it principally as an artistic tool to evoke a very specific objective reality—that is, the world (indeed the *mind*) of the Roman underclass—and to this end it worked very well. But it never merged enough with his sense of self to become a vehicle of lyric expression.

The linguistic philosophy that had led Pasolini originally to write poetry in dialect nevertheless figured greatly in his approach to his subsequent poems in Italian. And this was what might be best described as a belief in language—in this specific case Italian—as a fluid, not a fixed, entity. That is, just as he had presumed that he could do what he wished in inventing a poetry in the Friulian dialect of Casarsa, including borrowing at once from ancient Romance repertoires and foreign late-Romantic or premodern trends while freely selecting from the living speech around him, he likewise considered Italian an open field for plunder, with the entire tradition of forms, styles, discourses, and rhetorics being fair game for his use, along with whatever localisms, modern corruptions, experimentalisms, and jargons might be deemed appropriate at any given moment. Pasolini's Italian poetry thus fell within the bounds of what Gianfranco Contini called

48. Ibid.

plurilinguismo—defined by the literary historian, in the Italian context, as the poetic language issuing from Dante and consisting of a highly diverse lexicon of terms, registers, and even morphologies (including dialect) that varied and shifted according to expressive need, situation, location, and so on—as opposed to *monolinguismo*, which was the tradition of poetic usage issuing from Petrarch and consisting of a highly limited vocabulary of terms and expressions for specific lyric situations that, through their repeated use over time, conferred an enriched repertoire of associations on a rarefied verbal fabric. Pasolini was to make much of Contini's *plurilinguismo* in his own literary criticism, and clearly considered himself—with Contini's confirmation—a contemporary manifestation of this phenomenon, which was quite widespread among Italian writers after World War II.[49] As always, however, when appropriating concepts, he would eventually extend the notion beyond its original limits, in this case to include form, genre, and medium, which in his later production would all function as so many "languages" forever overlapping and contaminating one another.

For now, however, Pasolini's practice of *plurilinguismo* was restricted to literary mediums. More important, perhaps, was his fundamental notion of language as something that is always in the process of being born—and which, in coming to be, at once expresses and demiurgically shapes the reality in which it arises. As he put it several years later:

> language, let no one forget,
> though the fruit of dark origins, becomes one
> with what shall be but is not yet.
> And being this open mystery, this
> infinite wealth, it now shatters
> every limit reached, every legitimate form.
> —from "The Stylistic Reaction" (1960)

This linguistic intersection of past-present-future, of tradition and experimentation, is perhaps the most visible novelty of the new poetic vein Pasolini was beginning to explore in Rome, and it issues primarily from a combination of his own manneristic approach to poetry and the Gramscian emphasis on the role of the intellectual/artist in culling the forms of the "national-folk" culture and helping to shape it. We see this already in what

49. According to prominent critic Pier Vincenzo Mengaldo in *Profili di critici del novecento* (Turin: Bollati Bollinghieri, 1998), p. 80, "our current interest in modern dialect poetry in Italy [. . .] owes more to the erudite and critical excavations of Pasolini than to anyone else."

would prove to be the first example of Pasolini's original use of terza rima, the meditative poem entitled "L'Appennino" ("The Apennines"), which he completed toward the end of his second full year in Rome (1951), and which would eventually appear in the 1957 collection *Le ceneri di Gramsci*.

Modeled loosely on the terza rima *poemetti* of Pascoli—himself a "plurilinguist" whose Italian bears traces of the Romagnolo dialect, among other things—"L'Appennino" panoramically spans the Italian peninsula along the course of its principal mountain chain, embracing past glories and present squalor in its broad field of vision, all of it cast under the haunting shadow of Jacopo della Quercia's celebrated early-Renaissance funerary statue of Ilaria del Carretto, whose closed eyes symbolize the spiritual "sleep" into which the Italian nation has fallen since the now-lapsed state of grace embodied in the human perfection of her finely molded forms. The poem's own form, ultimately derived from Dante, incorporates this fall from grace through willful inconsistencies of meter and rhyme and sharp contrasts of subject and tone. For example, after a long, sweeping introduction that evokes the geographic and cultural riches of central Italy in elegant hendecasyllables, the poet homes in on the present, *his* present:

> Under closed eyelids, a little kid
> from Cassino, sold by his parents,
> laughs; he's being fed
>
> by a killer and a whore
> on the raging banks of the Aniene . . .

Following this dramatic drop in tone and language, which takes us from medieval and Renaissance landscapes to the Roman *borgate*, the poem becomes an elaborate counterpoint of high and low, with the exquisite tensions sometimes contained within a single sentence:

> Behind
> clearings of peonies, Rome in moonlight gilds
> Hellenic and Baroque remains and grimy
> faithless suburbs, where nobody knows
> anything but sex, and the caves are slimy
> with feces and children.

Still marginal in his immediate life situation, Pasolini here is already in full possession of his "public" voice, and, in the manner of Leopardi, uses it to express as much love as dismay for his people, the ambivalence burnt into his very language. With a full iconographic repertoire at his disposal, he can bring out this tension visually, wrapping the sordid present in the colors of past glory:

> against the plebian's laughter, all talk
> of redemption always was and still is
> fruitless. He beams in a careless blaze
>
> of seventeenth-century colors,
> as if his insolent presence alone,
> with his rags and gold chains, and the callous
>
> smile of loveless hovels in his eyes,
> sufficed to let him hold his own
> both in shadow and sunlight.

Here the young toughs of the *borgata* are a modern extension of the taverngoers whom Caravaggio used to illustrate his Gospel episodes: they bask in the same Roman light, lurk in the same shadows, equally excluded from instituted salvation—Christian or Communist—equally captured in vivid imagery for future generations.

When *Le ceneri di Gramsci* was published by Garzanti in 1957, the first edition sold out in fifteen days. This was no doubt due primarily to the notoriety that Pasolini had gained from the controversy and popularity of his first published novel, *Ragazzi di vita* (1956), for which he had been taken clamorously to court on charges of "obscenity" and acquitted. But there were other important reasons for the book's success. It spurred lively critical debate in most quarters, and won glowing praise from some reviewers and fellow writers. For Italo Calvino, *Le ceneri di Gramsci* was "one of the most important events in Italian literature since the end of the war, and certainly the most important in the field of poetry. [. . .] It is the first time in who knows how many years that a vast poetic composition has managed to express, with extraordinary success in its inventiveness and use of formal mediums, a conflict of ideas, a cultural and moral problematics in the face of a socialist conception of the world."[50]

After decades in which much Italian poetry, through the dominance of the Hermetic school, had been confined within highly personalized, often cryptic (though beautiful) language systems not easily understood by the common reader, Pasolini managed to treat subjects of broad concern in a style that relied at least in part on rational exposition, without relinquishing for an instant his highly personal presence within the work. In articu-

50. Quoted in Naldini, VP, 188.

lating his own doubts and contradictions concerning the socialist dream, which he addressed directly to Gramsci in the title poem, Pasolini was speaking for much of the literary and artistic intelligentsia of the age:

> The scandal of self-contradiction—of being
> with you and against you; with you in my heart,
> in the light, against you in the dark of my gut.
>
> Though a traitor to my father's station
> —in my mind, in a semblance of action—
> I know I'm bound to it in the heat
>
> of my instincts and aesthetic passion;

and yet he was also speaking only for himself, as in the lines that immediately follow:

> drawn to a proletarian life
> from before your time, I take for religion
>
> its joyousness, not its millennial
> struggle—its nature, not its
> consciousness.

Pasolini had successfully merged, at least for a moment, the public and personal veins. What was once narcissism here becomes lucid self-analysis, but with no repudiation of his principal passions. In these last five lines, in fact, Pasolini gives us a concise summary of his magnetic attraction to the common people, who, however formidable a political mass they may be, are for him a repository of ancient values and culture. His social vision spans the centuries, informed more by timeless agrarian traditions and natural cycles than by dry Marxist rationalizations of historical forces and relations of production. It is more humanistic and literary than purely political, and it unites his prior experience of Friuli with the picture he will later paint of the ancient peasant world in such films as *The Decameron, The Arabian Nights*, and *Medea*.

   With their unusual blend of collective vision and private reflection, traditional form and radical critique, hopeful idealism and disenchanted realism, the poems of *Le ceneri di Gramsci* thrust Pasolini's poetry into the center of the public arena for what would prove to be a relatively short while. Probably only for the four years between this volume and the one that followed in 1961, *La religione del mio tempo* (The Religion of My Time), was the formal, aesthetic, and philosophical importance of Pasolini's poetry given its proper due before his image as a controversial filmmaker, polemicist, and general enfant terrible—a caricature greatly exaggerated and largely fabricated by scandal sheets and gossip columnists, often with extreme-right sympathies—came to distract the reading public from the more essential aspects of his literary project. During this brief period, however, Pasolini became a sort of lightning rod for the tensions between the different schools and movements thriving or emerging at the time in Italian letters.

Much of the subject matter of the *Gramsci* poems—the working class, the peasantry, the landscapes of postwar industrialism, the nation's past—placed Pasolini within the Neorealist current, but his analytical treatment of these subjects, his constant self-referentiality, and his linguistic complexity set him apart and lent the work an aura of novelty and experiment that derived above all from the contrasts between the traditional form and the unorthodox content of the work. It should be remembered, of course, that the mingling of registers and languages practiced by Pasolini was not in itself anything new to Italian poetry, since one of the principal achievements of the literary *avanguardia storica*—represented predominantly by the Futurist poets in the early century and those immediate successors who absorbed their influence—was precisely the opening of poetry's field to include new languages more representative of the multifariousness of life in modern industrial society. What was paradoxically novel about Pasolini's work was its recuperation of such ancient traditional forms as terza rima—featured in all but two of the poems in the *Gramsci* volume—to embody a sensibility, philosophy, and language(s) that undermined the very institutions such forms had come to represent over time. It is the same strategy we saw in the poems of *The Nightingale of the Catholic Church*, except that here it has found an idiom of broader appeal.

Pasolini had occasion to expound upon this strategy in a 1957 essay, "La libertà stilistica" ("Stylistic Freedom"), which he wrote as an introduction to a *Piccola antologia neo-sperimentale*, edited by him. The essay was published as a special double issue of Pasolini's magazine, *Officina*,[51] which he had founded two years earlier with his old Bologna friends Francesco Leonetti and Roberto Roversi. Opening his review to a handful of "neo-experimental" poets, including three from the group that had formed around the Milanese review *Il Verri* and would soon be known as the *neoavanguardia*, Pasolini used the opportunity to distinguish himself from that group's positions and expound upon his own "experimentalism."

---

51. Numbers 9 and 10. The essay was reprinted with very slight revision in *Passione e ideologia* (Milan: Garzanti, 1960). The quotes that follow in the discussion of "La libertà stilistica" are from *Saggi sulla letterature e sull'arte*, vol. I, 1229–37.

Though written in the first-person plural, "La libertà stilistica" amounts to a personal literary declaration of independence from any specific "school" of poetry or thought and, coinciding with the resounding success of *Le ceneri di Gramsci*, it is a valuable document of the aesthetic and spiritual underpinnings of his poetry and, proleptically, of his film, theater, and other work.

Availing himself of Gramsci's concept and critique of *novecentismo* (intended, roughly speaking, as twentieth-century modernism), Pasolini is quick to draw up battle lines, even with those whose work he is presenting:[52] "We have never in any way identified the innovative spirit with the experimentalist one: neo-experimentalism [. . .] tends, if anything, to be imitative, not subversive, of the twentieth-century stylistic tradition." And yet, lest anyone misread him, he immediately lays claim to an experimentalism of his own, as part of "a small group of pure, predestined 'experimenters,' who, with a linguistic passion preconstituted in psychology, conduct an activity that, if not necessarily innovative, comes close to subversion and anarchism." Having thus established a clear political bent and a certain mysticism and exceptionalism in the adjective "predestined," he addresses his Marxism:

> [our] adoption of Marxist philosophy is due, at its origin, to an emotional and moral impetus, and is therefore continually permeable to the insurgence of the religious and, naturally, Catholic spirit that [this position] presupposes etc.
>
> Thus in the "experimentation" that we recognize as our own (to differentiate ourselves from the current neo-experimentalism), there remains a contradictory or negative aspect: that is, an indecisive, problematic, and dramatic attitude that coincides with the ideological independence hinted at above, which requires a continuous, painful effort to keep oneself equal to a present reality that one does not possess ideologically, as might a Catholic, a Communist, or a free-market capitalist. And this, then, implies a certain gratuitousness in our experimentation, a certain excess: that is, a surviving experimentalist bent.
>
> But also of import is a positive aspect, and that is the identification of experimentation with invention, with an implicit critical and ideo-

---

52. He was already engaged in a polemic with some of the *neosperimentali*, particularly Edoardo Sanguineti, one of the poets featured in his selection, and the dispute would become increasingly exacerbated over time. *Officina*, moreover, had from the start taken an editorial line that was generally *antinovecentista*—that is, rejecting the influence of the modern avant-gardism of Futurism, the *vociani*, and the so-called *frammentismo* defined by De Robertis.

logical opposition to instituted precedents—in other words, a cultural process [. . .] ideally preceding the poetic process.

Pasolini here delineates an artistic position, with all its contradictions and paradoxes, quite unique to himself in twentieth-century literature—that is, at once Marxist, anarchist, and Catholic, yet none of the above; keenly aware of the early century's precedent of experimentalism, whose procedures are no longer new, yet fiercely unwilling to forego his peculiar exercise of this option; tending to a "gratuitousness" and "excess" resulting from a modus operandi unfettered by "ideology," yet overcoming these aspects by relinquishing any specific claim to innovation and identifying *his own* experimentation with "invention." (*Inventare*, in the original, is a term strongly redolent of Classical *inventio*, though here it denotes an *inventio* opposed to "instituted precedent.") All in all, it is a lucid exercise in aesthetic self-awareness, one that well situates Pasolini's position within the immediate historical context.

Having thus qualified the "experimentalist" position, Pasolini turns to the question of poetic language, where he must of necessity deal with the still predominant influence of Hermeticism exercised by the older, major poets of his time (Ungaretti, Montale, Quasimodo, Luzi, etc.). Confronted with the fact that in Hermetic poetry "the language had been *raised entirely to the level of poetry* [his italics]," he writes, it now "tends to be lowered *entirely to the level of prose*, that is, of reason, logic, and history, entailing a stylistic direction diametrically opposed to the preceding one."

Again he is referring to his own work, and specifically to the procedure he adopted in *Le ceneri di Gramsci*, though even in these poems, written in what is surely the most "rational," "historicist" phase of his career, he occasionally allows himself what can only be called flights of lyric fancy. More important than any putative rationalism, however, is Pasolini's claim to "history," the effort to remain "equal to a present reality [*attualità*] that one does not possess ideologically." For whether or not he fully realized the goal of manifesting the historical moment in his verse, it was a purpose he liked to claim was his most significant contribution to the poetry of his time—one that would come to full fruition not so much in poetry as in his later *scritti corsari*, his "pirate writings," the highly caustic editorializing on current events that he practiced in mainstream periodicals in the last few years of his life.

But how, then, to make poetry of this language of prose? "From this derives," he goes on, "a readoption, probably unexpected, of pre–twentieth-century, or traditional—in the current sense of the term—stylistic modes [. . .]" (unexpected for his audience, perhaps, but certainly not for him, since such modes had been part of his strategy from the start). And, more specifically, how to make purportedly *experimental* poetry?

> These traditional stylistic modes become the mediums of an experimentation that is, for its part, with ideological awareness, absolutely anti-traditionalist: so much so as to call into question, by definition, and in a violent manner, the structure and superstructure of the State, and to condemn, in what is probably a tendentious act of passion, its tradition, which from the Renaissance to the Counter-Reformation to Romanticism has followed a social and political regression down to Fascism and the current situation.

Pasolini's project is thus nothing less than an attempt to recuperate traditional culture for revolutionary ends, and to do so in absolute freedom, without any guiding ideology other than what he calls a Continian "philological spirit"—in other words, a constant investigation and working of the very materials of language—since one goal of this "spirit" is, for Pasolini, to "abolish every form of positionalism at its origin," that is, to abolish any form of ideological instrumentalization of language at the heart of the language itself. Such "independence," he writes, is "painful," for it "suffers, as if in remorse [. . .] from its exclusion from all praxis or [. . .] action." And in this exclusion he takes his cue not from Marx but again from Gramsci, specifically "the 'imprisoned' Gramsci,[53] all the more free as he is secreted away from the world, outside the world, in a Leopardian situation in spite of himself, reduced to pure, heroic thought." Thus is Pasolini's personal status as social outsider—homosexual, artist, faithless mystic—converted, through the critical spirit, to poetic and moral dictum, even at his moment of popular literary triumph. The redemption from such solitude lies precisely in his own brand of "stylistic experimentalism," which actually "presupposes an innovative struggle not in the domain of style, but in that of culture and the spirit." He would thus transform mankind from the redoubt of his solitude through thought itself, through art, culture, *hegemony* in the specifically Gramscian sense of the term.[54] And from such experiment he would set out on "a road of love—physical and emotional love

53. Perhaps Gramsci's most influential writings are the more than three thousand pages of "notebooks" on Italian history and society that he wrote during his imprisonment from 1926 to 1934.
54. That is, specifically through culture and cultural persuasion, in the same manner as capitalism has maintained its sway.

for the phenomena of the world, and intellectual love for their spirit, history: which shall put us forever, '*in our feelings, at the point where the world is renewed.*'"[55]

*

Early in 1959, the first issue in a new series of *Officina* appeared under the imprint of the commercial publisher Bompiani, but problems arose at once because of a polemical poem by Pasolini: "A un papa" ("To a Pope"), a rhetorical invective against Pope Pius XII, Eugenio Pacelli, considered by many to have been compromised by his silence and inaction during the Fascist-Nazi epoch. As the publisher was close to the Vatican, the controversy created strife within the editorial board and subsequent issues were suspended. The poem itself, part of a series of what Pasolini called "epigrams," represented a new vein for him, merging politico-moral invective with verse, which he would tap with varying degrees of frequency for the rest of his life.

Also early in 1959, Pasolini's second "Roman" novel, *Una vita violenta*, was published to general critical acclaim and the now customary outcry of self-appointed moralists. When the book won the Premio Crotone later that year, the awards ceremony was marred by the vociferous protests of representatives of a broad swath of conservative groups from the Fascists to the Christian Democrats, the sort of spectacle that would become more and more frequent at Pasolini's public appearances. With his increasing visibility in such public forums as mass-market journalism and film, he was becoming more and more exposed to the insults and provocations of such parties. In early 1960, the right-wing group Azione Cattolica filed an official complaint against *Una vita violenta*, only to have the court dismiss it. Like the previous novel, *Ragazzi di vita*, it was a commercial success.

A new collection of poems, *La religione del mio tempo*, came out in 1961 to general approval from the literary milieu. Its opening sequence, "La Ricchezza" (here translated as "Riches"), and the title poem continue the panoramic vein so effectively mined in the poemetti of *Le ceneri di Gramci*, and further highlight an aspect peculiar to Pasolini among the poets of his time: the role of movement as a poetic device. Beginning, perhaps, with the 1951 poem "L'Appennino," or even with its predecessor, "L'Italia," Pasolini's longer poems cover vast areas of space and time, urban, geographic and personal, as though the speaking voice were soaring over the subject

55. Compare with part V, stanzas 7–12 of "The Cry of the Excavator" (pp. 211–13 below).

matter, able to descend upon individual scenes and details at will before drawing back to a desired distance. While surely a function of the rapid pace of the poet's life, this technique is also, and perhaps above all, derived from his growing familiarity with cinema, and it becomes increasingly pronounced in his poetry as his work in that medium increases. The very first line of "La Ricchezza," which opens the volume of *La religione del mio tempo*, unveils this motif: "He takes a few steps, raising his chin . . ." The movement then sweeps down through southern Tuscany and Umbria, over past artistic splendors and present human grace, before descending toward Rome in a stunning baroque image of a sunset, then descending further, down into the meanders of anonymous sex and prostitution in the shadows of the ancient Baths of Caracalla.

In "La Ricchezza," Pasolini is in full command of his hybrid, "contaminated" style, filling sonorous, ancient hendecasyllables with contemporary imagery and his now familiar public-private voice. The terza rima tercet here has merged into continuous lines undivided by stanzas, its presence moving in and out of the strings of cadences and occasional rhymes, sometimes disappearing into free verse, even prosaic sequences, before reemerging in quasi-archaic diction and strict metrics. Toward the end of "La Ricchezza," the cinema literally bursts into the poem in the form of Rossellini's *Open City*, in a full-throated paean—aesthetic and moral—to the seventh art, where "the present dissolves, cut off, / and the song of the *aedoi* becomes deafening."

In the title poem, as in "La Ricchezza," Pasolini's terza rima begins to break up. Though divided into tercets like the poemetti of *Gramsci*, "La religione del mio tempo" presents us with a further contaminated form, displaying frequent hypermetric and hypometric lines, inconsistent rhymes, and a retreat away from public themes into a more exasperated subjectivity. Here, too, images appear occasionally in cinematic form, moving, as it were, into and out of the picture frame:

> They appear around the corner of the block,
> upright but tired from the climb,
> disappear around the corner of another block,
>
> ankles vanishing behind them.

The poem is a final farewell to a form of religion, that of the age-old agrarian society that the poet once believed in but now sees as a world fast succumbing to industry and capitalism. But it's as though he realizes it was doomed even before he discovered it:

The church I loved in adolescence
had died over the centuries, living
only in the old and sorrowful scents

of the fields.

This disillusionment, and its rapid extension to the whole of society, will
become one of the dominant themes of Pasolini's subsequent work. It had,
of course, been present for a while, specifically in the critical, oppositional
stance of his "civic" poetry beginning with "L'Appennino." But in the latter
half of the volume *La religione del mio tempo*, the two sections comprising the
Epigrammi and the *Poesie incivili*,[56] it takes on a life of its own, to be further
explored by Pasolini in his essays.

These were the years—roughly from 1955 to 1960—when the "eco-
nomic miracle" of postwar Italy became a fait accompli and the country
basked in unprecedented prosperity. For Pasolini, however, it was the end
of an era of cultural history. The problem was not that the prospects for
the socialist dream had receded with the years, since the electoral repre-
sentation of the Communist and Socialist parties remained massive and
together equaled or surpassed that of the ruling Christian Democratic
party. It was that the Italian nation was undergoing what Pasolini would
later call an "anthropological transmutation." The triumph of consumer
capitalism—which Pasolini termed "neo-capitalism"—not only trans-
formed the paradigms of the class struggle as it had been conceived up
until then; more importantly, with its formidable arsenal of mass media
coupled with its visible economic success, it also changed the very minds
of those classes—the workers, the peasants, and especially the dispos-
sessed—who had always stood outside the power structures, so that they,
too, embraced the values of the new system, even as they remained ex-
cluded from the avenues of power. The ancient belief systems and struc-
tures by which Italian agrarian society had lived until then—which essen-
tially predated even the Christianization of the peninsula and had for the
most part survived the first phase of industrialization in the late nineteenth
and early twentieth centuries—were suddenly beginning to disappear
with the onset of mass production and mass distribution of the basics of
life, such as food, tools, and culture. To a poet like Pasolini, this meant
nothing less than the extinction of the reality on which the symbols and

56. A play on the word "civile," which can mean both "civic" and "civilized." Thus,
by *Poesie incivili*, Pasolini means both "Uncivic Poems" and "Uncivilized Poems."

myths of his culture had been based since time immemorial. It was as if his very concept of eternity had died.

In his everyday life, in Rome and in his cherished *borgate*, the effects of these rapid transformations and of Pasolini's resulting alarm were manifold. In his professional life, this period marked the beginning of his intellectual drift away from many of the Roman friends and literary colleagues who shared his leftist sympathies but not his darkening pessimism. Politically, it pushed him further away from an already distant Communist Party, which in the past had wrung its hands more than once over his "reactionary" tendencies. Aesthetically and personally, Pasolini perceived the new mass culture as a direct threat to his linguistic philosophy, as increasingly widespread means of mass communication tended to erode age-old regional speech habits and to flatten the Italian language to a uniform standard spoken by all classes. And this was, paradoxically, one of his reasons for embracing the cinema as a means of self-expression.

But it was among the lumpen classes he still frequented in and outside Rome that he most strongly felt the repercussions of these transformations. The vain, flippant, socially dispossessed young men he had once seen, perhaps naively, as content with their sensual vitality in the here-and-now, innocent in their spontaneity and absolutely untouched by middle-class Christian ethics, like a class of wanderers outside of history's determinant trends, were starting to become like everyone else. The "plebian" [*volgare*] whose "insolent presence alone . . . sufficed to let him hold his own / both in shadow and sunlight" now wanted more. He wanted a television, a refrigerator, a car, and would even resort to violence to obtain them. He became, in Pasolini's eyes, a reflection of the violence implicit in neocapitalism itself.

> Other fashions, other idols,
> the mass, not the people, the mass
> intent on being corrupted
> now looks out onto the world
> and transforms it, drinking its fill
> at every screen, at every video
> with utter greed, amorphous
> desire to be part of the feast.
> —from "Wisteria" (1960) in *The Religion of My Time*[57]

Pasolini knew that no forgotten nook or cranny of the peninsula would remain untouched by consumer culture. Only in his travels abroad, to Third

57. *Tutte le poesie*, vol. I, 1059.

World lands such as India, the African continent, and the Arabian peninsula, did he find examples of traditional societies that hadn't yet succumbed to the capitalist juggernaut. This is the meaning of the cri de coeur that ends, as if by interruption, the poem "To Death: A Fragment":

> Africa! My sole
> alternative . . . .
> . . . .

IV

Pasolini's first film, *Accattone*, shot in the spring of 1961 and unveiled at the Venice Film Festival in the autumn, captures the world of the *borgata* at the cusp of this "anthropological transmutation." Awaited with great anticipation, owing in large part to Pasolini's literary reputation and to the whiff of sulfur surrounding him in the popular press (there were far more journalists, for example, on the sets of his shoots than there normally would have been for a novice filmmaker), the film received mixed reviews in Italy and enthusiastic praise in Paris, with legendary French cineast Marcel Carné calling it "a marvelous film." Translating some of Pasolini's literary strategies to the screen, *Accattone* showcases the same downtrodden Roman suburbs and their colorful dialect in all their splendor, making a martyr of its lowlife pimp protagonist. Through a deft manipulation of the musical soundtrack, particularly Bach's *Saint-John's Passion*, and the frequent use of full frontal "hieratic" shots of the characters (an expedient adopted primarily because of his then limited knowledge of cinematic vocabulary), Pasolini is able, in the sharp juxtaposition of high and low registers, to confer an air of tragic nobility on a tale that might otherwise be seen as a story of petty criminals. Like the *romanesco* novels, *Accattone* was a commercial success.

By year's end Pasolini was already preparing to shoot another film, *Mamma Roma*, which would star Anna Magnani, one of the divas of Italian Neorealist cinema and the tragic heroine of Rossellini's *Open City*. In this film, which was more warmly received by critics when it premiered at Venice in the fall of 1962, Pasolini adopts many of the same "poetic" strategies as in *Accattone*. One of these is his characteristically simultaneous adoption and subversion of a manner or style, in this case Neorealism. One might think, for example, that the visual roughness of these two films — the stark contrasts, the blinding whites and opaque blacks — were the results of a limited budget, as in the early Neorealist films shot before the end of the World War II or immediately thereafter, or of the inexperience of a director who was still very much a beginner. In fact, they were a conscious "linguistic" choice on Pasolini's part. Much to the exasperation of his celebrated cinematographer, Tonino Delli Colli, the poet had him make three generations of copies of the original print of *Accattone* to obtain a visual harshness equal to that of the story he was filming: "He wanted it to look really dirty," says Delli Colli.[58] Pasolini repeated this procedure in *Mamma Roma*, with the difference that the close-ups of Magnani, at Delli Colli's insistence, were allowed a full spectrum of halftones. The stylistic purpose, however, remained the same; that is, first he "artificially" evokes the Neorealist manner, then he proceeds to turn it inside out, elevating the represented reality to the level of tragedy and myth. In *Mamma Roma*, Pasolini does this in several fashions, again with the soundtrack (Bach, Vivaldi, et al.), but even more strikingly with the soliloquies of Anna Magnani's title character, who, back out on the street against her will, vents her spleen in lyric streams of words as she pounds the pavement at a pace not likely to attract many johns. Most arresting of all is the image of Mamma Roma's son, the adolescent Ettore, at the moment of his death. Imprisoned for petty theft when already sick with tuberculosis, he is strapped down half-naked to a table by prison guards after becoming delirious with fever, then left there to die. In a cinematic tour de force, the sharply foreshortened shot of the boy's dead body, taken from below, becomes the very image of Andrea Mantegna's *Dead Christ*,[59] raising the needless death of an innocent at society's hands to the soaring heights of Christ's own sacrifice, and ennobling a symbol of the dispossessed with the art of the great masters. It is a culminating moment for Pasolini's poetics of making myth from reality, a procedure that began with his evocations of rural Friuli and his inner struggles and continued through his portraits of the underclasses, a people theretofore excluded from Italian literature, in whom and for whom "the myth is reborn / in all its power," thanks to the poet's art.

Just as the poetry informed the cinematic vision, Pasolini's work in cinema increasingly influenced the poetry. While working on *Mamma Roma* in 1962, Pasolini began writing the first of the poems that would go into his next book, *Poesia in forma di rosa* (Poem in the Shape of a Rose), published in 1964. These included the so-called "Poesie mondane" ("Worldly poems"), where the language is indeed "lowered entirely to the level of prose," this

58. In an interview included on disc 2 of the Criterion Collection edition of *Mamma Roma*.
59. *Cristo morto* (ca. 1490), considered a revolutionary realization of perspective foreshortening, is in the Pinacoteca di Brera (Milan).

time utterly stripped of traditional form. But it is not just any prose. In addition to the infiltration of technical film jargon (". . . try the seventy-five, then / track and end with a close-up"), the language becomes a veritable mosaic of every sphere of Pasolini's intellectual and artistic activity, combining references to art history, current events, journalism, his present and future works, and his personal life, like a seamless recording of the free association of his thoughts.

> Pontormo with his meticulous
> cameraman has cast streetcorners
> of yellowish buildings to cut through
> this soft, crumbly light
> falling from the yellow sky and turning brown
> speckled with gold over the world of the city . . .

Pasolini's poetry has entered a new phase. Recuperating the diaristic vein in a multifaceted language set down with the same apparent facility with which he wrote prose, the new style displays a visionary quality that has always been present but never fully embraced. Traces of the "old manner" of *Gramsci* remain in some of the other pieces in *Poesia in forma di rosa*, such as "La Guinea," in which the poet further explores, in anguished terza rima, the analogies between Africa and a traditional Italy poised on the brink of extinction. But the future inexorably lies in the breakdown of the form and the dissolution of the vision it once held, which in "La Guinea" occurs literally and cinematically, as images of Africa fade into images of Italy and vice versa. And on the personal level Pasolini's "public" voice is forced to acknowledge its powerlessness—against the world's transformations, and against a public image of himself beyond his control:

> Ah, I can no longer resist the extortions
> of an operation unequaled, I think,
> in turning my thoughts and my acts
>
> into something other than what they are,
> transforming my poor self at its root[.]

The poet who had sought to give voice to history must now succumb to its pitiless course. And as the purpose he had once invested in the *form* of his public expression, the terza rima, dies, so does the form itself. In the volume's title piece, "Poesia in forma di rosa," as Pasolini admits defeat even on linguistic questions—"I got it all wrong," the poem begins—the tercets devolve into little more than a visual device, with lines of widely varying length and rhythm, few rhymes, and strophes that stretch to four and five lines. This and another terza rima poem, "Persecution," are literally his farewell to the form and the "civic" voice it once represented, as the latter piece explores his now profound ostracism from not only the public world, but even from the people on the street. The reason and logic of "Discovering Marx" and *Gramsci* at this point are little more than a distant memory, and poetry itself is cast into doubt (in "La mancanza di richiesta di poesia" ["The Lack of Requests for Poetry"]) when even his fellow literati see henceforth only his distorted public image and cease to view him as a poet ("Your time as a poet is over . . ." "The Fifties are over in this world." "You're yellowing along with *Le ceneri di Gramsci*").

A phase of Pasolini's personal history thus merges with one of the overriding themes of *Poem in the Shape of a Rose*—already present in the *Poesie incivili* that close out *The Religion of My Time*—that is, what he variously calls "the end of History," "Posthistory," and the "new Prehistory." In the "anthropological transmutation" brought on by the booming consumerism that was sweeping away traditional lifestyles, the new, emergent society signaled the end for all of the West—and eventually the whole globe—of what had long been considered "history" in all its many meanings, from the Christian-Marxist teleological model to the more ancient, folkloric cyclical model. The "Revolution," at this point, is "nothing more than a feeling," he writes in the poem "Progetto di opere future" ("Plans for Future Works"). In a 1964 column responding to a reader in the periodical *Vie Nuove*, he explains:

> . . . the slow end of History [. . .] makes me a lonely man, faced with an equally desperate choice: losing myself in southern, African prehistory, in the realms of the Bandung, or throwing myself headlong into the prehistory of neocapitalism, into the mechanization of life for populations at the high industrial level, into the realms of Television. Our children will lose themselves in this future for one hundred, two hundred, two thousand, ten thousand, thirty thousand years.[60]

Already intimated in the final line of "Gramsci's Ashes" ("I know that our history has ended"), where it is one of the undercurrents of his doubts about Marxist historicism, this perception, now universal, here assumes cosmic dimensions. As a product of the old forms of history—humanism, philology, Catholicism, Marxism—Pasolini himself is a "force of the Past" extended into the present and future, privileged by culture and doomed by vocation to tell us of his and our disaster, which extends to Nature itself:

60. Quoted in G. Jori, *Pasolini*, 57.

. . . I see the twilights, the mornings
over Rome, the Ciociaria, the world,
as the first acts of Posthistory
to which I bear witness, by arbitrary
birthright, from the outer edge
of some buried age.

Prescient witness to neoliberalism in embryo, decades before its full
flowering, he sees the "future of mankind" in "the windows of a Bank" in
Rome:

Nobody knew any more about pity
or hope: all they knew,
in this dogged city,
was the future,
just as they had once known life.
It was in everyone's heart,
their daily passion, novelty
taken for granted, light of the new history.[61]

Among the works in *Poem in the Shape of a Rose*, this violent historical
break—both personal and cultural—finds its most fitting formal expres-
sion in the masterly sequence entitled "Una disperata vitalità" ("A Des-
perate Vitality"). Combining the verbal and visual jargons of cinema and
television with nearly every one of Pasolini's formal, rhetorical, poetic,
and narrative manners past and present (reminiscence, elegy, landscape,
motion, analysis, irony, Marxism, prophecy, etc.), the poem—actually
an interlocking suite of poems—recapitulates his entire life's experience,
reaching deep into the past, evoking a televisual present, and thrusting
vertiginously into the future. Opening with image sequences that mimic
cinematic montage,

as in a film by Godard:
        under a sun bleeding motionless
        unique,
the canal of the port of Fiumicino
—a motorboat returning unnoticed
—Neapolitan sailors covered in woolen rags
—a car accident, a few onlookers gathered round . . .

the poem is a microcosm of what Pasolini's artistic and intellectual project
had become: vast and teeming, open-ended, seemingly chaotic but rig-

61. From "La nuova storia," in *Tutte le poesie*, vol. I, 1284.

orously consistent and whole. The methods have changed—expanded, really—but the vision, which has always been one of clairvoyant realism, has remained essentially the same, changing only with the changing reality. Still utterly the poet—"Verse! I write verse! Verse! / [. . .] / verse NO LONGER IN TERCETS" (though the poem *does* contain a section in tercets)—Pasolini has turned to the forms, to the *language* of forms, most befitting his purpose: "I've gone straight back to the magma!" And from the bubbling mass he reemerges artistically whole, true to past and future, "more modern than any modern man, / in search of brothers no longer alive."[62] With its linguistic hodgepodge chosen not by chance but as the necessary image of a specific reality, his multimedia poem is a brilliant example of the "invention" by "experimentation" sought after in "La libertà stilistica"—not an abstract composition of words arranged at the author's whims, but a self-portrait throbbing with the pulse of life, casting its gaze "down through the centuries" into the future. In this single broad gesture, Pasolini leaves the *neoavanguardia* far behind in their willful semantic irrelevance and becomes a sort of one-man, "non-nominalistic"[63] avant-garde, without renouncing either his love of tradition, his desperate embrace of the present, or his will to change the world in the "domain of culture and the spirit."

Seen from the vantage of these poetics, dubbed the "avant-garde of tradition" by poet and critic Gianni D'Elia,[64] Pasolini's paradoxical sociocultural politics—his persistent support of a Communist party he never ceased to lambaste (and did not belong to), his primordial Christian mysticism in the face of Catholic groups that never ceased to persecute him—begin to gain clarity. Anticipating the European "green" left by a good decade, he is a Communist, he says, out of "Instinct of Preservation." He sees the capitalist credo of infinite economic growth as a death sentence for the multimillenary civilization from which all our cultural forms have arisen, a process of "genocide"[65] already underway. And while the orthodox ideologues and party hacks of Communism might be equally besotted with "productivity"—one motive for his constant criticism—he sees the cultural

62. From "Poesie mondane" (p. 313 below).
63. The term is Walter Siti's, in "L'opera rimasta sola," inter alia, postface to *Tutte le poesie*, vol. II, 1899–1944.
64. D'Elia, in *L'eresia di Pasolini. L'avanguardia della tradizione dopo Leopardi*, sees Pasolini as the direct heir of Leopardi in what he calls "the avant-garde of tradition," a concept he develops throughout this book.
65. The term is Pasolini's in "L'articolo sulle lucciole," *Scritti corsari* (Milan: Garzanti, 1975), 130, and elsewhere.

channels of the left as allowing at least the possibility to "coax" the mass "toward a solution," which, however unlikely, might at least spare the cities and countrysides from total commodification. But where Pasolini most fully embraces the socialist worldview is in the residual Judeo-Christian spirituality of its altruism and idealism. Again responding to a reader in *Vie Nuove*, he writes:

> The atheism of a militant communist is the flower of religion compared to the cynicism of a capitalist: in the former one can always find moments of idealism, desperation, psychological violence, cognitive will, and faith — which are elements, however dissociated, of religion; in the latter one finds only Mammon.[66]

But "Logic" (i.e., Marxist rationalism) "has gone out of fashion." Thus "the Revolution is now nothing more than a feeling." "Now," he says, "it's the age / of Psychagogics," that is, of spiritual development.[67] "I can only write in Prophecies / rapt by Music, / in an excess of semen or pity." And so with spiritualism and sensualism, twin poles of his art from the start, will he seek to shape creations with which he might *psychagogically* "coax" mankind — taking his pedagogical vocation to the metaphysical level — onto a "road of love."

*

The personal frustration and sense of persecution expressed in nearly all of *Poesia in forma di rosa* stem from specific developments in Pasolini's life at the time. As his fame as a filmmaker grew, he became an increasingly easy target for the vindictive Italian magistrature and the harassment of certain sectors of the public. He was subjected to false accusations and government censure alike, as when his short 1963 film, *La Ricotta*, was sequestered for many months. He did, however, enjoy a victory of sorts over his detrac-

66. Quoted in Jori, *Pasolini*, 56.
67. Pasolini no doubt intends the term in the full range of its Italian meaning, specifically as the *psicagogia* of ancient pre-Christian religions — that is, the propitiatory rites enacted to guide the souls of the dead in their journey to the underworld — and as the summoning of souls of the dead to the world of the living. He is thus evoking a "spiritual development," encompassing the full cycle of the soul's life before birth (as in section VII of "Una disperata vitalità"), during its time on earth ("Ah, for me this time on earth is but a visit!"; section IV) and thereafter (the "epitaph" that is section VIII, quoted here).

tors when his 1964 film, *The Gospel According to Matthew*, met with the over-
whelming approval of critics and public, with the notable exception of the
Communists and the intellectual left. By 1965 the film was a worldwide
success, and for a moment Pasolini seemed to have been granted a reprieve
from the normally hostile Italian press. In his idiosyncratic treatment of
the scriptural text, aimed at highlighting its most "realistic" and socially
revolutionary aspects, he had clearly touched a resonant chord. With its
agitated Christ, always on the move, at once furious and vulnerable, and
a subjectively "poetic," handheld camera[68] that gave the whole story the
look of a newsreel that had somehow come down through the ages, the
Gospel emerged from centuries of incense-beclouded Church rituals with
striking immediacy.

Pasolini, however, was quick to turn his back on commercial success
and popular acceptance. His next film, *Uccellacci e uccellini* (*Hawks and Spar-
rows* in English, 1965)—starring the celebrated Neopolitan comic Totò,
now in decline, opposite a boy the poet had met on the set of *La Ricotta*,
Ninetto Davoli, who had become his companion and would star in many
of his other films—was quite roughly produced and didactic in tone.
More importantly, it was the first in a series of films in which Pasolini con-
sciously tried to prevent his cinema from becoming just another "object of
consumption" like the common run of foreign and domestic films. Having
become, in his very person, an "object of consumption" for the national
yellow press, Pasolini was never to let up in his direct and indirect chal-
lenges to consumer culture, and the films that followed *Uccellacci*—*Oedipus
Rex*, *Teorema*, *Pigsty*, and *Medea*, among others—became, in his words,
increasingly "aristocratic and difficult, in that they could not be easily
exploited."[69]

These were years of increasingly frantic activity, even by Pasolini's
standards. From 1966 to 1969, for example, aside from the prolific writ-
ing (including essays on film, politics, and culture), he made no less than
five feature-length films and four shorts, many of them involving extensive
scouting for locations in places like Morocco, sub-Saharan Africa, Anatolia,
and India, always in search of timeless settings where a sense of the sacred
remained present in everyday reality. The fruits of these explorations be-

68. In the essay "Il cinema della poesia," in *Empirismo eretico*, Pasolini asserts that
the movement of the handheld camera implies subjectivity and therefore a "poetic"
point of view (*Saggi sulla letteratura e sull'arte*, vol. I, 1461–89).
69. J. Duflot, *Pasolini* (Paris: Editions Albatros, 1977), 74–75.

came increasingly palpable in the atmosphere of ritual and mysticism characterizing such films as *Oedipus Rex*, *Teorema* and, later, *Medea*. They are the visual translation of the "psychagogics" foretold in "A Desperate Vitality."

> Everything is holy, everything is holy, everything is holy. There is nothing natural in Nature, my boy, bear that well in mind. When nature comes to seem natural to you, everything will be finished. And something new will begin. Goodbye sky, goodbye sea. Look behind you, what do you see? Do you see anything natural? [. . .] Is there a single bit of it that seems natural to you, and not possessed by a god?[70]
> —The centaur (speaking to Jason), in *Medea* (1969)

In his cinematic and theatrical evocations of antiquity, Pasolini had found yet another language in which to express his "love for the phenomena of the world" and to evoke the myth that dwells, in embryo, in reality. Sainthood lies within the pimp Accattone just as Apollo guides the sun, just as the nymphs hide in the rushes. And when "nature comes to seem natural to you"—that is, when you see things only with the eyes of reason: the reason of the Enlightenment, of Marxist or capitalist materialism—you will not see the whole; you will have lost your link to a world that stretches back to the origins of language. This is the "new" life beginning for man. Once the utopia of Marxist reason dissolves in concordance with the equally rationalist triumph of the world-as-commodity, Pasolini can only return to the primordial truth of things and the secrets they hold: to see the world ideally as *ierofania*, as "hierophany," the presence of the sacred in everything. Only thus does one see the thing in full. He does not renounce reason per se; it is simply not the whole story. This is the meaning of Pasolini's "realism" and what it has become. "Only what is mythic is realistic, and only what is realistic is mythic," says the centaur to Jason. The poet's purpose is to record at once the thing as he sees it and *the vision in the thing*:

> What man saw in grain when he discovered agriculture, what he learned from this relationship, what he understood from the example of the seeds that lose their form underground in order to be reborn, all this

70. It is hard not to notice an echo here of Allen Ginsberg's 1955 poem, "Footnote to 'Howl'": "Holy! Holy! Holy! [. . .] Everything is holy! everybody's holy! everywhere is holy!" (*Collected Poems 1947–1980*. New York: Harper & Row, 1984.) Pasolini was an admirer of Ginsberg and met the American poet for the first time in New York in 1966. It is interesting to note how Pasolini takes Ginsberg's exaltation of universal sacrality back to a time not just before the modern age, but before the very existence of Christianity and Western Civilization, when it could exist unfettered by Reason.

represented the definitive lesson: resurrection, my dear boy. But now this definitive lesson serves no more purpose. What you see in grains, what you understand of the rebirth of seeds, is henceforth without meaning for you, like some faraway memory that no longer concerns you.

—The centaur (speaking to Jason) in Medea (1969)

"Something new" has indeed begun, analogous to the shift in the story of Medea from the archaic prehistory of Colchis to the Classical age of Greece. But behind the "reason" of Greece remained the irrational, archaic world of the gods, coexistent with it in memory, just as the centaur reappears twofold to the adult Jason: fully human on one side, half man and half horse on the other. "What is sacred," says the centaur, "is preserved alongside its new, profane form." What henceforth remains to Pasolini the poet—in film, essay, fiction, and poetry (as poetry)—is the task of preserving the old form alongside the new, preserving the memory of the sacred in the face of universal profanation, before the continuity is destroyed, even as it is destroyed.

This is one of the overriding themes of Pasolini's last complete book of new poems, *Trasumanar e organizzar* (Transhumanize and Organize), published in 1971 and featuring the lyrics he had begun composing with renewed vigor in 1968. As he says to Duflot in his 1969 book-length interview *Il sogno del centauro* (The Dream of the Centaur): "As I read the mystics, I am discovering more and more [. . .] that the other side of mysticism is indeed 'doing,' 'acting,' action. In fact my next collection of poems will be called *Trasumanar e organizzar*. What I mean by this expression is that the other side of 'transhumanization' (*trasumanar*: the word is Dante's, in its apocopated form)—that is, of spiritual ascent—is, indeed, organization."[71] The justification for Pasolini's radical activism as artist and intellectual thus lies no longer in historical materialism (i.e., "Logic"), but in pure, transcendent idealism.

The historical and metaphysical veins that have alternately informed Pasolini's poetry from the start, and that first began to merge in parts of *Poesia in forma di rosa*, fuse into a single vision in *Trasumanar e organizzar*. In a single linguistic stroke—the title—the poet has affirmed the spiritual need long ignored by the dominant ideologies of the left and forced the concerns of the transcendent spirit into the sphere of modern politics and history. The poetry's language is now more multifaceted and interdisciplinary

71. Duflot, *Pasolini*, 84; also in *Scritti sulla politica e sulla società*, 1462. On Pasolini's use of the Dantean term, see also the notes on the poems, p. 473, and p. 476 under the entry for line 75.

than ever, the verse utterly free, save for inevitable echoes of the old metrics. And for the first time we see a systematic use of fragmentation—of sentences, stanzas, thoughts—and the willful misuse (or lack) of punctuation, capitalization, morphology, and so on. But there is a new clarity in this formlessness, afforded by the serenity of conviction—a belief, however grim, in the cultural-spiritual tabula rasa wrought by the New Prehistory and its resultant, terrifying freedom:

> A freedom never before seen in history
> There is no model for this free image of me
> not in projections in heaven nor in projections on earth
> [. . .]
> Horrid, sad, dull freedom
> and yet never before in human history has there been
> any greater.
> —from "Introduction" (ca. 1970) in appendix
>   (posthumous) to *Trasumanar e organizzar*

Set adrift from prior moorings of religion and community, the alienated man of consumer society becomes a "free," cosmic nomad in the undefined universe of space and time, yet prey to the "totalitarian"[72] manipulations of that same society, and thus a "slave." The only possible salvation remaining is language itself:

> The final hierophany in the order of time,
> cheese on macaroni,
> is, ah, linguistic: I don't believe language
> has ever been assumed up to a godly sphere
> and become as such an object of ritual and prayer.
> The final spasm, in fact,
> has been the interpretation of all reality
> as *hierosemy*, which is even better than
> as *total hierophany*.

The poet has come full circle, from the sacred language of pure poetry in his youth, through its contamination by time and history, and "back" to *hierosemy*—that is, the holiness of the sign, in all its complexity and "impurity," its philological substrata. The sacred, at least for Pasolini, is still preserved alongside its profane form. But for how long? This is, after all, the "final spasm," and, "once this last / consecration is also exhausted, / there is no place [. . .] left where the Lord *might be*." Death shall be no longer

---

72. The word is Pasolini's, in *Scritti corsari* and elsewhere.

"mythic," and thus myth itself shall die. Bereft of consolation, Pasolini's only recourse is, as always, to bear witness: through language and its "consecration"—in poetry, essay, film—to leave one final monument to the tragedy of our demythification, his oeuvre.[73]

Thus, in *Trasumanar* Pasolini's poems assume the stark forms of our world: press releases, polemics, prayers, love lyrics, and documents—"often," writes Zanzotto, "of very high, unexpected quality: mud and snow, circle and vanishing point, submissiveness and stifled cry of presence, cracked orphic egg, and news editorializing as on a TV panel."[74] From the vantage of his growing isolation, awaiting the new, remembering the old, Pasolini lives out in "real time" the death of Western civilization's forms and our inability to make of ourselves any new, ideal forms. He gives us back our forms and myths such as they are, rickety and hollow, and as such they provoke horror and shock.

Or, worse, they elicit only indifference. Indeed, so absent was the critical response to *Trasumanar e organizzar* that Pasolini felt compelled to write his own *autorecensione*, or "self-review." It was as if nobody would forgive him—this most vital, most language-conscious of poets—for taking poetry onto the big screen and the front pages of newspapers. But no matter. The firm conviction, indeed the clairvoyance, present in *Trasumanar e organizzar* would illuminate all his subsequent work in other mediums, particularly the fierce sociometaphysical polemics he waged in columns in the weekly *Tempo* and the Milanese daily *Il Corriere della Sera*, in which he literally foresaw the waves of terror that would soon engulf the peninsula, and the official tolerance and collusion that made it all possible.

Not even the breakup with his beloved Ninetto, who decided to marry a Roman girl in 1971, would distract Pasolini from the creative and intellectual furor of his last four years, when he made the *Trilogy of Life*—the immensely successful films based on stories from *The Decameron*, *The Canterbury Tales*, and *The Arabian Nights*—and wrote most of the essays by which he is best known outside Italy today. This sad episode would, however,

73. G. Jori, in *Pasolini* (110), writes: "If, for Dante, Paul's fateful access to the supreme vision is achieved by providing a structural model of reality, Pasolini's ambition to a global 'hierosemy' leads, in *Trasumanar e organizzar*, in the Notes to *Petrolio-Vas*, and in his essayistic prose, to a cosmic 'structuralism' that freely, and poetically, contaminates semiology and devotion to history, and leads to an interpretation of the world through archetypes and absolute structures—marked by the insistence of capital letters—that coincide with the intuition of 'the other side of the heavens,' the 'divine.'"

74. Zanzotto, *Aure e disincanti*, 211.

inspire a long series, partly unfinished, of 112 sonnets in the great Italian tradition of unrequited love. Written between 1971 and 1973, and only recently available in full in *Tutte le poesie*, the sequence is a poignant farewell to a lapsed time of happiness, in a form from another age, composed as the poet roamed the world on film shoots.

In his last published book of poems, *La nuova gioventù* (The New Youth, 1975), Pasolini revisits another lapsed era, that of his Friulian youth. And in so doing, he renounces his long-cherished illusion of it. The time when he could see in the boys of Friuli "the laughter of their dead forebears" has been forever eclipsed. In a world where fireflies, for example, have definitively disappeared from the Italian landscape due to pollution, "an old man [. . .] can no longer recognize his own youth in the new youth."[75] What once belonged to human memory as far back as the mind could conceive, and still survived in 1940, no longer exists. The chain has been broken, and the world evoked in Pasolini's early poetry, real or not, is gone forever. Now that he stands on the far side of this epochal shift, never to return—now that we move "outside the circle, along [the] straight line" of history, having renounced all prior forms of rebirth—Pasolini, compelled as always to explain and redefine his positions, must rewrite the poems of the first and second parts of *La meglio gioventù*; that is, his first "adult" poems. And *La nuova gioventù* is to *La meglio gioventù* as darkness is to light. The village fountain in the dedicatory opening, originally a "fountain of rustic love," is now a "fountain of love for no one"; and where there was "no water fresher" than its own, now there is "no water older." What was once eternally refreshed is now forever old and irretrievable, soon to be beyond memory.

The only "forward-looking" poems in *La nuova gioventù* are in the cycle of new compositions at the end, entitled "Tetro entusiasmo" ("Grim Enthusiasm"), some of which combine Italian and Friulian for the first time. But the future into which they cast their gaze is grim indeed. Utterly resigned henceforth to the new capitalism's triumph across all sectors of society, Pasolini clings anew, and alone, to a socialist dream become a utopia, himself now reduced, like the imprisoned Gramsci, to "pure, heroic thought." Still, his poetic eye for pathos remains intact:

> Often I feel my heart
> break in the face of people's
> holiness: after all,

75. "L'articolo delle lucciole," in *Scritti corsari*, 129; also in *Saggi sulla politica e sulla società*, vol. II, 405.

being content with an extra
thousand lire in one's pocket[76]
is a form of holiness.
—from "Verses Dashed off in a Hurry"

And in the book's final poem, "Saluto e augurio" ("Goodbye and Best Wishes"), there is even a glimmer of light in the poet's resignation. Addressed to a hypothetical young "Fascist," it is an exhortation to love and defend the things dearest to the poet: the farmhouses and churches, the "intimacy with the sun and the rain," the poor and the "Gods of the fields," which are all things "of the past." Politics don't matter: "It's enough that the feeling / for life be the same for all." And having placed this burden on the young man's shoulders, he says: "Carry it yourself. It shines bright in the heart. / And I shall walk lightly on, always choosing / life, and youth."

It is this faint but profound ray of hope at the close of a book of darkness that, to my mind, gives the lie to the fatalism of those who see Pasolini's murder, a few months after the book came out, as somehow inevitable, willed, or even purposely staged by the poet himself.[77] For when Pasolini was found dead on the morning of November 2, 1975, severely beaten and run over by his own car on the same beach in Ostia where the previous year he had filmed one of the most joyously sensual scenes of *The Arabian Nights*,[78] there was a nearly unanimous rush in the mass media, and even among the intelligentsia, to deem this a fitting conclusion to a life always lived on the edge. They all cited the deep pessimism of his later years, the repeated imagery of death, his recantation of *The Trilogy of Life*, the cruelty and violence of his last film (the posthumously released *Salò, or the 120 Days of Sodom*), and his continued noctambulations in Rome's seediest quarters as signs of a conscious or unconscious solicitation of death, an unwillingness to go on living in a world with which he was perpetually at loggerheads. Forgotten were the circumstances of his creative and personal life at the time of his murder: the unfinished novel of a lifetime, *Petrolio*; the well advanced project for what was to be his most am-

---

76. A thousand lire in 1974–75 was equivalent to about eighty cents US.
77. Pasolini's lifelong personal friend, the painter Giuseppe Zigaina, has written several books advancing the argument that Pasolini had long planned to stage his own murder-suicide, and that his work is full of clues and foreshadowings of this fact. Cf. selected bibliography below for works by Zigaina.
78. Naldini, *Crono*, cxxvi.

bitious film, tentatively titled *Porno-Theo-Kolossal*; the new house he had bought on the beach with Moravia; the medieval tower he had bought and restored in the Viterbo province, where he hoped to withdraw and devote himself to the classics; and, perhaps most importantly, his lifelong commitment never to abandon his mother.

As for Pasolini's obsession with death, and the often haunting manner in which certain images in his writing seem to foreshadow the circumstances of his murder,[79] it must be remembered that death—his own and that of others—had been a dominant theme of his work since the days of his youth. Indeed, mortality, for him, was the most ennobling circumstance of human existence: "The only thing that grants man true greatness," he wrote, "is the fact that he dies."[80] That he envisioned his own death with increasing frequency in the last ten years of his life attests more to the growing prophetic quality of his work during this time,[81] and to the simple fact of aging, than to any fateful necessity in the occurrence of his death, which was murder, pure and simple.[82] On the other hand,

79. Cf. such poems in this volume as "My Former Life," "To Death: A Fragment,"; and "A Desperate Vitality" (pp. 112, 294, and 330, respectively, below). In a note to the posthumously published prose poem *La Divina Mimesis* (1975), Pasolini even imagines publishing the notebooks of a "writer beaten to death with a stick," thus prefiguring the situation in which the editor of his posthumous *Petrolio* found himself when putting the book together; cf. Jori, *Pasolini*, 101.

80. Quoted in De Ceccaty, *Pasolini* (Paris: Editions Gallimard, 2005), 174.

81. Aside from his own death, he foresaw, among other things, the total victory of American-style consumer capitalism as a global phenomenon, the concomitant fall of the Soviet system, the anti-Western rebellion of the Arab-Muslim world (see the poem "Prophecy," p. 362 below), and the collapse of much of the ruling Italian political class due to corruption and collusion in crimes of state (as later proven in the P2 Masonic lodge and *Tangentopoli* scandals, and by subsequent scholarship on the Piazza Fontana massacre and the Bologna train station bombing, which occurred after Pasolini's death). Cf., inter alia, Giorgio Boatti, *Piazza Fontana* (Milan: Feltrinelli, 1993, 2007).

82. The facts of Pasolini's murder have never been convincingly established, due above all to the lack of political and judicial will to get to the bottom of the case. The conviction of Pino Pelosi, the young hustler Pasolini had solicited that evening, as the lone killer, was based entirely on Pelosi's confession and elicited serious doubts from the start. But when the court of first instance, on the basis of inconsistencies between the young man's testimony and the forensic and medical evidence, concluded the likely involvement of other individuals in the crime and recommended further investigation in that direction, the court of second instance re-

such foreshadowings must be clearly distinguished from the terrible sense of personal danger he felt and expressed during the last year or so of his life. For example, on a trip to Sweden just days before he was killed, dur-

---

acted with an alacrity highly unusual for the Italian judiciary, to say the least, and rejected all the first court's findings out of hand without any further investigation.

It is above all the summary nature of the second court's action that has led some to believe that a political decision had been made to cover up the possible complicity of other parties in the murder, either because of the desire, not uncommon at the time in cases potentially involving right-wing extremists, to shield suspects of that political formation, or, in the worst of cases, because of complicity on the part of the state itself. In other words, it was not the demonstrated existence of evidence pointing to accomplices that in itself suggested a possible political crime, since group beatings and murders of homosexuals are unfortunately not an uncommon occurrence; it was, rather, the subsequent actions of the judiciary that suggested it. Moreover, even in 2005 when Pelosi recanted, claimed that there had indeed been accomplices, and gave information corroborating some of the original evidence and testimony, initial motions to reopen the case were ignored.

Many of Pasolini's friends believed from the start that it was a political assassination. (In a 1974 *Corriere* column Pasolini, without naming names, had openly accused the state of complicity in the terrorist massacres at Piazza Fontana in Milan in 1969 and on the Rome-Milan train in 1974, both of which crimes were ultimately attributed, after much evasion and even *dépistage* on the part of some law-enforcement figures, to right-wing extremists.) Others believe that Pasolini was the victim of blackmail.

From a legal standpoint, probably the best book on the poet's murder, replete with the related court documents, is by Marco Tullio Giordana, *Pasolini: Un delitto italiano* (Milan: Mondadori, 1994), which is accompanied by a film of the same name, also by Giordana. Also useful is Dario Bellezza, *Il poeta assassinato* (Venice: Marsilio, 1996), which hews close to the evidence and contradicts the same author's earlier thesis in *Morte di Pasolini* (Milan: Mondadori, 1981), which was more along the lines of the legendary murder-suicide hypothesis. B. D. Schwartz, himself a lawyer, also provides in his *Pasolini Requiem* a thorough account of the available material. René de Ceccaty, in his fine, concise biography *Pasolini*, likewise discusses the question in considerable detail. More hermeneutic approaches to the murder can be found, as mentioned in note 76 above, in several titles by Giuseppe Zigaina, particularly the two editions of *Pasolini e la morte*. Gianni d'Elia takes a similar approach, though basing his argument mostly on Pasolini's posthumous novel *Petrolio*, in *Il Petrolio delle Stragi* (Milan: Effigie, 2006). There is also *Pasolini: Cronaca giudiziaria, persecuzione, morte* (Milan: Garzanti, 1977), a compilation of testimonies, documents, analyses, chronologies, and so on edited by Pasolini's close friend and principal actress Laura Betti, which conveys a keen sense of the continual and

ing a question-and-answer period with the audience after a film screening, Pasolini said that he expected sooner or later to be murdered.[83] It was not the first time he'd made such a statement. His fear was based on a contemporary climate of violence and the very real harassment and threats he had endured for decades from right-wing agitators, which had increased as he directly took on the corrupt rulers of Italy from the front pages of *Il Corriere della Sera*, perhaps the country's most respected daily. But these passionate public harangues, however dangerous, were hardly a solicitation of death; rather, they denounced the culture of death proper to a consumer society "based on the idea of possession and the idea of destruction,"[84] in the name of a better, increasingly elusive life. "Here [in Italy] there is a desire to kill," Pasolini said in his last interview, given a few hours before he was murdered. "And this desire binds us together like sinister brothers in the sinister failure of an entire society. [. . .] We are all in danger."[85] His confrontation with this society was a clear rejection of what he saw as its debased reality, not a complacent self-indulgence in its same destructive whims. Pasolini was very clear about this: "Refusal has always been an

---

mounting persecution of the poet-cineast up until, and perhaps culminating in, his death.

The blackmail-setup thesis was prominently featured in a recent documentary by German filmmaker Andreas Pichler, titled *The Pasolini Affair* (Die Akte Pasolini, 2013). Pichler bases his account primarily on the testimony of Pasolini's close friend Sergio Citti (see p. 456 in notes on the poems in this volume), who had seen the poet/filmmaker earlier that same evening and claims that Pasolini had been driving frantically around the Rome metropolitan area that day and evening to meet with unnamed people, trying to recover two missing reels from what proved to his last film, *Salò, or the 120 Days of Sodom*, which were allegedly being held for ransom, or so Pasolini and Citti believed. Citti later came to believe that the reels were used as bait to lure Pasolini into the ambush that killed him. Finally, the convicted murderer, Giuseppe (Pino) Pelosi, wrote his own unfortunate book, *Io, angelo nero* (Rome: Sinnos, 1995), maintaining his original thesis of accidental homicide in self-defense, which, as mentioned, he was to recant ten years later during a national television interview, claiming that three "unknowns" with "Southern accents" had forced their way into Pasolini's car, killed the poet, and threatened to kill Pelosi's family if he told the truth. Whatever the reality, there would probably be enough material and secondhand witnesses still alive today to solve the case if only there were the political will to do so.

83. B. D. Schwartz, *Pasolini Requiem*, 10.
84. *L'ultima intervista di Pasolini*, by Furio Colombo and GianCarlo Ferretti (Rome: Avagliano Editore, 2005), 62 (also in *Saggi sulla politica e sulla società*, 1723).
85. Ibid., 57.

essential act. The saints, the hermits, but also the intellectuals, the few who made history, were those who said no."[86]

In a 1967 essay entitled "Observations on the Sequence Shot"—an allegorical meditation on real life as "unedited cinema," based on the Zapruder film of the assassination of John F. Kennedy—Pasolini wrote:

> It is absolutely necessary that we die, *because as long as we are alive, we lack meaning*, and the language of our lives [. . .] is untranslatable, a chaos of possibilities, an uninterrupted search for relationships and meanings. Death enacts an instantaneous montage of our lives: that is, it chooses the truly significant moments (which can no longer be modified by other possible contrary or inconsistent moments), and places them in sequence, creating from our present—which is infinite, unstable, and uncertain, and therefore linguistically indescribable—a past that is clear, stable, and certain, and therefore linguistically quite describable [. . .]. *Only thanks to death does our life let us express ourselves.*[87]

Pasolini's murder brought into focus, as no critical commentary ever could, an artistic career of which one of the dominant themes was the death of the innocent—from the "dead boy" of his first poem to the extinction of the peasant world, from the sacrifice of Christ to the wasted lives of the world's underclasses, to the victims of Fascist perversity in *Salò*. What we make of the sudden and violent "montage" of his life remains, however, up to us. Certainly his death halted a creative juggernaut, one of the great human and intellectual dramas of our time. On the other hand, his poetry, like his description of death, also chose "the truly significant moments" of his life and placed them "in sequence," to the point that he more than once referred to his own past works as "posthumous." As the years went by, moreover, his work had become more and more about the artistic process itself than about any single, finished product, and his sudden passing ensured that it would all remain open-ended. Yet if his death thus confirmed a creative mechanism long at work, the sudden void it created also underscored the vital force he had been. It deprived the world, in his own words, of "one less signature of importance in the pleas for peace,"[88] of a man who unflinchingly "state[d] / his case at great risk to his carcass."[89] For this, I

86. Ibid., 53.
87. "Osservazioni sul piano sequenza," *Saggi sulla letteratura e sull'arte*, vol. I, 1560–61. The italics in the quote are Pasolini's own.
88. "Una disperata vitalità" (p. 351 below).
89. From "La Guinea," in *Poesia in forma di rosa* (cited in *Tutte le poesie*, vol. I, 1085–92).

think, came the grief-stricken crowd of ten thousand on November 5, 1975, to pay their respects, in the shadow of Giordano Bruno in Rome's Campo de' Fiori,[90] to the latest in a succession of great Italian heretics—one who, amidst the storm, still preferred to "walk lightly on, always choosing / life, and youth."[91]

Stephen Sartarelli

90. Campo de' Fiori, in the historic heart of Rome, was the site where the philosopher Giordano Bruno (1548–1600) was burnt at the stake for heresy by the Papal Inquisition. In 1887 a statue was erected in his memory by Ettore Ferrari at the center of the square, and it was around this statue that the crowd, having issued from the nearby Communist Party headquarters in Via delle Botteghe Oscure, gathered to pay their last respects to Pasolini.
91. From "Saluto e augurio" ("Goodbye and Best Wishes"), p. 447 below.

ON THE TEXTS

Given Pasolini's vast poetic output, this volume does not pretend to be exhaustive or definitive. A great deal of his verse remains to be translated into English, particularly his early work in the Friulian dialect. The early poems in Italian and the many uncollected cycles now available in Walter Siti's edition *Tutte le poesie* (2003) likewise constitute a deep well yet to be tapped, to say nothing of the less known pieces in the principal collections Pasolini published during his lifetime. Here I have merely tried to give as representative a selection as possible, within the twin constraints of time and space, of the full range of Pasolini's highly diverse yet always recognizable voice. Of considerable help in my decisions was the anthology *Poesie scelte* (1997), edited by Nico Naldini and Francesco Zambon.

As for the translations, the broad diversity of Pasolini's poetic "manners" necessarily dictated a fluid and changeable approach in rendering his texts into reasonably faithful English. For example, the Friulian poems generally display a concision and verbal economy present only in the earliest of Pasolini's Italian texts, which were written when the poet was still under the influence of the dialect, while the bulk of his mature Italian compositions are famous for their combination of baroque floridity and prosaic sprawl. As a result, when translating the dialect poems, I have tended to eschew the rhyme, when it is present, in order to preserve as much as possible the simple meaning and plain, fable-like diction of the original. On the other hand, in the more discursive Italian pieces of his maturity, with their often serpentine, Latinate sentences, I felt much freer to search for rhymes that might convey the tension between form and content in the models. While this approach may seem inconsistent, I have nevertheless adopted it in an attempt to conform to the characteristics inherent in each specific text.

Pasolini himself, in his compositional approach, let the qualities proper to whatever language he happened to be using at any given moment guide him in his choices. This is, in fact, one of the principal reasons for the discrepancy between his Friulian and Italian poems, and for the similar divergence one finds between his Roman and Italian prose fiction. It is also one of the things that makes him, when writing in Italian, a most "Italian" writer — that is, given to expansiveness and complexity. With his language(s) as my guide, I have tried to convey these sometimes striking variations within the limits of my American English. Nevertheless, in those instances where I attempted to reproduce, at least in part, the original rhyme scheme (as in the terza rima poems), I also allowed myself the freedom to abandon the pattern when necessary and not to force the meaning too much for the sake of the form.

In any case, a careful reader will note that Pasolini's approach to closed forms is, in fact, quite open and variable. Among his many idiosyncrasies, he often uses off-rhymes, apocopated rhymes, and assonances in the place of rhymes; abandons rhyme schemes established at the start of a poem only to revive part or all of them later in the poem; temporarily abandons metrical schemes for rhetorical effect or semantic necessity; or leans, for certain passages, on internal and cross-rhymes more than end rhymes. In my own approach to his formal work, I have attempted to reproduce the spirit and, at least in part, the effect of this variable approach.

For the original texts, I have relied on Walter Siti's comprehensive annotated two-volume edition of *Tutte le poesie*, a veritable gift to Pasolini scholars and admirers.

I
Da *La meglio gioventù* /
From *The Best of Youth*
(The Friulian Poems)

Il nini muàrt

Sera imbarlumida, tal fossàl
a cres l'aga, na fèmina plena
a ciamina pal ciamp.

Jo ti recuardi, Narcìs, ti vèvis il colòur
da la sera, quand li ciampanis
a sùnin di muàrt.

David

Pognèt tal pos, puòr zòvin,
ti voltis viers di me il to ciaf zintìl
cu' un ridi pens tai vuj.

Ti sos, David, coma un toru ta un dì di Avrìl
che ta li mans di un frut ch'al rit
al va dols a la muàrt.

Tornant al Pàis

Où sont les neiges d'antan?
F. VILLON

    I

Fantassuta, se i fatu
sblanciada dongia il fòuc,
coma una plantuta
svampida tal tramònt?
«Jo i impiji vecius stecs
e il fun al svuala scur
disìnt che tal me mond
il vivi al è sigùr.»
Ma a chel fòuc ch'al nulìs
a mi mancia il rispìr,
e i vorès essi il vint
ch'al mòur tal pàis.

Dead Boy

Radiant evening, water rises
in the ditch, a woman with child
walks in the field.

I remember you, Narcissus; you were
the color of evening when the bells
tolled the knell.

David

Leaning on a well, poor lad,
you turn your graceful head toward me,
a solemn smile in your eyes.

You, David, are like a bull on an April day
in the hands of a laughing boy,
gently bound for slaughter.

Returning to the Village

Où sont les neiges d'antan?
F. VILLON

I

What are you doing
by the fire, girl,
pale as a sapling
fading in the dusk?
"I'm kindling old sticks.
The smoke rises dark
and tells me the world
I live in is safe."
But by the sweet-smelling fire
I cannot breathe.
I wish I were the wind
dying down in the village.

II

Il me viàs l'è finìt.
Dols odòur di polenta
e tris-c' sìgus di bòus.
Il me viàs l'è finìt.
«Ti vens cà di nualtris,
ma nualtris si vif,
a si vif quiès e muàrs
coma n'aga ch'a passa
scunussuda enfra i bars.»

III

A fiesta a bat a glons
il me pàis misdì.
Ma pai pras se silensi
ch'a puarta la ciampana!
Sempri chè tu ti sos,
ciampana, e cun passiòn
jo i torni a la to vòus.
«Il timp a no'l si mòuf:
jot il ridi dai paris,
coma tai rams la ploja,
tai vuj dai so frutìns.»

Ciant da li Ciampanis

Co la sera a si pièrt ta li fontanis
il me pàis al è colòur smarìt.

Jo i soj lontàn, recuardi li so ranis,
la luna, il trist tintinulà dai gris.

A bat Rosari, pai pras al si scunìs:
jo i soj muàrt al ciant da li ciampanis.

Forèst, al me dols svualà par il plan,
no ciapà pòura: jo i soj un spirt di amòur

che al so pàis al torna di lontàn.

II

My journey is over.
Sweet smell of polenta,
sad lowing of cattle.
My journey is over.
"You've come here among us,
but we only live,
live quiet and dead,
like water that trickles
unseen between hedges."

III

Midday chimes ring
festive in my village.
Yet what silence the bell
casts over the fields!
You haven't changed, bell;
in awe I return to your voice.
"Time does not move:
behold the fathers' smiles
in the children's eyes
like rain on the branches."

Song of the Bells

When evening dissolves in the fountains
my village turns a forgotten color.

From afar I remember the frogs,
the moon, the crickets' sad tremolo.

Rosario rings, trails off through the fields:
I have died to the song of the bells.

Stranger, do not fear my gentle flight
over the plain; I am a spirit of love

come back to his land from afar.

La domènia uliva

FÌ

> Mari, i vuardi ingropàt
> il vint che scur al mòur
> par di là dai vinc' àins
> dal me vivi cristiàn.
>
> Seris, àrbui bagnàs,
> frutìns lontàns ch'a sìghin,
> mari, chistu il paìs
> par là ch'i soj passàt.

MARI (*tal Sèil*)

> Parsé da li me vìssaris
> a no èisa nassuda
> la àgrima ch'al plans
> il me fì benedèt?
>
> Sarès to mari, àgrima,
> clara coma na stela,
> e al sun lizèir dal Espuj
> i ti cocolarès . . .
>
> Lui, ch'al ti plans, al è
> sempri sòul tal paìs,
> dut scur, tai pras verdùs,
> i fòucs, i vecius murs!

MARI-FRUTA (*puartànd pal paìs l'aulìf*)

> A bat misdì di Pasca!
>
> Fuèjs claris, sèil fresc.
>
> Fantàs, volèisu aulìf?
>
> Clara sera di Pasca.

66 *

Olive Sunday

SON

> Mother, I watch in dismay
> as the wind dies darkly
> past my twenty years
> of Christian life.
>
> Evenings, wet trees,
> children shouting far away,
> this, Mother, is the village
> I've left behind.

MOTHER (*in Heaven*)

> Why has my womb
> borne not a tear
> to weep for
> my blessèd son?
>
> I should be your mother,
> star-bright tear,
> and at the vespers' gentle sound,
> I should rock you in my lap . . .
>
> He who weeps for you
> is always alone in the village,
> dark amid the soft green fields,
> the fires and the ancient walls!

CHILD-MOTHER (*carrying olive branches round the village*)

> Easter's midday chimes are ringing!
>
> The leaves are bright, the sky is fresh.
>
> Children! Want some olive branches?
>
> Easter evening's bright, the sky is fresh.

Clara roja, sèil fresc.

Aulìf, aulìf, aulìf.

FÌ

Frututa da l'aulìf,
cor a dami na fras-cia.
Tu, colòur di rosa,
fra li fuèjs i ti ris.

Ma to mari a ti vif
la so passion tai vuj:
a si sblancia il pàis
e tu i ti trimis duta . . .

MARI-FRUTA

No, i no trimi fantàt:
al trima il sèil di fuèjs
cu'l soreli lizèir
ch'al rit tal nustri ciaf.

Al trima fresc il pòul,
al trima clar il fun,
al trima, muàrt tal lun,
di ghitaris il borc.

FÌ

Se ciàcaris! Na fras-cia,
no altri, i ài domandàt.
Sai ben jo se ch'a trima
tal pàis sensa pas.

Me mari a era fruta
e chistu muàrt sunsùr
al passava pal còur
sidìn dai vecius murs.

The canal is bright, the sky is fresh.

Olive branches, olive branches!

SON

> Olive-branch girl,
> come give me a branch.
> Face like a rose, you
> laugh between the leaves.
>
> But your mother's distress
> shines forth in her eyes:
> the village grows dim
> and you tremble all over . . .

CHILD-MOTHER

> No, my boy, I tremble not:
> the sky trembles with leaves,
> a soft sun laughs
> above our heads.
>
> The poplar trembles cool,
> the smoke trembles bright;
> dead in the light, the village
> trembles with guitars.

SON

> Such chatter! A branch
> is all I ask, no more.
> I know well what trembles
> in the restless village.
>
> When my mother was a girl
> this lifeless rumble
> shook the silent heart
> of the ancient walls.

MARI-FRUTA

A è la Pasca ch'a suna
pierduda pai rivàj,
in tal còur dal soreli
ch'al lus sui nustris maj.

Li cròus a si cujèrzin
di zemis, l'aria a è un ciant.
Pai ciamps i ciampanilis
a ciàntin il dì sant.

FÌ

Jo i no sai di cròus!
Pierdùt ta la me vòus
i sint sòl la me vòus
i cianti la me vòus.

MARI-FRUTA

E il sèil?

FÌ

Al lus sidìn.

MARI-FRUTA

E i àins?

FÌ

Muàrs.

MARI-FRUTA

I cuàrps?

CHILD-MOTHER

> It's Easter ringing
> madly along the banks,
> in the heart of the sun
> that shines on our troubles.
>
> The crosses are covered
> with buds, the air is a song.
> Over the fields the belfries
> sing the holy day.

SON

> I know nothing of crosses!
> Lost in my voice,
> I hear only my voice,
> I sing of my voice.

CHILD-MOTHER

> What of the heavens?

SON

> They shine in silence.

CHILD-MOTHER

> What of the years?

SON

> Dead.

CHILD-MOTHER

> And the bodies?

FÌ

Ah, dols Avril . . .

MARI-FRUTA

Li fèminis?

FÌ

SÒUL LA ME VÒUS.

MARI (*tornada spirt*)

Ah, Crist.

FÌ

Par sempri a mòur
ju pai pras scurs
la trista vòus
che jo i suspiri.

A no si ferma
sot il sèil mut,
a no si piert
cu'l vint lontàn.

Dutis li seris
la sint ch'a mòur
pai vecius murs
e pai pras scurs.

MARI (*tal Sèil*)

Fì, la to vòus no basta
a fati coma i paris:
li lòur peràulis claris
a ti vìvin tal sen.

SON

Ah, sweet April . . .

CHILD-MOTHER

And the women?

SON

ONLY MY VOICE.

MOTHER (*a spirit again*)

Ah, Christ.

SON

The sad voice
of my sigh
forever dies
across the darkened fields.

It does not stop
beneath the silent sky,
it is not lost
upon the distant wind.

I hear it die
every evening
over ancient walls
and darkened fields.

MOTHER (*in Heaven*)

Son, your voice alone
won't make you like our fathers:
their clear words
live on in your breast.

A son peràulis muartis
di ligrìa e prejera,
fì, ciàntilis cun me,
ciàntilis pal to ben.

MARI E FÌ

Pari nustri lontàn
ta la mari dal sèil
nu tal còur da la ciera
coma in sun ti ciantàn.

Benedèt il To Nòn
colàt tal nustri lavri
e tai lavris dai fradis
parsè si perdonani.

Dani il pan ogni dì
fin al dì da la muàrt
quan' chi'i vignìn tal sèil
par no vivi pì.

FÌ (tornàt sòul tal paìs)

A plòuf un fòuc
scur tal me sen:
no'l è soreli
e no'l è lus.

Dis dols e clars
a svuàlin via,
jo i soj di ciar
ciar di frutùt.

S'a plòuf un fòuc
scur tal me sen,
Crist al mi clama
MA SENSA LUS.

They are dead words
of joy and prayer.
Sing them with me, my Son,
sing them for your own good.

MOTHER AND SON

Our father far away
in heaven's womb,
we sing to you as in a dream
from the heart of the earth.

Blessed be thy name,
fallen from our lips
onto our brothers' lips
that they might forgive us.

Give us each day our bread
until our dying day
when we shall join the sky
never to live again.

SON (*alone again in the village*)

Fire rains dark
in my breast:
it is neither
sun nor light.

Days sweet and bright
fly away,
I am made of flesh,
a boy's flesh.

When fire rains
dark in my breast,
Christ calls to me,
BUT WITHOUT LIGHT.

Dansa di Narcìs

Jo i soj neri di amòur
nè frut nè rosignòul
dut intèir coma un flòur
i brami sensa sen.

Soj levàt ienfra li violis
intànt ch'a sclariva,
ciantànt un ciant dismintiàt
ta la not vualiva.
Mi soj dit: "Narcìs!"
e un spirt cu'l me vis
al scuriva la erba
cu'l clar dai so ris.

Pastorela di Narcìs

Jèir vistìt di fiesta
(ma i èrin di Vìnars)
i zevi par i tìnars
pras e i ciamps àrsis.
I tegnevi li mans
in sacheta . . . Cutuàrdis àins!
cuàrp cialt di belessa!
I tociavi le me cuessa
sot li plejs lìmpiis da la barghessa.

Na vòus a ciantava
ta l'ombrena dai poj.
Jo i ài sigàt: "Hoi!"
crodìnt ch'a fòssin fioj . . .
I soj zut là dongia
e a era na frutina bionda . . .
No: na fantata
cu na ciamesa scarlata
fant erba ic bessola ta la fumata.

Narcissus Dancing

I am black with love
neither boy nor nightingale
intact as a flower
I yearn without desire.

I arose amid violets
 at the day's first light,
sang a song forgotten
 in the unchanging night.
 I said to myself: "Narcissus!"
 and a spirit with my face
 darkened the grass
with the glow of his curls.

Narcissus Pastourelle

Yesterday dressed in my Sunday
best (though it was Friday)
I wandered through greening
meadows and dried-up fields,
hands in my pockets . . .
 Fourteen years old!
 a body warm with beauty!
Under my trousers' limpid folds
I was touching my thigh.

A voice was singing
in the shade of the poplars.
 "Hey!" I called out,
thinking it was my friends . . .
 As I drew near
I saw a girl with blond hair . . .
 No, it was a young woman
in a scarlet blouse,
alone in the mist, pulling up grass.

I olmi platàt . . .
 e al so post i soj jo:
mi jot sintàt ta un soc
 sot i rams dal pòul.
  I vuj di me mari
neris coma il fòns dal stali,
  il stomi lusìnt
 sot da l'abit risìnt,
e una man pojada sora il grin.

Il dì da la me muàrt

Ta na sitàt, Trièst o Udin,
 ju par un viàl di tèjs,
di vierta, quan' ch'a mùdin
 il colòur li fuèjs,
  i colarài muàrt
sot il soreli ch'al art
   biondu e alt
e i sierarài li sèjs,
lassànlu lusi, il sèil.

Sot di un tèj clìpit di vert
 i colarài tal neri
da la me muàrt ch'a dispièrt
 i tèjs e il soreli.
  I bièj zuvinùs
a coraràn ta chè lus
  chi'i ài pena pierdùt,
 svualànt fòur da li scuelis
 cui ris tal sorneli.

I spied on her unseen . . .
and in her place I saw
myself, sitting on a root,
under the poplars' branches . . .
with my mother's eyes
dark as the bottom of a manger,
chest glistening
under new clothes,
hand resting in my lap.

The Day of My Death

In a city, Trieste or Udine,
    along an avenue of lindens
when the leaves change
    color in spring,
    I shall fall down dead
under a sun burning
        blond and high
and close my eyes,
leaving the sky to its light.

Under a linden warm with green
    I shall fall into the black
of death, which the sun
    and lindens will dispel.
    Beautiful boys
will run in the light
        that I've just left,
        flying out of the schools,
        curls falling onto their brows.

Jo i sarài 'ciamò zòvin
    cu na blusa clara
e i dols ciavièj ch'a plòvin
    tal pòlvar amàr.
    Sarài 'ciamò cialt
e un frut curìnt pal sfalt
    clìpit dal viàl
    mi pojarà na man
    tal grin di cristàl.

Laris

Rivat dongia to mari
sintiratu enciamò
i me bussons tal lavri
ch'i ti ài dat coma un lari?

Ah, laris duciu doi!
No èria scur tal prat?
No robàvinu ai poj
la ombrena tal to sac?

I cunìns son restàs
sensa erba stasera,
e i to lavris robàs
bùssin la prima stela . . .

Conzèit

Romài essi lontàns a val,
Friul, essi scunussùs. A par
il timp dal nustri amòur un mar
    lustri e muàrt.
In ta la lus la to part
a è finida, no ài scur tal sen
par tignì la to ombrena.

I shall be still young
   in a bright shirt
my sweet hair streaming
   in the bitter dust.
   I shall be still warm,
and a boy running down
     the asphalt avenue
   shall lay a hand upon
   my crystal lap.

Thieves

Back home with your mother,
will you still feel the kisses
I left on your lips
like a thief?

Ah, thieves, both of us!
Was it not dark in the field?
Did we not steal the poplars'
shadow in your bag?

The rabbits will go
without grass tonight,
as your stolen lips
kiss the evening's first star.

Envoi

By now, Friuli, to be
far away is to be unknown.
The time of our love
is like a glistening
   dead sea.
Your part has ended in light
and I have no darkness in me
to hold your shadow.

II
Da *L'Usignolo della Chiesa Cattolica* / From *The Nightingale of the Catholic Church*

Le albe

È ancora buio, povere vecchie, e l'alba vi sbianca i visi di cera: con voi sono venuti in chiesa solo tre quattro giovinetti.

Dove sono volati gli anni che dividono il corpo di questi ragazzi da quello dei loro padri? Tu, Domenico, figlio di Stefano, non pregare col colore di quegli occhi, che mi fai tremare, se conto nel tuo grembo gli uomini del tuo sangue che furono qui piegati a pregare.

O piccolo servo! Corpo di tuo padre, labbra di tuo padre, petto di tuo padre, che morte risuona nel tuo canto, che vita nel tuo quieto non esistere?

Io guardo in questi ragazzi il riso dei loro morti quando venivano in chiesa, e, cantando, credevano di essere vivi per sempre. Ma gli anni spariti nel paese non sono mai trascorsi. Questa è una loro alba, e noi, noi siamo i morti.

La Passione

I

Cristo nel corpo
sente spirare
odore di morte.
Ah che ribrezzo
sentirsi piangere!
Marie, Marie,
albe immortali,
quanto dolore . . .
Io fui fanciullo
e oggi muoio.

II

Cristo, il tuo corpo
di giovinetta
è crocifisso
da due stranieri.
Sono due vivi

Dawns

Poor old women, it's still dark as dawn whitens your waxen faces.
Only three or four boys have come to church with you.

   What's become of the years separating the bodies of these boys
from those of their fathers? You, Domenico, Stefano's son, don't pray
with the color of your eyes. I tremble when I count in your loins the
men of your line who came here and knelt down to pray.

   O little servant with your father's body, your father's lips, your
father's chest! What death resounds in your song, what life in your
quiet nonexistence?

   In these boys I see the laughter of their dead forebears, who used
to come into church and, when they sang, thought they would live
forever. But the village's long-vanished years have never passed. This
dawn is theirs, and we, we are the dead.

The Passion

   I

Christ in his body
smells the odor
of death in the air.
Ah, how wretched
to hear oneself weep!
Marys, Marys,
undying dawns,
so much sorrow . . .
I was once a boy
and today I die.

   II

Christ, thy body
like a girl's
is crucified
by two foreigners.
They're two strapping

ragazzi e rosse
hanno le spalle,
l'occhio celeste.
Battono i chiodi
e il drappo trema
sopra il Tuo ventre . . .
Ah che ribrezzo
col caldo sangue
sporcarvi i corpi
color dell'alba!
Foste fanciulli,
e per uccidermi
ah quanti giorni
d'allegri giochi
e d'innocenze.

III

Cristo alla pace
del Tuo supplizio
nuda rugiada
era il Tuo sangue.
Sereno poeta,
fratello ferito,
Tu ci vedevi
coi nostri corpi
splendidi in nidi
di eternità!
Poi siamo morti.
E a che ci avrebbero
brillato i pugni
e i neri chiodi,
se il Tuo perdono
non ci guardava
da un giorno eterno
di compassione?

lads with shoulders
red and eyes
a heavenly blue.
They hammer the nails,
and the cloth upon
Thy belly trembles . . .
Ah, how wretched
to sully your bodies
the color of dawn
with my hot blood!
You once were boys
and now to kill me
oh! all those days
of cheerful games
and innocence.

III

Christ, in the peace
of Thy torment
naked dew
was Thy blood.
Placid poet,
wounded brother,
thou sawest us
when our splendid
bodies rested
in eternal nests!
Then we died.
For what purpose would
the fists and the black
nails have shone,
had Thy forgiveness
not looked down upon us
from an eternal day
of compassion?

IV

Cristo ferito,
sangue di viole,
pietà degli occhi
chiari dei Cristiani!
Fiore fiorente,
sul monte lontano
come possiamo
piangerti, o Cristo?
Il cielo è un lago
che mugge intorno
al muto Calvario.
O Crocifisso,
lasciaci fermi
a contemplarti.

V

Cristo, ai tuoi poveri
figli dispersi
nell'infinito
cielo del vivere,
ecco, morendo
Tu lasci questa
finita Immagine.
Soave faciullo,
corpo leggero,
ricci di luce . . .
è San Giovanni.
Perduti in nubi
d'indifferenza
in Sé ci chiama
e a Sé ci informa
questo Tuo Corpo.

IV

Christ wounded,
blood of violets,
pity in the fair eyes
of the Christians!
Flowering flower
on a distant hill,
how may we weep
for thee, O Christ?
The sky is a thundering
lake all around
silent Calvary.
O Crucifix,
keep us still
to gaze upon thee.

V

Christ, to thy poor
children scattered
in the infinite
sky of life,
thou, in dying
leavest us
this finite Image.
Gentle boy,
nimble body,
curls of light . . .
Saint John.
Lost in clouds
of indifference,
we are summoned,
we are moulded
by this thy Body.

VI

Cristo si abbatte
dentro il Suo corpo.
Da se remote
in quali ardenti
campagne ha sguardo
la Sua pupilla?
Qui è ben cieco,
fermo sull'ossa:
un uccelletto
insanguinato
su una proda.
Dietro, la luce
marcisce il cielo.
Per le vallate
e per le vette
non suona voce:
ultimo e dolce
fruscio la serpe
che si rintana.
O Dio che ombre
dentro il chiarore
delle saette!
La Samaria
annega al buio,
la morte tuona
s'un cimitero
di fresche aiuole!
Polvere e fronde
echi di voci
riversi al vento
nel mesto buio.
Ah siamo uomini
dimentichiamo.
Dietro di Cristo
sui monti morti
il cielo fugge,
è un cieco fiume.

VI

Christ falls down
into His body.
To what burning
heartlands far away
does His pupil
cast its gaze?
Now He's blind,
bones unmoving:
a bloodied
little bird
cast upon a shore.
Behind, the light
rots the sky.
Across the valleys
and mountaintops
no voice rings out:
a last, sweet
slithering, the snake
furrowing back home.
O God, what shadows
in the flashing
thunderbolts!
Samaria drowns
in darkness,
death thunders
over a graveyard
of fresh flower beds!
Dust and boughs,
echoes of voices
blown back on the wind
in the dismal gloom.
Alas, we forget
we are men.
Behind Christ
the sky flees
over dead mountains.
It is a blind river.

In Memoriam

Tu sei stato
come me:
abiti freschi e scarpe nuove.
O dolci Domeniche!
Tua madre cambiò viso mille volte
con te fanciullo
e giovinetto.
Ora
tu sai
l'orrendo momento,
l'ultimo respiro.
Forse
hai visto con altri occhi
QUESTI abiti e QUESTA camicia,
povero spirito
tremante sulle proprie spoglie
coi labbri ancora piegati
al riso
del giovane vivo.
Ma io
esperto del gioco,
non so coprirti di fiori . . .
È ridicolo!
È uno scherzo di certo!
Tu spirito?
Non ho di te
immagini di dolore.
Tu ridi,
ridi,
nel mio ricordo.
Cercherò,
nell'acqua e tra i sassi
il tuo viso di morto.
Ma credo
che non lo troverò.
Tu non senti suonare
le campane,

In Memoriam

You were once
like me:
fresh clothes and new shoes.
O sweet Sundays!
Your mother wore a thousand different faces
in your childhood
and youth.
Now
you know
the terrible moment,
the final breath.
Perhaps
you've seen THESE clothes, THIS shirt
with other eyes,
poor spirit
trembling over its own remains,
lips still curled
with the laughter
of the living boy.
But I
know the game well,
and cannot cover you in flowers . . .
It's ridiculous!
It's surely a joke!
You, a ghost?
I have no mournful images
of you.
You laugh,
laugh
in my memory.
I shall look
in the water, between the rocks
for your dead face.
But I don't think
I'll ever find it.
You cannot hear
the bells toll,

e la tua voce di lieto amico
non sa
che ti vuole il silenzio.

Litania

JANUA COELI

La porta s'apre
quando la pioggia
marcisce la sera.
Allora un raggio

rompe dai nuvoli.
Tu nuda, o Vergine,
specchi nell'umido
il viso azzurro.

SPECULUM JUSTITIAE

Specchio del cielo!
In te le nubi
i muri gli alberi
cadono immoti.

Spio capovolto . . .
Che pace paurosa!
Non c'è un sospiro
nel cielo, un alito.

MATER PURISSIMA

Poveri miei occhi
di giovinetto
chini s'un corpo
colore dell'alba!

and your happy, friendly voice
does not know
the silence wants you.

Litany

JANUA COELI

The door opens
as rain rots
the evening.
A ray then

breaks through the clouds.
You are naked, O Virgin,
your azure face
mirrored in the damp.

SPECULUM JUSTITIAE

Mirror of the sky!
In you the clouds,
the walls, the trees
fall motionless.

Upside down I watch . . .
What frightening calm!
Not a breath of wind
in the sky, not a sigh.

MATER PURISSIMA

My poor eyes
like a boy's
downcast on a body
the color of dawn!

Il gesto santo
del mio peccato
cade in un vespro
di castità.

MATER CASTISSIMA

Ahi crudeltà
non trapassarmi
con gli occhi il corpo!
Sì, esso è nudo

caldo e innocente . . .
Sotto quel crudo
amore degli occhi
mi sento morire.

MATER INVIOLATA

Dal tuo grembiule
accieca il figlio
un lume candido
di albe e gigli.

Madre! quel lume
è tanto puro
che la tua coscia
pare di neve.

TURRIS EBURNEA

Seni di avorio,
nidi di gigli,
non v'ha violato
mano di padre.

Fianchi lucenti
di nere nuvole
non vi fa scuro
la nostra pioggia.

The holy gesture
of my sin
falls in a vesper
of chastity.

MATER CASTISSIMA

Oh cruelty
do not pierce my body
with your eyes!
Yes, it is naked,

warm and innocent . . .
In the harsh love
of those eyes
I feel myself dying.

MATER INVIOLATA

Through your apron
shines a white light
of dawns and lilies
that blinds your son.

Mother! The light
is so pure
that your thigh
looks like snow.

TURRIS EBURNEA

Breasts of ivory,
nests of lilies,
no father's hand
has ever forced you.

Luminous contours
of black clouds,
our rain does not
darken you.

STELLA MATUTINA

Nel duro silenzio
rustici uccelli
pungono l'aria
e il casto cuore.

Che calma morte!
Su ridestiamoci,
che il nostro cuore
vuole peccare.

REGINA PACIS

O Inesistente
quante preghiere
strappate al cuore
per ricadere

sul nostro cuore!
Febbrile e vano
suono degli angelus
sul giorno umano.

Lingua

Fanciulletto perverso con le gemme
dell'Europa terse nel mio sesso,
morto di timidezza feci ingresso
nel museo vigilato dagli Adulti.
Amai la statua più nuda d'amore:
dov'ero carne essa era avorio.
Come farle indossare i maliziosi
calzoni che fasciavano l'ingenuo
mio fianco? E ancora io m'estenuo,
eterno fanciuletto, ad abbracciare
con uno sguardo il marmo che m'abbaglia.

STELLA MATUTINA

In stony silence
unruly birds
pierce the air
and the chaste heart.

What quiet death!
Come, let us wake
again, for our heart
wants to sin.

REGINA PACIS

O Unreality
all those prayers
wrenched from the heart,
only to fall back

on our hearts!
The Angelus chimes
feverish, empty
over the human day.

Language

A perverse young boy with Europe's buds
unsullied in my sex, so bashful
I could die, I entered the museum
under the watchful eyes of the Adults.
All my love was for the nudest statue:
where I was flesh, it was ivory.
How would I ever make it don
the impish trousers wrapping
my innocent loins? To this day, forever
the boy, I wear myself out trying to grasp
the blinding marble at a glance.

Diedi i miei ardori fidi e informi
a quella Forma preesistente, accesa
del mio amore, e crudelmente illesa.
Io amavo troppo! Era fanciullesca,
senza ironia, la mia dolce speranza:
non concessi la minima vacanza
ai miei sogni, né il minimo sorriso:
ma erano le Origini. E i miei baci
non corrisposti erano capaci
di distrarmi da una morte certa.
E la via della morte mi fu aperta.

Tu, orribile statua, sei la morte
Nel mio passato, io non voglio più
volerti, voglio il mio silenzio nudo,
il silenzio del fanciullo che un'Europa
senza statue accendeva con l'aurora,
del fanciullo che in dialetto vola
sul suo vergine cuore senza mondo.
Rinnego tutto quanto ho confessato
per commuoverti, rinnego il mio peccato
e il mio rimorso: sarò avorio anch'io,
avorio di un fanciullo ignoto a Dio.

Ripercorro a ritroso il mio cammino:
privo di te com'è dolce il paesaggio
padano, senza ombre di miraggi!
Il Livenza scatena le sue rose
verdi, l'Idria specchia inodorose
viole, il cielo senza azzurro guarda
le rogge casarsesi senza infanzia.
E tintinnano i coltelli nei pranzi
di Capodanno in un nitore lieto.
Geme senza echi il maggiolino
ai sensi del nascosto fanciullino.

I gave my true and formless passions
to that preexistent Form: aflame
with my love, it remained cruelly unscathed.
I loved too much! My sweet hope
was childish and without irony:
I granted my dreams not the slightest
respite, not the faintest smile.
But they were the Origins. And my
unreturned kisses had the power
to distract me from a sure death.
And thus I set out on death's path.

You, dreadful statue, are the death
in my past. I no longer want to want you,
I want only my naked silence,
the silence of a boy whom a statueless
Europe set aflame with the dawn,
the boy who flies in dialect
over his unworldly, virgin heart.
I renounce everything I confessed
trying to move you, I renounce my sin
and my remorse: I too shall become ivory,
an ivory boy unknown to God.

I retrace my path backwards:
how sweet the Po landscape
is without you, devoid of mirages!
The Livenza unleashes its green
roses, the Idria reflects unscented
violets, the blueless sky looks down
on the youthless canals of Casarsa.
And knives tinkle at dinners
in the happy clarity of New Year's Day.
The May-bug hums without echo
in the ears of the hiding boy.

Senza la tua minaccia d'alabastro
rivivrò gli slanci per mia madre,
le soggezioni pel mio grembo, ladro
di tenerezze e gentili vergogne . . .
Riproverò stupori senza ombra
per l'orologio, il topo, la fionda,
i compagni, la chiesa, la piazzetta.
Sarò il Narciso fiore che si specchia
amante senza amore, con l'orecchia
distratta dalle voci che l'amore
senza parole inventa per il fiore.

Ma tu, o endecasillabo di avorio,
o madrigale di viola, o statua
di poetiche, tra gli smalti e l'acqua
dell'Arcadia, eternamente adulta,
ami solo la gioia . . . e la purezza.
Non vuoi peccati, o pianto, di fanciulli!
E dunque? Può l'angelo pregare
nel Partenone? o il martire tornare
giglio? L'amore infine è aridità.
Ma sì, sarò reo d'averti amata,
o Autorità, io, l'Unico, il Segnato.

No, non ho madre, non ho sesso,
ho ucciso il padre col silenzio,
amo la mia pazzia di acqua e assenzio,
amo il mio giallo viso di ragazzo,
le innocenze che fingo e l'isterismo
che celo nell'eresia o lo scisma
del mio gergo, amo la mia colpa
che quando entrai nel museo degli adulti
era la piega dei calzoni, gli urti
del cuore timido: e tu rifiuti
ciò per cui ti amo, non mi muti.

Without your alabaster threat
I shall relive my passions for my mother,
my subjection to my groin, thief
of tenderness and sweet embarrassments . . .
I shall feel again a shadowless amazement
for clocks, mice, and slingshots,
for friends, the Church, and the town square.
I shall be the Narcissus flower reflected
as loveless lover, ear distracted
by the voices that a wordless love
invents for the flower.

Yet you, O ivory hendecasyllable,
O violet madrigal, O statue
of poetics among the enamels and the waters
of Arcadia, eternally adult—
you love only joy . . . and purity.
You don't want the sins or tears of children!
And so? Can an angel pray
in the Parthenon? Can a martyr turn
back into a lily? Love in the end is aridity.
And yes, I shall be guilty of having loved you,
O Authority—I, the Unique, the Branded.

No, I have no mother, I have no sex,
I've murdered my father with silence,
I love my madness of water and absinthe,
I love my sallow boyish face,
my feigned innocence and the hysterics
I cloak in heresy or the schism
of my jargon, I love my guilt,
which in the adults' museum
was the fold in my trousers and
the throbbing of my timid heart—and you disdain
what I love in you, and leave me unchanged.

Un Cristo

Non rinuncio alla gioia che con troppa
facilità discioglie, nel segreto
delle mie intimissime manovre,
il ghiaccio dei sudori e delle prove
mancate . . . Questo gioco mi è consueto:
non cambio la gioia col rimorso!

Eppure sento impedimento, piovre
che mi stringono . . . È Lui? Il Suo soccorso
non è divino, no: è puro gioco
che dentro il mio io scopro, come fuoco
nel fuoco, discorso nel discorso.
Il Suo piano è perfetto, non ha peso.

Io non Lo penso e certo non invoco
la Sua presenza! ed ecco che inattesi
compaiono i Suoi angeli stranieri.
Nella mia vita, freddi, i fili interi
spezzano, aggrovigliano i distesi:
salva, e inconscia, la mia preda ride . . .

(Quel giorno il Suo angelo fu un serio,
tranquillo contadino che MI VIDE.
altra volta fu un rapido uragano
che mi trattenne in camera, LONTANO . . .
E fu, ancora, la modesta effige
d'un Cristo che pendeva da uno spago

sul petto che sfioravo con la mano.)

Memorie

Torno alle giornate
più remote del nostro
amore, una marea
di muta gratitudine,
e disperati baci.

A Christ

I refuse to relinquish the joy
that in the stealth
of my innermost ploys
too easily melts the ice of my sweats
and failed attempts . . . I know the game well
and won't trade joy for regrets!

And yet I feel hindrances like octopi
holding me back . . . Is it Him?
His intercession is not divine. No, I
find it's purely a game I play within,
like fire within fire, words within words.
His plan is perfect, weightless.

He's not on my mind, and I certainly
don't summon Him! Yet suddenly
His alien angels appear before me.
Cold, they snap the unbroken threads
of my life, snag the ones outstretched:
Safe and oblivious, my quarry laughs . . .

(That day His angel was a serious,
placid peasant who SAW ME;
another time it was a sudden storm
that kept me AWAY, in my room . . .
Still another it was the modest form
of a Christ that hung from a string

on a chest my hand was lightly stroking.)

Memories

Now I go back
to the earliest days
of our love, a tide
of silent gratitude
and desperate kisses,

Tutta la mia infanzia
è sulle tue ginocchia
spaventata di perderti
e perdutamente
felice di averti.

Ho compiuto il viaggio
che tu non hai compiuto,
mia lodoletta, madre
fanciulla. Coraggio
di dolce indiziato,
invasato e imprudente
e cieco amore . . . Fui
un altro, al ritorno,
con in volto la maschera
della nostra dolcezza.

Una bellezza fonda
d'ombre nella fronte
pura e nell'onda
giovane dei capelli —
magra negli ossi
del mento e degli zigomi,
dura nella tenera
curva della faccia —
bellezza di ragazzo
o ladro — trasparente
e torbida — riempita
da una vecchia innocenza,
indurita dagli anni
ma, forse, ancora mite . . .
Ah, odiosa mitezza
adorabile in te
ch'eri davvero bella.

Ricordo i pomeriggi
di Bologna: al lavoro
cantavi nella casa
che non era che un'eco.

my whole childhood
spent in your lap,
afraid to lose you
and hopelessly
happy to have you.

I made the journey
you never could,
my little skylark, girl
of a mother. Courage
of the gentle defendant,
bedeviled, imprudent,
blind love . . . When I returned
I was somebody else,
wearing the mask
of our tenderness.

A beauty deep
with shadow in the smooth
brow and the youthful
wave of the hair —
lean in the bones
of chin and cheek,
hard in the tender
curve of the face —
a boyish, thieflike
beauty — limpid,
turbid — full of
an old innocence,
hardened by the years
but still meek, perhaps . . .
Ah, that hated meekness
so adorable in you
who were truly beautiful.

I remember the afternoons
in Bologna, when you would
sing while you worked, and
the house was one great echo.

Poi tacevi, e volata
nell'altra stanza (ah il bruno
tuo passo di bambina . . .)
riprendevi a cantare.
E il pomeriggio era
silenzio e rapimento:
già presagiva, forse,
di contare nel gioco
orrendo del destino.

Tu sai quanto fui puro . . .
quanto amavo una vita
troppo bella per me . . .
quanto ero deciso
a difendere e amare . . .
Ma tu di me conosci
gli abbandoni, l'aureola
di ingenue dedizioni,
la passione irrichiesta
e nobile . . . ne ignori
una rassegnazione
che è bassezza, gergo,
parola disonesta.
Nella storia del nostro
amore c'è un'ombra,
il rapporto unico,
la troppa confidenza
che non s'esprime, resta
parola, imputridisce . . .
La purezza perduta:
ecco la novità,
il terrible dato,
e la vecchia famiglia
ancora forse trepida
della storia padana,
della sua giovinezza
triste ed eroica . . .

Then you'd fall silent, fly
into another room (ah, your
dark, girlish steps . . .)
and resume your song.
And the afternoon was
all silence and rapture,
already forboding, perhaps,
a role in destiny's
terrible game.

You know how pure I was . . . .
how much I loved a life
too beautiful for me . . .
how determined I was
to love and protect . . . .
But you know me
for my fervors, the halo
of my naive devotions,
my unrequired, noble
passion . . . You don't know
the resignation in me,
the baseness, the jargon,
the dishonest words.
In the story of our
love lurks a shadow:
the unique bond,
the excessive intimacy
never expressed remains
only words, and festers . . .
Purity lost:
that was the novelty,
the terrible fact,
for an age-old family
still unsure, perhaps,
of its history by the Po,
its unhappy,
heroic youth . . .

Il mondo è nell'ombra
del tuo tiepido riso
di madre giovinetta.
Ah, non so nulla e tutto
della tua floridezza,
le tue vesti fragranti
di mode impure e timide,
la tua bianca gola,
simile all'eroine
dell'epoca . . . Tu, sola,
davi la solitudine
a chi, nella tua ombra,
provava, per il mondo,
un troppo grande amore.

Mi innamoro dei corpi
che hanno la mia carne
di figlio — col grembo
che brucia di pudore —
i corpi misteriosi
d'una bellezza pura
vergine e onesta, chiusi
in un gioco ignaro
di sorrisi e di grazia
(aria che li rischiara
coi loro deliziosi
capelli, in prati impuri
della loro innocenza),
corpi spenti dai tremiti
della carne, uno spettro
di batticuori senza
pietà, spada affondata
nella rosa disfatta
della gola che sanguina,
i corpi dei figli
coi calzoni felici,
col bruno o il biondo
delle madri nei passi,
e un troppo grande amore,
nel cuore, per il mondo.

In the shadow of your
languid laugh, girlish
mother, lies the world.
Oh, I know nothing and everything
about your bloom,
your dresses fragrant
with fashions indecent and shy,
your white neck
so like those of the heroines
of the time . . . . You alone
granted solitude to one
who, in your shadow,
felt too great a love
for the world.

I fall in love with bodies
that have my same
filial flesh—loins
burning with modesty—
mysterious bodies
of a pure and virgin,
honest beauty, trapped
inside unknowing games
of smiles and grace
(the air that brightens them
and their lovely hair
in impure meadows
of their innocence),
bodies drained in shudders
of the flesh, spectre
of pitiless heartbeats,
sword thrust deep
in the blown rose
of the bleeding throat,
bodies of sons
in happy trousers,
with their mothers' dark
or fair hair in their steps
and too great a love of the world
in their hearts.

L'ex-vita

In un debole lezzo di macello
vedo l'immagine del mio corpo:
seminudo, ignorato, quasi morto.
È così che mi volevo crocifisso,
con una vampa di tenero orrore,
da bambino, già automa del mio amore.
Ma dietro questa nebbia di midolla
(da quanti anni o secoli qui immobile?)
o Individuo, o Sosia, tu ti trovi
fatto di me, del mio calore, e ostile
di una morte anteriore al mio morire.

Io giungo a te da un viaggio inebbriante.
Toccai, in giorni tutti luce, i muri
anneriti di Casarsa e l'erbe umide.
Con negligente gesto di guerriero
offersi il corpo nudo al tempo fresco
antichissimo, languido, del Meschio
del Livenza, del Po . . . Giocai sull'orlo
di un'intera pianura, nei suoi prati
brucianti, sotto cieli sterminati,
nelle case godute in grembo a un'iride
di mille odori affettuosi, sottili.

Ed entro nel tuo cerchio, amaro, fresco
come mia madre al vespro nel varcare
la soglia, imperlata d'erbe aride,
e con me porto un vento di paesaggi,
una superba leggerezza, un candido
coraggio di straniero. E tu non spandi
che silenzio. O sconosciuto ch'eri tutto:
il ragazzo perduto nella casa,
il giovane borghese che cullava
i falsi amori dell'amato cuore,
ora sei nulla, IL NULLA, il puro errore.

My Former Life

Amidst a faint stench of butchery,
I see an image of my body:
half-naked, forgotten, near death.
Such was how I wished to be crucified
— in a flash of heartrending horror —
as a child, already my love's automaton.
Yet behind this fog of the marrow
(immobile for how many years or centuries?)
O Individual, O Double, you find yourself
fashioned from me, from my heat, defiant
with a death from before my own dying.

I come to you after a thrilling journey.
On days when all was light, I touched
the charred walls and damp grass of Casarsa.
With a warrior's nonchalance
I offered my naked body to the ancient
cool of the Meschio, the Livenza,
the Po . . . I played at the edge
of a great plain, in its burning
fields, under limitless skies
in houses treasured in the bosom of a spectrum
of a thousand loving, subtle scents.

I enter your circle, bitter and fresh
as my mother crossing the threshold
in the evening, bejeweled with dry grass.
I bring with me a wind of landscapes,
weightless and proud, and a foreigner's
innocent courage. And you emit only silence.
O stranger, you once were everything,
the boy losing his way in the house,
the young bourgeois cherishing
false loves in his beloved heart,
and now you are nothing, NOTHINGNESS, pure wrong.

Così, o affamato, o desiderio oscuro,
con uno sguardo di ere pre-umane
esprimi la tua vita di maniaco.
La tua mania è la vita del mondo.
Tu vuoi solo da me che corrisponda
al tuo folle sforzo di annullarti,
ignori ogni attrazione del mio secolo,
ogni vacanza, ogni passione appresa
negli anni di una vita di sé accesa:
non vuoi saperne che, nel tempo, a feste
quasi eterne l'eternità si presti!

Ma ignori anche giochi più vitali:
confessare le voglie del maschio,
l'amore per mia madre, che TU amasti,
luce che stagna nel fondo della notte
dell'infanzia . . . (Oh ultimo candore
di questo mio esibirmi! E tu lo ignori.)
Amai solo coloro che tu odiavi.
Eternai l'ombra di me giovinetto
per rimpiangervi, avido, gli affetti
tutti speranza, gli ardori di giglio,
che infiammavano la mia carne di figlio.

Per te, in un deserto di sereno,
il povero segreto del mio sesso
disonoro, e, incurante, lo confesso.
Non so per che miracolo, tranquillo
e infine onesto, dalla mia nevrosi
suscito puri cieli, inodorosi
luoghi, in cui—Materia o Morte—muori.
Sì, spesso sei morto, e allegro torna
il ragazzo nel grembo, e alla forma
soavissima il mitomane entusiasta,
se solo la vita gli è rimasta.

Thus, O starveling, O obscure desire,
you express your maniacal life
with a gaze from pre-human ages.
Your mania is the living world.
All you want from me is to comply
with your mad effort to negate yourself.
You shun all my century's attractions,
all forms of leisure, every passion
learned over a life enflamed with itself.
And you will have none of the near endless
feasts eternity, in time, may offer us!

Yet you shun even more essential games:
admitting the longings for men,
the love for my mother, whom YOU loved,
light fading in the heart of the night
of childhood . . . (O final candor
of my self-exposure! Which you ignore.)
I loved only those you hated,
immortalized the ghost of my boyhood self
that I might mourn his hopeful
affections, the ardor, lily-fresh,
enflaming my filial flesh.

In a desert of serenity, for you
I tarnish the poor secret of my loins,
and own up to it without a care.
I don't know what miracle allows me,
untroubled and forthright, to summon
perfect skies from my neurosis, odorless
places in which—as Matter or Death—you die.
Yes, very often you're dead, and the boy
happily returns to the womb,
the burning mythomaniac to gentle form,
when life is all that's left to him.

Ma tu, nel fondo del tempo, qui mi attendi,
nell'interno, dove ventre e muscoli
ammorba un lezzo morbido di muschi
o di escrementi; e mentre un nudo buio
da sottoscale o bivacco di nomadi
s'infoltisce, ti vedo, mummia, automa,
e tu mi vedi. Oh nostalgia mortale
per chi non ti conobbe, e ignorando,
o puro Vivo, le tue angoscie di orango,
si perdeva col suo destino giocondo,
il cuore ignoto in un ignoto mondo.

Ballata del delirio

Solo, solo, una statua di cera
indurita dal vecchio raggio
della mia vita già leggera . . .
E torna l'aria della sera
muta nel cuore del linguaggio.
Con sospiri d'anni è svanita
in lucidi orizzonti, aria
alitata da gole d'angeli,
l'esistenza — e torna alle nari
del mio cadavere, mare
di giorni dagli Ave agli Angelus.

Tutto stona, parola, ascolto
il disaccordo delle tenebre,
pazzo e sadico sgomento
nella parola, tromba ebbra di
dissonanze — è il fallimento,
anonimo, del mondo. Batte
cieca la luce delle stelle
nelle cucine spente, attratte
dal fetore le jene grattano
àtone . . .

Yet here you await me, in the depths
of time, within, where a mild stench
of excrement or musk pollutes the guts
and muscles; and as a naked darkness
of stairwells and nomads' camps
grows thick, I see you—mummy, automaton—
and you see me. O fatal yearning
for one who never knew you, and who—O pure and
living thing—not knowing your apelike anguish,
could disappear into his happy lot,
an unknown heart in an unknown world.

The Ballad of Delirium

Alone, alone, waxen statue
hardened by the old glint
of my once weightless life . . .
The evening air returns, voiceless
in the heart of language.
Vanished with the sighs of years
over bright horizons, air
soughed through angels' throats,
existence returns to my dead
body's nostrils, ocean
of days from Ave to Angelus.

It's all out of tune, speech and hearing
the shadows in discord,
mad, sadistic dismay
at words, trumpet drunk
on dissonance—it's the world's
anonymous failure. Blind
the starlight throbs
in blacked-out kitchens, drawn
by the stench, hyenas scratch
atonic. . .

Ecco, ti sento e non mi scuoto,
diapason tremante d'anni,
punta di diamante fioco
che incide l'orlo dell'anima;
devo ancora restare immoto:
ormai sono vivo nello specchio,
sono la mia immagine immersa
nella vita di luce cieca
nello specchio del giovinetto
prigioniero del lume terso.

Sono dentro lo specchio muto
— un azzurro pesce stretto
dal ghiaccio, col guizzo perduto
nella bara di eterno vetro —
l'allarme che sibila acuto
nei grembi vaghi della parola
non incrina la superficie
dello specchio: e appena sfiora
gli occhi dell'immagine sola
che vive . . .

Dentro il silenzio pastorale
dello specchio con il candido
colore dell'alba natale,
quanto innocente, mia domanda
d'irresponsabile mortale!
Dove corrono i treni, arsi
di ferro per la pianura umida,
dove guardano i lumi sparsi
nell'orizzonte, dove puntano i salsi
piroscafi e dove i fumi

delle fabbriche, dove tende
la vita se non all'acheronte
che nello specchio si distende?
I vizi e le viltà, mia fonte,
hanno in te freschezze stupende?
E che stupendi assassinii
compie l'infante nel segreto

Tuning fork humming with years,
blunt diamond point cutting
the edge of the soul,
I hear you but don't stir:
I still have to keep still:
I now live inside the mirror,
I am my own image immersed
in the life of the blind light
in the mirror of the boy
imprisoned in the glare.

Inside the voiceless mirror
I'm a blue fish surrounded
by ice, darting tail frozen
in this eternal glass tomb —
the siren shrieking shrill
in the vague wombs of speech
does not crack the mirror's
surface, barely skimming
the eyes of the lone image
alive . . .

In the pastoral silence
of the mirror white
as the dawn of birth,
how innocent my question is!
Foolish mortal!
Where go the trains of burning
steel across the humid plain,
where gaze the scattered lights
on the horizon, where sail
the sooty steamships, where floats

the smoke of factories, where tend
our lives if not toward
the Acheron inside the mirror?
Are vice and cowardice, my source,
amazingly renewed in you?
And what amazing murders does
the newborn infant fashion deep inside

del corpo di fresco carminio? . . .
(Voce squisita, così incrini
il barbaro nel vetro quieto,

così incanti l'estremo rosa
di chi parlava un'altra lingua
e s'è ammutolito alla nuova,
così sei l'ombra che cinge,
funebre sciopero del cuore,
le pazzie impietrite dell'anima;
così sei l'estrema eleganza
della foglia che sfiora gli anni
dando ai silenzi troppo umani
del selvaggio una finta fragranza.)

       Lo specchio in frantumi
     i sensi liberi nel reale ec
  comi al mondo! Ah ritorno! sono vostro
     coetaneo è finita la quarantena, il dera
      gliamento non era che oggetto della
        Sociologia . . . Ma io ritorno, che scan
   dalosa impudenza, al quotidiano
ritento il Salto Qualitativo a rovescio, la
   vecchia caduta dell'angelo, che scandalo!
     Oh, miei dolci coetanei, come
  per voi, tra me e il reale c'è un ordine stupendo
    A CUI APPARTENNI, l'ingenuità.

Poco più che corpo, o futuri
Vivi che vivrete al mio posto
al tepore di questi muri,
altro amore in me non conosco
che l'Azzurro dei giorni scuri,
altro il tempo non è che Azzurro
dietro le spalle del morente,
un paesaggio soave e brullo,
un ossessionante sussurro,
fisica immagine sul Niente.

its body of fresh rosy flesh?
(And thus, delicious voice, you crack
the brute inside the silent glass,

thus you cast a spell upon the final blush
of one who used to speak a different tongue
and then fell mute in the new language,
thus you are the shadows
that envelop the soul's petrified insanities,
dark abdication of the heart,
you are the final elegance
of leaves that skim across the years,
giving false fragrance to the savage's
all-too-human silences.)

> *The mirror shattered,*
> *senses freed into reality, here*
> *I am in the world! Ah, I'm back! I'm your*
> *contemporary, the quarantine is over, the de-*
> *railment was merely a subject for*
> *Sociology. . . But I'm back, what scan-*
> *dalous cheek, every day I re-attempt*
> *the Qualitative Leap backwards, the old*
> *angel-fall, what a scandal!*
> *Oh my sweet contemporaries, between me*
> *and reality — the same as for you — lies an amazing realm*
> TO WHICH I ONCE BELONGED: *naivety.*

Little more than body, O future
Beings who shall live in my stead
inside the warmth of these walls,
I've known no other love in me
except the blue sky on dark days —
time is nothing more than the Azure
behind a dying man's back,
a gentle, barren landscape,
haunting whisper of a voice,
physical image of Nothingness.

La scoperta di Marx

Io so che gli intellettuali nella gioventù sentono realmente
l'inclinazione fisica verso il popolo e credono che questo sia amore.
Ma questo non è amore: è meccanica inclinazione verso la massa.
M. GOR'KIJ

I

Può nascere da un'ombra
con viso di fanciulla
e pudore di viola

un corpo che m'ingombra
o, da un grembo azzurro
una conscienza — sola

dentro il mondo abitato?
Fuori dal tempo è nato
il figlio, e dentro muore.

II

Sangue mediterraneo,
alta lingua romanza
e cristiana radice

nel perfetto estraneo
nato nella stanza
d'una città felice.

Tu eri irreligiosa,
barbara, o ingenua sposa
e infante genitrice.

III

Come sono caduto
in un mondo di prosa
s'eri una passeretta,

Discovering Marx

I know that intellectuals in their youth feel a truly physical attraction towards the people and believe that this is love. But it is not love: it is a mechanical attraction to the mass.
MAXIM GORKY

I

Can this burdensome body
be born of a shadow
with the face of a girl

chaste as a violet?
Can an azure womb beget
a conscience — alone

in a populous world?
Out of time the son
is born, and in it he dies.

II

Of Mediterranean blood,
high Romance tongue
and Christian stock

is the perfect outsider
born in the home
in a city of joy.

You were without religion,
uncouth, O naive bride,
infant mother.

III

How did I fall
into a world of prose
when you were a sparrow

un'allodola, e muto
alla storia—una rosa—
o madre giovinetta

era il tuo cuore? in questo
ordine manifesto
da te il mondo mi accetta?

IV

M'hai trasmesso nel cuore
già adulto di un tempo
di cui, adolescente,

cercai arso d'amore
le fonti. Ah educazione
conforme il prepotente

senso del mio secolo,
senso unico, eco
del Cuore preesistente!

V

E ogni giorno affondo
nel mondo ragionato,
spietata istituzione

degli adulti—nel mondo
da secoli arenato
al suono di un Nome:

con esso m'imprigiono
nello stupendo dono
ch'è ormai solo ragione.

a skylark, your heart
mute to history, a rose,
O child mother of mine?

Will the order revealed
by your very existence
grant me a place in mankind?

   IV

To my already adult
heart you handed down
a time that, in adolescence,

burning with love, I sought
to unearth at its source.
An upbringing true

to the way of my century,
the only way, echo
of the Heart that came before!

   V

Now each day I plunge
into the world of reason,
that ruthless institution

of adults — a world
long ago run aground
on the sound of a Noun;

and I lock myself up
in the marvelous gift
that Reason has now become.

VI

Ma il peso di un'età
che forza la conscienza
e modella il dovere,

quando in me avrà
vinto la resistenza
del mio cuore leggero?

se, con te, non ho anima
d'amore, ma una fiamma
di lieve carità?

VII

Non pensavi che il mondo
di cui sono un figlio
cieco e innamorato

non fosse un giocondo
possesso di tuo figlio,
dolce di sogni, armato

di bontà — ma un'antica
terra altrui che alla vita
dà l'ansia dell'esilio?

VIII

La lingua (di cui suona
in te appena una nota,
nell'alba del dialetto)

e il tempo (a cui dona
la tua ingenua e immota
pietà) son le pareti

VI

But when will the weight of an age
that compels the conscience
and spurs one to duty

overcome the resistance
that still has its way
with my frivolous heart?

—since in you I obey
not a spirit of love
but gentle charity's flame?

VII

Didn't you know that the world
whose blind, enamored son
I am, was not some joyous

possession of mine
full of sweet dreams
laden with goodness,

but an ancient land
belonging to others, where
life has the anguish of exile?

VIII

Language (which barely chimes
a note in your fine
morning song in dialect)

and time (which your childlike,
steadfast devotion
uplifts) are the two walls

tra cui sono entrato,
sedizioso e invasato,
coi tuoi occhi mansueti.

IX

Non soggetto ma oggetto
madre! un inquieto fenomeno,
non un dio incarnato

con i sogni nel petto
di ansioso figlio! anonima
presenza, non desolato

io! M'hai espresso
nel mistero del sesso
a un logico Creato.

X

Ma c'è nell'esistenza
qualcos'altro che amore
per il proprio destino.

È un calcolo senza
miracolo che accora
o sospetto che incrina.

La nostra storia! morsa
di puro amore, forza
razionale e divina.

between which I entered the world,
seditious, possessed,
and with your gentle eyes.

IX

Not a subject, but an object,
Mother! a restless phenomenon,
not a god in the flesh

with the dreams of a distressed
son in his heart! An anonymous
presence, not a desolate

self! Through the mystery of sex
you brought me to life
in a logical Universe.

X

But in life there is more
than mere love
of one's destiny.

There is a calculus
free of troubling miracles
and corrosive mistrust.

Our history! vice grip
of pure love, force
of reason and divinity.

Poesiole notturne

I

Non ha fondo questo vuoto
che spalanca la stagione,
rinnovata nell'ignoto
assillante la ragione,

se vaneggia su animali
sensi desti ai nuovi spazi.
Quando un poco necessari
eravamo, come sazi,

è bastata questa ala
di tepore, perché vano
ci paresse ogni segnale

dell'ancora sconosciuto
nostra essere: e lontano
il reale tempo umano.

II

Si allarga senza fine
nel buio della notte
del sabato, il confine
dentro cui le corrotte

nostre presenze sono
umane: nel silenzio
altro silenzio, e suono
cosmico nel morente

suono della contrada.
Ingigantito un mio
gesto si propaga

Little Night Poems

    I

There's no end to the void
opened up by the season
renewed in the mysteries
that disquiet reason,

as it yawns over animal
senses aroused to new spaces.
When, being sated, a minimal
sense of necessity was ours,

all it took was this wing
of warmth to make any
sign of our still unknown

being seem pointless to us,
and the real human day
seem so far away.

    II

In the darkness of Saturday
night, the boundaries
within which our decayed
forms find humanity

expand without end:
in the silence, still more
silence, and cosmic
sounds in the moribund

sounds of the street.
I make a move which,
magnified, soon extends

fino a dove Dio
non è: e ormai nel cuore
è il puro terrore.

III

Quando è più duro vivere
la vita è più assoluta?
Sulle serali rive
dei sensi muti è muta

la vecchia ragione
in cui mi riconosco:
è un corso interiore
un sordo sottobosco

dove tutto è natura.
Faticoso travaglio
del sussistere oscuro

solo tu sei necessario . . .
E mi travolgi piano
oltre il confine umano.

IV

Lievità misteriosa
del peso ormai morto
della vita, candore
del cuore sporco . . .

Sono i sensi un ricamo,
dopo la mezzanotte,
quando ritorna a casa,
muta, la puttana . . .

È davvero un vento
questo dell'interna
vita, che non cade
mai, e monotono alterna

to where there is
no God — and horror
fills me to the core.

III

When it's harder to live,
is life more absolute?
On my muted senses'
evening shores, also mute

is the old reason
defining my selfhood:
it is an inner path
a silent underwood

where all is nature.
Toilsome labor
of obscure existence,

you alone are necessary . . .
And gently you drive me
beyond human boundaries.

IV

Mysterious lightness
of life's now dead
weight, pure whiteness
of the unclean heart . . .

The senses are embroidered
after midnight, when
the prostitute quietly
returns home . . .

It's really a wind
of the life within,
one that never dies down,
monotonously shifting

i sentimenti: ora,
chissà perché felice
(di nulla, e anzi,
come una meretrice,

torno da un disperato
giro) ardo gloriosamente
di vita: preda di forze
ora vive ora spente . . .

our feelings: even now,
inexplicably happy
(over nothing: in fact,
like a whore I'm just back

from a desperate walk),
I feel gloriously vibrant
with life, prey to forces
now living, now spent . . .

III
Da *I Diari* /
From *The Diaries*

Adulto? Mai—mai, come l'esistenza
che non matura—resta sempre acerba,
di splendido giorno in splendido giorno—
io non posso che restare fedele
alla stupenda monotonia del mistero.
Ecco perché, nella felicità,
non mi sono abbandonato—ecco
perché, nell'ansia delle mie colpe
non ho mai toccato un rimorso vero.
Pari, sempre pari con l'inespresso,
all'origine di quello che io sono.

                          *

Sarebbe così facile svelare
questa luce o quest'ombra . . . Una parola:
e l'esistenza che in me esiste sola
sotto le voci che ogni uomo inventa
per avvicinarsi a verità
fuggenti, sarebbe espressa, infine.
Ma questa parola non esiste.
Se tuttavia ascolto nel rumore
che sale dal rione, un suono un poco
più terso—o aspiro nell'odore
della stagione un più preciso alito
di foglie fradice, di pioggia, allora,
allusa, l'indicibile mia vita
mi si disegna, per un solo instante . . .
E non so sopportarla . . . Ma un giorno,
ah un giorno, urlerò, a quella vista,
sarà un urlo la rivelazione . . .

Adult? Never, never — like life itself,
which never matures, forever green
from splendid day to splendid day,
I cannot help but remain true
to the wondrous monotony of mystery.
This is why, when happy,
I've never given up on myself — and why
in my anguish over all I've done wrong
I've never felt any real remorse.
Forever equal to what is left unsaid,
at the origin of what I am.

*

It would be so easy to unveil
this light or this shadow . . . One word,
and the life that lives alone in me,
beneath the voices every man invents
to get closer to fugitive
truths, would be expressed at last.
But no such word exists.
If, however, in the din rising up
from the streets I hear a sound slightly
clearer than the rest — or if I inhale
among the season's scents a sharper breath
of leaves, awash with rain, then,
by suggestion, my ineffable life
looms before me, for only an instant . . .
And I can't bear it . . . But one day,
oh, one day, that sight will make me shout,
and my shout will be a revelation . . .

Pieno di confidenza e di tepore
è il senso degli odori che nell'aria
mattutina la festa rinverdisce:
odori di campagne d'altri anni
nella città che l'afa della pioggia
rinverdisce e preme contro un corpo
adolescente . . . Siamo a Sacile . . . A Idria . . .
i castagni traspirano; l'interno
della casa è invaso da un vapore
tenero; la vita famigliare
è immersa nel suo senso inconsapeveole,
e assoluto. Dalle fessure entra
l'odore dell'aperto, afoso e fresco,
di stelle; le nuvole perdute
oltre i vetri s'incagliano leggere
in un cielo deterso, controluce
tra le piante lavate. Non son più
in quel tempo, e quel tempo è sempre.
Ragazzo mi ridesto, e mi ritrovo
vecchio, la freschezza che m'innonda
e il tepore di festa, sono resti
d'una vita che specchia la sua ombra.

*

Full of intimacy and warmth
are the smells the holiday
revives in the morning air,
country smells of years ago
revived in the city by the haze
of the rain and sticking to an adolescent
body. . . And we're in Sacile . . . In Idria . . .
The chestnut trees sweat;
a tender vapor invades
the house; family life
is steeped in unawareness,
absolute. Through the cracks
the smell of outdoors, hazy and cool
with stars, filters in; clouds lost behind
the windowpanes gently stall
in a purified sky, backlit
between laundered plants. I'm not
in that time anymore, and that time is forever.
I reawaken as a boy, and realize
I'm old; the cool washing over me,
the holiday warmth, are remnants
of a life that mirrors its shadow.

*

Chiusa la festa su una Roma sorda
a ogni ingenua attesa, chiuso il giorno,
come immondizie al vento i passi
del ritorno, le voci, i fischi, vanno
morendo vasti per le strade, radi
negli androni. È la sosta della cena:
poi, più tardi, con l'inquieto peso
dell'ombra sporca, senz'aria, nelle
vesti festive di una gente estranea,
là dove il caos della città si gela
in chiarori di lumi costellati
lungo strade murate da una pace
di morte, torna l'antica sera . . .
Per i lungofiumi abbandonati
smaglianti corone di fanali,
qualche stella ai fianchi delle nubi —
e sulle periferie, da Testaccio
a Monteverde, stagna stanco e umido
un vibrare di voci di passanti
e motori — sperduta incrostazione
del nostro mondo sul muto universo.

*

La pioggia ha verniciato la terra
intorno all'Aniene. Quasi voce
dell'inquieto sereno, c'è un ragazzo
che tra mucchi di calce e di mattoni,
sfrega un filo di ferro sopra un triste
coperchio. Con i camion lontani
vibra confusa la periferia, e
muore il giorno inutile; inutili
cantano il silenzio le cicale
nella mesta penombra incendiata.

*

At holiday's end, in a Rome deaf
to all naive expectation, at day's end
like litter in the wind, the footsteps
heading home, the voices, the whistles
slowly recede, vast in the streets, faint
in the doorways. It's the suppertime lull.
Later, heavy and restless
as the dirty, airless shadow, dressed
in the festive garb of a foreign people,
where the city's chaos congeals
in glimmering constellations of lights
along streets walled in by a peace
like death, the ancient evening returns . . .
Down deserted riverside avenues,
brilliant coronas of headlights,
a few stars next to clouds—
and on the city's edge, from Testaccio
to Monteverde, voices of passersby
and motors quaver stagnant
and damp—stray encrustations
of our world upon the silent universe.

*

Rain has varnished the earth
around the Aniene. Like a voice
of the restless calm, there's a boy
between piles of lime and bricks
scraping a metal wire over a miserable
barrel-top. The city's periphery shakes
in a havoc of distant trucks, and
the useless day comes to an end.
Useless cicadas intone the silence
in the fiery gloom of twilight.

Se qualcuno mi chiede (e qualcuno
me lo chiede) dove vado con me
risponderei di non saperlo. Ho avuto
fin nel ventre materno, con la gioia,
questa sicurezza in una vera,
assoluta, inconoscibile irrealtà.

*

Interrotto nel momento più limpido
nel momento in cui il cuore si prepara
a darsi al mondo che gli è stato dato
—le passioni ossessioni, le fedi incubi,
i doveri dogmi,—vidi che il mondo
per me era irreale. Restai per qualche anno
dentro un sua ombra. Ma mi era dato,
e in me nacque il caos: sulla purezza
passava il peccato senza scalfirla,
sull'ignoto il noto come un elemento
estraneo, sulla carne il pentimento
come parte di essa: tutto finiva
in me, deposito di un mare
anche a sé assente, in un notte estiva.

*

Come in uno spasimo del pensiero,
balenante, veri vedo a un tratto
gli uomini. Sordidi . . . innocenti . . . e incapaci
a uscire dalla fusione col mondo
—col loro mondo di cui sono i vivi . . .
Io, che nascendo li ho visti nati, mai
fui capace, come in un sogno, a crederli
semplicemente la mia specie.
Ma nel futuro . . .

*

Should anyone ask me (and ask me
they do) where I am going,
I answer I don't know. Ever since
my mother's womb I've had, along with
the joy, this firm belief in a true,
absolute, unknowable reality.

*

Interrupted at the clearest of moments,
the moment when the heart prepares
to give itself to the world it was given
— the passion-obsessions, nightmare beliefs,
imperative dogmas — I saw that the world
was unreal for me. I remained a few years
in its shadow. But it was mine to have,
and chaos was born within me: sin passed
over purity without leaving a trace,
the known over the unknown
like something foreign, penance over flesh
as though part of it: and everything ended
in me, sediment of a sea
absent even to itself, on a summer night.

*

As in a spasm of thought,
a flash, I suddenly see people
as real. Sordid . . . innocent . . . and unable
to step out of their fusion with the world
— the world in which they are the living . . .
I, who saw them born in my own birth,
was never able, as in a dream, to think
of them even as my kind.
But in the future . . .

*

Correvo nel crepuscolo fangoso
dietro a scali sconvolti, a mute
impalcature, tra rioni bagnati
nell'odore del ferro, degli stracci
riscaldati, che dentro una crosta
di polvere, tra casupole di latta
e scoli, inalzavano pareti
recenti e già annerite, contro un fondo
di stinta metropoli.
                        Sull'asfalto
scalzato, tra i peli di un'erba acre
di escrementi e spianate
nere di fango — che la pioggia scavava
in infetti tepori — le dirotte
file dei ciclisti, dei rantolanti
camion di legname, si sperdevano
di tanto in tanto, in centri di sobborghi
dove già qualche bar aveva cerchi
di bianchi lumi, e sotto la liscia
parete di una chiesa si stendevano
viziosi, i giovani.
                        Intorno ai grattacieli
popolari, già vecchi, i marci orti
e le fabbriche irte di gru ferme
stagnavano in un febbrile silenzio;
ma un po' fuori dal centro rischiarato,
al fianco di quel silenzio, una strada
blu d'asfalto, pareva tutta immersa
in una vita immemore ed intensa
quanto antica. Benché radi, brillavano
i fanali d'una cadente luce,
e le finestre ancora aperte erano
bianche di panni stesi, palpitanti
di voci interne. Alle soglie sedute
stavano le vecchie donne, e limpidi
nelle tute o nei calzoncini quasi
di festa, scherzavano i ragazzi,
ma abbracciati fra loro, con compagne
di loro più precoci.

*

I was running in the muddy twilight
past decrepit railyards and silent
scaffolds, through wet neighborhoods
that smelled of iron and reheated rags
hoisted up—in the dust-laden spaces
between tin shacks and sewage
canals—on newly built, already
blackened walls against the backdrop
of a colorless metropolis.
                              Over broken
asphalt, through clumps of grass pungent
with excrement and black stretches
of mud—dotted with warm, foul pools
dug out by the rain—queues of cyclists
and wheezing trucks bearing wood
scattered headlong here and there
into suburban centers where
a few cafes already glowed
with circles of light, and under the smooth
walls of a church some young people
lay mischievously about.
                              Around already old
low-income high-rises, rotting gardens
and construction sites bristling with motionless cranes
stagnated in feverish silence.
But a bit outside the well-lit center,
beside the silence, a blue asphalt
street appeared wholly immersed
in a life as oblivious and intense
as it was ancient. Though few in number,
the streetlamps glowed with a falling light,
and the still-open windows were white
with laundry hung out to dry and vibrant
with voices inside. Old women sat
in the doorways, as a group of boys
huddled together, brightly dressed
in overalls or almost festive shorts,
joking with girls who were
younger than they.

Tutto era umano,
in quella strada, e gli uomini vi stavano
aggrappati, dai vani al marciapiede,
coi loro stracci, le loro luci . . .

Sembrava che fino dentro l'intima
e miserabile sua abitazione, l'uomo fosse
solo accampato, come un'altra razza,
e attaccato a questo suo rione
dentro il vespro unto e polveroso,
non fosse Stato il suo, ma confusa
sosta.
     Tuttavia chi passava e guardava
privo dell'innocente necessità,
cercava, estraneo, una comunione,
almeno nella festa del passare e del guardare.
Non c'era intorno che la vita: ma in quel morto
mondo, per lui, ricominciava la Realtà.

             Everything on that street
was human, and the people all clung
to it tightly, in the windows, on the sidewalks
with their rags and their lights . . .

It seemed as though man, even deep
in his wretched abode, were merely
encamped here, like another species,
and that his bond with this place,
in the grimy, dusty evening,
were not an Existence, but a random
stop.
      Yet the passerby looking on
without the innocence of need
sought, as a stranger, communion there,
at least in the joy of passing and looking.
All around was only life, and in that dead
world, for him, Reality was reborn.

IV
Da *Le ceneri di Gramsci* /
From *Gramsci's Ashes*

L'Appennino

I

Teatro di dossi, ebbri, calcinati,
muto, è la muta luna che ti vive,
tiepida sulla Lucchesia dai prati

troppo umani, cocente sulle rive
della Versilia, così intera sul vuoto
del mare — attonita su stive,

carene, vele rattrappite, dopo
viaggi di vecchia, popolare pesca
tra l'Elba, l'Argentario . . .

La luna, non c'è altra vita che questa.
E vi si sbianca l'Italia da Pisa
sparsa sull'Arno in una morta festa

di luci, a Lucca, pudica nella grigia
luce della cattolica, superstite
sua perfezione . . .

Umana la luna da queste pietre
raggelate trae un calore
di alte passioni . . . È, dietro

il loro silenzio, il morto ardore
traspirato dalla muta origine:
il marmo, a Lucca o Pisa, il tufo

a Orvieto . . .

II

Non vi accende
la luna che grigiore, dove azzurri
gli etruschi dormono, non pende

The Apennines

I

Silent theatre of mountaintops chalky
and rapt, the silent moon lives your life,
tepid over the Lucchesia

and its all-too-human fields, white-hot over
Versilia's shores, so full over the empty
expanse of the sea—dumbstruck over

keels and holds, over sails shriveled up
after age-old, humble fishing runs
between Elba and the Argentario . . .

The moon is the only life there is.
And its gaze whitens Italy from Pisa
scattered on the Arno in a lifeless feast

of lights, to Lucca, modest in the gray
light of her surviving Catholic
perfection . . .

Human, the moon draws a heat
of high passion from these frozen
stones . . . It is the lifeless

ardor behind their silence,
exhaled by their voiceless source:
marble in Lucca and Pisa, tufa

in Orvieto . . .

II

Here the moon
lights up only gloom, Etruscans blue
in sleep . . . It hangs overhead

che a udire voci di fanciulli
dai selciati di Pienza o di Tarquinia . . .
Sui dossi risuonanti, brulli

ricava in mezzo all'Appennino
Orvieto, stretto sul colle sospeso
tra campi arati da orefici, minia-

ture, e il cielo. Orvieto illeso
tra i secoli, pesto di mura e tetti
sui vicoli di terra, con l'esodo

del mulo tra pesti giovinetti
impastati nel tufo.

Chiusa nei nervi, nel lucido passo,
tra sgretolate muraglie e scoscese
case, la bestia sale su dal basso

con ai fianchi le tinozze d'accesa
uva, sotto il busto di Bonifacio
prossimo a farsi polvere, difeso

da barocca altezza nella medioevale
nicchia della muraglia.

        III

È assente al suo gesto Bonifacio,
dal reggere la fionda nella grossa
mano Davide, e Ilaria, solo Ilaria . . .

Dentro nel claustrale transetto
come dentro un acquario, son di marmo
rassegnato le palpebre, il petto

dove giunge le mani in una calma
lontananza. Lì c'è l'aurora
e la sera italiana, la sua grama

just to hear the voices of children
rising up from the cobbles of Pienza
or Tarquinia . . . Over stark and echoing crests,

it carves from the heart of the Apennines
Orvieto, city huddled on a rise
over fields furrowed by goldsmiths,

miniatures, and the sky. Orvieto unmarred
through the centuries, a jumble of walls and roofs
over tight earthen streets, as a mule

departs amidst a jumble of boys
moulded from the rock . . .

Hunching its muscles and stepping with care,
the animal climbs between crumbling walls
and steep-faced houses, tubs of bright-colored

grapes slung over its sides, passing
under a bust of Boniface
about to turn to dust, sitting

safe at a baroque height
in the wall's medieval niche.

III

Boniface is absent from his gesture,
David missing from the sling he holds
in his great hand, and Ilaria, only Ilaria . . .

In the secluded transept
as in an aquarium, her eyelids
are of patient marble, her hands

folded on her breast in the placid
distance. Here we see Italy's dawn
and evening, her wretched

nascita, la sua morte incolore.
Sonno, i secoli vuoti: nessuno
scalpello potrà scalzare la mole

tenue di queste palpebre.

Jacopo con Ilaria scolpì l'Italia
perduta nella morte, quando
la sua età fu più pura e necessaria.

IV

Sotto le palpebre chiuse ride
tra i pidocchi il mammoccio di Cassino
comprato ai genitori; per le rive

furenti dell'Aniene, un assassino
e una puttana lo nutrono, nelle
coloniali notti in cui Ciampino

abbagliato sotto sbiadite stelle
vibra di aeroplani di regnanti,
e per i lungoteveri che sentinelle

del sesso battono in spossanti
attese intorno a terree latrine,
da San Paolo, a San Giovanni, ai canti

più caldi di Roma, si sentono supine
suonare le ore del mille
novecento cinquantuno, e s'incrina

la quiete, tra i tuguri e le basiliche.

Nelle chiuse palpebre d'Ilaria trema
l'infetta membrana delle notti
italiane . . . molle di brezze, serena

birth, and her colorless death.
Centuries of emptiness, sleep: no
chisel will ever manage to undo

the delicate mass of those eyelids.

In Ilaria Jacopo sculpted an Italy
lost in death, at her purest,
most imperative age.

IV

Under closed eyelids, a little kid
from Cassino, sold by his parents,
laughs; he's being fed

by a killer and a whore
on the raging banks of the Aniene,
on colonial nights as Ciampino,

dazzled under faded stars, shakes
from the roar of our rulers' airplanes,
and along the Tiber the sentries of sex

pace about on their nightly campaigns,
wearily waiting by earthen latrines
from San Paolo to San Giovanni and

to Rome's hottest streets, and nineteen
fifty-one slavishly chimes
its hours, shattering the serene

air round the shanties and basilicas.

Behind Ilaria's eyelids quivers
the festering membrane of Italy's nights . . .
soft in the breezes, peaceful in silvery

di luci . . . grida di giovanotti
caldi, ironici e sanguinari . . . odori
di stracci caldi, ora bagnati . . . motti

di vecchie voci meridionali . . . cori
emiliani leggeri tra borghi e maceri . . .
Dalla provincia viziosa ai cuori

bianchi dei globi dei bar salaci
delle periferie cittadine,
la carne e la miseria hanno placidi

ariosi suoni. Ma nelle veline
e massicce palpebre d'Ilaria, nulla
che non sia sonno. Forme mattutine

che, precoce, la morte alla fanciulla
legò al marmo. All'Italia non resta
che la sua morte marmorea, la brulla

sua gioventù interrotta . . .

Sotto le sue palpebre, nel suo
sonno, incarnata, la terra alla luna
ha un vergine orgasmo nell'argenteo buio

che sulla frana dell'Appennino sfuma
scosceso verso coste dove imperla
il Tirreno o l'Adriatico la spuma.

Dentro il rotondo recinto di pelli
e di metallo, isolato tra le fratte
in cerchio in una radura d'erba

verdissima sui dossi del Soratte,
dorme un umido, annerito gregge,
e il pastore con le membra contratte

nel calcare.

lights . . . sarcastic cries of hot-blooded
violent youths . . . odors of hot, wet rags . . .
old Southern voices making wisecracks

in the dark . . . weightless Emilian choirs
between villages and retting vats . . .
From the vicious province to the white cores

of globe lamps in the seedy bars
along the city's outskirts,
flesh and poverty make a placid,

melodious sound. But under Ilaria's
gauzy, massive eyelids there is nothing
but sleep. Forms of a morning

that a girl's early death cast
in stone. All that Italy has left
is her marble death, her barren

interrupted youth . . .

Under her eyelids, in her sleep,
the earth made flesh in the moonlight
virginally climaxes down the steep

and silvery dark of the Apennines' slide
toward shores where the froth adorns
the Tyrrhenian and Adriatic like pearls.

In a round enclosure of animal hides
and sheet metal, in a secluded
clearing of bright green grass

amid the scrub on the Soratte's heights,
a damp and blackened flock sleeps
in a circle, their shepherd tightly

curled up in the limestone . . .

V

Sotto le sue palpebre chiuse Luni
all'addiaccio, e le trepide
città dove l'Appennino profuma

più umano nelle cesellate siepi,
tra i caldi arativi della Toscana,
o dove più selvaggio le vecchie pievi

assorbe nell'etrurio—s'allontanano
sull'ala dei vergini, chiari
suoni serali. Ed essa si dipana,

la catena, nei solchi secolari
delle vene del Serchio, dell'Ombrone
e, dietro rudi imbuti e terrei fari

d'albore, il Tevere, nel polverone
appenninico, pagano ancora . . .
Roma, dietro radure di peoni,

ruderi alessandrini e barocchi indora
alla luna, e disfatte borgate
irreligiose, dove tutto si ignora

che non sia sesso, grotte abitate
da feci e fanciulli; i lungofiumi
dal Pincio, all'Aventino, alle scarpate

dello spoglio San Paolo dove i lumi
ingialliscono la calda atmosfera,
risuonano dei passi che le umide

pietre macchiano, e la romana sera
echeggiandone, come una membrana
grattata da un vizioso dito, svela

più acuto l'odore dell'orina.

V

Under her closed eyelids and the night skies
ancient Luni and the tremulous
cities where the Apenines rise

fragrant and more human among hedgerows
and Tuscany's arable warmth,
or where more wildly they swallow

up old country churches in Etrurian
folds, fade on the wings of evening's
clear and virgin sounds. Then the chain

unwinds in the ancient furrows
of the Serchio's and Ombrone's veins,
and past the craggy hollows and livid

beacons of dawn flows the Tiber, still
pagan in the Apenninic dust . . . Behind
clearings of peonies, Rome in moonlight gilds

Hellenic and Baroque remains and grimy
faithless suburbs, where no one knows
anything but sex, and the caves are slimy

with feces and children. From the Pincio
to the Aventine, to the embankments
of naked San Paolo, where the glow

of the lights turns the warm environment
yellow, the riverside echoes
with footsteps that stain the damp stones,

resonating in the Roman night
that like a membrane scratched
by an indecent finger ignites

with a powerful smell of urine.

VI

Un esercito accampato nell'attesa
di farsi cristiano nella cristiana
città, occupa una marcita distesa

d'erba sozza nell'accesa campagna:
scendere anch'egli dentro la borghese
luce spera aspettando una umana

abitazione, esso, sardo o pugliese,
dentro un porcile il fangoso desco
in villaggi ciechi tra lucide chiese

novecentesche e grattacieli.

Sotto le sue palpebre chiuse questo
assedio di milioni d'anime
dai crani ingenui, dall'occhio lesto

all'intesa, tra le infette marane
della borgata.

VII

Si perde verso il bianco Meridione,
azzurro, rosso, l'Appennino, assorto
sotto le chiuse palpebre, all'alone

del mare di Gaeta e di Sperlonga . . .

Dietro il Massico stende Sparanise
candelabri di ulivi, tra festoni
di piante rampicanti sulle elisie

radure, dove lucono i lampioni
a San Nicola . . . Si spalanca il golfo
affricano di Napoli, nazione

nel ventre della nazione . . .

VI

Outside the Christian city camps
an army waiting to become Christian;
they occupy a rotten expanse

of dirty grass across the hot countryside;
Sardinians, Apulians, they too hope
to descend into the bourgeois light,

expecting to find a human abode,
mud-covered tables in pigsties
in dead-end villages between bright

twentieth-century churches and highrises.

Under her closed eyelids lies
this siege of millions of souls
with ingenuous minds but eyes

that learn fast, among the foul
gutters of the shantytowns.

VII

Toward the white South the Apennines scatter
blue and red, rapt under closed cyclids,
in the aura of the sea at Gaeta

and Sperlonga . . .

Behind Mount Massico, Sparanise
displays her olive-tree candelabra,
amid creepers festooned across Elysian

glades where streetlamps shine
at San Nicola . . . Below sprawls
the African bay of Naples, nation

in the womb of a nation . . .

E non più Jacopo (più recente è il sonno
di Ilaria) sotto le palpebre fonde
in civile forma il popolare mondo

italiano, e contro gli sfondi
del suo paesaggio, non più scarnisce
in luce di intelletto — che non nasconde

la buia materiale — una mano che unisce
a Dio il povero rione. Quaggiù
tutto è preumano, e umanamente gioisce,

contro il riso del volgare fu
ed è inutile ogni parola
di redenzione: splende nella più

ardente indifferenza dei colori
seicenteschi, quasi che al sole
o all'ombra non bastasse che la sola

sfrontata presenza, di stracci, d'ori,
con negli occhi l'incallito riso
dei bassi digiuni d'amore.

Ragazzi romanzi sotto le palpebre
chiuse cantano nel cuore della specie
dei poveri rimasta sempre barbara

a tempi originari, escluse alle vicende
segrete della luce cristiana,
al succedersi necessario dei secoli:

e fanno dell'Italia un loro possesso,
ironici, in un dialettale riso
che non città o provincia ma ossesso

poggio, rione, tiene in sé inciso,
se ognuno chiuso nel calore del sesso,
sua sola misura, vive tra una gente

Under those eyelids Jacopo no longer
casts the Italian people's world
in civilized mould (Ilaria's slumber

is of more recent date); against the background
of their landscape, in the intellect's light
— which does not hide dark matter — he no longer

unfleshes a hand linking God
to the impoverished slum. Down here
all is prehuman and knows human joy;

against the plebian's laughter, all talk
of redemption always was and still is
fruitless. He beams in a careless blaze

of seventeenth-century colors,
as if his insolent presence alone,
with his rags and gold chains, and the callous

smile of loveless hovels in his eyes,
sufficed to let him hold his own
both in shadow and sunlight.

Under closed eyelids the boys of Rome sing
at the heart of the race of the dispossessed,
a barbarous breed still living

in primordial times, unblessed
by the secret affairs of Christianity's light
in the inexorable course of the ages;

they're making Italy a thing of their own,
with an irony and laughing dialect
that bears the mark of no province or town

but only some bedeviled hillside or district,
each enclosed in the heat of sex,
his sole yardstick, living among people

abbandonata al cinismo più vero
e alla più vera passione; al violento
negarsi e al violento darsi; nel mistero

chiara, perché pura e corrotta . . .

Se ognuno sa, esperto, l'ingenuo linguaggio
dell'incredulità, della insolenza,
dell'ironia, nel dialetto più saggio

e vizioso, chiude nell'incoscienza
le palpebre, si perde in un popolo
il cui clamore non è che silenzio.

1951

Le ceneri di Gramsci

I

Non è di maggio questa impura aria
che il buio giardino straniero
fa ancora più buio, o l'abbaglia

con cieche schiarite . . . questo cielo
di bave sopra gli attici giallini
che in semicherchi immensi fanno velo

alle curve del Tevere, ai turchini
monti del Lazio . . . Spande una mortale
pace, disamorata come i nostri destini,

tra le vecchie muraglie l'autunnale
maggio. In esso c'è il grigiore del mondo,
la fine del decennio in cui ci appare

tra le macerie finito il profondo
e ingenuo sforzo di rifare la vita;
il silenzio, fradicio e infecondo . . .

given to the most genuine cynicism,
the most genuine passion, brutal both
in withholding and sharing themselves, clear

in their mystery, at once pure and corrupt . . .

Every one of them has learned to speak
the naive language of disbelief, insolence
and irony, in the wisest, most indiscreet

dialect, and when their eyelids shut
in mindless sleep, they vanish into
a people whose clamor is only silence.

1951

Gramsci's Ashes

I

It's not May that brings this impure air,
makes the darkness of the foreign garden
darker still, or dazzles with the glare

of blind sunbursts . . . this frothy sky
over pale-yellow penthouses
in vast semicircles that deny

a view of the Tiber's meanders and
Latium's deep-blue hills . . . Between these old
walls the autumnal May extends

a deathly peace as unloved as our
destinies. It carries all the grayness
of the world, the close of a decade where

we saw our keen, naive attempts
to remake life end up among the ruins
and a sodden, sterile silence . . .

Tu giovane, in quel maggio in cui l'errore
era ancora vita, in quel maggio italiano
che alla vita aggiungeva almeno ardore,

quanto meno sventato e impuramente sano
dei nostri padri—non padre, ma umile
fratello—già con la tua magra mano

delineavi l'ideale che illumina
(ma non per noi: tu, morto, e noi
morti ugualmente, con te, nell'umido

giardino) questo silenzio. Non puoi,
lo vedi?, che riposare in questo sito
estraneo, ancora confinato. Noia

patrizia ti è intorno. E, sbiadito,
solo ti giunge qualche colpo d'incudine
dalle officine di Testaccio, sopito

nel vespro: tra misere tettoie, nudi
mucchi di latta, ferrivecchi, dove
cantando vizioso un garzone già chiude

la sua giornata, mentre intorno spiove.

II

Tra i due mondi, la tregua, in cui non siamo.
Scelte, dedizioni . . . altro suono non hanno
ormai che questo del giardino gramo

e nobile, in cui caparbio l'inganno
che attutiva la vita resta nella morte.
Nei cerchi dei sarcofaghi non fanno

che mostrare la superstite sorte
di gente laica le laiche iscrizioni
in queste grige pietre, corte

In the May of your youth, when to be mistaken
was still part of life, in that Italian
May when life had yet its share of passion,

you, less reckless and impurely healthy
than our fathers—no father but a humble
brother—already with your slender hand

you outlined the ideal that sheds
its light upon this silence (but not for us:
you are dead and we are likewise dead

with you, in this humid garden). Only
here, you see, on foreign ground, may you rest,
still the outcast. Patrician ennui

is all around you. The clanging of anvils,
faint in the late afternoon, is all
that reaches you here from the mills

of Testaccio, where between run-down sheds,
stark piles of sheet metal and iron scraps,
a shop-boy sings playfully, already

ending his day as the rain outside stops.

    II

Between the two worlds, a truce not our own.
Choices, commitments . . . by now only
echo the sounds of this lonely,

noble garden, where the illusion that softened
the life stubbornly persists in death.
The lay inscriptions in the round bands

of tombstones reveal only what's left
of the fate of these laymen
among gray stones majestic

e imponenti. Ancora di passioni
sfrenate senza scandalo son arse
le ossa dei miliardari di nazioni

più grandi; ronzano, quasi mai scomparse,
le ironie dei principi, dei pederasti,
i cui corpi sono nell'urne sparse

inceneriti e non ancora casti.
Qui il silenzio della morte è fede
di un civile silenzio di uomini rimasti

uomini, di un tedio che nel tedio
del Parco, discreto muta: e la città
che, indifferente, lo confina in mezzo

a tuguri e a chiese, empia nella pietà,
vi perde il suo splendore. La sua terra
grassa di ortiche e di legumi dà

questi magri cipressi, questa nera
umidità che chiazza i muri intorno
a smorti ghirigori di bosso, che la sera

rasserenando spegne in disadorni
sentori d'alga . . . quest'erbetta stenta
e inodora, dove violetta si sprofonda

l'atmosfera, con un brivido di menta,
o fieno marcio, e quieta vi prelude
con diurna malinconia, la spenta

trepidazione della note. Rude
di clima, dolcissimo di storia, è
tra questi muri il suolo in cui trasuda

altro suolo; questo umido che
ricorda altro umido; e risuonano
—familiari da latitudini e

and blunt. With unbridled passions
creating no scandal still burn the bones
of these rich men of nations

greater than ours. Never quite gone,
the sarcasms of princes and pederasts
whose bodies in the scattered urns

are now ash, but not yet chaste,
seethe in the air. Here death's silence confirms
the civic silence of men who remained

men, a tedium that in the graveyard's
tedium is quietly transformed
while the indifferent city that discards

it among shanties and churches here
loses its splendor, piously impious.
Its earth rich in nettles and verdure

yields these lean cypresses, the black
dampness staining the walls that surround
the colorless swirls of boxwood

smothered by evening's brightness in stark
scents of algae . . . this spare, unscented
grass into which the twilight sinks

with a shudder of mint or rancid
hay, placidly foreshadowing,
wistful as the day, night's unlit

trepidation. Harsh in climate, deep
in gentle history, through the soil within
these walls another soil seeps;

this dampness recalls another
like it; and from regions
and horizons where English woods

orizzonti dove inglesi selve coronano
laghi spersi nel cielo, tra praterie
verdi come fosforici biliardi o come

smeraldi: "And O ye Fountains . . ." — le pie
invocazioni . . .

III

Uno straccetto rosso, come quello
arrotolato al collo ai partigiani
e, presso l'urna, sul terreno cereo,

diversamente rossi, due gerani.
Lì tu stai, bandito e con dura eleganza
non cattolica, elencato tra estranei

morti: Le ceneri di Gramsci . . . Tra speranza
e vecchia sfiducia, ti accosto, capitato
per caso in questa magra serra, innanzi

alla tua tomba, al tuo spirito restato
quaggiù tra questi liberi. (O è qualcosa
di diverso, forse, di più estasiato

e anche di più umile, ebbra simbiosi
d'adolescente di sesso con morte . . .)
E, da questo paese in cui non ebbe posa

la tua tensione, sento quale torto
— qui nella quiete delle tombe — e insieme
quale ragione — nell'inquieta sorte

nostra — tu avessi stilando le supreme
pagine nei giorni del tuo assassinio.
Ecco qui ad attestare il seme

non ancora disperso dell'antico dominio,
questi morti attaccati a un possesso
che affonda nei secoli il suo abominio

crown lakes scattered in the heavens
over meadows green as phosphorescent
billiard-cloth or emeralds, the pious

invocations—"And O ye Fountains . . ."
—familiarly resound . . .

III

A red cloth like those the Partisans
once wore around their necks; and beside the urn
on softened ground, two geraniums

a rather different shade of red.
And you, here, banished with your hard, un-
Catholic grace, registered among the dead

foreigners: Gramsci's ashes . . . Torn
between hope and disillusion, I draw near,
having chanced into this spare green corner,

before your grave, before your spirit left
down here among the free. (Or perhaps it's something
else, more ecstatic but more modest

too, some drunken adolescent
symbiosis between sex and death . . .)
And in this country where your ferment

knew no rest, I sense how wrong you were
—here in the quiet of the tombs—and yet
how right as well—about our unsure

lot—when writing those last splendid
pages during the days of your murder.
And here to attest to the still unscattered

seed of the ancient dominion are
these dead men, still attached to possessions
whose infamy and grandeur reach far

e la sua grandezza: e insieme, ossesso,
quel vibrare d'incudini, in sordina,
soffocato e accorante — dal dimesso

rione — ad attestarne la fine.
Ed ecco qui me stesso . . . povero, vestito
dei panni che i poveri adocchiano in vetrine

dal rozzo splendore, e che ha smarrito
la sporcizia delle più sperdute strade,
delle panche dei tram, da cui stranito

è il mio giorno: mentre sempre più rade
ho di queste vacanze, nel tormento
del mantenermi in vita; e se mi accade

di amare il mondo non è che per violento
e ingenuo amore sensuale
così come, confuso adolescente, un tempo

l'odiai, se in esso mi feriva il male
borghese di me borghese: e ora, scisso
— con te — il mondo, oggetto non appare

di rancore e quasi di mistico
disprezzo, la parte che ne ha il potere?
Eppure senza il tuo rigore, sussisto

perché non scelgo. Vivo nel non volere
del tramontato dopoguerra: amando
il mondo che odio — nella sua miseria

sprezzante e perso — per un oscuro scandalo
della coscienza . . .

IV

Lo scandalo del contraddirmi, dell'essere
con te e contro te; con te nel cuore,
in luce, contro te nelle buie viscere;

back over centuries; while the obsessive
ringing of anvils — however softened,
muted, heartrending — from that submissive

neighborhood attests to its end.
And here, too, am I . . . poor and wearing
clothes the poor like to eye in shop windows

splendidly crass, their fabric now brown
with the filth of the loneliest streets
and the benches on trolleys that confound

my days — while these sorts of respites
grow ever more rare in the torment
of trying to stay alive; and if it's

true I love the world, it's only with a violent,
ingenuous, sensual love, like what
once drove me, as a confused adolescent,

to hate it, whenever its bourgeois evil
offended my bourgeois self; and now split
— with you — doesn't the world seem to merit

rancor and almost mystical contempt,
at least the part that holds power?
And yet, lacking your rigor, I get

on by not choosing. I live by not wanting,
as in the postwar years now past, loving
the world that I hate — in its misery,

scornful and lost — through some dark scandal
of conscience . . .

IV

The scandal of self-contradiction — of being
with you and against you; with you in my heart,
in the light, against you in the dark of my gut.

del mio paterno stato traditore
—nel pensiero, in un'ombra di azione—
mi so ad esso attaccato nel calore

degli istinti, dell'estetica passione;
attratto da una vita proletaria
a te anteriore, è per me religione

la sua allegria, non la millenaria
sua lotta: la sua natura, non la sua
coscienza; è la forza originaria

dell'uomo, che nell'atto s'è perduta,
a darle l'ebbrezza della nostalgia,
una luce poetica: ed altro più

io non so dirne, che non sia
giusto ma non sincero, astratto
amore, non accorante simpatia . . .

Come i poveri povero, mi attacco
come loro a umilianti speranze,
come loro per vivere mi batto

ogni giorno. Ma nella desolante
mia condizione di diseredato,
io possiedo: ed è il più esaltante

dei possessi borghesi, lo stato
più assoluto. Ma come io possiedo la storia,
essa me possiede; ne sono illuminato:

ma a che serve la luce?

V

Non dico l'individuo, il fenomeno
dell'ardore sensuale e sentimentale . . .
altri vizi esso ha, altro è il nome

Though a traitor to my father's station
—in my mind, in a semblance of action—
I know I'm bound to it in the heat

of my instincts and aesthetic passion;
drawn to a proletarian life
from before your time, I take for religion

its joyousness, not its millennial
struggle—its nature, not its
consciousness. It is man's primordial

strength, having been lost in the act,
that gives this faith the joy of nostalgia,
the glow of poetry. More than that

I cannot say, without being right
but insincere, expressing abstract
love, not heartbreaking sympathy . . .

Poor as the poor myself, I cling tight,
like them, to demeaning hopes;
like them, every day of my life I fight

just to live. Yet in my disheartening
condition as one of the dispossessed,
I still possess—and it's the most thrilling

of bourgeois possessions, the ultimate
state of being. Yet as I possess history,
I am possessed by it, enlightened by it:

but what good is the light?

        V

I don't mean the individual, that phenomenon
of sensual and emotional fervor . . .
He has other vices; his sin

e la fatalità del suo peccare . . .
Ma in esso impastati quali comuni,
prenatali vizi, e quale

oggettivo peccato! Non sono immuni
gli interni e esterni atti, che lo fanno
incarnato alla vita, da nessuna

delle religioni che nella vita stanno,
ipoteca di morte, istituite
a ingannare la luce, a dar luce all'inganno.

Destinate a esser seppellite
le sue spoglie al Verano, è cattolica
la sua lotta con esse: gesuitiche

le manìe con cui dispone il cuore;
e ancor più dentro: ha bibliche astuzie
la sua coscienza . . . e ironico ardore

liberale . . . e rozza luce, tra i disgusti
di dandy provinciale, di provinciale
salute . . . Fino alle infime minuzie

in cui sfumano, nel fondo animale,
Autorità e Anarchia . . . Ben protetto
dall'impura virtù e dall'ebbro peccare,

difendendo una ingenuità di ossesso,
e con quale coscienza!, vive l'io: io,
vivo, eludendo la vita, con nel petto

il senso di una vita che sia oblio
accorante, violento . . . Ah come
capisco, muto nel fradicio brusio

del vento, qui dov'è muta Roma,
tra i cipressi stancamente sconvolti,
presso te, l'anima il cui graffito suona

has another name and predetermined fate. . .
Yet what common, prenatal vices
he's made of, what

objective sin! The actions that originate
within him and without, and make him
life made flesh, are immune to none

of the religions that are part of life,
death's collateral, and founded
to deceive the light and give light to deception.

His mortal remains destined for burial
at Verano, he wages a Catholic
struggle against them, with Jesuitical

manias directing his heart; further
inside, in his conscience, lie Biblical
wiles . . . and ironic, liberal fervor . . .

and to go with his dislikes as a provincial
dandy, a crude glow of provincial
good health . . . down to the infinitesimal

details where, in his animal depths, lurk
Authority and Anarchy . . . Well-protected
from impure virtue and drunken

sin, and defending an obsessive
naivety—conscientiously!—so lives
the ego: so live I, eluding life,

with that sense of life as poignant, violent
oblivion in my breast . . . Mute
while the wind wetly stirs up the somnolent

cypresses, here next to you, where
Rome herself is mute, oh how
I understand the soul whose inscription rings

Shelley . . . Come capisco il vortice
dei sentimenti, il capriccio (greco
nel cuore del patrizio, nordico

villeggiante) che lo inghiottì nel cieco
celeste del Tirreno; la carnale
gioia dell'avventura, estetica

e puerile: mentre prostrata l'Italia
come dentro il ventre di un'enorme
cicala, spalanca bianchi litorali,

sparsi nel Lazio di velate torme
di pini, barocchi, di giallognole
radure di ruchetta, dove dorme

col membro gonfio tra gli stracci un sogno
goethiano, il giovincello ciociaro . . .
Nella Maremma, scuri, di stupende fogne

d'erbasaetta in cui si stampa chiaro
il nocciòlo, pei viottoli che il buttero
della sua gioventù ricolma ignaro.

Ciecamente fragranti nelle asciutte
curve della Versilia, che sul mare
aggrovigliato, cieco, i tersi stucchi,

le tarsie lievi della sua pasquale
campagna interamente umana,
espone, incupita sul Cinquale,

dipanata sotto le torride Apuane,
i blu vitrei sul rosa . . . Di scogli,
frane, sconvolti, come per un panico

di fragranza, nella Riviera, molle,
erta, dove il sole lotta con la brezza
a dar suprema soavità agli olii

Shelley . . . How I understand the whirlwind
of feelings, the whimsy (Greek
in the heart of the Northern, patrician

sojourner) that swallowed him up
in the blind Tyrrhenian blue; the fleshly
joy of adventure, aesthetic

and puerile—as the shores of an Italy
prostrate as though in the belly
of a giant cicada, stretch silvery

white in Latium, dotted with airy throngs
of evergreens, baroque, and yellowy
clearings of rocket greens in which a young

Ciociaro sleeps in a Goethian dream,
member swollen under his rags . . .
—or dark in Maremma with wondrous streams

of arrowhead where the hazels stand in bright
relief on bridle paths the herdsman fills,
oblivious, with all his youth . . .

—or blindly fragrant in the dry
bends of Versilia's shore, which by
the blind and tangled sea displays

the vivid stuccoes and soft inlays
of a paschal, fully human landscape
darkening over the Cinquale

and unraveling under the torrid
Apuan Alps, glassy blues over the red . . .
of rocks, landslides, spilt as in a scented

panic down into the Riviera
steep and soft, where sunlight wrestles
with the breeze to make the oils of the sea

del mare . . . E intorno ronza di lietezza
lo sterminato strumento a percussione
del sesso e della luce: così avvezza

ne è l'Italia che non ne trema, come
morta nella sua vita: gridano caldi
da centinaia di porti il nome

del compagno i giovinetti madidi
nel bruno della faccia, tra la gente
rivierasca, presso orti di cardi,

in luride spiaggette . . .

Mi chiederai tu, morto disadorno,
d'abbandonare questa disperata
passione di essere nel mondo?

    VI

Me ne vado, ti lascio nella sera
che, benché triste, così dolce scende
per noi viventi, con la luce cerea

che al quartiere in penombra si rapprende.
E lo sommuove. Lo fa più grande, vuoto,
intorno, e, più lontano, lo riaccende

di una vita smaniosa che del roco
rotolìo dei tram, dei gridi umani,
dialettali, fa un concerto fioco

e assoluto. E senti come in quei lontani
esseri che, in vita, gridano, ridono,
in quei loro veicoli, in quei grami

caseggiati dove si consuma l'infido
ed espansivo dono dell'esistenza —
quella vita non è che un brivido;

more utterly sweet . . . And everywhere
the vast percussion instrument of sex
and light reverberates with happiness:

Italy's so used to it she does not
even tremble, as though dead in life;
from hundreds of ports, kids hotly

call out to their friends among the people
of the shore, their brown faces
dripping wet, near gardens of thistle

or dirty little beaches . . .

Would you, in death unadorned,
have me abandon my desperate
passion for being in the world?

VI

I'm going. I'll leave you to the evening
which, however sad, descends so sweetly
for us, the living, its faint light cleaving

to the shadows of the neighborhood,
stirring it up, making it bigger, empty
all around and, in the distance, rekindling

a restless life that with the rumble
of the trams, the human shouts
in dialect, creates a concert muffled

and absolute. You can feel that
in these living beings—yelling, laughing
in their vehicles, inside their wretched

tenements in which the sinister,
expansive gift of life is burning up—
this life is nothing but a shudder;

corporea, collettiva presenza;
senti il mancare di ogni religione
vera; non vita, ma sopravvivenza

—forse più lieta della vita—come
d'un popolo di animali, nel cui arcano
orgasmo non ci sia altra passione

che per l'operare quotidiano:
umile fervore cui dà un senso di festa
l'umile corruzione. Quanto più è vano

—in questo vuoto della storia, in questa
ronzante pausa in cui la vita tace—
ogni ideale, meglio è manifesta

la stupenda, adusta sensualità
quasi alessandrina, che tutto minia
e impuramente accende, quando qua

nel mondo, qualcosa crolla, e si trascina
il mondo, nella penombra, rientrando
in vuote piazze, in scorate officine . . .

Già si accendono i lumi, costellando
Via Zabaglia, Via Franklin, l'intero
Testaccio, disadorno tra il suo grande

lurido monte, i lungoteveri, il nero
fondale, oltre il fiume, che Monteverde
ammassa o sfuma invisibile sul cielo.

Diademi di lumi che si perdono,
smaglianti, e freddi di tristezza
quasi marina . . . Manca poco alla cena;

brillano i rari autobus del quartiere,
con grappoli d'operai agli sportelli,
e gruppi di militari vanno, senza fretta,

a bodily, collective presence;
you can feel the lack of any true
religion; not life, but subsistence

— perhaps happier than life — as if they
were a race of animals whose arcane
thrill lay in no other passion

than that of daily labor:
a humble fervor that humble corruption
grants a sense of celebration. The more

useless all ideals — in this historic
void, this teeming pause where life falls
silent — the more manifest the terrific,

sunburnt, almost Alexandrian
sensuality illuminating all,
igniting everything impurely

as a bit of our world collapses
and the world drags on, in shadow, back
into the empty squares and desolate workshops . . .

Lights are coming on already, sparkling
in Via Zabaglia, Via Franklin, all over
Testaccio, naked from its great mountain

of refuse to the *lungoteveri*
and the black backdrop past the river,
which Monteverde gathers and dissolves in the sky.

Diadems of light scatter and glimmer,
cold with a sadness almost like that
of the sea . . . Soon it will be time for dinner;

the few running buses glitter in the dusk,
clusters of workers hang out the doors;
groups of soldiers in no particular rush

verso il monte che cela in mezzo a sterri
fradici e mucchi secchi d'immondizia
nell'ombra, rintanate zoccolette

che aspettano irose sopra la sporcizia
afrodisiaca: e, non lontano, tra casette
abusive ai margini del monte, o in mezzo

a palazzi, quasi a mondi, dei ragazzi
leggeri come stracci giocano alla brezza
non più fredda, primaverile; ardenti

di sventatezza giovanile la romanesca
loro sera di maggio scuri adolescenti
fischiano pei marciapiedi, nella festa

vespertina; e scrosciano le saracinesche
dei garages di schianto, gioiosamente,
se il buio ha reso serena la sera,

e in mezzo ai platani di Piazza Testaccio
il vento che cade in tremiti di bufera,
è ben dolce, benché radendo i capellacci

e i tufi del Macello, vi si imbeva
di sangue marcio, e per ogni dove
agiti rifiuti e odore di miseria.

È un brusio la vita, e questi persi
in essa, la perdono serenamente,
se il cuore ne hanno pieno: a godersi

eccoli, miseri, la sera: e potente
in essi, inermi, per essi, il mito
rinasce ... Ma io, con il cuore cosciente

di chi soltanto nella storia ha vita,
potrò mai più con pura passione operare,
se so che la nostra storia è finita?

1954

head to the mount, where between muddy
dirt heaps and dry piles of rubbish
in shadow hide little whores, angrily

waiting at the top of the aphrodisiac
filth. Not far away, between illegal
shanties at the edge of the hill,

or between buildings like other worlds,
kids light as rags play in a spring breeze
no longer cold. Burning with youthful

brashness on their Roman evening
in May, dark adolescents
whistle down the sidewalks in the twilight

celebration; the rolling shutters of garages
crash and thunder suddenly, joyously,
after darkness has quieted the night;

and through the plane trees of Piazza Testaccio,
dying in shudders, as in a squall, the wind
is sweet as it sweeps over the *cappellaccio*

and tufa of the Slaughterhouse,
steeping in rotten blood and everywhere
stirring up trash and the smell of despair.

Life is commotion; and these people are
lost in it, and untroubled when they lose it,
since their hearts are full of it. There they are,

poor things, enjoying the evening, helpless;
yet in them and for them, myth is reborn
in all its power . . . But I, with the conscious

heart of one who lives only in history,
can I ever act with pure passion again,
when I know that our history has ended?

                                        1954

Il pianto della scavatrice

I

Solo l'amare, solo il conoscere
conta, non l'aver amato,
non l'aver conosciuto. Dà angoscia

il vivere di un consumato
amore. L'anima non cresce più.
Ecco nel calore incantato

della notte che piena quaggiù
tra le curve del fiume e le sopite
visioni della città sparsa di luci,

echeggia ancora di mille vite,
disamore, mistero, e miseria
dei sensi, mi rendono nemiche

le forme del mondo, che fino a ieri
erano la mia ragione d'esistere.
Annoiato, stanco, rincaso, per neri

piazzali di mercati, tristi
strade intorno al porto fluviale,
tra le baracche e i magazzini misti

agli ultimi prati. Lì mortale
è il silenzio: ma giù, a viale Marconi,
alla stazione di Trastevere, appare

ancora dolce la sera. Ai loro rioni,
alle loro borgate, tornano su motori
leggeri—in tuta o coi calzoni

di lavoro, ma spinti da un festivo ardore—
i giovani, coi compagni sui sellini,
ridenti, sporchi. Gli ultimi avventori

The Cry of the Excavator

I

Only loving, only knowing matter.
Not the fact of having loved, or
having known. We become only sadder

living out a love that's over.
The soul can no longer grow.
And now in the enchanted night, hot

and full, as countless lives still echo
here between the river's bends
and sleepy visions of a city aglow

with scattered lights, a disaffection,
mystery, and sensual misery
turn me against these reflections

of the world, even though just yesterday
they were my reason for living.
Bored and tired, I head home, making my way

through dark market squares and gloomy streets
around the river's port, past shacks thrown
together with warehouses in the midst

of the country's last fields. Here
a deathly silence reigns, but farther down,
on Viale Marconi, or at Trastevere

Station, the evening still looks sweet.
Smiling, unwashed—in overalls or work trousers,
but spurred on by a festive heat—

the young return to their quarters,
their slums, on small motorbikes, friends
seated behind. Here and there,

chiacchierano in piedi con voci
alte nella notte, qua e là, ai tavolini
dei locali ancora lucenti e semivuoti.

Stupenda e misera città,
che m'hai insegnato ciò che allegri e feroci
gli uomini imparano bambini,

le piccole cose in cui la grandezza
della vita in pace si scopre, come
andare duri e pronti nella ressa

delle strade, rivolgersi a un altro uomo
senza tremare, non vergognarsi
di guardare il denaro contato

con pigre dita dal fattorino
che suda contro le facciate in corsa
in un colore eterno d'estate;

a difendermi, a offendere, ad avere
il mondo davanti agli occhi e non
soltanto in cuore, a capire

che pochi conoscono le passioni
in cui io sono vissuto:
che non mi sono fraterni, eppure sono

fratelli proprio nell'avere
passioni di uomini
che allegri, inconsci, interi

vivono di esperienze
ignote a me. Stupenda e misera
città che mi hai fatto fare

esperienza di quella vita
ignota: fino a farmi scoprire
ciò che, in ognuno, era il mondo.

standing at tables in cafes still bright
but half empty, the evening's last clients
loudly converse in the night.

Stunning, wretched city,
you've taught me what men learn
as children, lighthearted and fierce,

the small things that let one discover
life's greatness in peace, how
to step hard and ready into the fray

of the streets, to go up to another man
without trembling, how without shame
to examine the change handed lazily back

by the bus's sweaty ticketman,
as behind him the façades stream by
with the unending colors of summer;

how to defend myself, how to offend,
how to keep the world before my eyes
and not just in my heart; how to realize

that few people know the passions
I have lived—and while they may
not treat me in brotherly fashion

they are my brothers simply because
they have human passions
and, lighthearted, unknowing, and whole,

they thrive on experiences
unknown to me. Stunning, wretched
city, you've let me experience

this unknown life—and in the end
let me discover what is
the world in every one of us.

Una luna morente nel silenzio,
che di lei vive, sbianca tra violenti
ardori, che miseramente sulla terra

muta di vita, coi bei viali, le vecchie
viuzze, senza dar luce abbagliano
e, in tutto il mondo, le riflette

lassù, un po' di calda nuvolaglia.
È la notte più bella dell'estate.
Trastevere, in un odore di paglia

di vecchie stalle, di svuotate
osterie, non dorme ancora.
Gli angoli bui, le pareti placide

risuonano d'incantati rumori.
Uomini e ragazzi se ne tornano a casa
—sotto festoni di luci ormai sole—

verso i loro vicoli, che intasano
buio e immondizia, con quel passo blando
da cui più l'anima era invasa

quando veramente amavo, quando
veramente volevo capire.
E, come allora, scompaiono cantando.

II

Povero come un gatto del Colosseo,
vivevo in una borgata tutta calce
e polverone, lontano dalla città

e dalla campagna, stretto ogni giorno
in un autobus rantolante:
e ogni andata, ogni ritorno

The moon fades in silence, giving life
to the stillness, shining white amid violent
glimmers that dazzle without shedding light

upon an earth in a hush with its fine
avenues, its narrow old streets, as a few
warm banks of cloud on the skyline

cast reflections all over the world.
It's the most beautiful night of the summer.
Amid a smell of the straw of old stables

and taverns emptied of clientele,
Trastevere is not yet asleep:
the dark corners, placid walls

still echo with magical sounds.
Men and boys are coming home
—under garlands of lights now alone—

to narrow streets choked with darkness
and garbage, walking with the same
soft steps that used to fill my soul

when I truly loved, when
I truly wanted to understand. And they
disappear singing, as they did back then.

    II

Poor as a cat in the Colosseum,
I lived in a suburban slum all whitelime
and dust clouds, far from the city,

far from the country, crammed each day
into a wheezing city bus;
and every ride, whether on the way

era un calvario di sudore e di ansie.
Lunghe camminate in una calda caligine,
lunghi crepuscoli davanti alle carte

ammucchiate sul tavolo, tra strade di fango,
muriccioli, casette bagnate di calce
e senza infissi, con tende per porte . . .

Passavano l'olivaio, lo straccivendolo,
venendo da qualche altra borgata,
con l'impolverata merce che pareva

frutto di furto, e una faccia crudele
di giovani invecchiati tra i vizi
di chi ha una madre dura e affamata.

Rinnovato dal mondo nuovo,
libero — una vampa, un fiato
che non so dire, alla realtà

che umile e sporca, confusa e immensa,
brulicava nella meridionale periferia,
dava un senso di serena pietà.

Un'anima in me, che non era solo mia,
una piccola anima in quel mondo sconfinato,
cresceva, nutrita dall'allegria

di chi amava, anche se non riamato.
E tutto si illuminava, a questo amore.
Forse ancora di ragazzo, eroicamente,

e però maturato dall'esperienza
che nasceva ai piedi della storia.
Ero al centro del mondo, in quel mondo

di borgate tristi, beduine,
di gialle praterie sfregate
da un vento sempre senza pace,

to work or back, was a nightmare of sweat
and anguish. Long walks in the warm haze,
long twilights in front of papers

piled on my desk, between muddy roads,
low walls, and whitewashed little houses
with no window frames, and curtains for doors . . .

The olive man and ragman would come
from some other outlying slum
bearing dusty goods that looked as though

stolen, wearing the cruel expression
of youngsters who'd grown old as the vice-
ridden children of a hard, hungry mother.

Renewed by this new world,
and free — a flame, a breath
I can't explain gave a sense of untroubled

holiness to a reality teeming
humble and dirty, vast and confused
on the city's southern periphery.

A soul inside me, not only my own,
a little soul was growing in that boundless
world, nourished by the joy of one

who loved, though unrequited.
And all was lit up by this love
— still a boy's love, perhaps, and heroic,

yet seasoned by the experience
coming to life at history's feet.
I was at the center of the world,

in a world of sad, bedouin suburbs,
yellow grasslands lashed
by a wind forever restless

venisse dal caldo mare di Fiumicino,
o dall'agro, dove si perdeva
la città fra i tuguri; in quel mondo

che poteva soltanto dominare,
quadrato spettro giallognolo
nella giallognola foschia,

bucato da mille file uguali
di finestre sbarrate, il Penitenziario
tra vecchi campi e sopiti casali.

Le cartacce e la polvere che cieco
il venticello trascinava qua e là,
le povere voci senza eco

di donnette venute dai monti
Sabini, dall'Adriatico, e qua
accampate, ormai con torme

di deperiti e duri ragazzini
stridenti nelle canottiere a pezzi,
nei grigi, bruciati calzoncini,

i soli africani, le piogge agitate
che rendevano torrenti di fango
le strade, gli autobus ai capolinea

affondati nel loro angolo
tra un'ultima striscia d'erba bianca
e qualche acido, ardente immondezzaio . . .

era il centro del mondo, com'era
al centro della storia il mio amore
per esso: e in questa

maturità che per essere nascente
era ancora amore, tutto era
per divenire chiaro—era,

either blowing from the warm sea waters
of Fiumicino or from the *agro*, where
the city disappeared amid the shanties —

in a world over which only
the Penitentiary — square yellow
specter in the yellowy haze,

pierced by a thousand identical
windows with bars — could preside,
between ancient fields and sleepy hamlets.

The waste paper and dust cast about
here and there by the breeze,
the meager, echoless voices

of little women come down from
Sabine hills and Adriatic seas,
and now encamped here, with swarms

of withered, tough little children
screaming in their ragged T-shirts
and their drab, faded shorts,

the African sun, the violent downpours
that turned the streets into rivers
of mud, the city buses foundering

in their corners at the terminus,
between the last strip of white grass
and some acrid, burning garbage heap . . .

This was the center of the world, just
as my love for it was at the center
of history; and in this ripeness

— which, being newborn,
was still love — everything was
about to become clear — it *was*

chiaro! Quel borgo nudo al vento,
non romano, non meridionale,
non operaio, era la vita

nella sua luce più attuale:
vita, e luce della vita, piena
nel caos non ancora proletario,

come la vuole il rozzo giornale
della cellula, l'ultimo
sventolio del rotocalco: osso

dell'esistenza quotidiana,
pura, per essere fin troppo
prossima, assoluta per essere

fin troppo miseramente umana.

III

E ora rincaso, ricco di quegli anni
così nuovi che non avrei mai pensato
di saperli vecchi in un'anima

a essi lontana, come a ogni passato.
Salgo i viali del Gianicolo, fermo
da un bivio liberty, a un largo alberato,

a un troncone di mura—ormai al termine
della città sull'ondulata pianura
che si apre sul mare. E mi rigermina

nell'anima—inerte e scura
come la notte abbandonata al profumo—
una semenza ormai troppo matura

per dare ancora frutto, nel cumulo
di una vita tornata stanca e acerba . . .
Ecco Villa Pamphili, e nel lume

clear! This suburb naked to the wind,
not Roman, not Southern,
not working-class, was life

in its most current light:
life, and life's light, complete
in a chaos not yet proletarian,

as the crude newssheet
of the local cell, the latest
offset flyer, would have it: backbone

of daily existence,
pure in being all too
near, absolute in being

all too wretchedly human.

    III

And now I head home, enriched by times
still so fresh I should never have guessed
I would see them grow old in a soul

now as far from them as from all the past.
I walk up the Janiculum's avenues, stop
at an Art Nouveau junction, in a piazza

with trees, at a remnant of wall, by now
at the edge of the city, on the plain
rolling down to the sea. And in my soul,

dark and inert as the night giving in
to its fragrance, a seed now too old
to bear fruit germinates again

in the accumulated mass of a life
long since turned weary and bitter . . .
Here's Villa Pamphili and, in the light

che tranquillo riverbera
sui nuovi muri, la via dove abito.
Presso la mia casa, su un'erba

ridotta a un'oscura bava,
una traccia sulle voragini scavate
di fresco, nel tufo — caduta ogni rabbia

di distruzione — rampa contro radi palazzi
e pezzi di cielo, inanimata,
una scavatrice . . .

Che pena m'invade, davanti a questi attrezzi
supini, sparsi qua e là nel fango,
davanti a questo canovaccio rosso

che pende a un cavalletto, nell'angolo
dove la notte sembra più triste?
Perché, a questa spenta tinta di sangue,

la mia coscienza così ciecamente resiste,
si nasconde, quasi per un ossesso
rimorso che tutta, nel fondo, la contrista?

Perché dentro in me è lo stesso senso
di giornate per sempre inadempite
che è nel morto firmamento

in cui sbianca questa scavatrice?

Mi spoglio in una delle mille stanze
dove a via Fonteiana si dorme.
Su tutto puoi scavare, tempo: speranze

passioni. Ma non su queste forme
pure della vita . . . Si riduce
ad esse l'uomo, quando colme

that quietly makes the new walls glitter,
the street that I live on.
Near my home, on a bit of grass little

more than a dingy froth,
a trickle over chasms freshly
dug out of the tufa—the wrath

of destruction now silent—there rises lifeless
against sundry buildings and shreds of sky,
an excavator . . .

What is this sorrow that fills me, at the sight
of these tools strewn about here and there
in the mud, and that scrap of red cloth

hung from a trestle in a corner
where the night seems grimmest?
Why, seeing that faded, bloody color,

does my conscience so blindly resist
and take cover, as if distressed
to its core by some wild remorse?

Why do I have the same presentiment
inside, of days forever unfulfilled,
as I sense in the dead firmament

over that sun-whitened excavator?

I undress in one of countless rooms
in Via Fontenaia where people sleep.
Time, you may cut deep into everything—

hopes, passions—but not into these pure
forms of life . . . They become one
with man himself, when experience

siano esperienza e fiducia
nel mondo . . . Ah, giorni di Rebibbia,
che io credevo persi in una luce

di necessità, e che ora so così liberi!

Insieme al cuore, allora, pei difficili
casi che ne avevano sperduto
il corso verso un destino umano,

guadagnando in ardore la chiarezza
negata, e in ingenuità
il negato equilibrio — alla chiarezza

all'equilibrio giungeva anche,
in quei giorni, la mente. E il cieco
rimpianto, segno di ogni mia

lotta col mondo, respingevano, ecco,
adulte benché inesperte ideologie . . .
Si faceva, il mondo, soggetto

non più di mistero ma di storia.
Si moltiplicava per mille la gioia
del conoscerlo — come

ogni uomo, umilmente, conosce.
Marx o Gobetti, Gramsci o Croce,
furono vivi nelle vive esperienze.

Mutò la materia di un decennio d'oscura
vocazione, se mi spesi a far chiaro ciò
che più pareva essere ideale figura

a una ideale generazione;
in ogni pagina, in ogni riga
che scrivevo, nell'esilio di Rebibbia,

and faith in the world are at their height.
Oh, the days of Rebibbia,
which I had thought lost in a light

of necessity, and which I now know were so free!

Like my heart, which through the difficult
straits that had thrown it off
the path to a human destiny

gained through fervor a clarity
denied, and through naivety
an unlikely balance—my mind,

too, those days, attained clarity
and balance. And thus blind
regret, the mark of all my

struggles with the world, was kept
at bay by adult but untried ideologies . . .
The world was becoming a subject

no longer of mystery but of history.
The joy of knowing it—with the humble
knowledge that every man has—

increased a thousandfold.
Marx and Gobetti, Gramsci and Croce
were alive in the experience of life.

The stuff of ten years of obscure
vocation changed, when I strove to bring
to light what seemed like the ideal figure

for an ideal generation;
every page, every line I wrote
during my exile in Rebibbia

c'era quel fervore, quella presunzione,
quella gratitudine. Nuovo
nella mia nuova condizione

di vecchio lavoro e di vecchia miseria,
i pochi amici che venivano
da me, nelle mattine o nelle sere

dimenticate sul Penitenziario,
mi videro dentro una luce viva:
mite, violento rivoluzionario

nel cuore e nella lingua. Un uomo fioriva.

    IV

Mi stringe contro il suo vecchio vello,
che profuma di bosco, e mi posa
il muso con le sue zanne di verro

o errante orso dal fiato di rosa,
sulla bocca: e intorno a me la stanza
è una radura, la coltre corrosa

dagli ultimi sudori giovanili, danza
come un velame di pollini . . . E infatti
cammino per una strada che avanza

tra i primi prati primaverili, sfatti
in una luce di paradiso . . .
Trasportato dall'onda dei passi,

questa che lascio alle spalle, lieve e misero,
non è la periferia di Roma: «*Viva
Mexico!*» è scritto a calce o inciso

sui ruderi dei templi, sui muretti ai bivii,
decrepiti, leggeri come osso, ai confini
di un bruciante cielo senza un brivido.

displayed this eagerness, this presumption,
this gratitude. I was new
to my new situation

of old labor and old poverty,
and the few friends who called on me
on forgotten mornings and evenings

up by the Penitentiary,
saw me in a brilliant light:
a gentle, violent revolutionary

in heart and language. A man in bloom.

IV

He holds me close to his aging fleece,
which smells of the woods, and places his snout,
with its boarlike tusks or the teeth

of a stray bear with breath like roses,
over my mouth — and the room around me
turns into a glade, and the blanket, corroded

by the last sweats of youth, dances
like a cloud of pollen . . . Actually
I'm walking down a road that advances

through the first fields of spring
as they vanish in heavenly light . . .
Carried away by the waves of my footsteps,

what I'm leaving behind me, wretched,
lighthearted, is not Rome's periphery: everywhere
I see "*Viva Mexico!*" written in whitewash, or etched

into the ruined temples and decrepit
walls, airy as bones, at the crossroads
and the edges of a burning, shudderless sky.

Ecco, in cima a una collina
fra le ondulazioni, miste alle nubi,
di una vecchia catena appenninica,

la città, mezza vuota, benché sia l'ora
della mattina, quando vanno le donne
alla spesa—o del vespro che indora

i bambini che corrono con le mamme
fuori dai cortili della scuola.
Da un gran silenzio le strade sono invase:

si perdono i selciati un po' sconnessi,
vecchi come il tempo, grigi come il tempo,
e due lunghi listoni di pietra

corrono lungo le strade, lucidi e spenti.
Qualcuno, in quel silenzio, si muove:
qualche vecchia, qualche ragazzetto

perduto nei suoi giuochi, dove
i portali di un dolce Cinquecento
s'aprano sereni, o un pozzetto

con bestioline intarsiate sui bordi
posi sopra la povera erba,
in qualche bivio o canto dimenticato.

Si apre sulla cima del colle l'erma
piazza del comune, e fra casa
e casa, oltre un muretto, e il verde

d'un grande castagno, si vede
lo spazio della valle: ma non la valle.
Uno spazio che tremola celeste

o appena cereo . . . Ma il Corso continua,
oltre quella famigliare piazzetta
sospesa nel cielo appenninico:

There, atop a hill, between clouds
and the undulant contours
of an ancient ridge of Apennines,

lies the town, half empty even at this hour
of the morning, when the women go
shopping — or in evening's golden glow

when children run to their mothers
from the courtyards of the schools.
The streets fill with deep silence,

the slightly disconnected cobbles blur,
old as time, gray as time,
and two long, stone walkways,

shiny, lifeless, flank the streets.
Someone, in the silence, is moving:
an old woman, a little boy

lost in play, who sees perhaps
a charming Cinquecento portal
open gently, or a small well

with little creatures carved along the rim
resting on the meager grass
at some forgotten crossroads or corner.

At the top of the hill, the town's main square
lies deserted, and between the houses,
behind a low wall and the green

of a great chestnut, you can see the space
of the valley below, but not the valley.
A space that shimmers pale blue

or slightly ashen . . . But the Corso continues
beyond the familiar piazzetta
suspended in the Apennine sky,

s'interna fra case più strette, scende
un po' a mezza costa: e più in basso
—quando le barocche casette diradano—

ecco apparire la valle—e il deserto.
Ancora solo qualche passo
verso la svolta, dove la strada

è già tra nudi praticelli erti
e ricciuti. A manca, contro il pendio,
quasi fosse crollata la chiesa,

si alza gremita di affreschi, azzurri,
rossi, un'abside, pèsta di volute
lungo le cancellate cicatrici

del crollo—da cui soltanto essa,
l'immensa conchiglia, sia rimasta
a spalancarsi contro il cielo.

È lì, da oltre la valle, dal deserto,
che prende a soffiare un'aria, lieve, disperata,
che incendia la pelle di dolcezza . . .

È come quegli odori che, dai campi
bagnati di fresco, o dalle rive di un fiume,
soffiano sulla città nei primi

giorni di bel tempo: e tu
non li riconosci, ma impazzito
quasi di rimpianto, cerchi di capire

se siano di un fuoco acceso sulla brina,
oppure di uve o nespole perdute
in qualche granaio intiepidito

dal sole della stupenda mattina.
Io grido di gioia, così ferito
in fondo ai polmoni da quell'aria

makes its way through huddled houses
and halfway down the slope: farther down
— as the small baroque houses thin out —

one sees, at last, the valley — and the wild.
Take a few more steps toward the bend,
where the road already runs through stark

little meadows, scrubby and steep,
and on the left, against the hillside,
as if a church had collapsed there,

stands an apse full of frescoes
blue and red, scrolls shattered
all along the eroded scars

of the collapse — which only it,
an enormous shell, has survived
to gape against the sky.

And here a wind begins to blow
from the wild beyond the valley, light,
desperate, burning the skin with sweetness . . .

It's like those smells of just-
watered fields or riverbanks
that blow over the city on the first

days of fair weather, and you
don't know what it is but, almost
mad with regret, you wonder

if it's from a fire burning over the frost
or from grapes or medlars forgotten
in some barn loft now warming

in the sun of that stupendous morning.
I cry out for joy, so much does it hurt,
deep in my lungs, to breathe the air

che come un tepore o una luce
respiro guardando la vallata

. . . .

            V

Un po' di pace basta a rivelare
dentro il cuore l'angoscia,
limpida, come il fondo del mare

in un giorno di sole. Ne riconosci,
senza provarlo, il male
lì, nel tuo letto, petto, coscie

e piedi abbandonati, quale
un crocifisso — o quale Noè
ubriaco, che sogna, ingenuamente ignaro

dell'allegria dei figli, che
su lui, i forti, i puri, si divertono . . .
il giorno è ormai su di te,

nella stanza come un leone dormente.

Per quali strade il cuore
si trova pieno, perfetto anche in questa
mescolanza di beatitudine e dolore?

Un po' di pace . . . E in te ridesta
è la guerra, è Dio. Si distendono
appena le passioni, si chiude la fresca

ferita appena, che già tu spendi
l'anima, che pareva tutta spesa,
in azioni di sogno che non rendono

niente . . . Ecco, se acceso
alla speranza — che, vecchio leone
puzzolente di vodka, dall'offesa

like warmth or light
as I gaze upon the valley

. . . .

    V

A little peace is all one needs to see
the anguish within the heart,
limpid as the bottom of the sea

on a sunny day. You recognize,
but do not feel, the evil there
in your bed, with chest, thighs

and feet exposed in air
as on a crucifix — or like the drunken
Noah dreaming, naïvely unaware

of his mirthful sons, who,
strong and pure, make light over him . . .
The day now looms over you,

like a sleeping lion in your room.

By what roads will the heart gain
fulfilment and perfection, even
in this mix of bliss and pain?

A little peace . . . And in you war,
and God, are reawakened. No sooner are
the passions quelled, a fresh wound healed,

than at once you deplete your soul
— which had seemed already depleted —
in feats of dream that don't yield

anything . . . When, for example, kindled
by hope — as Khrushchev, old lion
stinking of vodka, makes vows to the world

sua Russia giura Krusciov al mondo —
ecco che tu ti accorgi che sogni.
Sembra bruciare nel felice agosto

di pace, ogni tua passione, ogni
tuo interiore tormento,
ogni tua ingenua vergogna

di non essere — nel sentimento —
al punto in cui il mondo si rinnova.
Anzi, quel nuovo soffio di vento

ti ricaccia indietro, dove
ogni vento cade: e lì, tumore
che si ricrea, ritrovi

il vecchio crogiolo d'amore,
il senso, lo spavento, la gioia.
E proprio in quel sopore

è la luce . . . in quella incoscienza
d'infante, d'animale o ingenuo libertino
è la purezza . . . i più eroici

furori in quella fuga, il più divino
sentimento in quel basso atto umano
consumato nel sonno mattutino.

    VI

Nella vampa abbandonata
del sole mattutino — che riarde,
ormai, radendo i cantieri, sugli infissi

riscaldati — disperate
vibrazioni raschiano il silenzio
che perdutamente sa di vecchio latte,

from his offended Soviet Union—
you suddenly realize you are dreaming.
It's as if your every passion,

your every inner torment, all
your naive shame at not being
present, in your heart, at the renewal

of the world, were burning
in the happy peace of August.
In fact the new wind blowing

drives you backwards, to where
there's no wind at all; and there, like
a tumor reforming, you repair

to love's ancient cauldron,
sensation, terror, joy.
And in that same oblivion

is light . . . in that unconsciousness
of infants, beasts, or naive libertines
is purity . . . in that flight

the most heroic frenzies, the most divine
emotions—in a lowly human act
performed in the sleep of a morning.

VI

In the blaze of the morning
sun's abandon—now glancing
hot over the construction sites,

warming the fixtures—frantic
tremors scrape at the silence,
which smells hopelessly of old milk,

di piazzette vuote, d'innocenza.
Già almeno dalle sette, quel vibrare
cresce col sole. Povera presenza

d'una dozzina d'anziani operai,
con gli stracci e le canottiere arsi
dal sudore, le cui voci rare,

le cui lotte contro gli sparsi
blocchi di fango, le colate di terra,
sembrano in quel tremito disfarsi.

Ma tra gli scoppi testardi della
benna, che cieca sembra, cieca
sgretola, cieca afferra,

quasi non avesse meta,
un urlo improvviso, umano,
nasce, e a tratti si ripete,

così pazzo di dolore, che, umano,
subito non sembra più, e ridiventa
morto stridore. Poi, piano,

rinasce, nella luce violenta,
tra i palazzi accecati, nuovo, uguale,
urlo che solo chi è morente,

nell'ultimo istante, può gettare
in questo sole che crudele ancora splende
già addolcito da un po' d'aria di mare ...

A gridare è, straziata
da mesi e anni di mattutini
sudori—accompagnata

dal muto stuolo dei suoi scalpellini,
la vecchia scavatrice: ma, insieme, il fresco
sterro sconvolto, o, nel breve confine

empty squares, and innocence.
The jolts have been growing with the sun
since at least seven o'clock. Present

are a dozen scraggly aging workers,
their rags and T-shirts burning
with sweat. Their scattered voices

and their struggles with the sliding dirt
and clods of mud strewn about
seem to be undone by all the shaking.

But between the stubborn bursts
of the backhoe, as it blindly shatters,
blindly shovels, blindly scoops

as if to no purpose, a sudden,
human cry rings out,
then repeats itself at intervals,

so wild with sorrow that at once
it seems no longer human, but
only a lifeless screech. Then it slowly

starts anew, in the violent sun,
between the blinded buildings, same
as before, a cry that only someone

in the last moments before death might emit
in the cruel rays still shining down
and softened, now, by a light sea breeze . . .

What's wailing, wracked by months
and years of early morning sweat
in the company of its mute

throng of stonecutters, is
the old excavator; but it's
also the fresh-ravaged earth,

dell'orizzonte novecentesco,
tutto il quartiere . . . È la città,
sprofondata in un chiarore di festa,

—è il mondo. Piange ciò che ha
fine e ricomincia. Ciò che era
area erbosa, aperto spiazzo, e si fa

cortile, bianco come cera,
chiuso in un decoro ch'è rancore;
ciò che era quasi una vecchia fiera

di freschi intonachi sghembi al sole,
e si fa nuovo isolato, brulicante
in un ordine ch'è spento dolore.

Piange ciò che muta, anche
per farsi migliore. La luce
del futuro non cessa un solo istante

di ferirci: è qui, che brucia
in ogni nostro atto quotidiano,
angoscia anche nella fiducia

che ci dà vita, nell'impeto gobettiano
verso questi operai, che muti innalzano,
nel rione dell'altro fronte umano,

il loro rosso straccio di speranza.

1956

or the whole district in the confines
of the modern skyline . . . It's
the city, bathed in a festive light

—it's the world. What cries is all that ends
and begins again. What used to be
a stretch of grass, an open expanse,

and is now a courtyard white as snow
enclosed within walls of resentment,
what used to be a kind of sideshow

of fresh plaster façades askew in the sun
and is now a new city block, bustling
with an order made of dull misfortune.

What cries is whatever changes, even
for the better. The light of the future
never stops wounding us, not even

for an instant: it's right here, burning
in our every daily gesture,
tormenting even the confidence

that gives us life, the passion of Gobetti
for these workers as they hoist,
in this street on the other front of humanity,

their red tatter of hope.

1956

V

Da *La Religione del mio tempo* /
From *The Religion of My Time*

La Ricchezza

1.

Gli affreschi di Piero a Arezzo — Viaggio nel brusio vitale —
Il ventre campestre dell'Italia — Nostalgia della vita

Fa qualche passo, alzando il mento,
ma come se una mano gli calcasse
in basso il capo. E in quell'ingenuo
e stento gesto, resta fermo, ammesso
tra queste pareti, in questa luce,
di cui egli ha timore, quasi, indegno,
ne avesse turbato la purezza . . .
Si gira, sotto la base scalcinata,
col suo minuto cranio, le sue rase
mascelle di operaio. E sulle volte
ardenti sopra la penombra in cui stanato
si muove, lancia sospetti sguardi
di animale: poi su noi, umiliato
per il suo ardire, punta un attimo i caldi
occhi: poi di nuovo in alto . . . Il sole
lungo le volte così puro riarde
dal non visto orizzonte . . .
Fiati di fiamma dalla vetrata a ponente
tingono la parete, che quegli occhi
scrutano intimoriti, in mezzo a gente
che ne è padrona, e non piega i ginocchi,
dentro la chiesa, non china il capo: eppure
è così pio il suo ammirare, ai fiotti
del lume diurno, le figure
che un altro lume soffia nello spazio.

Riches

1.

Piero's frescoes in Arezzo — Journey into life's commotion —
The rustic womb of Italy — Nostalgic for life

He takes a few steps, raising his chin,
but as though a hand were pressing
down on his head. And in that naive,
labored pose, he holds still, granted entry
inside these walls, into a light
he fears, as if, unworthy soul,
he had troubled its purity . . .
Under the crumbling base he turns
his tiny head, his shaven
workman's jowls. And into vaults aflame
above the half-light through which he passes
as though flushed from a den, he casts
suspicious animal glances; then, ashamed
of his boldness, he briefly turns his burning eyes
on us; then looks back up again . . . Again
the sun blazes pure in the vaults
from an invisible horizon . . .
Breaths of flame from the stained glass to the west
color the wall, and those eyes
look on in fear, surrounded by people
well versed in such things; but he does not kneel
in the church, does not bow his head — and yet
so pious is his wonder, in the waves
of daylight, at the figures
another light breathes into the space.

Quelle braccia d'indemoniati, quelle scure
schiene, quel caos di verdi soldati
e cavalli violetti, e quella pura
luce che tutto vela
di toni di pulviscolo: ed è bufera,
è strage. Distingue l'umiliato sguardo
briglia da sciarpa, frangia da criniera;
il braccio azzurrino che sgozzando
si alza, da quello che marrone ripara
ripiegato, il cavallo che rincula testardo
dal cavallo che, supino, spara
calci nella torma dei dissanguati.

Ma di lì già l'occhio cala,
sperduto, altrove . . . Sperduto si ferma
sul muro in cui, sospesi,
come due mondi, scopre due corpi . . . l'uno
di fronte all'altro, in un'asiatica
penombra . . . Un giovincello bruno,
snodato nei massicci panni, e lei,
lei, l'ingenua madre, la matrona implume,
Maria. Subito la riconoscono quei
poveri occhi: ma non si rischiarano, miti
nella loro impotenza. E non è, a velarli,
il vespro che avvampa nei sopiti
colli di Arezzo . . . È una luce
— ah, certo non meno soave
di quella, ma suprema — che si spande
da un sole racchiuso dove fu divino
l'Uomo, su quell'umile ora dell'Ave.

Those limbs of the demon-possessed, those dark
backs, that chaos of green soldiers
and violet horses, the pure
light veiling everything
in shades of fine dust: it's havoc,
it's butchery. The humbled gaze distinguishes
bridle from sash, forelock from mane,
the light blue arm raised to cut a man's throat
from the brown one bent to parry the blow,
the horse stubbornly backpedaling
from the horse, upended, kicking
hard into the bleeding throng.

Yet already the eye, bewildered, looks
down, turns elsewhere . . . Bewildered it comes
to rest on a wall where it discovers,
suspended like two worlds, two bodies . . . one
in front of the other, in an Asian
penumbra . . . a dark-haired youth,
limber in his bulky clothes, and she,
she, the innocent mother, matron unfledged,
Mary. Those lowly eyes recognize her
at once. But, meek in their impotence,
they do not brighten. And it's not the sunset
blazing in the sleepy hills of Arezzo
that veils them . . . It's a light
—oh, no less sweet than this,
surely, but supreme—shed
by a cloistered sun where Man became God,
now shining on this humble hour of prayer.

Che si spande, più bassa,
sull'ora del primo sonno, della
notte, che acerba e senza stelle Costantino
circonda, sconfinando dalla terra
il cui tepore è magico silenzio.
Il vento si è calmato, e, vecchio, erra
qualche suo soffio, come senza
vita, tra macchie di noccioli inerti.
Forse, a folate, con scorata veemenza,
fiata nel padiglione aperto
il beato rantolo degli insetti,
tra qualche insonne voce, forse, e incerti
mottetti di ghitarre . . .
Ma qui, sul latteo tendaggio sollevato,
la cuspide, l'interno disadorno,
non c'è che il colore ottenebrato
del sonno: nella sua cuccetta dorme,
come una bianca gobba di collina,
l'imperatore dalla cui quieta forma
di sognante atterrisce la quiete divina.

*

Schiuma è questo sguardo che servile
lotta contro questa Quiete; e, ormai,
rassegnato, sbircia se sia giunto
il momento di uscire, se il via vai
che qui ronza attutito, lo richiami
agli atti quotidiani, ai gai
schiamazzi della sera. Schiuma gli sciami
di borghesi che dietro i calcinacci
dell'altare, con le mani
si fanno specchio, stirano le faccie
affaticate, presi dalla sete
(che li trascende, li mette sulle traccie
d'altra testimonianza) d'essere i fedeli
testimoni d'un passato che è loro.

And shining, below,
on the hour of first sleep, in the young
and starless night enfolding Constantine
and emanating from an earth
whose warmth is an enchanted silence.
The wind has abated, while a few
of its dying breaths wander as though
lifeless through thickets of motionless hazels.
Perhaps with mournful vehemence the insects'
joyous wheezing rasps in gusts inside
the open tent, amid voices unsleeping, perhaps,
and some vague ballads with guitars . . .
Yet here, over the milky, raised curtain,
the apex, the unadorned interior,
there is only the darkening color
of sleep, as in his camp bed
like a white humpbacked hill
lies the emperor, whose peaceful, dreaming form
reflects the fearsome peace of God.

*

Froth are the eyes that slavishly
fight this Peace and, by now resigned,
squint to see if it's time
yet to leave, if the bustle here
and its muffled hum will take him back
to everyday life and the cheerful
noises of evening. Froth the bands
of bourgeois behind the crumbling altar,
shielding their eyes with their hands,
stretching their tired faces,
overcome by a thirst
(which transcends them and sends them
rushing after other testimonials) to bear
faithful witness to a past that is theirs.

Schiuma—sotto i mattoni già neri
di San Francesco, sui selciati che il sole
allaga lontano di una luce
ormai perdutamente incolore—
gli stanchi rumori dei posteggi,
i caffè semivuoti . . .
Schiuma, benché più fervida, e anzi,
felice, questo fermento
di tanta vita perduta, e troppo bella
se ritrovata qui, fuggevolmente
e disperatamente, in una terra
che è solo visione . . .
Non si sente, nella piazza, dentro il cerchio
delle trecentesche case, che un sospeso
chiasso di ragazzi: se ti guardi intorno,
con visucci di figli provinciali,
pudichi calzoncini, non ne conti
meno di mille; e poiché i ferri e i pali
dei palchi per il palio
fanno della piazza quasi una gabbia,
eccolo brulicante saltellare,
con un sussurro che nella sera impazza,
quel disperato stuolo d'uccellini . . .

Ah, fuori, riapparso tempo della pia
sera provinciale, e, dentro,
riaperte ferite della nostalgia!
Sono questi i luoghi, persi nel cuore
campestre dell'Italia, dove ha peso
ancora il male, e peso il bene, mentre
schiumeggia innocente l'ardore
dei ragazzi, e i giovani sono virili
nell'anima offesa, non esaltata,
dalla umiliante prova
del sesso, dalla quotidiana
cattiveria del mondo. E se pieni
d'una onestà vecchia come l'anima,
qui gli uomini restano credenti
in qualche fede—e il povero fervore
dei loro atti li possiede tanto

Froth—under San Francesco's
bricks already black, on cobblestones
a distant sun drowns in a light
now hopelessly colorless—
the weary sounds of parking lots
and half-empty cafés . . .
Froth, though hotter, indeed
happier, the ferment
of all this life, lost and all too beautiful
when rediscovered here so fleetingly,
desperately, in a land
that is only vision . . .
In the square, inside the circle of Trecento
houses, a din of children's voices hangs
in air, the only sound: if you look around,
you'll count no less than a thousand of them,
sons of the provinces, with their little faces
and their prudish shorts; and as the rods and planks
of grandstands for the Palio
have turned the piazza into a kind of cage,
they now swarm and flit about,
their murmur running riot in the evening,
a frantic flock of little birds . . .

Ah, outside, a time of pious country
evenings returns, while inside,
old wounds of nostalgia reopen!
These are places, lost in the rural
heart of Italy, where good and evil
still mean something, as the fervor
of youngsters froths in innocence,
and the young men are virile
in souls offended, not exalted,
by the mortifying test
of sex, the ordinary
wickedness of the world. And if,
full of honesty ancient as the soul,
the men here keep believing
in some kind of faith—and the humble
fervor of their acts so grips them

da perderli in un brusio senza memoria —
più poetico e alto
è questo schiumeggiare della vita.
E più cieco il sensuale rimpianto
di non essere senso altrui, sua ebbrezza antica.

2.

Tre ossessioni: testimoniare, amare, guadagnare — Ricordi di miseria —
La ricchezza del sapere — Il privilegio del pensare

Tra orizzonti che il tramortito blu
umbro copre di assolate fiumare
e crinali arati che si perdono su
nel cielo, così tersi da incrinare
la cornea, o in valli che aprono
lucidità di baie, tu, ignara
macchina — per cui non sono che gravitante
peso nel cuoio — e tu, che la guidi,
e che in quel peso al tuo fianco
— mentre gli parli, intenditore e prodigo —
vedi fin troppa vita . . . , c'è qualcosa
che, irrelato, misto di tenerezza e odio,
di sgomento entusiasmo e di smaniosa
noia, accade invisibile a voi.

E in questo accadere una mostruosa
distruzione si compie, pur splendendo di gioia.
È l'io che brucia. E, poiché è impotente,
cieco, prigione dell'eccesso
della visione, chi il suo incendio sente
come da un'altra vita, ne avesse
solo pietà o simpatia! E non l'orrore
per l'uomo perduto nel regresso
che gli costa la sua vecchia, puerile passione!

that they lose themselves in a commotion without memory—
then higher still, and more poetic
is this froth of life.
And blinder the sensual regret
not to be what others feel, that ancient drunkenness.

2.

*Three obsessions: bearing witness, loving, earning — Memories of misery —
The wealth of knowledge — The privilege of thinking*

Between horizons that the senseless blue
of Umbria enfolds in sunlit torrents
and deep-furrowed crests that fade
far up into the sky, so sharp they cut
the cornea, or down in valleys opening
in bright pools like bays, you, unknowing
car—for whom I'm just a leaden weight
upon the leather seat—and you, behind
the wheel, who in that weight beside you see
all-too-much life and speak to it, extravagant,
as one who knows . . . , there's some unstated thing
combining tenderness and hatred, horrified
excitement and impatient ennui,
something happening you cannot see.

And in this thing a monstruous
devastation is occuring, yet radiant with joy.
It's the ego burning. Yet how blind
and powerless it is, prisoner to eyes
that see too much! If only he who feels
its blaze as though inside another life
could feel some pity or compassion for it!
And not just horror for the man in decline,
lost and bereft of his old, boyish passion!

E fosse solo, a bruciare, sotto queste
vesti sciupate, questa fronte che introna
la corsa, la smania—manifesta—
a testimoniare. La religiosa, pazza
conscienza che fa immota la festa
della vita inconsciente, della razza
bambina, i cui volti, fuggendo,
ridono caldi contro le terrazze
delle colline, sul vuoto dei torrenti
tra millenarie vigne e casolari . . .
Sì che questi chiari momenti
d'oscuro amore, abbandonati,
non si perdano, nel mondo, in cui rimane
persa nella sua purezza
la luce delle gesta quotidiane.

O fosse, insieme, a bruciare—ardente
legna di questa antica ansia
di testimoniare—la carne, che sente
in ogni voce di questi festanti
paesaggi, una voce d'amore,
che vede in ogni atto—con cui avanzi
o resti indietro un nuovo corpo, bello
di giovinezza—un atto d'amore . . .
Ed è amore—voglia disperata
dei sensi, lucido isterismo—questo
che cola oro e marrone sui declivi,
dietro i cespugli e i fossi, nel modesto
splendore del meriggio e il vivo
buio della sera.
Questo che accende
una gota, con le tinte dell'ulivo
o del garofano, che al sole radente
brilla—imberbe o appena ombrata
dalla prima peluria—gaiamente
fischiettando . . . o il ciuffo d'una testa
ben tosata, che balza alto e dolcemente sghembo
su due allegri occhi . . . o la mano posata
negligente e ironica su un grembo . . .

If only all that burned under these
threadbare clothes, inside this head benumbed
by the drive, were the urge — so keen —
to bear witness, the mad, religious
conscience that brings to a standstill the feast
of unconscious life, that race of children
whose faces laugh hot as they flee
against the terraced hillsides,
over chasms of torrents flowing
between thousand-year vineyards and farmsteads . . .
So that these shining moments of shadowy
love, once abandoned, might not
be forgotten, in a world where the light
of everyday exploits is lost
in all its purity.

Or if only what burned — fiery
wood of the ancient yearning
to bear witness — were also the flesh
that hears in each voice of these jubilant
landscapes a voice of love,
that sees in each act — by which a new
body, with the beauty of youth, moves
forward or stays behind — an act of love . . .
For it *is* love — the senses' desperate
longing, the lucid hysteria — this thing
melting gold and brown over the slopes,
behind shrubs and ditches, in the humble
afternoon splendor and the evening's
vivid dark.
This thing that enflames
a cheek in shades of olive
or carnation as it glows
in the incident sunlight — beardless or just barely
shaded with fresh down — merrily
whistling . . . or a fringe of hair on a close-cropped
head, bouncing high and sweetly aslant
over two carefree eyes . . . or a hand casually
resting, ironic, on a lap . . .

Questo che vede la morte in ogni proda
che scompare, per sempre, nel lembo
di ogni strada che tra soglie si snoda,
corre tra liete gioventù, per sempre
è perduta . . .

                    *

Ché qualcos'altro, ancora, brucia il cuore:
fuoco, anche questo, di cui io, vile,
non vorrei parlare: come di un dolore
troppo interiore e misero, per dire
l'interiore e misera grandezza
che pure ha in sé ogni nostro dolore.

Il desiderio di poter contare
sul pane, almeno, e un po' di povera lietezza.
Ma preme senza vita l'ansia che più serve
a stare in vita . . . Quanta vita mi ha tolto
l'essere stato per anni un triste
disoccupato, una smarrita vittima
di ossesse speranze. Quanta vita
l'essere corso ogni mattina tra resse
affamate, da una povera casa, perduta
nella periferia, a una povera scuola
perduta in altra periferia: fatica
che accetta solo chi è preso alla gola,
e ogni forma dell'esistenza gli è nemica.

Ah, il vecchio autobus delle sette, fermo
al capolinea di Rebibbia, tra due
baracche, un piccolo grattacielo, solo
nel sapore del gelo o dell'afa . . .
Quelle faccie dei passeggeri
quotidiani, come in libera uscita
da tristi caserme, dignitosi e seri
nella finta vivacità di borghesi
che mascherava la dura, l'antica
loro paura di poveri onesti.

This thing that sees death in every shore
that vanishes, forever, at the edge
of every road that wends between front doors,
races through the happy days of youth, forever
lost . . .

*

For still another thing burns the heart:
fire, yet again, which, coward that I am,
I'd rather not discuss—as if it were
a pain too inward and paltry to express
the inward, paltry greatness
in every pain we suffer.

Wishing one could count on bread,
at least, and a bit of modest happiness.
And yet the concern most vital to staying alive
looms lifeless . . . . So much life I've wasted
being sad and jobless for so many
years, a bewildered victim
of obsessive hopes. So much life
spent rushing every morning through
ravenous throngs from a modest home lost
on the outskirts to a modest school
lost in still other outskirts, a grind
accepted only by someone caught by the throat,
for whom every form of existence is unkind.

Ah, the old seven o'clock bus, waiting
at Rebibbia terminus between two
shacks and a small high-rise, alone
amidst the smell of frost or torrid heat . . .
And the faces of the daily passengers,
looking as if they're out on leave
from gloomy barracks, dignified
and serious, feigning middle-class
ebullience to mask the hard, ancient
fear of poor, honest people.

Era loro la mattina che bruciava,
sul verde dei campi di legumi intorno
all'Aniene, l'oro del giorno,
risvegliando l'odore dei rifiuti,
spargendo una luce pura come uno sguardo
divino, sulle file delle mozze casette,
assopite insieme nel cielo già caldo . . .
Quella corsa sfiatata tra le strette
aree da costruzione, le prodaie bruciate,
la lunga Tiburtina . . . Quelle file di operai,
disoccupati, ladri, che scendevano
ancora unti del grigio sudore
dei letti — dove dormivano da piedi
coi nipoti — in camerette sporche
di polvere come carrozzoni, biechi e gai . . .
Quella periferia tagliata in lotti
tutti uguali, assorbiti dal sole
troppo caldo, tra cave abbandonate,
rotti argini, tuguri, fabbrichette . . .

                              *

Ma in questo mondo che non possiede
nemmeno la coscienza della miseria,
allegro, duro, senza nessuna fede,
io ero ricco, possedevo!
Non solo perché una dignità borghese
era nei miei vestiti e nei miei gesti
di vivace noia, di repressa passione:
ma perché non avevo la coscienza
della mia ricchezza!

L'essere povero era solo un accidente
mio (o un sogno, forse, un'inconscia
rinuncia di chi protesta in nome di Dio . . .).
Mi appartenevano, invece, biblioteche,
gallerie, strumenti d'ogni studio: c'era
dentro la mia anima nata alle passioni,
già, intero, San Francesco, in lucenti
riproduzioni, e l'affresco di San Sepolcro,
e quello di Monterchi: tutto Piero,

The morning was theirs as it burned
over green fields of vegetables around
the Aniene, daylight's golden rays
awakening the smell of garbage,
shedding a light as pure as a god's gaze
over rows of stunted little houses
dozing together in a sky already hot . . .
The breathless rush past tight
construction sites, scorched embankments,
the long Tiburtina . . . The queues of workers,
unemployed, and thieves, who came out
still greasy with the gray sweat
of beds in which they'd slept head-to-foot
with nephews in dusty rooms grimy
as freight cars, cheerful and sullen . . .
The surburban slum cut up into so many
identical lots steeped in a sun
too hot, between abandoned quarries,
crumbling banks, shanties, small factories . . .

                              *

Yet in this world, which has nothing,
not even the awareness of poverty,
I, cheerful, hard, and lacking all faith,
was rich. I had something!
Not only because there was a bourgeois dignity
in my clothes and my gestures of lively
boredom and repressed passion,
but because I didn't know
I was rich!

Being poor was only an accident
for me (or a dream, perhaps, the unconscious
refusal of one protesting in God's name . . .)
Whereas I possessed libraries, museums,
tools of every sort of study. Born
to the passions, my soul already
housed Saint Francis, whole, in bright
reproductions, and the frescoes of San
Sepolcro and Monterchi: all of Piero

quasi simbolo dell'ideale possesso,
se oggetto dell'amore di maestri,
Longhi o Contini, privilegio
d'uno scolaro ingenuo, e, quindi,
squisito . . . Tutto, è vero,
questo capitale era già quasi speso,
questo stato esaurito: ma io ero
come il ricco che, se ha perso la casa
o i campi, ne è, dentro, abituato:
e continua a esserne padrone . . .

Giungeva l'autobus al Portonaccio,
sotto il muraglione del Verano:
bisognava scendere, correre attraverso
un piazzale brulicante di anime,
lottare per prendere il tram,
che non arrivava mai o partiva sotto gli occhi,
ricominciare a pensare sulla pensilina
piena di vecchie donne e sporchi giovanotti,
vedere le strade dei quartieri tranquilli,
Via Morgagni, Piazza Bologna, con gli alberi
gialli di luce senza vita, pezzi di mura,
vecchie villette, palazzine nuove,
il caos della città, nel bianco
sole mattutino, stanca e oscura . . .

*

Ah, raccogliersi in sé, e pensare!
Dirsi, ecco, ora penso — seduti
sul sedile, presso l'amico finestrino.
Posso pensare! Brucia gli occhi, il viso,
dalle marcite di Piazza Vittorio,
il mattino, e, misero, adesivo,
mortifica l'odore del carbone
l'avidità dei sensi: un dolore terribile
pesa nel cuore, così di nuovo vivo.

Bestia vestita da uomo — bambino
mandato in giro solo per il mondo,
col suo cappotto e le sue cento lire,

as the symbol of ideal possession,
object of love of my teachers —
Longhi, Contini — privilege
of a naive and thus exquisite
pupil. True, all this capital
had already been almost depleted,
this condition elapsed; but I was
like the rich man who, if he loses his home
or his fields, remains accustomed to them inside
and still feels as if he owns them . . .

The bus would pull up at Portonaccio,
under the Campo Verano's great wall:
it was time to get off, to run through
the piazza teeming with souls,
fight to get on the tram,
which wouldn't come or would leave before our eyes,
to start thinking again on the platform
crowded with old women and dirty young men,
look out on the streets of the quieter neighborhoods,
Via Morgagni, Piazza Bologna, with trees
yellow with a lifeless light, fragments of wall,
old houses, new villas,
the chaos of a city weary and dim
in the white morning sun . . . .

*

Oh, to withdraw into oneself and think!
To say to oneself: there, now I'm thinking — sitting
on the bench, beside the friendly window.
I can think! The morning burns the eyes,
the face, from the wet lawns of Piazza Vittorio,
while a smell of coal, nasty and sticky,
mortifies the avid senses. A terrible sorrow
weighs on the heart so newly alive.

A beast dressed like a man — a child
sent out alone into the world,
with his overcoat and his one hundred lire,

eroico e ridicolo me ne vado al lavoro,
anch'io, per vivere . . . Poeta, è vero,
ma intanto eccomi su questo treno
carico tristemente di impiegati,
come per scherzo, bianco di stanchezza,
eccomi a sudare il mio stipendio,
dignità della mia falsa giovinezza,
miseria da cui con interna umiltà
e ostentata asprezza mi difendo . . .

Ma penso! Penso nell'amico angoletto,
immerso l'intera mezzora del percorso,
da San Lorenzo alle Capannelle,
dalle Capannelle all'aeroporto,
a pensare, cercando infinite lezioni
a un solo verso, a un pezzetto di verso.
Che stupendo mattino! A nessun altro
uguale! Ora fili di magra
nebbiolina, ignara tra i muraglioni
dell'acquedotto, ricoperto
da casette piccole come canili,
e strade buttate là, abbandonate,
al solo uso di quella povera gente.
Ora sfuriate di sole, su praterie di grotte
e cave, naturale barocco, con verdi
stesi da un pitocco Corot; ora soffi d'oro
sulle piste dove con deliziose groppe marrone
corrono i cavalli, cavalcati da ragazzi
che sembrano ancor più giovani, e non sanno
che luce è nel mondo intorno a loro.

    3.

Riapparizione poetica di Roma

Dio, cos'è quella coltre silenziosa
che fiammeggia sopra l'orizzonte . . .
quel nevaio di muffa — rosa
di sangue — qui, da sotto i monti
fine alle cieche increspature del mare . . .

heroic and ridiculous, I head off to work,
me too, to live . . . A poet, it's true,
yet meanwhile here I am on a train
depressingly full of clerks,
as in some kind of joke, tired and pale;
here I am sweating for my salary,
pride of my spurious youth,
misery from which I defend myself,
humble inside and bitter outside . . .

But I do think! I think in my friendly little corner,
engrossed the whole half hour of the journey
from San Lorenzo to Le Capannelle
and Le Capannelle to the airport,
thinking, looking for infinite meanings
in just one line of poetry, in part of a line.
What a magnificent morning! Like
no other! Slender threads
of witless fog between the great walls
of an aquaduct covered
with little houses small as kennels
and roads thrown down right there and left
to the use of those humble people alone.
Outbursts of sunlight on grasslands of caves
and quarries, nature's baroque, with greens
applied by a poor man's Corot, gusts of gold
on bridle paths over which horses with beautiful
brown cruppers run, mounted by boys
who look younger still, and know not
what light is in the world around them.

3.

Rome Poetically Reappears

God, what is that silent blanket
aflame on the horizon . . . .
that expanse of snowy moss—pink
with blood—from here beneath the hills
all the way to the blindly rippling sea . . .

quella cavalcata di fiamme sepolte
nella nebbia, che fa sembrare il piano
da Vetralla al Circeo, una palude
africana, che esali in un mortale
arancio . . . È velame di sbadiglianti, sudice
foschie, attorcigliate in pallide
vene, divampanti righe,
gangli in fiamme: là dove le valli
dell'Appennino sboccano tra dighe
di cielo, sull'Agro vaporoso
e il mare: ma, quasi arche o spighe
sul mare, sul nero mare granuloso,
la Sardegna o la Catalogna,
de secoli bruciate in un grandioso
incendio, sull'acqua, che le sogna
più che specchiarle, scivolando,
sembrano giunte a rovesciare ogni
loro legname ancora ardente, ogni candido
bracere di città o capanna divorata
dal fuoco, a smorire in queste lande
di nubi sopra il Lazio.
Ma tutto ormai è fumo, e stuperesti
se dentro quel rudere d'incendio,
sentissi richiami di freschi
bambini, tra le stalle, o stupendi
colpi di campana, di fattoria
in fattoria, lungo i saliscendi
desolati, che già intravedi dalla Via
Salaria — come sospesa in cielo —
lungo quel fuoco di malinconia
perduto in un gigantesco sfacelo.
Ché ormai la sua furia, scolorando, come
dissanguata, dà più ansia al mistero,
dove, sotto quei rósi polveroni
fiammeggianti, quasi un'empirea coltre,
cova Roma gli invisibili rioni.

that cavalcade of flames, buried
in fog, making the plain
between Vetralla and the Circeo look like
an African swamp exhaling a lethal
orange light? It's a veil of yawning,
sooty mists all twisted into livid
veins, burning folds, ganglia
on fire, down where the Apennine
valleys open between sky dikes
onto the hazy Agro
and the sea. And sliding over the water
as in a dream more than a reflection,
like arches or spikes over the sea,
the black and grainy sea,
Sardinia, or Catalonia,
burnt up centuries ago in some majestic
blaze, look as if they've cast out every
last still-glowing timber, every white-hot
brazier of cities and hovels devoured
by flames, to die in this wasteland
of clouds over Latium.
But now it's all smoke, and you'd be surprised
if you heard, inside that fiery ruin,
the shouts of fresh-faced children
in stables or a tremendous
pealing of bells from farm to farm
up and down the desolate hills
already visible from the Via Salaria—
which hangs as though suspended in air—
all along that great blaze of gloom
dispersed in one gigantic disintegration,
its fury now fading as though drained
of blood, feeding the mystery's anguish,
and under jagged clouds of flaming
dust like a heavenly blanket,
Rome broods over invisible boroughs.

4.

Serata romana — Verso le Terme di Caracalla — Sesso, consolazione della
miseria — Il mio desiderio di ricchezza — Trionfo della notte

Dove vai per le strade di Roma,
sui filobus o i tram in cui la gente
ritorna? In fretta, ossesso, come
ti aspettasse il lavoro paziente
da cui a quest'ora gli altri rincasano?
È il primo dopocena, quando il vento
sa di calde miserie familiari
perse nelle mille cucine, nelle
lunghe strade illuminate,
su cui più chiare spiano le stelle.
Nel quartiere borghese, c'è la pace
di cui ognuno dentro si contenta,
anche vilmente, e di cui vorrebbe
piena ogni sera della sua esistenza.
Ah, essere diverso — in un mondo che pure
è colpa — significa non essere innocente . . .
Va, scendi, lungo le svolte oscure
del viale che porta a Trastevere:
ecco, ferma e sconvolta, come
dissepolta da un fango di altri evi
— a farsi godere da chi può strappare
un giorno ancora alla morte e al dolore —
hai ai tuoi piedi tutta Roma . . .

Scendo, attraverso Ponte Garibaldi,
seguo la spalletta con le nocche
conto l'orlo rosicchiato della pietra,
dura nel tepore che la notte
teneramente fiata, sulla volta
di caldi platani. Lastre d'una smorta
sequenza, sull'altra sponda, empiono
il cielo dilavato, plumbei, piatti,
gli attici dei caseggiati giallastri.
E io guardo, camminando per i lastrici
slabbrati, d'osso, o meglio odoro,

4.

Roman evening — To the Baths of Caracalla — Sex, consolation of the poor —
My desire for wealth — Triumph of the night

Where are you going down the streets of Rome,
on trolley-buses and trams taking people home?
—Hurried, possessed, as if
on your way to an exacting job
such as the others have just left?
It's right after supper, and the wind
smells of warm family miseries
lost in the thousands of kitchens
down the long, well-lit streets
as the stars shine brighter above.
In the affluent wards reigns a peace
with which all are happy inside,
even meanly, and they wish every night
of their lives could be full of it.
But being different—even in a world that is quite
in the wrong—means not being innocent.
Go on, go down the dark bends
of the avenue that leads to Trastevere:
there, unmoving, unsettled, as though
unearthed from the mud of past eras
—offering herself to anyone who can still
wrest a day from death and sorrow—
all of Rome lies at your feet . . .

I go down and cross the Ponte Garibaldi,
rap my knuckles along the parapet,
against the notched edge of stone
hard in the warmth the night exhales
softly over a vault of hot plane-
trees. On the far bank, pale
slabs in sequence fill the colorless
sky—the penthouses, leaden and flat,
of yellowish apartment buildings.
And, walking on a shattered
pavement of bone, I look out on,

prosaico ed ebbro—punteggiato d'astri
invecchiati e di finestre sonore—
il grande rione familiare:
la buia estate lo indora,
umida, tra le sporche zaffate
che il vento piovendo dai laziali
prati spande su rotaie e facciate.

E come odora, nel caldo così pieno
da esser esso stesso spazio,
il muraglione, qui sotto:
da ponte Sublicio fino sul Gianicolo
il fetore si mescola all'ebbrezza
della vita che non è vita.
Impuri segni che di qui sono passati
vecchi ubriachi di Ponte, antiche
prostitute, frotte di sbandata
ragazzaglia: impure traccie
umane che, umanamente infette,
son lì a dire, violente e quiete,
questi uomini, i loro bassi diletti
innocenti, le loro misere mete.

*

Vanno verso le Terme di Caracalla
giovani amici, a cavalcioni
di Rumi o Ducati, con maschile
pudore e maschile impudicizia,
nelle pieghe calde dei calzoni
nascondendo indifferenti, o scoprendo,
il segreto delle loro erezioni . . .
Con la testa ondulata, il giovanile
colore dei maglioni, essi fendono
la notte, in un carosello
sconclusionato, invadono la notte,
splendidi padroni nella notte . . .

or rather I smell—prosaic and drunk—
the great family quarter, dotted
with aging asters and noisy windows
and gilded in damp summer
darkness, between the fetid gusts
that the wind from Latian meadows
rains down upon tram rails and façades.

And what a smell—in heat so thick
it fills the space all by itself—
from the embankment below:
from the Ponte Sublicio as far as the Janiculum
the stench mingles with the thrill
of a life that is not life.
Indecent signs that old drunkards
of Ponte, ancient prostitutes,
scattered packs of young toughs,
have passed this way: indecent human
traces, humanly tainted, that are there
to tell us, with quiet violence,
of these men, their lowly, innocent
pleasures, their miserable intents.

*

To the Baths of Caracalla go
young friends straddling Rumi
or Ducati motorbikes with manly
modesty and manly immodesty,
indifferently hiding or revealing
in the warm folds of their pants
the secrets of their erections . . .
With wavy hair and youthfully
bright sweaters, they cleave
the night, invade the night
on an unending merry-go-round,
night's glorious masters . . .

Va verso le Terme di Caracalla,
eretto il busto, come sulle natìe
chine appenniniche, fra tratturi
che sanno di bestia secolare e pie
ceneri di berberi paesi — già impuro
sotto il gaglioffo basco impolverato,
e le mani in saccoccia — il pastore migrato
undicenne, e ora qui, malandrino e giulivo
nel romano riso, caldo ancora
di salvia rossa, di fico e d'ulivo . . .

Va verso le Terme di Caracalla,
il vecchio padre di famiglia, disoccupato,
che il feroce Frascati ha ridotto
a una bestia cretina, a un beato,
con nello chassì i ferrivecchi
del suo corpo scassato, a pezzi,
rantolanti: i panni, un sacco,
che contiene una schiena un po' gobba,
due coscie certo piene di croste,
i calzonacci che gli svolazzano sotto
le saccoccie della giacca pese
di lordi cartocci. La faccia
ride: sotto le ganasce, gli ossi
masticano parole, scrocchiando:
parla da solo, poi si ferma,
e arrotola il vecchio mozzicone,
carcassa dove tutta la giovinezza
resta, in fiore, come un focaraccio
dentro una còfana o un catino:
non muore chi non è mai nato.

Vanno verso le Terme di Caracalla
· ·

To the Baths of Caracalla,
straight-backed as on his native
Apennine slopes between sheep tracks
smelling of centuries of animals
and the sacred ashes of Berber villages,
already unchaste in his loutish, dusty
black beret, hands in his pockets, goes
the young shepherd who moved here at age eleven,
now impish and gay with the laughter of Rome,
still warm with red sage, figs, and olives . . .

To the Baths of Caracalla goes
the old family man out of a job
whom cruel Frascati has reduced
to a dim-witted beast, a holy fool
with the old metal of his broken-down
body in pieces that rattle around
in his chassis, his clothing a sack
holding a slightly hunched back
and two surely scab-covered thighs,
ragged trousers fluttering under
jacket pockets stuffed full
of filthy paper bags. His face
smiles: bones creak under jaw muscles
as they mutter some words;
he talks to himself, then stops
and rolls his old butt-end,
a carcass in which all of youth
remains in bloom, like an ember
in a coffer or basin:
he cannot die who was never born.

To the Baths of Caracalla go
. . . .

*

Sesso, consolazione della miseria!
La puttana è una regina, il suo trono
è un rudere, la sua terra un pezzo
di merdoso prato, il suo scettro
una borsetta di vernice rossa:
abbaia nella notte, sporca e feroce
come un'antica madre: difende
il suo possesso e la sua vita.
I magnaccia, attorno, a frotte,
gonfi e sbattuti, coi loro baffi
brindisini o slavi, sono
capi, reggenti: combinano
nel buio, i loro affari di cento lire,
ammiccando in silenzio, scambiandosi
parole d'ordine: il mondo, escluso, tace
intorno a loro, che se ne sono esclusi,
silenziose carogne di rapaci.

Ma nei rifiuti del mondo, nasce
un nuovo mondo: nascono leggi nuove
dove non c'è più legge; nasce un nuovo
onore dove onore è il disonore...
Nascono potenze e nobiltà,
feroci, nei mucchi di tuguri,
nei luoghi sconfinati dove credi
che la città finisca, e dove invece
ricomincia, nemica, ricomincia
per migliaia di volte, con ponti
e labirinti, cantieri e sterri,
dietro mareggiate di grattacieli,
che coprono interi orizzonti.

Sex, consolation of the poor!
The whore is queen, her throne
a Roman ruin, her land a patch
of shit-strewn field, her sceptre
a red patent-leather handbag.
She barks in the night, dirty and fierce
as an ancient mother, protecting
her domain and her life.
Gathered round in groups, the pimps,
swollen and haggard with Brindisian
or Slavic moustaches, are
chieftains, rulers: they swing
their hundred-lire deals in the dark,
winking in silence, exchanging
passwords: the world around them
keeps still, shut out just like them,
silent carrion of predators.

Yet from the world's refuse, a new
world is born: new laws are born
where there is no more law, new honor
born where honor is dishonor . . .
Powers and nobilities rise
from the piled-up shanties,
in the endless expanses where you think
the city ends, but where in fact it begins
all over again, inimical, begins a thousand
times over again, with bridges
and mazes, excavations and scaffolds
behind great waves of high-rises
that cover entire horizons.

Nella facilità dell'amore
il miserabile si sente uomo:
fonda la fiducia nella vita, fino
a disprezzare chi ha altra vita.
I figli si gettano all'avventura
sicuri d'essere in un mondo
che di loro, del loro sesso, ha paura.
La loro pietà è nell'essere spietati,
la loro forza nella leggerezza,
la loro speranza nel non avere speranza.

*

Vado anch'io verso le Terme di Caracalla,
pensando—col mio vecchio, col mio
stupendo privilegio di pensare . . .
(E a pensare in me sia ancora un dio
sperduto, debole, puerile:
ma la sua voce è così umana
ch'è quasi un canto.) Ah, uscire
da questa prigione di miseria!
Liberarsi dall'ansia che rende
così stupende queste notti antiche!
C'è qualcosa che accomuna chi sa l'ansia
e chi non la sa: l'uomo ha umili desideri.
Prima d'ogni altra cosa, una camicia candida!
Prima d'ogni altra cosa, delle scarpe buone,
dei panni seri! E una casa, in quartieri
abitati da gente che non dia pena,
un appartamento, al piano più assolato,
con tre, quattro stanze, e una terrazza,
abbandonata, ma con rose e limoni . . .

Solo fino all'osso, anch'io ho dei sogni
che mi tengono ancorato al mondo,
su cui passo quasi fossi solo occhio . . .
Io sogno, la mia casa, sul Gianicolo,
verso Villa Pamphili, verde fino al mare:
un attico, pieno del sole antico
e sempre crudelmente nuovo di Roma;
costruirei, sulla terrazza una vetrata,

When love is easy
the pauper feels like a man;
he grounds his faith in life,
scorning those who live differently.
The children cast themselves to the winds,
confident they live in a world
that fears them and their sex.
Their pity lies in having no pity,
their strength in frivolity,
their hope in having no hope.

*

I, too, head for the Baths of Caracalla,
thinking — with my old, magnificent
privilege of thinking . . .
(And let there still be a god in me that thinks,
lost, weak, and childish,
yet whose voice is so human
it is almost a song.) Oh, to leave
this prison of poverty!
To be free of the yearning
that makes these ancient nights so splendid!
He who knows yearning, and he who does not,
have something in common: man's desires are humble.
First of all: a clean white shirt!
First of all: some nice new shoes,
and serious clothes! And a home, in a neighborhood
inhabited by people who don't make any trouble,
an apartment on the most sunlit floor,
with three, four bedrooms, and a terrace,
neglected, but with roses and lemon trees . . .

Alone down to my bones, I too have dreams
that keep me anchored to the world,
over which I pass as if I were all eyes . . .
I dream of a house on the Janiculum,
near Villa Pamphili, green all the way to the sea:
a penthouse, bathed in the ancient
and ever cruel new sun of Rome.
On the terrace I would build a glass porch

con tende scure, di impalpabile tela:
ci metterei, in un angolo, un tavolo
fatto fare apposta, leggero, con mille
cassetti, uno per ogni manoscritto,
per non trasgredire alle fameliche
gerarchie della mia ispirazione . . .
Ah, un po' d'ordine, un po' di dolcezza,
nel mio lavoro, nella mia vita . . .
Intorno metterei sedie e poltrone,
con un tavolinetto antico, e alcuni
antichi quadri, di crudeli manieristi,
con le cornici d'oro, contro
gli astratti sostegni delle vetrate . . .
Nella camera da letto (un semplice
lettuccio, con coperte infiorate
tessute da donne calabresi o sarde)
appenderei la mia collezione
di quadri che amo ancora: accanto
al mio Zigaina, vorrei un bel Morandi,
un Mafai, del quaranta, un De Pisis,
un piccolo Rosai, un gran Guttuso . . .
. . . .

                        *

La catasta dei ruderi arancione
che la notte con il fresco colore
del tartaro infanga, dei bastioni
di leggera pomice, erborei,
monta nel cielo: e più vuote
sotto, le Terme di Caracalla al bruciore
della luna spalancano l'immoto
bruno dei prati senza erbe, dei pesti
rovi: tutto svapora e si fa fioco
tra colonnati di caravaggesca polvere,
e ventagli di magnesio,
che il cerchietto della luna campestre
scolpisce in fumate iridescenti.
Da quel grande cielo, ombre grevi,
scendono i clienti, soldati pugliesi
o lombardi, o giovincelli di Trastevere,

with dark curtains of very fine canvas;
in one corner I would put a desk,
custom-made and light, with a thousand
drawers, one for each manuscript,
so as not to breach the ravenous
hierarchies of my inspiration . . .
Oh, to give a little order, a little charm
to my work, my life . . .
Around it I would put some chairs and armchairs,
a small antique table, a few old
paintings by cruel Mannerists,
with gold frames, against
the abstract supports of the panes . . .
In the bedroom (a simple little
bed, with floral coverlets
woven by Calabrian or Sardinian women)
I would hang my painting collection,
which I still love: alongside
my Zigaina, I would like a fine Morandi,
a Mafai from '40, a De Pisis,
a small Rosai, a big Guttuso . . .

. . . .

*

A heap of orange ruins
muddied by night to the color
of fresh tartar, grass-covered
bastions of light pumice,
rises up into the sky. Below,
the Baths of Caracalla, hollow and burning
in moonlight, gape onto the unmoving
brown of grassless meadows and trampled
briars, the whole picture fading amidst
columns of Caravaggesque dust
and cones of magnesium light
which the rustic moon's little disk
sculpts into iridescent clouds of smoke.
From that big sky descend heavy shades,
the customers, soldiers from Apulia
or Lombardy, or boys from Trastevere,

isolati, a bande, e nel basso piazzale
sostano dove le donne, arse e lievi
come stracci scossi dall'aria serale,
rosseggiano, urlando — quale bambina
sordida, quale innocente vecchia, e quale
madre: e in cuore alla città che vicina
preme con raschi di tram e groppi
di luci, aizzano, nella loro Caina,
i calzoni duri di polvere che spingono,
capricciosi, agli sprezzanti galoppi
sopra rifiuti e livide rugiade.

    5.

Continuazione della serata a San Michele — Il desiderio di ricchezza del
sottoprletariato romano — Proiezione al "Nuovo" di Roma città aperta

Testimone e partecipe di questa
bassezza e miseria, ritorno
lungo la corallina spalletta,
contratto nel batticuore — supino
nella sete di sapere, nell'ansia di capire,
che non ha, nella vita, mai fine
anche se la vita, pur febbrile,
è recidiva monotonia, vizio
del ricadere e del cieco risentire . . .

E come se Roma o il mondo avesse inizio
in questa vecchia sera, in questi odori
millenari, cammino lungo il precipizio
che barbaro il Tevere apre tra dormitori
sordidi, e spagnoleschi quartieri
di terracotta, piazzali dagli splendori
ridotti a qualche barocca e cerea
voluta di chiesa sconsacrata
e ora magazzino, tra vicoli neri
che polvere, luna, vecchiezza, empietà
coprono di biancore — cartilagine
che fa sonori i selciati alla pedata.

alone or in groups, and they wait in the square
below, where the women, dry and light
as rags blown about by the evening air,
turn red in the face as they shout—one
a dirty little girl, one an old innocent,
one a mother in the heart of a city
bearing down hard with screeching trams
and clusters of lights, they stir up the dust-
stiffened trousers in their Circle of Cain,
who, on a whim, break into a jeering charge
over rubbish and the livid dew.

    5.

The evening continues at San Michele—The Roman subproletariat's
desire for wealth—Projection of Open City *at the "Nuovo"*

Witness and participant in this
baseness and misery, I return
along the coralline parapet,
tense and heart racing—abject
in the thirst to know and understand,
which in life has no end,
even when life, however frantic,
is repetitive monotony, the vice
of backsliding and blind reliving . . .

As if Rome or the world had begun
with this old evening, these ancient
smells, I walk along the precipice
the barbarous Tiber cleaves through squalid
dormitories and Spanishlike quarters
of brick, large squares with splendors
reduced to a few faded, Baroque
scrolls on some deconsecrated church
now a warehouse, between black little streets
that dust, moonlight, old age, and godlessness
cover with white—a cartilage that makes
the cobblestones crackle underfoot.

Imbocco San Michele, tra muraglie
basse, quasi di casematte, piazze
granulose su cui la luna abbaglia
come su decrepita ghiaia, terrazze
dove occhieggia un garofano
o una testa d'aruta, che ragazze
in vestaglia annacquano: e l'aria muta
porta le loro voci di prigioniere
tra mura di tufo con porte come buche
e bifore sbilenche. Ma risuonano fiere
le grida dei maschi ancora teneri che
rincasano dai primi spettacoli, canottiere
e magliette svolazzanti sopra le
vite strette e discinte . . . Nella piazzetta
sotto casa, sostano, intorno al caffè
già vuoto, o più in là tra le carrette
o i camion ruggini in file inanimate
dove più arde la luna, e i vicoletti,
sboccando, sono più bui — o illuminati
appena per svelare, di sbieco,
in una pietra leggera e disossata
come spugna, qualche gonfia parete
incrostata di rosoni e bugnati;
e, su questo messicano rione, rispecchia
il cielo il suo incanto ignorato,
con vapori freschi come buccia di mela,
sulle casupole del proletariato
che festeggia, rissoso e umile, la sera.

*

Li osservo, questi uomini, educati
ad altra vita che la mia: frutti
d'una storia tanto diversa, e ritrovati,
quasi fratelli, qui, nell'ultima forma
storica di Roma. Li osservo: in tutti
c'è come l'aria d'un buttero che dorma
armato di coltello: nei loro succhi
vitali, è disteso un tenebrore intenso,
la papale itterizia del Belli,
non porpora, ma spento peperino,

I turn onto San Michele, pass between low
walls like casemates, past grainy
piazzas with the moon glaring above
as though over weather-worn gravel,
balconies with carnations and clumps
of rue poking out, watered by girls in
dressing gowns. The mute air conveys
these prisoners' voices between walls
of tufa with doors like holes and warped
mullion windows, while the shouts
of still tender-aged males, coming home
from the early picture show, tank tops
and T-shirts fluttering over their slim and
unbuckled waists, proudly ring out . . .
They stop in the little piazza near home,
around the already empty café or farther away
among carts and rusty trucks in lifeless
rows where the moon burns brightest
and the narrow streets beckon darkest —
or lit just enough to reveal,
obliquely, a few swollen stone walls,
light and fleshy as sponge,
and studded with rosettes and bosses.
Over this Mexican district the sky
mirrors its unseen enchantments,
fresh emanations of apple peel
over hovels of proletarians celebrating,
raucous and humble, the evening.

*

I watch them, these men brought up
to another life than my own, fruit
of a history so different, rediscovered
like brothers, here, in Rome's
latest historical form. I watch them:
they all have something of the herdsman
who sleeps with his dagger: their
vital fluids steeped in deep gloom,
Belli's papal jaundice,
not purple but spent peperino,

bilioso cotto. La biancheria, sotto,
fine e sporca; nell'occhio, l'ironia
che trapela il suo umido, rosso,
indecente bruciore. La sera li espone
quasi in romitori, in riserve
fatte di vicoli, muretti, androni
e finestrelle perse nel silenzio.
È certo la prima delle loro passioni
il desiderio di ricchezza: sordido
come le loro membra non lavate,
nascosto, e insieme scoperto,
privo di ogni pudore: come senza pudore
è il rapace che svolazza pregustando
chiotto il boccone, o il lupo, o il ragno;
essi bramano i soldi come zingari,
mercenari, puttane: si lagnano
se non ce n'hanno, usano lusinghe
abbiette per ottenerli, si gloriano
plautinamente se ne hanno le saccocce piene.
Se lavorano — lavoro di mafiosi macellari,
ferini lucidatori, invertiti commessi,
tranvieri incarogniti, tisici ambulanti,
manovali buoni come cani — avviene
che abbiano ugualmente un'aria di ladri:
troppa avita furberia in quelle vene . . .

Sono usciti dal ventre delle loro madri
a ritrovarsi in marciapiedi o in prati
preistorici, e iscritti in un'anagrafe
che da ogni storia li vuole ignorati . . .
Il loro desiderio di ricchezza
è, così, banditesco, aristocratico.
Simile al mio. Ognuno pensa a sé,
a vincere l'angosciosa scommessa,
a dirsi: "È fatta," con un ghigno di re . . .
La nostra speranza è ugualmente ossessa:
estetizzante, in me, in essi anarchica.
Al raffinato e al sottoproletario spetta
la stressa ordinazione gerarchica
dei sentimenti: entrambi fuori dalla storia,

bilious brick. Underclothes fine
but dirty; in the eyes, an irony
that shines through the wet, red,
indecent burning. The evening reveals
them as if in hermitages, refuges
made up of alleys, low walls, doorways
and dormers lost in silence.
Surely their primary passion
is the desire for wealth: as filthy
as their unwashed bodies
at once hidden and visible,
devoid of all modesty; as immodest
as the raptor that hovers above, quietly
foretasting his meal, or the wolf or the spider.
They lust after money like gypsies,
mercenaries, or whores, complain
when they don't have it, stoop
to base flattery to get it, gloat like Plautian
actors when their pockets are full.
Even when they work — as bullying butchers,
savage shoeshiners, queer salesmen,
devious ticketmen, consumptive
peddlers, laborers good as dogs —
they still look like thieves.
Too much congenital cunning in those veins . . . .

Straight from their mothers' womb
they found themselves on the street or in
prehistoric meadows, registered in offices
that would have them shunned by all history . . .
Their desire for wealth
is thus banditlike, aristocratic.
Like my own. Everyone thinks of himself,
of winning the anguishing wager,
of saying: "It's done," with a kingly sneer . . .
Our hopes are equally obsessive:
mine aesthetic, theirs anarchic.
The aesthete and the subproletarian
are subject to the same hierarchy
of sentiment. Both stand outside history,

in un mondo che non ha altri varchi
che verso il sesso e il cuore,
altra profondità che nei sensi.
In cui la gioia è gioia, il dolore dolore.

*

Ma che colpo al cuore, quando, su un liso
cartellone . . . Mi avvicino, guardo il colore
già d'un altro tempo, che ha il caldo viso
ovale, dell'eroina, lo squallore
eroico del povero, opaco manifesto.
Subito entro: scosso da un interno clamore,
deciso a tremare nel ricordo,
a consumare la gloria del mio gesto.
Entro nell'arena, all'ultimo spettacolo,
senza vita, con grige persone,
parenti, amici, sparsi sulle panche,
persi nell'ombra in cerchi distinti
e biancastri, nel fresco ricettacolo . . .
Subito, alle prime inquadrature,
mi travolge e rapisce . . . l'intermittence
du cœur. Mi trovo nelle scure
vie della memoria, nelle stanze
misteriose dove l'uomo fisicamente è altro,
e il passato lo bagna col suo pianto . . .
Eppure, dal lungo uso fatto esperto,
non perdo i fili: ecco . . . la Casilina,
su cui tristemente si aprono
le porte della città di Rossellini . . .
ecco l'epico paesaggio neorealista,
coi fili del telegrafo, i selciati, i pini,
i muretti scrostati, la mistica
folla perduta nel daffare quotidiano,
le tetre forme della dominazione nazista . . .
Quasi emblema, ormai, l'urlo della Magnani,
sotto le ciocche disordinatamente assolute,
risuona nelle disperate panoramiche,
e nelle sue occhiate vive e mute
si addensa il senso della tragedia.
È lì che si dissolve e si mutila il presente,
e assorda il canto degli aedi.

in a world with no outlets
but sex and the heart,
no depth but in the senses.
Where joy is joy, and sorrow sorrow.

*

What a flutter in my heart when, on
a faded poster . . . I draw near, study the color
— already from another era — of the heroine's
warm oval face, the heroic squalor
of that shabby, opaque placard.
I go inside at once, stirred by an inner clamor,
determined to tremble in remembrance,
to consummate the glory of my act.
I enter the theater for the last show,
lifeless among a crowd of gray people,
relatives and friends scattered about in the seats
and lost in the shadow in distinct, whitish
circles in the cool of the pit . . .
At once, upon seeing the first frames,
I am overwhelmed, swept away by . . .
l'intermittence du coeur. I find myself
on the dark roads of memory, in mysterious
rooms where man is physically other,
and the past bathes him in its tears . . .
And yet, by now an expert of long acquaintance,
I don't lose the thread: here is . . . the Casilina,
onto which the gates of Rossellini's
city sadly open . . . here's the epic
neorealist landscape, the telegraph
wires, cobblestones, and pine trees,
the crumbling walls, the mystical
crowd lost in its everyday chores,
the dark forms of the Nazi occupation . . .
Practically a symbol by now, Magnani's cry,
under her disheveled, absolute shock of hair,
rings out in the desperate pan shots,
while the meaning of tragedy
crystallizes in her vivid, silent stare.
And here the present dissolves, cut off,
and the song of the aedoi becomes deafening.

6.

Un'educazione sentimentale — La Resistenza e sua luce — Lacrime

Chi fui? Che senso ebbe la mia presenza
in un tempo che questo film rievoca
ormai così tristemente fuori tempo?
Non posso farlo ora, ma devo
prima o poi sviscerarlo fino in fondo,
fino a un definitivo sollievo . . .
Lo so: ero appena partorito a un mondo
dove la dedizione d'un adolescente
— buono come sua madre, improvvido
e animoso, mostruosamente
timido, e ignaro d'ogni altra omertà
che non fosse ideale — era avvilente
segno di scandalo, santità
ridicola. Ed era destinata
a farsi vizio: ché marcisce l'età
la mitezza, e fa dell'accorato
dono di sé, ossessione. E se ho trovato
di nuovo un'accorata purezza
dell'amare il mondo, il mio
non è che amore, nudo amore, senza
futuro. Troppo perduto nel brusio
del mondo, troppo cosparso dell'amaro
di un pur triste, chapliniano riso . . .
È resa. Umile ebbrezza del contemplare,
partecipe, sviscerato — e inattivo.
Umile riscoperta d'un allegro restare
degli altri uomini al male: il reale,
vissuto da loro in un empireo di luoghi
miseri, ridenti, sulle rive
di gai torrenti, sui gioghi
di monti luminosi, sulle terre oppresse
dall'antica fame . . .
È senso della grandezza, questo senso
che mi strugge sui minimi atti
di ogni nostro giorno: riconoscenza
per questo loro riapparire intatti

6.

A sentimental education — *The Resistance and its light* — *Tears*

Who was I? What did it mean that I was present
at the time evoked in this film
and now so sadly outside of time?
Though I can't do so right now, sooner
or later I must get to the bottom of this,
until I find definitive relief . . .
I know: I had just come into a world
where the devotion of an adolescent
— one with his mother's goodness, heedless
and spirited, monstrously shy,
and ignorant of all complicity
that wasn't idealistic — was humiliating
cause for scandal, a ridiculous
sanctity. It was destined
to turn into vice: for age corrodes
meekness, and makes an obsession
of mournful self-giving. And if
I've rediscovered a mournful purity
in loving the world, mine
is only love, naked love, with no
future — too lost in the world's
commotion, too peppered with a bitter
laughter, however sad and Chaplinesque . . .
It's a surrender. The humble thrill of beholding,
as heartfelt — and inactive — participant.
The humble rediscovery of other men's
blithe acceptance of wrong: reality,
which they live out in a paradise of humble,
splendid places, on the banks
of joyful torrents, at the tops
of luminous mountains, in lands oppressed
by ancient hunger . . .
It's a sense of greatness, this feeling
that consumes me in the smallest acts
of each day of our lives — gratitude
to them for having reappeared whole

a me sopravvissuto, e pieno ancora
di stantio pianto . . .

*

Non è Amore. Ma in che misura è mia
colpa il non fare dei miei affetti
Amore? Molta colpa, sia
pure, se potrei d'una pazza purezza,
d'una cieca pietà vivere giorno
per giorno . . . Dare scandalo di mitezza.
Ma la violenza in cui mi frastorno,
dei sensi, dell'intelletto, da anni,
era la sola strada. Intorno
a me alle origini c'era, degli inganni
istituiti, delle dovute illusioni,
solo la Lingua: che i primi affanni
di un bambino, le preumane passioni,
già impure, non esprimeva. E poi
quando adolescente nella nazione
conobbi altro che non fosse la gioia
del vivere infantile — in una patria
provinciale, ma per me assoluta, eroica —
fu l'anarchia. Nella nuova e già grama
borghesia d'una provincia senza purezza,
il primo apparire dell'Europa
fu per me apprendistato all'uso più
puro dell'espressione, che la scarsezza
della fede d'una classe morente
risarcisse con la follia ed i tópoi
dell'eleganza: fosse l'indecente
chiarezza d'una lingua che evidenzia
la volontà a non essere, incosciente,
e la cosciente volontà a sussistere
nel privilegio e nella libertà
che per Grazia appartengono allo stile.

*

to me, a survivor still full
of old tears . . .

*

It's not Love. But what fault is it of mine
if my affections do not become
Love? Very much my fault, I would say,
when I can live from day to day
on mad purity, blind pity . . .
Make a scandal of meekness.
But the violence of the senses and intellect
that has confounded me for years
was the only way. In the beginning,
all around me was only the Language:
that of established deception, the required
illusions, which could not express
a small boy's first yearnings, his already
tainted, prehuman passions. And when
in adolescence I learned something
about my country other than the joy
of childhood living—in a provincial
homeland that for me was absolute, heroic—
it was anarchy. In the new and already grim
bourgeoisie of a province devoid of purity,
Europe first appeared to me
as an apprenticeship in a purer
manner of expression, one that might offset
the scant faith of a moribund class
with madness and the topoi
of elegance: so that an indecent
clarity of language might highlight
the will, unconscious, to nonbeing,
and the conscious will to carry on
in the privilege and freedom
that by Grace belong to style.

*

Così giunsi ai giorni della Resistenza
senza saperne nulla se non lo stile:
fu stile tutta luce, memorabile coscienza
di sole. Non poté mai sfiorire,
neanche per un istante, neanche quando
l'Europa tremò nella più morta vigilia.
Fuggimmo con le masserizie su un carro
da Casarsa a un villaggio perduto
tra rogge e viti: ed era pura luce.
Mio fratello partì, in un mattino muto
di marzo, su un treno, clandestino,
la pistola in un libro: ed era pura luce.
Visse a lungo sui monti, che albeggiavano
quasi paradisiaci nel tetro azzurrino
del piano friulano: ed era pura luce.
Nella soffitta del casolare mia madre
guardava sempre perdutamente quei monti
già conscia del destino: ed era pura luce.
Coi pochi contadini intorno
vivevo una gloriosa vita di perseguitato
dagli atroci editti: ed era pura luce.
Venne il giorno della morte
e della libertà, il mondo martoriato
si riconobbe nuovo nella luce . . .

Quella luce era speranza di giustizia:
non sapevo quale: la Giustizia.
La luce è sempre uguale ad altra luce.
Poi variò: da luce diventò incerta alba,
un'alba che cresceva, si allargava
sopra i campi friulani, sulle rogge.
Illuminava i braccianti che lottavano.
Così l'alba nascente fu una luce
fuori dall'eternità dello stile . . .
Nella storia la giustizia fu coscienza
d'una umana divisione di ricchezza,
e la speranza ebbe nuova luce.

*

Thus I came to the days of the Resistance
knowing nothing about it except its style.
A style that was all light, unforgettable
awareness of the sun. It could never fade,
not for an instant, not even when
Europe trembled in the deadest of wakes.
With our furniture on a cart, we fled
Casarsa for a remote village lost between
canals and vineyards. And it was pure light.
One quiet morning in March,
my brother left, on a train, in secret,
his pistol inside a book. And it was pure light.
He lived a long time in the mountains, which
gleamed white in the pale blue gloom
of the Friulian plain. And it was pure light.
From the attic of our country cottage, my mother
never stopped desperately eyeing those mountains,
already privy to destiny. And it was pure light.
With the few peasants around us,
I lived a glorious life as the victim
of terrible edicts. And it was pure light.
Then the day of death and freedom
came, and the tortured world
saw itself reborn in light . . .

That light was the hope of justice,
I didn't know what kind: Justice.
Light is always the same as all other light.
Then it changed: the light became uncertain dawn,
a dawn that grew and spread
over the fields and canals of Friuli.
It lit up the laborers in their struggle.
Thus the newborn dawn was a light
outside the eternity of style . . .
Justice in history was awareness
of a human division of wealth,
and hope had new light.

*

Ecco quei tempi ricreati dalla forza
brutale delle immagini assolate:
quella luce di tragedia vitale.
Le pareti del processo, il prato
della fucilazione: e il fantasma
lontano, in cerchio, della periferia
di Roma biancheggiante in una nuda luce.
Gli spari; la nostra morte, la nostra
sopravvivenza: sopravvissuti vanno
i ragazzi nel cerchio dei palazzi lontani
nell'acre colore del mattino. E io,
nella platea di oggi, ho come un serpe
nei visceri, che si torce: e mille lacrime
spuntano in ogni punto del mio corpo,
dagli occhi ai polpastrelli delle dita,
dalla radice dei capelli al petto:
un pianto smisurato, perché sgorga
prima d'essere capito, precedente
quasi al dolore. Non so perché trafitto
da tante lacrime sogguardo
quel gruppo di ragazzi allontanarsi
nell'acre luce di una Roma ignota,
la Roma appena affiorata dalla morte,
superstite con tutta la stupenda
gioia di biancheggiare nella luce:
piena del suo immediato destino
d'un dopoguerra epico, degli anni
brevi e degni d'un'intera esistenza.
Li vedo allontanarsi: ed è ben chiaro
che, adolescenti, prendono la strada
della speranza, in mezzo alle macerie
assorbite da un biancore ch'è vita
quasi sessuale, sacra nelle sue miserie.
E il loro allontanarsi nella luce
mi fa ora raggricciare di pianto:
perché? Perché non c'era luce
nel loro futuro. Perché c'era questo
stanco ricadere, questa oscurità.
Sono adulti, ora: hanno vissuto
quel loro sgomentante dopoguerra

Behold those times re-created by
the brutal power of sunlit images,
the light of life's tragedy.
The walls of the trial, the field
of the firing squad; and the distant
ghost of Rome's suburbs in a ring,
gleaming white in naked light.
Gunshots: our death, our survival.
Survivors, the boys enter a ring
of distant buildings in the harsh
color of morning. While I, in the pit
of today, have a kind of snake in my guts,
twisting about, and a thousand tears
dripping from every point in my body
from my eyes to my fingertips,
from the roots of my hair to my chest.
My weeping knows no bounds: it wells up
before I can understand it, almost
preceding the sorrow. I don't know why
I'm wracked by all these tears as I glimpse
that group of boys walking away
in the harsh light of an unknown Rome,
a Rome just resurfacing from death,
surviving with all the magnificent joy
of gleaming white in the light,
full of its immediate destiny
as postwar epic, of brief years
worth a whole lifetime.
I see them walking away, and it's quite
clear that, as adolescents, they're on the road
of hope, in the midst of ruins
engulfed in a whiteness that is life,
almost sexual life, sacred in its misery.
And as they walk away in the light
I shudder, on the verge of tears: Why?
Because there is no light
in their future. Because there's only
weary backsliding, only darkness.
They're grown up now. They've lived
their dreadful postwar years

di corruzione assorbita dalla luce,
e sono intorno a me, poveri uomini
a cui ogni martirio è stato inutile,
servi del tempo, in questi giorni
in cui si desta il doloroso stupore
di sapere che tutta quella luce,
per cui vivemmo, fu soltanto un sogno
ingiustificato, inoggettivo, fonte
ora di solitarie, vergognose lacrime.

Da *La Religione del mio tempo*

. . . Due giornate di febbre! Tanto

da non poter più sopportare l'esterno,
se appena un po' rinnovato dalle nubi
calde, di ottobre, e così moderno

ormai—che mi pare di non poterlo più
capire—in quei due che salgono la strada,
là in fondo, all'alba della gioventù . . .

Disadorni, ignorati: eppure fradici
sono i loro capelli d'una beata crosta
di brillantina—rubata nell'armadio

dei fratelli maggiori; oppure losca
di millenari soli cittadini
la tela dei calzoni al sole d'Ostia

e al vento scoloriti; eppure fini
i lavori incalliti del pettine
sul ciuffo a strisce bionde e sulla scrima.

Dall'angolo d'un palazzo, eretti,
appaiano, ma stanchi per la salita,
e scompaiono, per ultimi i garretti,

of corruption engulfed in light
and now they surround me, poor men
for whom every agony proved useless,
servants of time, at a moment
when we awake to the painful surprise
of learning that all that light
for which we lived was only a dream,
unjustified, unobjective, wellspring
now of lonely tears of shame.

From *The Religion of My Time*

. . . Two days of fever! Enough to make me

unable to stand the world outside
despite its faint revival by some
warm October clouds. And it's lately

so modern, I feel I no longer understand it:
like those two over there, in the first light
of youth, coming up the street . . .

Plain, neglected: yet their hair is bright
with a joyous crust of brilliantine —
stolen from their older brothers, right

out of the armoire — their canvas slacks
are seedy from age-old city suns,
bleached by the wind and sunlight

of Ostia; and the callused diligence
with which they comb the blond-streaked forelock
and the parting shows great refinements.

They appear around the corner of the block,
upright but tired from the climb,
disappear around the corner of another block,

all'angolo di un'altro palazzo. La vita
è come se non fosse mai stata.
Il sole, il colore del cielo, la nemica

dolcezza, che l'aria rabbuiata
da redivive nubi, ridà alle cose,
tutto accade come a una passata

ora del mio esistere: misteriose
mattine di Bologna o di Casarsa,
doloranti e perfette come rose,

riaccadono qui nella luce apparsa
a due avviliti occhi di ragazzo,
che altro non conosce se non l'arte

di perdersi, chiaro nel suo buio arazzo.
E non ho mai peccato: sono
puro come un vecchio santo, ma

neppure ho avuto; il dono
disperato del sesso, è andato
tutto in fumo: sono buono

come un pazzo. Il passato
è quello che ebbi per destino,
niente altro che vuoto sconsolato . . .

e consolante. Osservo, chino
sul davanzale, quei due nel sole
andare, lievi; e sto come un bambino

che non geme per ciò che non ha avuto solo,
ma anche per ciò che non avrà . . .
E in quel pianto il mondo è odore,

nient'altro: viole, prati, che sa
mia madre, e in quali primavere . . .
Odore che trema per diventare, qua

ankles vanishing behind them.
And it's as though I'd never been alive.
The sun, the color of the sky, the grim

sweetness the air again overcast
with clouds gives back to things—
all this unfolds as if in some past

moment of my existence: mysterious
mornings in Bologna or Casarsa,
painful and perfect as roses,

unfold again here, in the light
before the disheartened eyes of a boy
who knows nothing more than the art

of losing his way, bright in his darkness.
And I have never sinned: I am pure
as an old saint, though this

has got me nothing; the hopeless
gift of sex has all gone up
in smoke: mine is the goodness

of a madman. My past is what
I was given by destiny,
nothing but a disconsolate

—and consoling—emptiness . . . Leaning
on my window sill, I watch those two
walk lightly on, and I'm like a child groaning

not only for what he can't have,
but also for what he shall never have . . .
And in that lament the world is nothing more

than a scent—of violets and meadows
my mother knows well, in such springtimes . . .
A scent that will quiver and metamorphose,

dove il pianto è dolce, materia
d'espressione, tono . . . la ben nota
voce della lingua folle e vera

ch'ebbi nascendo e nella vita è immota.

*

L'ossessione è perduta, è divenuta
odorante fantasma che si stende
in giorni di luce grande e muta,

quando così debole si accende
l'azzurro che bianco è quasi,
ai rumori dispersi si rapprende

l'assurdo silenzio di stasi
naturali, e agli odori dei pranzi,
dei lavori, si mischiano randagi

soffi di bosco, sepolti nei canti
più ombrosi o più assolati
delle prime colline — stanchi

moti quasi di altre età, ora beati
in questa, che vuole nuovo amore.
Da bambino sognavo a questi fiati,

già freschi e intiepiditi dal sole,
frammenti di foreste, celtiche
quercie, tra sterpaglia e rovi di more

sfrondati, nel rossore, quasi svèlti
dall'autunno assolato — e seni
di fiumi nordici ciecamente deserti

dove pungeva l'odore dei licheni,
fresco e nudo, come di Pasqua le viole . . .
Allora la carne era senza freni.

where sorrow is sweetest, into the stuff
of expression and tone . . . the well-
familiar voice of the mad, true tongue

I was given at birth, which in life never changes

*

The obsession is gone, has now become
a fragrant ghost that spreads across
the days of great and voiceless light

when the blue so faintly ignites
that it's almost white, and scattered noises
crystallize into the senseless

silence of natural pauses,
and odors of lunches and labors
blend with stray woodland breezes

emerging from burial in shady
recesses or the sunniest spots
in the first gentle hills—lazy

stirrings as of other ages, now blessed
in our own, which demands a new love.
As a child I would dream of these breaths

already fresh and warmed from above
by the sun, fragments of forests, Celtic
oaks amid brushwood and blackberry

brambles red and bare as though stripped
by the bright autumn sun, and inlets
of blindly deserted Northern rivers

with the pungent smell of lichens,
cool and naked, like violets at Easter . . .
The flesh knew no restraint then.

E la dolcezza ch'era nel colore
del giorno, si faceva dolcezza
un poco anche in quel dolore.

La gioventù bendata, rozza, retta
delle famiglie barbare che andavano
emigrando, per la sommessa

selva o l'allagata plaga
consolavano la solitudine
del mio lettuccio, della mia strada.

La storia, la Chiesa, la vicissitudine
d'una famiglia, così, non sono
che un po' di sole profumato e nudo,

che riscalda una vigna in abbandono,
qualche filo di fieno tra i boschetti
corrosi, qualche casa tramortita al suono

delle campane . . . I giovinetti
antichi, essi soltanto vivi, se pieni
della primavera ebbero i petti

nelle età più belle, erano insieme
sogni del sesso e immagini bevute
dalla vecchia carta del poema

che di volume in volume, in mute
febbri di novità suprema,
—erano Shakespeare, Tommaseo, Carducci . . . —

faceva d'ogni mia fibra un solo tremito.

*

Avrei voluto urlare, e ero muto;
la mia religione era un profumo.
Ed eccolo ora qui, uguale e sconosciuto,

And the sweetness in the color
of the day became a little
sweetness even in that sorrow.

The tattered youth, crude and honest,
of barbarous families forever
migrating through placid forest

and flooded plain, brought consolation
to my lonely little bed,
the lonely road I traveled on.

History, the Church, the tribulations
of a family were thus no more
than a bit of fragrant, naked sun

warming an abandoned vineyard
or a few shoots of hay between withered
thickets, or some houses benumbed

by the ringing of bells . . . The boys
of past ages, coming only alive
when the spring filled their breasts

at the best time of life, were at once
a dream of sex, and images drunk
from old pages of poetry

that in book after book, in silent
fevers of absolute novelty
— Shakespeare, Tommaseo, Carducci . . . —

made every fiber in me tremble as one . . .

*

I wished I could shout, but I had no voice:
my religion was but a fragrance.
And here it is again, that fragrance,

quel profumo, nel mondo, umido
e raggiante: e io qui, perso nell'atto
sempre riuscito e inutile, umile

e squisito, di scioglierne l'intatto
senso nelle sue mille immagini . . .
Mi ritrovo tenero come un ragazzo

all'entusiasmo misterioso, selvaggio,
come fu in passato, e stente
lacrime mi bagnano la pagina

alla vista, nel solicello ardente,
di quei due, che — loro sì ragazzi —
si perdono svelti, beatamente,

nella ricca periferia, sotto terrazzi
pieni di sereno cielo di mare,
mattutini balconi, attici

dorati da un sole già serale . . .
Il senso della vita mi ritorna
com'era sempre allora, un male

più cieco se stupendamente colmo
di dolcezza. Perché, a un ragazzo, pare
che mai avrà ciò che egli solo

non ha mai avuto, E in quel mare
di disperazione, il suo furioso sogno
di corpi, crede di dover pagare

con l'essere follemente buono . . .

Così, se bastano due giorni
di febbre, perché la vita sembri
perduta e intero torni

in this world, unchanged and unknown, moist
and radiant—with me here lost
in the always successful, useless act,

precious and meek, of gleaning intact
the meaning from its countless images . . .
I find myself young again, a boy

with the same mild, mysterious
enthusiasm I had in the past,
as bitter tears dampen the page

at the sight of those two—who really
are boys—in the wan, burning sun,
before they quickly, blissfully

vanish into the rich outer city
under terraces full of the sea's
cloudless sky, early morning balconies,

penthouses already gold with evening light . . .
The meaning of life comes back to me
as it always was then, a blight

always blinder when splendidly brimming
with sweetness. For to a boy it can seem
that he shall never have what he alone

has never had. And in that sea
of despair he may believe he needs
to atone for his wild dreams of bodies

by being insanely good . . .

So, if two days of fever are all
it takes to make life seem
lost and to bring the world back

il mondo (e niente m'inebbri
altro che rimpianto) al mondo io,
nel grande e muto sole di settembre,

morendo, non saprei che dire addio . . .

Eppure, Chiesa, ero venuto a te.
Pascal e i Canti del Popolo Greco
tenevo stretti in mano, ardente, come se

il mistero contadino, quieto
e sodo nell'estate del quarantatre,
tra il borgo, le viti e il greto

del Tagliamento, fosse al centro
della terra e del cielo;
e lì, gola, cuore e ventre

squarciati sul lontano sentiero
delle Fonde, consumavo le ore
del più bel tempo umano, l'intero

mio giorno di gioventù, in amori
la cui dolcezza ancora mi fa piangere . . .
Tra i libri sparsi, pochi fiori

azzurrini, e l'erba, l'erba candida
tra le saggine, io davo a Cristo
tutta la mia ingenuità e il mio sangue.

Cantavano gli uccelli nel pulviscolo
in una trama complicata, incerta,
assordante, prede dell'esistere,

povere passioni perse tra i vertici
umili dei gelseti e dei sambuchi
e io, come loro, nei luoghi deserti

whole (with regret as my only thrill),
then all I can say to the world
as I die in the great, silent sun

of September, is goodbye . . .

And yet, Church, I came to you,
clutching Pascal and the *Songs of the Greeks*
in my passionate hands, as though

the mystery of peasant life, hushed
and deaf in the summer of '43
between the village, the vineyards

and the Tagliamento's banks, were
the center of the earth and heavens;
and there, with throat, heart and stomach

straining down the distant trail
to the Fonde, I frittered away
the hours of life's greatest years,

the entire day of my youth, in loves
whose sweetness still moves me to tears . . .
Between a few scattered books, some pale blue

flowers and the immaculate
grass amid the sorghum, I gave
all my innocence and blood to Christ.

The birds sang in the dust
in an elaborate weave, ambiguous,
deafening, prey to existence,

poor passions lost between the modest
summits of groves of mulberry and elder;
and I, like them, in secluded places

destinati ai candidi, ai perduti,
aspettavo che scendesse la sera,
che si sentissero intorno i muti

odori del fuoco, della lieta miseria,
che l'Angelus suonasse, velato
del nuovo, contadino mistero

nell'antico mistero consumato.

Fu una breve passione. Erano servi
quei padri e quei figli che le sere
di Casarsa vivevano, così acerbi

per me, di religione: le severe
loro allegrezze erano il grigiore
di chi, pur poco, ma possiede;

la chiesa del mio adolescente amore
era morta nei secoli, e vivente
solo nel vecchio, doloroso odore

dei campi. Spazzò la Resistenza
con nuovi sogni il sogno delle Regioni
Federate in Cristo, e il dolceardente

suo usignolo . . . Nessuna delle passioni
vere dell'uomo si rivelò
nelle parole e nelle azioni

della Chiesa. Anzi, guai a chi non può
non essere ad essa nuovo! Non dare
ad essa ingenuo tutto ciò

che in lui ondeggia come un mare
di troppo trepidante amore.
Guai a chi con gioia vitale

reserved for the lost and pure,
would wait for evening to fall,
for the silent smells of fire

and joyous misery to fill the air,
for the Angelus bell to toll, veiled
in the new peasant mystery

fulfilled in the ancient mystery.

It was a brief passion. They were servants,
those fathers and sons enjoying the evenings
in Casarsa, and to me they seemed

so green with religion: their somber
joys had the gloom of people
who owned something, however little.

The church I loved in adolescence
had died over the centuries, living
only in the old and sorrowful scents

of the fields. The Resistance came, and new
dreams swept away the dream of the Regions
Federated in Christ and their sweet

fervent nightingale . . . None of man's true
passions were revealed
in the words and actions

of the Church. On the contrary, woe
unto him who can only be
new to her! And offer her everything

swelling inside him like a sea
of too much trembling love!
Woe unto him who with vital glee

vuole servire una legge ch'è dolore!
Guai a chi con vitale dolore
si dona a una causa che nulla vuole

se non difendere la poca fede ancora
rimasta a dar rassegnazione al mondo!
Guai a chi crede che all'impeto del cuore

debba l'impeto della ragione rispondere!
Guai a chi non sa essere misero
nel misurare nell'anima i fondi

piani dell'egoismo e le derise
pazzie della pietà! Guai a chi crede
che la storia ad una eterna origine

—per candore piuttosto che per fede—
si sia interrotta, come il sole
del sogno; e non sa che è erede

la chiesa di ogni secolo creatore,
e difenderne gli istituiti beni,
l'orribile, animale grigiore

che vince nell'uomo luce e tenebra!
Guai a chi non sa che è borghese
questa fede cristiana, nel segno

di ogni privilegio, di ogni resa,
di ogni servitù; che il peccato
altro non è che reato di lesa

certezza quotidiana, odiato
per paura e aridità; che la Chiesa
è lo spietato cuore dello Stato.

[. . .]

1957-59

would want to serve a law of sorrow!
Woe unto him who with vital sorrow
gives himself to a cause that wants

only to defend the little faith left
to teach the world resignation!
Woe unto him who believes the heart's

élan should be matched by reason's!
Woe unto him who cannot be mean
as he plumbs the soul to nether regions

of selfishness and the ridiculous
follies of pity! Woe unto him who believes
—more out of innocence than faith—

that history was interrupted
at its eternal beginning, like the sun
in dreams, and doesn't know it's the Church

has inherited every age of creation
and defends its appointed estate,
the horrible, animal gloom

that defeats light and darkness in man!
Woe unto him who doesn't know
that this Christian faith is middle-class,

its sign in every privilege, in every surrender,
in every thralldom; and that sin
is nothing more than the crime of offending

everyday certitudes, hated
in fear and barrenness; and that the Church
is the pitiless heart of the State.

[. . .]

Appendice alla "Religione": Una luce

Pur sopravvivendo, in una lunga appendice
di inesausta, inesauribile passione
—che quasi in un altro tempo ha la radice—

so che una luce, nel caos, di religione,
una luce di bene, mi redime
il troppo amore nella disperazione . . .

È una povera donna, mite, fine,
che non ha quasi coraggio di essere,
e se ne sta nell'ombra, come una bambina,

coi suoi radi capelli, le sue vesti dimesse,
ormai, e quasi povere, su quei sopravvissuti
segreti che sanno, ancora, di violette;

con la sua forza, adoperata nei muti
affanni di chi teme di non essere pari
al dovere, e non si lamenta dei mai avuti

compensi: una povera donna che sa amare
soltanto, eroicamente, ed essere madre
è stato per lei tutto ciò che si può dare.

La casa è piena delle sue magre
membra di bambina, della sua fatica:
anche a notte, nel sonno, asciutte lacrime

coprono ogni cosa: e una pietà così antica,
così tremenda mi stringe il cuore,
rincasando, che urlerei, mi toglierei la vita.

Tutto intorno ferocemente muore,
mentre non muore il bene che è in lei,
e non sa quanto il suo umile amore,

Appendix to "Religion": A Light

Though I survive, in a long extension
of unexhausted, inexhaustible passion
— whose roots lie almost in another age —

I know that, in the chaos, a light of religion,
of goodness, redeems the excess
of love in my hopelessness . . .

This light is a poor woman, dainty and mild,
who has barely the heart to exist
and remains in the shadows like a child,

with her thinning hair, her now modest,
almost shabby clothes, which hide surviving
secrets that still smell of violets,

and a strength she summons in the silent
troubles of one afraid to be no longer
equal to her tasks. But she never laments

rewards she's never known. Poor woman,
she knows only how to love, heroically.
Motherhood is all she could ever have given.

The house is full of her skinny, girlish
limbs, full of her exertions:
Even at night, in her sleep, dry tears wash

over everything; a pity so ancient and rife
so breaks my heart when I return home
that I could scream or take my own life.

As all around us fiercely dies
the good inside her never dies;
she has no idea that her humble love

—poveri, dolci ossicini miei—
possano nel confronto quasi farmi morire
di dolore e vergogna, quanto quei

suoi gesti angustiati, quei suoi sospiri
nel silenzio della nostra cucina,
possano farmi apparire impuro e vile . . .

In ogni ora, tutto è ormai, per lei, bambina,
per me suo figlio, e da sempre, finito:
non resta che sperare che la fine

venga davvero a spegnere l'accanito
dolore di aspettarla. Saremo insieme,
presto, in quel povero prato gremito

di pietre grige, dove fresco il seme
dell'esistenza dà ogni anno erbe e fiori:
nient'altro ormai che la campagna preme

ai suoi confini di muretti, tra i voli
delle allodole, a giorno, e a notte,
il canto disperato degli usignoli.

Farfalle e insetti ce n'è a frotte,
fino al tardo settembre, la stagione
in cui torniamo, lì dove le ossa

dell'altro figlio tiene la passione
ancora vive nel gelo della pace:
vi arriva, ogni pomeriggio, depone

i suoi fiori, in ordine, mentre tutto tace
intorno, e si sente solo il suo affanno,
pulisce la pietra, dove, ansioso, lui giace,

poi si allontana, e nel silenzio che hanno
subito ritrovato intorno muri e solchi,
si sentono i tonfi della pompa che tremando

—poor, sweet little bones of mine—
could make me die of sorrow and shame
in the comparison, how her confined

gestures, the sighs she heaves
in the silence of the kitchen,
can make me feel impure and craven . . .

Nowadays everything, for her, the girl,
and me, the son, is over, has always been:
The only hope is that the end

will really come and stop the dogged
pain of waiting. Soon we'll be
together, in that humble meadow dotted

with gray stones, where every year the seed
of life makes the grass and flowers grow:
These days nothing but the countryside

bears down upon the little walls around it,
between the soaring skylarks in the day
and the hopeless song of nightingales at night.

There, insects and butterflies are legion
until late September, the season when
we return to the place where passion

keeps the bones of the other son
alive in the cold and stillness.
Every afternoon she goes there and sets

her flowers down in order, and all around
is silent, except her labored breath; she cleans
the stone where he lies restless underground,

then walks away, and in the silence that falls
at once over nearby walls and furrows,
you can hear the thuds of the pump, which with all

lei spinge con le sue poche forze,
volonterosa, decisa a fare ciò che è bene:
e torna, attraversando le aiuole folte

di nuova erbetta, con quei suoi vasi pieni
d'acqua per quei fiori . . . Presto
anche noi, dolce superstite, saremo

perduti in fondo a questo fresco
pezzo di terra: ma non sarà una quiete
la nostra, ché si mescola in essa

troppo una vita che non ha avuto meta.
Avremo un silenzio stento e povero,
un sonno doloroso, che non reca

dolcezza e pace, ma nostalgia e rimprovero,
la tristezza di chi è morto senza vita:
se qualcosa di puro, e sempre giovane,

vi resterà sarà il tuo mondo mite,
la tua fiducia, il tuo eroismo:
nella dolcezza del gelso e della vite

o del sambuco, in ogni alto o misero
segno di vita, in ogni primavera, sarai
tu; in ogni luogo dove un giorno risero,

e di nuovo ridono, impuri, i vivi, tu darai
la purezza, l'unico giudizio che ci avanza,
ed è tremendo, e dolce: ché non c'è mai

disperazione senza un po' di speranza.

1959

her feeble might she works with trembling hands,
willful and determined to do what's right:
and she returns, crossing the dense bands

of young grass in the parterres, carrying
vases full of water for her flowers . . . Soon
we, too, sweet survivor, shall be lying

lost at the bottom of this fresh patch
of earth: but ours won't be a quiet rest,
for it shall harbor still too much

of a life lived without purpose.
Ours shall be a paltry, labored silence,
our sleep full of sorrow, allowing

no comfort or peace, but only yearning
and regret, the sadness of those who die
without having lived; and if something

pure and always young is left behind,
it shall be your gentle world, your faith
and heroism: in the sweet mulberry, vines

and elder, in every high or lowly
sign of life, in every springtime, you
shall live on; everywhere the living

once laughed and laugh again, impurely,
you shall bring purity, sole judgement left
to us; and it is awesome, and sweet, for surely

no despair is of every hope bereft.

Al principe

Se torna il sole, se discende la sera,
      se la notte ha un sapore di notti future,
se un pomeriggio di pioggia sembra tornare
      da tempi troppo amati e mai avuti del tutto,
io non sono più felice, né di goderne né di soffrirne:
      non sento più, davanti a me, tutta la vita . . .
Per essere poeti, bisogna avere molto tempo:
      ore e ore di solitudine sono il solo modo
perché si formi qualcosa, che è forza, abbandono,
      vizio, libertà, per dare stile al caos.
Io tempo ormai ne ho poco: per colpa della morte
      che viene avanti, al tramonto della gioventù.
Ma per colpa anche di questo nostro mondo umano,
      che ai poveri toglie il pane, ai poeti la pace.

A Bertolucci

Sopravvivenza: anch'essa. Essa, la vecchia campagna,
      ritrovata, quassù, dove, per noi, è più eterna.
Sono gli ultimi giorni, o, è uguale, gli ultimi anni,
      dei campi arati con le file dei tronchi sui fossi,
del fango bianco intorno ai gelsi appena potati,
      degli argini ancora verdi sulle rogge asciutte.
Anche qui: dove il pagano fu cristiano, e con lui
      la sua terra, il suo campo coltivato.
Un nuovo tempo ridurrà a non essere tutto questo:
      e perciò possiamo piangerlo: con i suoi bui
anni barbarici, i suoi romanici aprili.
      Chi non la conoscerà, questa superstite terra,
come ci potrà capire? Dire chi siamo stati?
      Ma siamo noi che dobbiamo capire lui,
perchè lui nasca, sia pure perso a questi chiari giorni,
      a queste stupende stasi dell'inverno,
nel Sud dolce e tempestoso, nel Nord coperto d'ombra . . .

To the Prince

If the sun returns, if evening falls,
        if night has the taste of nights to come,
if a rainy afternoon seems to hail from times
        too beloved and never fully possessed,
I am none the happier whether I enjoy or suffer them:
        I no longer feel my whole life before me . . .
To be a poet, one needs a lot of time:
        hours and hours of solitude are the only way
to give shape to something that is strength, abandon,
        vice, freedom—to lend style to chaos.
I no longer have much time, thanks to death
        which fast approaches as youth declines.
But also thanks to this our human world,
        which leaves no bread to the poor, and to the poets no peace.

To Bertolucci

Survival: that too. It's the old landscape, rediscovered
        up here, where, for us, it's more eternal.
These are the last days, or—which amounts to the same—the last years,
        of plowed fields with tree trunks in rows over ditches,
of white mud around mulberry trees just pruned,
        of embankments still green over dry canals.
Even here, where a pagan was once Christian, and with him
        his land, his cultivated field . . .
A new age, with its dark years of barbarism,
        its Romanesque Aprils, shall reduce all this
to nothingness, and so we may weep for it.
        How can those who will not know this surviving earth
ever understand us? Or say who we once were?
        Yet it is we who must understand them,
that they might be born, however lost to these bright days,
        these magnificent winter stillnesses,
in the sweet, tempestuous South, the shadow-covered North . . .

Alla mia nazione

Non popolo arabo, non popolo balcanico, non popolo antico,
        ma nazione vivente, ma nazione europea:
e cosa sei? Terra di infanti, affamati, corrotti,
        governanti impiegati di agrari, prefetti codini,
avvocatucci unti di brillantina e i piedi sporchi,
        funzionari liberali carogne come gli zii bigotti,
una caserma, un seminario, una spiaggia libera, un casino!
        Milioni di piccoli borghesi come milioni di porci
pascolano sospingendosi sotto gli illesi palazzotti,
        tra case coloniali scrostate ormai come chiese.
Proprio perché tu sei esistita, ora non esisti,
        proprio perché fosti cosciente, sei incosciente.
E solo perché sei cattolica, non puoi pensare
        che il tuo male è tutto il male: colpa di ogni male.
Sprofonda in questo tuo bel mare, libera il mondo.

Frammento alla morte

Vengo da te e torno a te,
sentimento nato con la luce, col caldo,
battezzato quando il vagito era gioia,
riconosciuto in Pier Paolo
all'origine di una smaniosa epopea:
ho camminato alla luce della storia,
ma, sempre, il mio essere fu eroico,
sotto il tuo dominio, intimo pensiero.
Si coagulava nella tua scia di luce
nelle atroci sfiducie
della tua fiamma, ogni atto vero
del mondo, di quella
storia: e in essa si verificava intero,
vi perdeva la vita per riaverla:
e la vita era reale solo se bella . . .

La furia della confessione,
prima, poi la furia della chiarezza:
era da te che nasceva, ipocrita, oscuro

To My Country

Not an Arab people, not a Balkan people, not an ancient people
       but a living nation, a European nation,
and what are you? A land of babies, starving, corrupt,
       politicians working for landowners, reactionary governors,
petty lawyers with slicked-back hair and smelly feet,
       free-market bureaucrats mean as your bigoted uncles and aunts,
a barracks, a seminary, a public beach, a stinking mess!
       Millions of petits-bourgeois like millions of pigs
shoving one another as they graze near immaculate buildings
       between farmhouses now dilapidated as churches.
It's because you once existed that you do not now exist;
       because you once were conscious that you are now unconscious.
And it's only because you're Catholic that you cannot conceive
       that your evil is all evil: the sin of every evil.
Sink into this beautiful sea of yours and set the world free.

To Death: A Fragment

From you I come and to you I return,
sentiment born with the light and the heat,
baptized in a wail of joy,
identified as Pier Paolo
at the start of a frenzied epic:
I walked in the light of history,
but my being was heroic, always,
and under your sway, innermost thought.
In your luminous wake, in the dreadful
unease of your flame
every true act of the world
and its history
took form—and proved whole therein,
losing life in order to regain it:
and life was only real if beautiful . . .

First the mania for confession,
then the mania for clarity,
issued from you, dark, hypocritical

sentimento! E adesso,
accusino pure ogni mia passione,
m'infanghino, mi dicano informe, impuro
ossesso, dilettante, spergiuro:
tu mi isoli, mi dai la certezza della vita:
sono nel rogo, gioco la carta del fuoco,
e vinco, questo mio poco,
immenso bene, vinco quest'infinita,
misera mia pietà
che mi rende anche la giusta ira amica:
posso farlo, perché ti ho troppo patita!

Torno a te, come torna
un emigrato al suo paese e lo riscopre:
ho fatto fortuna (nell'intelletto)
e sono felice, proprio
com'ero un tempo, destituito di norma.
Una nera rabbia di poesia nel petto.
Una pazza vecchiaia di giovinetto.
Una volta la tua gioia era confusa
con il terrore, è vero, e ora
quasi con altra gioia,
livida, arida: la mia passione delusa.
Mi fai ora davvero paura,
perché mi sei davvero vicina, inclusa
nel mio stato di rabbia, di oscura
fame, di ansia quasi di nuova creatura.

Sono sano, come vuoi tu,
la nevrosi mi ramifica accanto,
l'esaurimento mi inaridisce, ma
non mi ha: al mio fianco
ride l'ultima luce di gioventù.
Ho avuto tutto quello che volevo, ormai:
sono anzi andato anche più in là
di certe speranze del mondo: svuotato,
eccoti lì, dentro di me, che empi
il mio tempo e i tempi.

sentiment! Let them now
condemn my every passion, let them
drag me through the mud, call me twisted,
foul pervert, dilettante, perjurer;
you keep me apart, give me life's assurance:
I burn at the stake, play the card of fire
and win: I win this small,
vast possession, my infinite,
miserable pity
which makes even righteous anger my friend.
And I can do this because I've endured you too long!

To you I return, the way
an emigrant returns and rediscovers his homeland:
I've made my fortune (in the mind)
and am happy, just the way
I used to be, stripped of rules.
Inside me is a poet's black rage.
A crazed adolescent's old age.
Your joy used to verge on
terror, it's true, and now
it nearly merges with another joy,
livid and arid: my disappointed passion.
You really do frighten me now,
for you're really very close to me,
enclosed within my state of rage, my dark
hunger, my thrashing like some newborn creature.

I'm in good health, the way you like it;
my neurosis spreads all around me;
exhaustion dries me out but
hasn't beat me yet: beside me
laughs the last light of youth.
I've got all that I wanted, by now.
I've even gone beyond
some of the world's expectations: a hollow
shell, I've got you now inside me, filling
my time and our times.

Sono stato razionale e sono stato
irrazionale: fin in fondo.
E ora . . . ah, il deserto assordato
dal vento, lo stupendo e immondo
sole dell'Africa che illumina il mondo.

Africa! Unica mia
alternativa. . . . .
. . . .

La Rabbia

Vado sulla porta del giardino, un piccolo
infossato cunicolo di pietra al piano
terra, contro il suburbano
orto, rimasto lì dai giorni di Mameli,
coi suoi pini, le sue rose, i suoi radicchi.
Intorno, dietro questo paradiso di paesana
tranquillità, compaiono
la facciate gialle dei grattacieli
fascisti, degli ultimi cantieri:
e sotto, oltre spessi lastroni di vetro,
c'è una rimessa, sepolcrale. Sonnecchia
al bel sole, un po' freddo, il grande orto
con la casetta, in mezzo, ottocentesca,
candida, dove Mameli è morto,
e un merlo cantando, trama la sua tresca.

Questo mio povero giardino, tutto
di pietra . . . Ma ho comprato un oleandro
— nuovo orgoglio di mia madre —
e vasi di ogni specie di fiori,
e anche un fraticello di legno, un putto
obbediente e roseo, un po' malandro,
trovato a Porta Portese, andando
a cercare mobili per la nuova casa. Colori,
pochi, la stagione è così acerba: ori
leggeri di luce, e verdi, tutti i verdi . . .
Solo un po' di rosso, torvo e splendido,

I've been rational and I've been
irrational, through and through.
And now . . . ah, the deafening wind
of the desert, the stunning, squalid
sun of Africa that lights up the world.

Africa! My sole
alternative . . . .
. . . .

Rage

I come to the garden's entrance, a small
sunken passage of stone on the ground
floor, facing a suburban
park that's been there since the days of Mameli,
with its pines, roses, and chicory.
All around, behind this heaven of peasant
tranquility, soar
the yellow façades of Fascist
high-rises and the latest construction sites.
Below, behind thick panes of glass,
is a tomblike storeroom. In the fine sun
and slight chill the great park dozes
around a nineteenth-century cottage,
pure white, where Mameli died,
as a blackbird weaves his plot in song.

My poor garden, all made
of stone . . . But I've bought an oleander
— my mother's new pride —
and pots of every kind of flower,
and even a little wooden friar, and a pink
cherub, obedient though a bit impish,
which I found at the flea market when I went
looking for furniture for the new house. Not many
colors, the season is still so young: soft
golden glows, and greens, every kind of green . . .
Only a little red, splendid and fierce,

seminascosto, amaro, senza gioia:
una rosa. Pende umile
sul ramo adolescente, come a una feritoia,
timido avanzo d'un paradiso in frantumi ...

Da vicino, è ancora più dimessa, pare
una povera cosa indifesa e nuda,
una pura attitudine
della natura, che si trova all'aria, al sole,
viva, ma di una vita che la illude,
e la umilia, che la fa quasi vergognare
d'essere così rude
nella sua estrema tenerezza di fiore.
Mi avvicino più ancora, ne sento l'odore ...
Ah, gridare è poco, ed è poco tacere:
niente può esprimere una esistenza intera!
Rinuncio a ogni atto ... So soltanto
che in questa rosa resto a respirare,
in un solo misero istante,
l'odore della mia vita: l'odore di mia madre ...

Perché non reagisco, perché non tremo
di gioia, o godo di qualche pura angoscia?
Perché non so riconoscere
questo antico nodo dela mia esistenza?
Lo so: perché in me è ormai chiuso il demone
della rabbia. Un piccolo, sordo, fosco
sentimento che m'intossica:
esaurimento, dicono, febbrile impazienza
dei nervi: ma non ne è libera più la coscienza.
Il dolore che da me a poco a poco mi aliena,
se io mi abbandono appena,
si stacca da me, vortica per conto suo,
mi pulsa disordinato alle tempie,
mi riempie il cuore di pus,
non sono più padrone del mio tempo ...

half-hidden, bitter, and joyless:
a rose. Hanging humbly
from an adolescent branch as from a loophole,
timid vestige of a shattered paradise . . .

Up close, it's even more modest,
like some poor defenseless thing, naked,
a pure attitude
of nature, thrust into the air and sun,
alive, but with a life that deludes
and humbles it, makes it almost ashamed
to be so crude
as a flower so utterly tender.
I draw closer still, smell its scent . . .
Ah, there's no point in shouting, no point in silence—
nothing can express an entire existence!
I forgo all action . . . I only know
that in this rose I inhale,
in a single, wretched instant,
the scent of my life: the scent of my mother . . .

Why don't I react, why don't I tremble
for joy, or revel in a fit of pure anguish?
Why can't I acknowledge
this ancient core of my existence?
I know why: because from now on the demon
of rage is inside me. A small, deaf, grim
emotion is poisoning me:
exhaustion, I'm told, the feverish fretting
of nerves—but that doesn't free my mind of it.
The pain estranging me from myself bit by bit
the moment I let myself go
breaks away from me, spins off by itself,
chaotically throbs in my temples,
filling my heart with pus,
and I am no longer in control of my time . . .

Niente avrebbe potuto, una volta, vincermi.
Ero chiuso nella mia vita come nel ventre
materno, in quest'ardente
odore di umile rosa bagnata.
Ma lottavo per uscirne, là nella provincia
campestre, ventenne poeta, sempre, sempre
a soffrire disperatamente,
disperatamente a gioire . . . La lotta è terminata
con la vittoria. La mia esistenza privata
non è più racchiusa tra i petali d'una rosa,
—una casa, una madre, una passione affannosa.
È pubblica. Ma anche il mondo che m'era ignoto
mi si è accostato, familiare,
si è fatto conoscere, e, a poco a poco,
mi si è imposto, necessario, brutale.

Non posso ora fingere di non saperlo:
o di non sapere come esso mi vuole.
Che specie di amore
conti in questo rapporto, che intese infami.
Non brucia una fiamma in questo inferno
di aridità, e questo arido furore
che impedisce al mio cuore
di reagire a un profumo, è un rottame
della passione . . . A quasi quarant'anni,
io mi trovo alla rabbia, come un giovane
che di sé non sa altro che è nuovo,
e si accanisce contro il vecchio mondo.
E, come un giovane, senza pietà
o pudore, io non nascondo
questo mio stato: non avrò pace, mai.

Nothing, before, could ever defeat me.
I was enclosed in my life as in a mother's
womb, inside a burning
scent of wet and humble rose.
But I struggled to break out, there in a pastoral
province, a poet of twenty, always, always
suffering desperately,
desperately rejoicing. . . The struggle ended
in victory. My private existence
is no longer enclosed within the petals of a rose
— a house, a mother, an arduous passion.
It's public. Now even the world I never knew
has come up to me, familiarly,
revealed itself and, little by little,
prevailed over me, imperative and brutal.

I cannot now pretend not to know it,
or not to know what it wants from me —
what sort of love
is at stake in this rapport, what sort of vile consents.
No flame burns in this arid
inferno, and the arid frenzy
that prevents my heart
reacting to a fragrance is a ruin
of passion . . . At almost forty years of age,
I find myself in a rage like a young man
who knows nothing of himself but his youth
and rails against the old world.
And, like a young man, without pity
or shame, I do not hide
my condition: I shall never find peace. Never.

VI
Da *Poesia in forma di rosa* /
From *Poem in the Shape of a Rose*

Da *"Poesie mondane"*

Una coltre di primule. Pecore
controluce (metta, metta, Tonino,
il cinquanta, non abbia paura
che la luce sfondi—facciamo
questo carrello contro natura!).
L'erba fredda tiepida, gialla tenera,
vecchia nuova—sull'Acqua Santa.
Pecore e pastore, un pezzo
di Masaccio (provi col settantacinque,
e carrello fino al primo piano).
Primavera medioevale. Un Santo eretico
(chiamato Bestemmia, dai compari.
Sarà un magnaccia, al solito. Chiedere
al dolente Leonetti consulenza
su prostituzione Medioevo).
Poi visione. La passione popolare
(una infinita carrellata con Maria
che avanza, chiedendo in umbro
del figlio, cantando in umbro l'agonia).
La primavera porta una coltre
di erba dura tenerella, di primule. . .
e l'atonia dei sensi mista alla libidine.
Dopo la visione (gozzoviglie
mortuarie, empie—di puttane),
una «preghiera» negli ardenti prati.
Puttane, magnaccia, ladri, contadini
con le mani congiunte sotto la faccia
(tutto con il cinquanta controluce).
Girerò i più assolati Appennini.
Quando gli Anni Sessanta
saranno perduti come il Mille,
e, il mio, sarà uno scheletro
senza più neanche nostalgia del mondo,
cosa conterà la mia «vita privata»,
miseri scheletri senza vita
né privata né pubblica, ricattatori,
cosa conterà! Conteranno le mie tenerezze,

From "Worldly Poems"

April 23, 1962

A blanket of primroses. Sheep
against the light (come on, come on, Tonino,
use the fifty, don't worry about the light
burning through—we're going to do
this tracking shot against nature!).
The grass—cold and tepid, yellow and
soft, old and new—over Acqua Santa.
Sheep and shepherd, a Masaccio
piece (try the seventy-five, then
track and end with a close-up).
Medieval spring. A heretical Saint
(called Blasphemy, by his cronies.
He'll be a pimp, as usual. Ask
long-suffering Leonetti for help
on prostitution in the Middle Ages).
Then, a vision. The Passion, peasant-style
(an endless traveling shot with Mary
coming forward, asking about her son
in Umbrian, singing her torment in Umbrian).
Spring brings a blanket of hard,
young grass and primroses . . .
and sensual languor mixed with libido.
After the vision (sacrilegious
revelries of death and whores),
a "prayer" in the burning meadows.
Whores, pimps, thieves, peasants
with hands folded under their faces
(all backlit, shot with the fifty).
I'll film the sunniest Apennines.
When the Sixties are as forgotten
as the Year One Thousand,
and *my* skeleton feels not
the slightest nostalgia for the world,
what will my "private life" matter!
Miserable skeletons with no life,
private or public, blackmailers,
what will it matter! My tenderness will matter.

sarò io, dopo la morte, in primavera,
a vincere la scommessa, nella furia
del mio amore per l'Acqua Santa al sole.

Quando una troupe invaderà le strade
di stanotte, sarà una nuova epoca.
Perciò: goditi anche questo dolore.
L'idea di fare un film sul tuo suicidio,
tuona nei millenni. . . si ricongiunge, indietro,
a Shakespeare. . . è sesso, grandezza
della libidine, sua soavità. . .
Il protagonista è macellato:
una bolla d'aria gonfia la sua pelle,
potrebbe volare per il terrore.
Una spaccatura gli scende dal palato
allo sterno, e irradia dei tremiti
per tutto il corpo: l'intossicazione
gli buca lo stomaco, gli dà la diarrea.
Suicidarsi, è la più semplice idea
che gli possa venire: entra, frattanto,
in un cinema (son anni che non lo fa,
così, da solo) e sui brevi spazi
del suo spasimo viscerale, ecco,
in montaggio alterno, gli enormi
spazi a colori della pubblicità.
Frigoriferi, dentifrici, gote
sorridenti. Poi andrà fuori.
La notte, col profumo dei tigli,
benché sia tardo aprile, quasi maggio.
Ma quell'anno la primavera stentava
a farsi avanti. La città era lucida,
e tremavano fanali, in quel lucore
di facile effetto—umido, pesante,
più pesante dell'odore stesso dei tigli
compressi, sprofondati nell'aria—
tremavano fanali di tram e automobili
come per una fuga atomica, per l'ultima
cena del mondo, o per la più recente,

I myself, after death, in springtime,
shall win the bet, with my furious
love of Acqua Santa in the sun.

April 25, 1962

When the cast invades the streets
tonight, a new epoch will dawn.
So enjoy this pain, too.
The idea of making a film about your suicide
thunders down the millennia . . . and links back up
with Shakespeare . . . it's sex, the libido's
greatness, its sweetness . . .
The protagonist is butchered:
his skin swells with air like a bubble,
he could fly from the terror of it.
He is split from the palate down
to the sternum, shudders radiating
throughout his body; the poison
bores through his stomach and gives him diarrhea.
Suicide seems the simplest thing
he can think of: meanwhile he enters
a movie theater (it's been years since he's done it
like this, alone), and in the brief intervals
between the spasms in his entrails, lo,
in alternating sequence, the huge colorful
intervals of the sponsors' commercials.
Refrigerators, toothpastes, smiling
cheeks. Later he'll go outside.
Scent of linden in the night air,
though it's late April, almost May.
But that year the spring had trouble
advancing. The city sparkled,
lights flickered in a facile
visual effect—damp and heavy,
even heavier than the scent of the lindens
compressed and stretching deep into the air—
headlights of trolleys and cars flickered
as in a rush of atoms, or the world's
last supper, or the most recent one,

con silenzioso orgasmo: mucchi
di luci in corsa, sgranati
lungo le curve d'una circonvallazione.
Con montaggio illogico, si vedrà,
poi, lui che cammina in una periferia
ancora più remota: siepi
gocciolanti, muretti di vecchi
casolari. . . e, un improvviso spazio
sereno, quasi primaverile, magari
con la luna su rappacificate nuvole:
in mezzo a quell'odoroso spazio,
quel vuoto di libertà campestre,
ecco cani che abbaiano, voci festose
di ragazzi — quelli del Mille,
o del futuro più lontano. Un piccolo
colpo di pistola. E «Fine». Ah,
siepi gocciolanti, china gonfia
della spudorata erba primaverile,
su monticelli traforati di cave,
dolci Tebaidi dove la natura ignorata
dagli uomini nuovi, festeggia l'aprile.

                    10 giugno 1962
. . . Fai pochi passi, e sei sull'Appia
o sulla Tuscolana: lì tutto è vita,
per tutti. Anzi, meglio è complice
di quella vita, chi stile e storia
non ne sa. I suoi significati
si scambiano nella sordida pace
indifferenza e violenza. Migliaia,
migliaia di persone, pulcinella
d'una modernità di fuoco, nel sole
il cui significato è anch'esso in atto,
si incrociano pullulando scure
sugli accecanti marciapiedi, contro
l'Ina-Case sprofondate nel cielo.
Io sono una forza del Passato.
Solo nella tradizione è il mio amore.
Vengo dai ruderi, dalle chiese,

in silent orgasm; clusters
of lights racing by, unleashed
along the curves of the beltway.
Then, in an illogical montage, we'll see
him walking in some even more
remote periphery: sodden
hedgerows, low walls of old
farmsteads . . . and suddenly a tranquil
space, almost springlike, maybe with
the moon above newly placid clouds:
in the midst of this fragrant space,
this vacuum of rustic freedom,
dogs suddenly barking, cheerful
voices of boys — in the year One Thousand
or in some more distant future. A quick
pistol-shot. And "The End." Ah,
sodden hedgerows, knolls swollen
with the shameless grass of spring
on hillsides pierced with caves,
sweet Thebaids where, unknown to the new
humanity, nature celebrates April.

June 10, 1962

. . . Take a few steps and you're on the Appia
or Tuscolana, where all is life
for all. But to be this life's
accomplice, better to know
no style or history. Its meanings
deal in apathy and violence
in sordid peace. Under a sun
whose meaning is also unfolding,
thousands and thousands of people,
buffoons of a modern age of fire,
cross paths, teeming dark
along the blinding sidewalks, against
housing projects stretching to the sky.
I am a force of the Past.
My love lies only in tradition.
I come from the ruins, the churches,

dalle pale d'altare, dai borghi
abbandonati sugli Appennini o le Prealpi,
dove sono vissuti i fratelli.
Giro per la Tuscolana come un pazzo,
per l'Appia come un cane senza padrone.
O guardo i crepuscoli, le mattine
su Roma, sulla Ciociaria, sul mondo,
come i primi atti della Dopostoria,
cui io assisto, per privilegio d'anagrafe,
dall'orlo estremo di qualche età
sepolta. Mostruoso è chi è nato
dalle viscere di una donna morta.
E io, feto adulto, mi aggiro
più moderno di ogni moderno
a cercare fratelli che non sono più.

12 giugno 1962

Ci vediamo in proiezione, ed ecco
la città, in una sua povera ora nuda,
terrificante come ogni nudità.
Terra incendiata il cui incendio
spento stasera o da millenni,
è una cerchia infinita di ruderi rosa,
carboni e ossa biancheggianti, impalcature
dilavate dall'acqua e poi bruciate
da nuovo sole. La radiosa Appia
che formicola di migliaia di insetti
—gli uomini d'oggi—i neorealistici
ossessi delle Cronache in volgare.
Poi compare Testaccio, in quella luce
di miele proiettato sulla terra
dall'oltretomba. Forse è scoppiata,
la Bomba, fuori dalla mia coscienza.
Anzi, è così certamente. E la fine
del Mondo è già accaduta: una cosa
muta, calata nel controluce del crepuscolo.
Ombra, chi opera in questa èra.
Ah, sacro Novecento, regione dell'anima
in cui l'Apocalisse è un vecchio evento!
Il Pontormo con un operatore

the altarpieces, the villages
abandoned in the Apennines or foothills
of the Alps where my brothers once lived.
I wander like a madman down the Tuscolana,
down the Appia like a dog without a master.
Or I see the twilights, the mornings
over Rome, the Ciociaria, the world,
as the first acts of Posthistory
to which I bear witness, by arbitrary
birthright, from the outer edge
of some buried age. Monstrous is the man
born of a dead woman's womb.
And I, a fetus now grown, roam about
more modern than any modern man,
in search of brothers no longer alive.

June 12, 1962

We meet in the screening room, and there
behold the city, poor in its hour of nakedness,
terrifying as all nakedness is.
A scorched earth whose blaze, extinguished
this evening or a few millennia ago,
is an unending circle of rose-colored ruins,
whitening coals and bones, scaffoldings
bleached by rain and then burnt
by new sun. The radiant Appia
teems with thousands of insects
— today's human beings — the neorealist
madmen of News in the vernacular.
Then Testaccio appears, in that honied
light projected onto the earth
from beyond the grave. Maybe the Bomb
has gone off without my knowing.
Yes, that must certainly be it. And the World
has already ended — but silently,
slipped in against the light of the sunset.
A shadow works the camera in this age.
Ah, sacred Twentieth Century, realm of the soul
where the Apocalypse is already old news!
Pontormo with his meticulous

meticoloso, ha disposto cantoni
di case giallastre, a tagliare
questa luce friabile e molle,
che dal cielo giallo si fa marrone
impolverato d'oro sul mondo cittadino...
e come piante senza radice, case e uomini,
creano solo muti monumenti di luce
e d'ombra, in movimento: perché
la loro morte è nel loro moto.
Vanno, come senza alcuna colonna sonora,
automobili e camion, sotto gli archi,
sull'asfalto, contro il gasometro,
nell'ora, d'oro, di Hiroscima,
dopo vent'anni, sempre più dentro
in quella loro morte gesticolante: e io
ritardatario sulla morte, in anticipo
sulla vita vera, bevo l'incubo
della luce come un vino smagliante.
Nazione senza speranze! L'Apocalisse
esploso fuori dalle coscienze
nella malinconia dell'Italia dei Manieristi,
ha ucciso tutti: guardateli — ombre
grondanti d'oro nell'oro dell'agonia.

Supplica a mia madre

È difficile dire con parole di figlio
ciò a cui nel cuore ben poco assomiglio.

Tu sei la sola al mondo che sa, del mio cuore,
ciò che è stato sempre, prima d'ogni altro amore.

Per questo devo dirti ciò ch'è orrendo conoscere:
è dentro la tua grazia che nasce la mia angoscia.

Sei insostituibile. Per questo è dannata
alla solitudine la vita che mi hai data.

cameraman has cast streetcorners
of yellowish buildings to cut through
this soft, crumbly light
falling from the yellow sky and turning brown
speckled with gold over the world of the city . . .
and like plants without roots, buildings and people
create only monuments of light
and shadow in motion—because
their death is in their movement.
As if with no soundtrack at all, cars
and trucks pass under the arches,
over the asphalt, against the gasometer
at the hour, the golden hour, of Hiroshima
twenty years later, driving ever farther
into their gesticulating death: while I,
arriving late to death and early
to real life, I drink down the light's
nightmare like a dazzling wine.
Nation without hope! Exploding outside
people's consciousness in the melancholy
Italy of the Mannerists, the Apocalypse
has killed them all—look at them: shadows
oozing gold in golden agony.

Plea to My Mother

It's hard to express in the words of a son
what, at heart, I'm not really like.

You alone in all the world know what love
has always come first in my heart.

This is why there's something terrible you should know:
it's from your grace that springs my sorrow.

You are irreplaceable. This is why the life you blessed
me with will always be condemned to loneliness.

E non voglio esser solo. Ho un'infinita fame
d'amore, dell'amore di corpi senza anima.

Perché l'anima è in te, sei tu, ma tu
sei mia madre e il tuo amore è la mia schiavitù:

ho passato l'infanzia schiavo di questo senso
alto, irrimediabile, di un impegno immenso.

Era l'unico modo per sentire la vita,
l'unica tinta, l'unica forma: ora è finita.

Sopravviviamo: ed è la confusione
di una vita rinata fuori dalla ragione.

Ti supplico, ah, ti supplico: non voler morire.
Sono qui, solo, con te, in un futuro aprile. . .

La persecuzione

Tornavo per la Via Portuense. Lasciai
(lucido nello stordimento della festa
degli altri, nemica, senza luce, mai

per me—rifiuto anche ciò che mi resta),
la macchina, nel sole dominato dalla sera,
su un marciapiede sbriciolato, nella mesta

confusione di un capolinea periferico. Era
tenerissima l'aria, e della gente
oziava, in una torbida miseria

di siepi attorno a un bar: era una spenta
parete perduta contro una visione
indicibile di sole, tuguri, fondamenta. . .

Intorno a quei tavoli, c'erano persone
che la sera, ancora torrida, rendeva
quasi spiriti: madri, con la loro passione

And I don't want to be alone. I have an infinite
thirst for love, for bodies pure and soulless.

For the soul is in you, it is you, but you are
my mother, and in your love are my fetters.

I went through childhood enslaved to a sentiment,
lofty and incurable, of overwhelming commitment.

It was the only way to feel alive, the only color,
the only form, and now it's over.

Still, we survive—in the confusion
of a life reborn outside of reason.

I beg you, oh, I beg you: don't wish for death.
I'm here, alone, with you, in an April to come.

Persecution

I was returning by way of Via Portuense.
Lucid amidst the tumult of other people's
celebration (offputting, devoid of light,

never for me—I even spurn what is left me),
I parked the car on a crumbling sidewalk
in the waning evening sun, in the gloomy

chaos of a suburban terminus. The air
was soft as could be, people were idling
about in the shadow of a wretched

hedgerow around a café—a lifeless
barrier against an unspeakable
vision of sun, shanties, and construction pits . . . .

Around those tables sat people
whom the still torrid evening seemed to turn
into spirits: mothers with trampled affections—

avvilita—figlie, con vesti in cui stringeva
il cuore l'allegra, borghese povertà
—vicini di casa... Insomma, chi poteva

concedersi la gioia d'una spesa, là
dove il loro lontano quartiere
riproduceva i grandi centri della città.

Io, entravo dentro quel bar, per caso, a bere
un qualcosa, consumato dal sole,
senza forza, sfatto di dolore e di sapere.

Ma—camminando controluce—scorsi, il sole,
oscurarsi, sui bambini e i giovinetti
che giocavano, lungo il muro, nel calore

immedicabile: e scendere dai tetti,
dalle siepi, dalle piante coperte di polvere
o carbonizzate, dagli sterpi secchi,

dalle dolci ondulazioni che dissolvono
l'agro verso il mare, un vento buio
e formicolante, ombra torbida,

alito mostruoso, che presto fu
quello di sempre: una brezza della sera,
che a quegli spiriti, perduti giù

nel cuore della vita, fu lieve bandiera
accennante dalle estati della morte.
Subito, quegli ignari giovincelli, in schiera

quasi a urlare che è innocente chi è forte,
misero nel loro juke-box un gettone:
e una musica nuova cantò la loro sorte.

Quella sorte, ascoltavo, nella mia passione
consumata fino a un'impaurita tenerezza,
anonimo ospite davanti alla sua consumazione...

daughters in dresses whose cheerful,
bourgeois shabbiness broke my heart—
neighbors . . . Anyone, in short, who could

afford the pleasure of spending money
at a place that made their faraway borough
seem like the great city centers.

By chance I went into this café to get
something to drink, worn out by the sun,
listless and wilting from sorrow and knowledge.

Then, walking against the light, I saw
the sun darken over the children and teenagers
playing along the wall in the incurable

heat; and from the roofs, the hedges,
the dust-covered or heat-blasted trees,
from the dried-up underbrush

and the sweet rolling hills that break up
the countryside down to the sea, there came
a dark, seething wind, a murky shadow,

a monstrous exhalation that soon became
what it had always been: an evening breeze,
which for those spirits lost down there

in the heart of life was a faint banner
beckoning from a summer of death.
Suddenly banding together as if to shout

that strength lies in numbers, those artless
youngsters put a token in the jukebox,
and a new song sang of their fate.

My passion consumed to a state of frightened
tenderness, I listened to that fate,
an anonymous guest at its consumption.

Ascoltavo la vita dalla mia sopravvivenza.
Ma era sempre cara, quella vita!
quella vita di sempre, senza odio e senza

amore, perduta nella sua forma infinita!
Popolo, borghesia, grossolana invasione
di Ferragosto, come intimidita

in quel suo sole da un' oscura ossessione,
infima espressione della massa, minutaglia
sperduta nel suo ancora paesano rione,

superstite ai margini dell'immensa battaglia:
e i figli ridono, i più piccoli giocando,
i più grandi ascoltando nella sterpaglia

il juke-box all'aperto, forti, candidi,
e così vivi da parere ancor più vivi
al fiato buio che sta su loro alitando. . .

Esco dal bar, io, triste tra quei giulivi,
carne tra quegli spiriti: e succede
qualcosa di tremendo. . . Oh, solo un brivido,

una sensazione, un nulla. . . Si vede,
ero stordito da tutto quel sole domenicale. . .
Come, uscendo dall'interno, misi un piede

oltre il recinto delle siepi del bar,
tutto fu alle mie spalle. La gente
ai tavoli, la gioventù con le sue ignare

bellezze, i figli cuccioli: niente
m'era più di fronte: e, quasi un canto
per la mia solitudine—a quel vento

lieve ch'era incominciato d'incanto—
il juke-box sollevava la sua voce al cielo.
Alle mie spalle: e io andavo avanti,

I was listening to life as a survivor.
But how precious that life still was!
The same life as ever, without hatred, without

love, lost in its infinite form!
The working and middle classes, crass invasion
of the August holiday, as though intimidated,

in that sun, by some dark obsession —
lowliest expression of the masses, little people lost
in their still villagelike neighborhood,

surviving on the margins of the great battle:
the children laugh, the youngest playing
and the bigger ones listening to the jukebox

in the open air, in the bushes, strong, pure,
so alive as to seem even more alive
in the dark breath blowing over them . . .

I exited the café — a sad presence among
the revelers, flesh among those spirits —
and something tremendous happened . . . Just a shudder,

mind you, a feeling, nothing, really . . . Clearly
I was dazed by all that Sunday sun . . .
As I stepped outside, into the enclosure

of hedges around the café,
everything was behind me. The people
at their tables, the youngsters with their ignorant

beauty, the puplike children: nothing was
before me anymore, and like a song
for my loneliness — in the gentle wind

that had stirred up as if on cue —
the jukebox raised its voice to the skies.
Behind me. And I went forward.

perché? Per che ragione vera?
Solo, come un feto, come all'ideali
fonti d'una vita, o una carriera. . .

Solo come un cane, per dir meglio, arido
come paglia secca, o come luce
che non dà luce a nulla. No, guardare

indietro non potevo, le perdute
forme dell'esistere: era certo
che sarebbero rimaste crudelmente mute

a guardarmi andare. Debole, scoperto,
le lasciavo alle spalle, ancora vive,
ancora calde, morto ancora incerto

d'essere veramente giunto alla fine.
Il sole tramontando colorava
davanti a me un po' di polvere, supine

case, abbandonati muriccioli: e dava
a me, radiato dall'ordine degli uomini
—solo a barcollare, gobbo, nella bava

dolcissima di quei luoghi senza nome,
festivi, estivi—l'angoscia del linciaggio:
e intanto un riso. . . un mite spettro comico

d'amore. . . un corpo vivo di coraggio. . .
cresceva in me, come statua in una statua.
E riprendevo così i primi passi del mio viaggio.

Avrei potuto cercare la pietà,
la resa, in quel momento: negarmi,
rinnegarmi, rifugiarmi in una Chiesa, correre là

dove da secoli si gettano le armi. . .
Invece, per fortuna, quella vita alle spalle,
mescolata ai funerei, almi

Why? For what reason, really?
Alone, like a foetus at the mythic
origins of a life, or a career . . . .

Alone as a dog, or better yet, barren
as dry straw, as light that sheds
no light on anything. No, I could not

look back, at the lost forms
of existence: I knew for certain
they would only have been cruelly silent

as they watched me leave. Weak, exposed,
I left them behind me, still alive,
still warm, a dead man still not sure

he'd really reached the end.
The setting sun colored the dust, the low
buildings, the squat, abandoned drywalls

before me, and in its light, struck from the ranks
of men, hunched and swaying, all alone
in the delicious froth of those nameless,

festive places of summer, I felt in danger
of being lynched—but then a laugh . . .
a gentle, comic specter of love . . . .

a body alive and fearless . . . .
rose up inside me, like a statue inside a statue.
And I set out on my way again.

I could have sought pity, could have surrendered
at that moment: denied myself, disowned
myself, taken refuge in a Church, fled to where

for centuries men have laid down their arms . . .
But instead, to my luck, that life behind me,
combined with the mournful, vital

raggi del crepuscolo, sopra lotti e stalle,
mi liberò: non ha diritti, l'uomo.
Non ha realtà, il suo paese, la sua valle. . .

E la mia «querelle» risuonò, come sempre risuona,
ormai senza più necessità, ingenuamente
ostinata, mostro di ragione e di passione.

Risuonò un po' pazza, come rivolta a quella gente;
che non c'entrava o, misera, non poteva capire,
innocente oggetto dell'odio d'un innocente.

«Come hanno tanto potuto tradire,
    i loro pastori, l'amore e l'onore?
Ah, è la ferocia forse che difende l'ovile.

Perché egli sa che non fingevano le loro parole:
non era che un calcolo elementare
e perciò adulto. . . Non ha diritti, il cuore!

E non ci voleva nulla, ahi, a deformare
questa sua forma, già incerta ai loro sguardi
di anime sicure, ironiche, ignare,

—come bambini sotto gli occhi dei padri
bonari verso le loro antiche
crudeltà, le loro stupide rabbie. . .

E fu facile trovare i complici del mito:
questi "più realisti del re," questi strazianti
confinati di Ina-Case e borgate, col corpo nutrito

da povere minestre, da grassi umilianti,
la camicia con un filo di sporcizia
sul collo, i figli urlanti

in fondo a caseggiati neri come ospizi,
le deboli nuche gialle di brillantina,
o tormentate da precoci calvizie,

rays of evening over the lots and stables,
set me free: Man has no rights.
No reality, no town, no valley his own . . .

And my grievance rang out, as it always does,
as henceforth unnecessary, naively
stubborn, a monster of reason and passion.

It rang a bit mad, as though addressed to people
whom it didn't concern or were too wretched to understand,
innocent objects of an innocent's hatred.

"How could they have so betrayed
their pastors, their honor, their love?
Ah, maybe it's ferocity protects the flock.

For he knows their words were sincere:
it was all but a simple and thus mature
calculation . . . . No, the heart has no rights!

And it took very little, alas, to deform the form
of this heart, which was already uncertain
in the eyes of those cocksure, ironic, ignorant souls

like children under the gaze of fathers
who look kindly on their ancient
cruelties, their stupid rages . . . .

And it was easy to find them complicit in the myth,
these people 'more royalist than the king,'
heartrending captives of public housing and slums,

their bodies fed on meager soups and wretched fats,
their shirts stained with rings of dirt
around the collar, their children screaming

deep inside apartments black as hospices,
the napes of their fragile necks yellow with pomade
or tortured by premature bald spots,

la loro nazionale assassina. . .
e cattolici! e fascisti!, per poter dire:
Anch'io son io, anche a me destina

la vita un compito non vile!
anche i miei atti sono consacrati
dalla coscienza di un eroico servire!

E, se tra essi, a bere, mescolati
nella cocente, minacciosa brezza,
ci fossero degli uomini fraterni, impegnati

a combattere, con lui, per l'interezza
dell'uomo. . . troverebbero l'opera compiuta:
un uomo che gli uomini disprezzano.

E darebbero la sua presenza per perduta.
Non ha diritti, il puro. . . Ogni ragione
avrebbero, essi di rivolgere duro

e quasi ostile — offeso nella sua passione
intransigente — lo sguardo, a lui che ha perso
il suo oscuro gioco con la pubblica opinione.

Egli può, oh sì, dentro di sé, urlare, immerso
nel terrore di un'ipocrisia
che è la norma dell'umile universo:

ma, di fronte agli altri, egli sa che non c'è via
che accettare la fine di quanto finì
nell'umiliazione, o in un po' di poesia. . .

Così, un esercito era pronto — chi
per vivere, chi per possedere in pace —
a incasellare questa persona, ora e qui,

nei cartelli del male, dove ora giace.
Ah, masse feroci, ch'egli tanto ama,
terra morta, di cui tanto gli piace

their murderous national cigarette . . .
And some are Catholics! And Fascists!
Which lets them say: I too am my own man, I too

am granted my not-unworthy task in life!
My actions, too, are blessed by the knowledge
that to serve is heroic!

And if, among their number drinking there
in the scorching, threatening breeze, there
were some brotherly men, engaged,

like him, in the fight to make man whole . . .
they would find the finished work before them:
a man despised by other men.

And they would see him as lost in that crowd.
The pure man has no rights . . . Their unbending
passion offended, they would have every reason

to cast a harsh and almost hostile
eye on him, the man who's lost
his obscure game with public opinion.

Oh, he can scream to himself all he wants,
immersed in the terror of the hypocrisy
that is the norm in this humble universe:

but in front of others he knows there is
no choice but to accept the outcome of all
that ends in humiliation, or in a little poetry . . .

Thus an army was ready — some so they could live,
others so they could own in peace —
to relegate this person, here and now,

to the ranks of evil, where he now lies.
O savage masses, whom he loves so much,
O dead land whose life, the naked sun

la vita, il nudo sole italiano!
Eccolo servito nella sua dolcezza:
è disonorante porgergli la mano.»

La mia vittoria, la mia sconfitta, la mia interezza!
Tutto è ora alle mie spalle... È bastato un nero
fiato di vento sopra questa ebbrezza

infima e infinita, volgare e austera,
di un pomeriggio di Ferragosto,
perché io, finendo, ritornassi vero.

Occhi, tornate occhi! Io riconosco
ciò che conobbi: sole e solitudine.
Sensi, tornate sensi, il posto

della vita è nuovo, atrocemente nudo.
Risalgo in macchina, rimetto in moto,
corro: la sera brucia, sudicia,

una clinica, con imposte verdi, il vuoto
d'uno sterro, con canne di torrenti,
la Parrocchietta sola contro il fuoco,

il Trullo, un detrito di facciate identiche,
colore dello sterco, una fiumana
di macchine di ritorno da torbidi frangenti,

Roma spalmata come fango sulla lama
infiammata cel cielo, ragazzi in fiore,
tutta l'estate nella maglietta grama,

ah vergogna e splendore, vergogna e splendore!
Mille nubi di pace accerchiano il cielo,
amore, mai non finirai d'essere amore.

1961

of Italy, he cherishes so much!
Here is meet reward for his tenderness:
it is a dishonor to shake his hand."

My victory, my defeat, my wholeness!
Everything is now behind me . . . . All it took
was a breath of black wind over the lowly,

endless, vulgar, austere merriment
of a mid-August holiday afternoon,
to make me, in my ending, real again.

Eyes, be eyes again! I now recognize
what I knew before: sun and solitude.
Senses, be senses again; life has a new,

atrociously naked place in the world.
I get back in my car, start up the engine,
and speed off: the grimy evening burns

a green-shuttered clinic, the void
of a foundation pit with river reeds,
the Parrocchietta alone against the fire,

the Trullo a detritus of identical façades
the color of excrement, a stream of cars
returning from troubled shoals,

Rome smeared like mud on the fiery blade
of the sky, young boys in bloom,
in the same wretched T-shirt all summer,

ah, shame and splendor, shame and splendor!
A thousand clouds of peace surround the sky.
Love, you shall never cease to be love.

Una disperata vitalità

I

(*Stesura, in «cursus» di linguaggio «gergale» corrente, dell'antefatto:
Fiumicino, il vecchio castello e una prima idea vera della morte.*)

Come in un film di Godard: solo
in una macchina che corre per le autostrade
del Neo-capitalismo latino—di ritorno dall'aeroporto—
[là è rimasto Moravia, puro fra le sue valige]
    solo, «pilotando la sua Alfa Romeo»
        in un sole irriferibile in rime
          non elegiache, perché celestiale
          —il più bel sole dell'anno—
come in un film di Godard:
        sotto quel sole che si svenava immobile
        unico,
     il canale del porto di Fiumicino
     —una barca a motore che rientrava inosservata
     —i marinai napoletani coperti di cenci di lana
     —un incidente stradale, con poca folla intorno...

—come in un film di Godard—riscoperta
del romanticismo in sede
di neocapitalistico cinismo, e crudeltà—
al volante
per la strada di Fiumicino,
ed ecco il castello (che dolce
mistero, per lo scenggiatore francese,
nel turbato sole senza fine, secolare,
questo bestione papalino, coi suoi merli,
sulle siepi e i filari della brutta campagna
dei contadini servi)...

—sono come un gatto bruciato vivo,
pestato dal copertone di un autotreno,
impiccato da ragazzi a un fico,

A *Desperate Vitality*

 I

(*Draft, in a cursus in present-day jargon, of what has just transpired: Fiumicino, the old castle, and a first real idea of death.*)

As in a film by Godard: alone
in a car speeding down the motorways
of Latin neo-capitalism—returning from the airport—
[where Moravia stayed behind, a pure soul with his bags]
    alone, "racing his Alfa Romeo"
        in sunlight so heavenly it cannot be put
        into rhymes not elegiac
        —the finest sun we've had all year—
as in a film by Godard:
        under a sun bleeding motionless
        unique,
    the canal of the port of Fiumicino
    —a motorboat returning unnoticed
    —Neapolitan sailors covered in woolen rags
    —a car accident, a few onlookers gathered round . . .

—as in a film by Godard—romanticism
rediscovered in a time
of neocapitalist cynicism and cruelty—
behind the wheel
along the road from Fiumicino—
there's the castle (what sweet
mystery for the French scriptwriter,
this papal colossus in the troubled, endless,
age-old sun, with its battlements
over hedges and plantation rows in an ugly landscape
of peasant serfs) . . .

—I am like a cat burnt alive,
crushed by a tractor-trailer's wheels,
hung by boys from a fig tree,

ma ancora almeno con sei
delle sue sette vite,
come un serpe ridotto a poltiglia di sangue
un'anguilla mezza mangiata

—le guance cave sotto gli occhi abbattuti,
i capelli orrendamente diradati sul cranio
le braccia dimagrite come quelle di un bambino
—un gatto che non crepa, Belmondo
che «al volante della sua Alfa Romeo»
nella logica del montaggio narcisistico
si stacco dal tempo, e v'inserisce
Se stesso:
in immagini che nulla hanno a che fare
con la noia delle ore in fila. . .
col lento risplendere a morte del pomeriggio. . .

La morte non è
nel non poter comunicare
ma nel non poter più essere compresi.

E questo bestione papalino, non privo
di grazia—il ricordo
delle rustiche concessioni padronali,
innocenti, in fondo, com'erano innocenti
le rassegnazioni dei servi—
nel sole che fu,
nei secoli,
per migliaia di meriggi,
qui, il solo ospite,

questo bestione papalino, merlato
accucciato tra pioppeti di maremma,
campi di cocomeri, argini,

questo bestione papalino blindato
da contrafforti del dolce color arancio
di Roma, screpolati
come costruzioni di etruschi o romani,

sta per non poter più essere compreso.

but with eight
of its nine lives still left,
like a snake reduced to a bloody pulp,
a half-eaten eel

—cheeks hollow under despondent eyes,
hair thinning frightfully at the crown,
arms now skinny as a child's
—a cat that won't croak, Belmondo
"at the wheel of his Alfa Romeo"
who in the narcissistic logic of the montage
steps outside of time and inserts
Himself
in images that have nothing do
with the boredom of hours on end . . .
or the afternoon's slow resplendence unto death . . .

Death lies not
in not being able to communicate
but in no longer being understood.

And that papal colossus, not without
grace—memory
of land concessions from the nobles,
innocent gifts, as innocent
as the serfs' submission—
in a sun that
over centuries
over thousands of noontides
was the only guest here,

that papal colossus, huddling
with its battlements amid coastal groves
of poplar, watermelon patches, dykes,

that papal colossus sheathed
in buttresses the sweet orange color
of Rome, crumbling
like a Roman or Etruscan structure,

is about to be no longer understood.

II

(*Senza dissolvenza, a stacco netto, mi rappresento in un atto —
privo di precedenti storici — di «industria culturale».*)

Io volontariamente martirizzato. . . e,
lei di fronte, sul divano:
campo e controcampo, a rapidi flash,
«Lei — so che pensa, guardandomi,
   in più domestica-italica M.F.
   sempre alla Godard — lei, specie di Tennessee!»,
il cobra col golfino di lana
      (col cobra subordinato
         che screma in silenzio magnesio).
   Poi forte: «Mi dice che cosa sta scrivendo?»

«Versi, versi, scrivo! versi!
   (maledetta cretina,
   versi che lei non capisce priva com'è
   di cognizioni metriche! Versi!)
   versi NON PIÙ IN TERZINE!

      Capisce?
   Questo è quello che importa: non più in terzine!
   Sono tornato tout court al magma!
   Il Neo-capitalismo ha vinto, sono
   sul marciapiede
         come poeta, ah [singhiozzo]
         e come cittadino [altro singhiozzo].»

E il cobro con il biro:
«Il titolo della Sua opera?» «Non so. . .
   [Egli parla ora sommesso come intimidito, rivestendo
   la parte che il colloquio, accettato, gli impone di
   fare: come sta poco
   a stingere
   la sua grinta
   in un muso di mammarolo condannato a morte]
   — forse. . . "La Persecuzione"
         o. . . "Una nuova preistoria" (o Preisroria)

II

(In a jump-cut, without fade-in, I show myself enacting—
with no historical precedent—the "culture industry.")

I, the voluntary martyr . . . and
she across from me, on the couch:
shot/reverse shot, in quick flashes,
"You"—I know what she's thinking, looking at me—
then a homegrown Italian MS,
also à la Godard—"You're a kind of Tennessee!"
this cobra in her little wool sweater
          (with a subordinate cobra,
            slithering in magnesium silence).
Then aloud: "Could you tell me what you're writing now?"

"Verse! I write verse! Verse!
(goddamned idiot,
verse you would never understand, since
you know nothing about metrics! Verse!)
verse NO LONGER IN TERCETS!

          Understand?
That's the important part: no longer in tercets!
I've gone straight back to the magma!
Neocapitalism has won, and I'm
out on the street
          as poet, ah [sob]
            and as citizen [another sob]."

The cobra with the ballpoint:
"And the title of your work?" "I don't know . . .
[He's speaking softly now, as though intimidated, playing
the part the interview, which he accepted, has forced him
to play: how little it takes
to shrink
his snarl
to the sulk of a mama's boy on death row]
—maybe . . . 'Persecution'
          or . . . 'A New Prehistory' (or just 'Prehistory')

335 *

o. . .
[E qui si inalbera, riacquista
la dignità dell'odio civile]
    "Monologo sugli Ebrei". . .»
        [Casca
il discorso come la debolezza dell'arsi
dell'ottonario scombinato: magmatico!]
«E di che parla?»
«Beh, della mia. . . della Sua, morte.
Non è nel non comunicare, [la morte]
ma nel non essere compresi. . .

    (Se lo sapesse, il cobra
    ch'è una fiacca pensata
      fatta tornando da Fiumicino!)
Sono quasi tutte liriche, la cui composizione
di tempo e luogo
consiste, strano!, in una corsa in automobile. . .
meditazioni dai sessanta ai centoventi all'ora. . .
con veloci panoramiche, e carrellate
a seguire o a precedere
su significativi monumenti, o gruppi
di persone, spronanti
a un oggettivo amore. . . di cittadino
(o utente della strada). . .»
«Ah, ah—[è la cobra con la biro che ride]—e. . .
chi è che *non comprende?*»
«Coloro che non ci appartengono più.»

    III

Coloro che non ci appartengono più!
Trascinati da un nuovo soffio della storia
ad altre vite, con le loro innocenti gioventù!

Ricordo che fu. . . per un amore
che m'invadeva gli occhi castani e gli onesti calzoni,
la casa e la campagna, il sole del mattino e il sole

or . . .
[and here he bristles, recovering
the dignity of civic hatred]
        'Monologue on the Jews' . . ."
                        [The conversation
 sags like a languid arsis
 in a muddled octosyllable: magmatic!]
"And what's it about?"
"Well, its about my . . . I mean your, death.
 Which lies not in not being able to communicate [death],
 but in not being understood . . .

        (If the cobra only knew that this
        is just some flimsy thought that came to me
        on the way back from Fiumicino!)
 They're almost all lyric poems whose arrangement
 of time and place
 derives—how strange!—from a ride in a car . . .
 meditations at forty to seventy miles per hour . . .
 with quick pans and tracking shots
 —before and after—
 of important monuments or groups
 of people, spurring
 an objective love . . . in the citizen
 (or motorist) . . ."
"Ha, ha"—[it's the cobress with the ballpoint laughing]—"and
 who is it that *doesn't understand*?"
"Those who no longer belong to us."

        III

Those who no longer belong to us!
Swept away to other lives, along with their
innocent youth, by a new breath of history!

I remember it was . . . for a love
that invaded my brown eyes and respectable
trousers, my house and country, the morning

della sera. . . nei sabati buoni
del Friuli, nelle. . . Domeniche. . . Ah!, non posso
neanche pronunciare questa parola delle passioni

vergini, della mia morte (vista in un fosso
secco formicolante di primule,
tra filari tramortiti dall'oro, a ridosso

di casolari scuri contro un azzurro sublime).

Ricordo che in quell'amore mostruoso
giungevo a gridare di dolore
per le domeniche quando dovrà splendere

«sopra i figli dei figli, il sole!»

Piangevo, nel lettuccio di Casarsa,
nella camera che sapeva di orina e bucato
in quelle domeniche che splendevano a morte. . .

Lacrime incredibili! Non solo
per quello che perdevo, in quel momento
di struggente immobilità dello splendore,

ma per quello che avrei perso! Quando
nuove gioventù—che non potevo neanche pensare,
così uguali a quelle che ora si vestivano

di calzettoni bianchi e di giubbetti inglesi,
col fiore all'occhiello—o di stoffe
scure, per nozze, trattate con figliale gentilezza,

—avrebbero popolato la Casarsa delle vite future,
immutata, coi suoi sassi, e il suo sole
che la copriva di moribonda acqua d'oro. . .

Per un impeto epilettico di dolore
omicida, protestavo
come un condannato all'ergastolo, chiudendomi
in camera,

and evening sun . . . on fine Saturdays
in the Friuli and . . . on Sundays . . . Ah! I can't
even utter that word of virgin passions,

that word of my death (glimpsed in a dry ditch
teeming with primroses
between tree rows numbed by the gold, behind

darkened cottages against a sublime blue sky).

I remember how, in that monstrous love,
I would actually howl in sorrow
for the Sundays when the sun shall shine

"upon the sons of sons!"

I would weep in my cot in Casarsa,
in a room that smelled of urine and laundry
on Sundays resplendent unto death . . .

Incredible tears! not only
for what I was losing at that moment
of splendor in heartrending stillness,

but for what I had yet to lose! When new
youths—whom I couldn't even imagine,
so like the ones now dressed

in thick white socks and English blazers,
flower in the lapel, or in dark
fabrics for weddings, prepared with filial care—

would people Casarsa with future lives
but leave it unchanged, with its stones and
its sun covering everything in dying golden water . . . .

In an epileptic fit of murderous
pain, I protested
like one imprisoned for life, shutting myself up
in my room

senza che del resto nessuno lo sapesse,
a urlare, con la bocca
tappata dalle coperte annerite
per le bruciature del ferro da stiro,
le care coperte di famiglia,
su cui covavo i fiori della mia gioventù.

E un dopopranzo, o una sera, urlando
sono corso,
per le strade della domenica, dopo la partita,
al cimitero vecchio, là dietro la ferrovia,
a compiere, e a ripetere, fino al sangue
l'atto più dolce della vita,
io solo, sopra il mucchietto di terra
di due o tre tombe
di soldati italiani o tedeschi
senza nome sulle croci di assi
—sepolti lì dal tempo dell'altra guerra.

E la notte, poi, tra le secche lacrime i corpi
sanguinanti di quei poveri ignoti
vestiti di panni grigioverdi

vennero in grappolo sopra il mio letto
dove dormivo nudo e svuotato,
a sporcarmi di sangue, fino all'aurora.

Avevo vent'anni, neanche—diciotto,
diciannove... ed era già passato un secolo
dacché ero vivo, una intera vita

consumata al dolore dell'idea
che non avrei mai potuto dare il mio amore
se non alla mia mano, o all'erba dei fossi,

o magari al terriccio di una tomba incustodita...
Vent'anni, e, con la sua storia umana, e il suo ciclo
di poesia, era conclusa una vita.

—without anyone's knowing it—
and screaming, mouth
stuffed with blankets
blackened with iron burns,
those precious family blankets
on which I nursed the flowers of my youth.

And one afternoon or evening, I ran
screaming
down the Sunday streets, after the game,
to the old cemetery behind the railroad tracks,
to perform and repeat, until I bled,
the sweetest act there is in life,
myself alone, atop a little mound of earth,
some two or three graves
of Italian or German soldiers
nameless on the wooden crosses,
buried there in the previous war.

Then that night, between dry tears
the bloody bodies of those wretched strangers
dressed in olive drab

came in swarms over my bed,
where I slept naked and drained,
to soil me with blood until dawn.

I was twenty years old, not even, eighteen,
nineteen . . . and already a century had passed
since I was alive—an entire life

consumed in sorrow at the thought
that I could only ever give my love
to my hand, or to the grass in the ditch

or the mound of earth of an untended grave . . .
Twenty years old, and a life, with its human
history, its cycle of poetry, was already over.

IV

(*Ripresa dell'intervista, e confuse spiegazioni sulla funzione
del marxismo, ecc.*)

(Ah, non è che una visita al mondo, la mia!)

Ma ritorniamo alla realtà.

[Lei è qui, con la faccia visibilmente preoccupata ma alleggerita
dalla buona educazione, che aspetta, nell'inquadratura «grigia»,
secondo la buona regola del classicismo francese. Un Léger.]

«Secondo lei allora—fa, reticente,
    mordicchiando il biro—qual'è
la funzione del marxista?» E si accinge a notare.

«Con. . . delicatezza da batteriologo. . . direi [balbetto,
        preso da impeti di morte]
    spostare masse da eserciti napoleonici, staliniani. . .
        con miliardi di annessi. . .
    in modo che. . .
        la massa che si dice conservatrice
        [del Passato] lo perda:
        la massa rivoluzionaria, lo acquisti
        riedificandolo nell'atto di vincerlo. . .
        È per l'Istinto di Conservazione
        che sono comunista!
            Uno spostamento
    da cui dipende vita e morte: nei secoli dei secoli.
    Farlo pian piano, come quando
        un capitano del genio svita
    la sicura di una bomba inesplosa, e,
per un attimo, può restare al mondo
(coi suoi moderni caseggiati, intorno al sole)
        o esserne cancellato per sempre:

        una sproporzione inconcepibile
        tra i due corni!

IV

(*Resumption of interview, with some confused explanations
on the role of Marxism, etc.*)

(Ah, for me this time on earth is but a visit!)

But let's get back to reality.

[She's here, face visibly worried though tempered by good breeding,
waiting on the "gray set," in keeping with the rules of good French
Classicism. A Léger.]

  "In your opinion," she asks reticently,
  nibbling her ballpoint, "what is the role
  of the Marxist?" And she gets ready to take notes.

  "With . . . the discretion of a bacteriologist . . . I'd say [I stammer,
      overcome by death wishes]
    it's to shift human masses as great as Napoleon's or Stalin's armies . . .
      with billions of adjuncts . . .
  in such a way that . . .
      the mass that claims to preserve
      [the Past] will lose it,
      and the revolutionary mass will gain it,
      rebuilding it in the act of winning it . . .
      It's the Instinct of Preservation
      that makes me a Communist!
         This shift
    is a matter of life and death, down through the centuries.
    To be made ever so gently, like the captain
      of the army corps of engineers, who,
    when unscrewing the safety on an unexploded bomb,
could either, in that instant, remain alive on earth
(with its modern buildings round the sun)
      or be struck forever from its surface:

      the inconceivable disproportion
      between the horns of the dilemma!

Uno spostamento
da fare piano piano, tirando il collo,
        chinandosi, raggricciandosi sul ventre,
        mordendosi le labbra o stringendo gli occhi
                come un giocatore di bocce
    che, dimenandosi, cerca di dominare
        il corso del suo tiro, di rettificarlo
                verso una soluzione
        che imposterà la vita nei secoli.»

        V

La vita nei secoli. . .
A questo alludeva
dunque — ieri sera. . .
rattrappito nel breve segmento del suo gemito —
quel treno lontano. . .

Quel treno che gemeva
sconsolato, come stupito di esistere,
(e, insieme, rassegnato — perché ogni atto
della vita è un segmento già segnato in una linea
che è la vita stessa, chiara solo nel sogno)

gemeva quel treno, e l'atto del gemere
— impensabilmente lontano, oltre le Appie
e i Centocelle del mondo —
si univa a un altro atto: unione casuale,
mostruosa, cervellotica
e tanto privata
che solo oltre la linea dei miei occhi
magari chiusi, è possibile averne conoscenza. . .

Atto d'amore, il mio. Ma perso nella miseria
di un corpo concesso per miracolo,
nella fatica del nascondersi, nell'ansare
lungo una cupa strada ferrata, nel pestare il fango
in una campagna coltivata da giganti. . .

A shift
to be made very gently, neck craned,
        bending forward, hunching over,
        biting one's lip or squinting hard
                like a bocce player
who with body English tries to control
        the path of his toss, to coax it
                towards a solution
        that will determine life through the centuries."

V

Life through the centuries . . .
So that was
the meaning—compressed
in its brief segment of wailing—
of that faraway train last night . . .

The train wailed
disconsolate, as though surprised to exist
(and also resigned—for every act
in life is a segment, already marked, in the line
that is life itself, clear only in dream)

and as the train wailed—inconceivably far away,
beyond the Appias and the Centocelles of the world—
that act of wailing
joined with another act: a chance union,
monstrous, delirious
and so private
that only beyond my line of vision, perhaps
even with eyes closed, could I ever imagine it . . . .

The act of love. My own. But lost in the misery
of a body miraculously granted,
lost in the effort to hide itself, in the panting
by a gloomy railroad track, trudging through the mud
in a countryside farmed by giants . . . .

La vita nei secoli . . .
come una stella cadente
oltre il cielo dei giganteschi ruderi,
oltre le proprietà dei Caetani o dei Torlonia,
oltre le Tuscolane e le Capannelle del mondo —
quel gemito meccanico diceva:
la vita nei secoli. . .

E i miei sensi erano lì ad ascoltarlo.

Accarezzavo una testa arruffata e polverosa,
del color biondo che bisogna avere nella vita,
del disegno che vuole il destino,
e un corpo di cavallino agile e tenero
con la ruvida tela dei vestiti che sanno di madre:
compivo un atto d'amore,
ma i miei sensi stavano ad ascoltare:

la vita nei secoli. . .

Poi la testa bionda del destino disparve
da un pertugio,
nel pertugio fu il cielo bianco della notte,
finché, contro quel lembo di cielo, apparve
un'altra pettinatura, un'altra nuca,
nera, forse, o castana: e io
nella grotta perduta nel cuore dei possessi
dei Caetani o i Torlonia
tra i ruderi construiti da giganti seicenteschi
in giorni immensi di carnevale, io
ero coi sensi ad ascoltare. . .

la vita nei secoli. . .

Più volte nel pertugio contro il biancore
della notte che si perdeva
oltre le Casiline del mondo,
sparì e riapparve la testa del destino,
con la dolcezza ora della madre meridionale
ora del padre alcolizzato, sempre la stessa

Life through the centuries . . .
like a falling star
beyond the sky of gigantic ruins,
beyond the domains of the Caetani and the Torlonia,
beyond the Tuscolanas and the Capannelles of the world—
that mechanical wail said:
life through the centuries . . .

And my senses were there to listen.

I was stroking a tousled, dusty head,
blond as life demands,
shaped as destiny wants,
and a coltlike body, agile and tender
in rough clothing that told of a mother:
I was performing an act of love,
but my senses kept listening:

life through the centuries . . . .

Then destiny's blonde head disappeared
through a hole,
and in the hole was the white sky of night,
until against that patch of sky appeared
another head of hair, another nape,
black, perhaps, or chestnut: and I
in a cave lost deep in the heart
of the Caetani or Torlonia domains,
among ruins built by seventeenth-century giants
on vast days of Carnival, I
with my senses kept listening . . .

life through the centuries . . .

Then in the hole, against the whiteness
of the night that stretched beyond
the Casilinas of the world, destiny's
head appeared and disappeared several times,
with the sweetness of a Southern mother
and then a drunken father, still the same

testolina arruffata e polverosa, o già
composta nella vanità di una giovinezza popolare:
e io,
ero coi sensi ad ascoltare

la voce di un altro amore
—la vita nei secoli—
che si alzava purissima nel cielo.

   VI

(*Una vittoria fascista*)

   Mi guarda con pena.
«E. . . allora lei. . .—[sorriso mondano, goloso,
con coscienza della golosità e cattivante
ostentazione—occhi e denti fiammanti—
di un leggero titubante disprezzo infantile
verso di sé]—allora lei, è molto infelice!»

«Eh (devo ammetterlo)
sono in uno stato di confusione, signorina.

Rileggendo il mio libro dattiloscritto
di poesia (questo, di cui parliamo)
ho avuto la visione. . . oh, magari fosse
solo di un caos di contraddizioni—le rassicuranti
contraddizioni. . . No, è la visione
di un'anima confusa. . .

Ogni falso sentimento
produce la sicurezza assoluta di averlo.
Il mio falso sentimento era quello. . .
della salute. Strano! dicendolo a lei
—incomprensiva per definizione,
con quel viso di bambola senza labbra—
verifico ora con chiarezza clinica
il fatto
di non aver mai avuto, io, alcuna chiarezza.
È vero che alle volte può bastare,

little head, tousled and dusty, or perhaps already
groomed as the vanity of common youth would have it,
while I
with my senses kept listening

to the voice of another love
— life through the centuries —
rising ever so pure in the sky.

VI

(A *fascist victory*)

She looks at me sadly.
"And so . . . you . . . — [a worldly, greedy smile,
conscious of its greed and the charming
ostentation — eyes and teeth flashing —
of her slightly hesitant and childish
self-deprecation] — you are very unhappy!"

"Yeah (I have to admit),
I'm in a state of confusion, Miss.

Rereading the typscript of my book
of poems (this one, which we're talking about),
what I saw there was — ah, if only it was
just a jumble of contradictions, reassuring
contradictions . . . No, what I saw was
a soul in confusion . . .

Every mistaken feeling
makes you absolutely certain of that feeling.
Mine was to think I was . . .
healthy. Strange! Telling you this
— you who by definition, with that lipless, doll-like
face of yours, cannot understand
— I now realize, with clinical clarity,
the fact
that I, myself, have never been clear at all.
It's true that sometimes, to be healthy

per essere sani (e chiari)
credere di esserlo... Tuttavia
(scriva, scriva!) la mia confusione
attuale è la conseguenza
di una vittoria fascista.

    [nuovi, incontrollati, fedeli
     impeti di morte]

Una piccola, secondaria vittoria.
Facile, poi. Io ero solo:
con le mie ossa, una timida madre
spaventata, e la mia volontà.

L'obbiettivo era umiliare un umiliato.
Devo dirle che ci sono riusciti,
e senza neanche molta fatica. Forse
se avessero saputo che era così semplice
si sarebbero scomodati di meno, e in meno!

(Ahi, parlo, vede, con un plurale generico: Essi!
con l'amore ammiccante del matto verso il proprio male.)

I risultati di questa vittoria, poi,
anch'essi, contano ben poco: una firma
autorevole in meno negli appelli di pace.
Beh, *a parte objecti*, non è molto.
A *parte subjecti*... Ma lasciamo stare:
ho descritto fin troppo,
e mai oralmente,
i miei dolori di verme pestato
che erige la sua testina e si dibatte
con ingenuità ripugnante, ecc.

Una vittoria fascista!
Scriva, scriva: sappiano (*essi!*) che lo so:

con la coscienza di un uccello ferito
che mitemente morendo non perdona.»

(and clear), it's enough
to think it . . . However
(write! write!) my present
confusion is the result
of a Fascist victory
        [new, uncontrollable, unfailing
        death wishes]

A small, minor victory.
And easy, too. I was alone:
with my bones, a shy, frightened
mother, and my will.

The point was to humiliate a humiliated man.
I must say they succeeded,
and without even much effort. Maybe
if they'd known it would be so simple,
they would have gone to less trouble, and less of them at that!

(Ah, I'm using a generic plural, you see: Them!
with the madman's complicitous love of his illness.)

The upshot of this victory, in any case,
matters little: one less signature
of importance in the pleas for peace.
Well, *a parte objecti*, it's not much.
A *parte subjecti* . . . never mind.
I've already spoken too much,
aloud as never before,
about my pain as a crushed worm
raising its little head and struggling
with repugnant naiveté, etc.

A Fascist victory!
Write, write. Let them know (*them!*) that I know:

conscious as an injured bird
that gently dies but never forgives."

VII

Non perdona!

C'era un'anima, tra quelle che ancora
dovevano scendere nella vita
—tante, e tutte uguali, povere anime—
un'anima, in cui nella luce degli occhi castani,
nel modesto ciuffo pettinato da un'idea materna
della bellezza maschile,
ardeva il desiderio di morire.

La vide subito, colui
che non perdona.

La prese, la chiamò vicino a sé,
e, come un artigiano,
lassù nei mondi che precedono la vita,
le impose le mani sul capo
e pronunciò la maledizione.

Era un'anima candida e pulita,
come un ragazzetto alla prima comunione,
saggio della saggezza dei suoi dieci anni,
vestito di bianco, di una stoffa
scelta dall'idea materna della grazia maschile,
con negli occhi tiepidi il desiderio di morire.

Ah, la vide subito, colui
che non perdona.

Vide l'infinita capacità di obbedire
e l'infinita capacità di ribellarsi:
la chiamò a sé, e operò su lei
—che lo guardava fiduciosa
come un agnello guarda il suo giusto carnefice—
la consacrazione a rovescio, mentre
nel suo sguardo cadeva
la luce, e saliva un'ombra di pietà.

VII

Never forgives!

There was once a soul, among those
still waiting to descend into life
— so many, poor souls, and all the same —
a soul in the light of whose brown eyes
and in whose modest forelock, combed by a mother's idea
of masculine beauty,
there burned a longing for death.

He saw it at once, did the one
who never forgives.

He took this soul, called it to his side
and like a craftsman,
up there in the worlds that precede life,
laid his hands on its head
and uttered the curse.

The soul was clean and innocent,
like a boy at First Communion,
wise with the wisdom of ten years of life,
dressed in white, in a fabric chosen
by a mother's idea of masculine grace,
a longing for death in his warm eyes.

Ah, he saw it at once, did
the one who never forgives.

He spotted his endless capacity for obedience,
and his endless capacity for rebellion,
called him over and performed
— as he looked on him trustfully
the way a lamb looks at its righteous butcher —
a reverse ordination, as
the light went out in his eyes,
and a shadow of pity rose up in its place.

«Tu scenderai nel mondo,
e sarai candido e gentile, equilibrato e fedele,
avrai un'infinita capacità di obbedire
e un'infinita capacità di ribellarti.
Sarai puro.
Perciò ti maledico.»

Vedo ancora il suo sguardo
pieno di pietà — e del leggero orrore
che si prova per colui che la incute,
— lo sguardo con cui si segue
chi va, senza saperlo, a morire,
e, per una necessità che domina chi sa e chi non sa,
non gli si dice nulla —
vedo ancora il suo sguardo,
mentre mi allontanavo
— dall'Eternità — verso la mia culla.

VIII

*(Conclusione funerea: con tavola sinottica — ad uso
della facitrice del «pezzo» — della mia carriera di poeta, e uno
sguardo profetico al mare dei futuri millenni.)*

«Venni al mondo al tempo
dell'Analogica.
Operai
in quel campo, da apprendista.
Poi ci fu la Resistenza
e io
lottai con le armi della poesia.
Restaurai la Logica, e fui
un poeta civile.
Ora è il tempo
della Psicagogica.
Posso scrivere solo profetando
nel rapimento della Musica
per eccesso di seme o di pietà.»

"You shall descend into the world,
  be innocent and kind, faithful and fair;
  you shall have an endless capacity for obedience,
  and an endless capacity for rebellion.
  You shall be pure.
  For this I curse you."

I still see those eyes of his,
full of pity—and the faint horror
one feels at those who arouse it—
the eyes of someone watching
another on his way, unknowing, to die,
and who, out of some need that grips those who know and those who don't,
says nothing to him—
I still see those eyes of his
as I headed off
—away from Eternity—toward my cradle.

VIII

*(Funereal conclusion, with synoptic table—for use
by the lady creating the "piece"—of my career as a poet and
a prophetic look at the sea of future millennia.)*

"I entered the world in the age
of Analogics.
I worked
as an apprentice in the field.
Then came the Resistance
and I
fought with the weapons of poetry,
I reinstated Logic and became
a civic poet.
Now it's the age
of Psychagogics.
I can only write in prophecies
rapt by Music,
in an excess of semen or pity."

*

«Se ora l'Analogica sopravvive
e la Logica è passata di moda
(e io con lei:
non ho più richiesta di poesia),
la Psicagogica
c'è
(ad onta della Demagogia
sempre più padrona
della situazione).
È così
che io posso scrivere Temi e Treni
e anche Profezie;
da poeta civile, ah sì, sempre!»

*

«Quanto al futuro, ascolti:
i suoi figli fascisti
veleggeranno
verso i mondi della Nuova Preistoria.
Io me ne starò là,
qual è colui che suo dannaggio sogna
sulle rive del mare
in cui ricomincia la vita.
Solo, o quasi, sul vecchio litorale
tra ruderi di antiche civiltà,
Ravenna
Ostia, o Bombay — è uguale —
con Dei che si scrostano, problemi vecchi
— quale la lotta di classe —
che
si dissolvono. . .
Come un partigiano
morto prima del maggio del '45,
comincerò piano piano a decompormi,
nella luce straziante di quel mare,
poeta e cittadino dimenticato.»

*

"Though Analogics survive
and Logic has gone out of fashion
(I to her, aside:
nobody asks me for poetry anymore),
Psychagogics
remain
(in spite of Demagogy,
increasingly master
of the situation).
That is how
I can write Themes and Threnodies
and Prophecies too;
as a civic poet, oh yes, always!"

*

"As for the future, listen:
your Fascist sons
will sail on
towards the worlds of the New Prehistory.
I shall stay behind,
as one who dreams his own downfall
on seashores
where life begins anew.
Alone, or almost, on an old coastline
among ruins of ancient civilizations,
Ravenna
Ostia or Bombay—it makes no difference—
with decrepit Gods, and old problems
—such as the class struggle—
dissolving . . .
Like a Resistance fighter
dead before May '45,
I shall begin to decompose
ever so slowly
in the harrowing light of this sea,
a poet and citizen forgotten."

IX

(*Clausola*)

«Dio mio, ma allora cos'ha
   lei all'attivo? . . .»
      «Io? — [un balbettio, nefando
         non ho preso l'optalidon, mi trema la voce
            di ragazzo malato] —
      Io? Una disperata vitalità.»

Marilyn

Del mondo antico e del mondo futuro
era rimasta solo la bellezza, e tu,
povera sorellina minore,
quella che corre dietro ai fratelli più grandi,
e ride e piange con loro, per imitarli,
e si mette addosso le loro sciarpette,
tocca non vista i loro libri, i loro coltellini,

tu sorellina più piccola,
quella bellezza l'avevi addosso umilmente,
e la tua anima di figlia di piccola gente,
non ha mai saputo di averla,
perché altrimenti non sarebbe stata bellezza.
Sparì, come un pulviscolo d'oro.

Il mondo te l'ha insegnata.
Così la tua bellezza divenne sua.

Dello stupido mondo antico
e del feroce mondo futuro
era rimasta una bellezza che non si vergognava
di alludere ai piccoli seni di sorellina,
al piccolo ventre così facilmente nudo.
E per questo era bellezza, la stessa
che hanno le dolci mendicanti di colore,

IX

(Coda)

"My God, then, what have you got
  to show for yourself? . . ."
    "Me? — [a stammer, treacherous —
      I forgot to take my Optalidon, my voice quakes
        like a sick boy's] —
Me? A desperate vitality."

Marilyn

Of the ancient world and the future world
all that remained was the beauty, and you,
poor little sister,
the one always running after your older brothers,
laughing and crying when they did, who liked
to wear their scarves and touch
their penknives and books when nobody was looking,

you, poor little sister,
daughter of simple people,
you wore that beauty humbly,
and in your simple soul
you never knew you had it,
or else it would not have been beauty.
Like fine gold dust it vanished.

The world taught it to you.
And thus your beauty became its own.

Of the stupid ancient world
and the ferocious future world
there remained a beauty that was not ashamed
to call attention to its small, kid-sisterly breasts,
its little belly so easily bared.
And that was why it was beauty, the same
you see in gentle black vagabonds

le zingare, le figlie dei commericanti
vincitrici ai concorsi a Miami o a Roma.
Sparì, come una colombella d'oro.

Il mondo te l'ha insegnata,
e così la tua bellezza non fu più bellezza.

Ma tu continuavi ad essere bambina,
sciocca come l'antichità, crudele come il futuro,
e fra te e la tua bellezza posseduta dal potere
si mise tutta la stupidità e la crudeltà del presente.
Te la portavi sempre dentro, come un sorriso tra le lacrime,
impudica per passività, indecente per obbedienza.
L'obbedienza richiede molte lacrime inghiottite.
Il darsi agli altri,
troppi allegri sguardi, che chiedono la loro pietà.
Sparì, come una Bianca ombra d'oro.

La tua bellezza sopravvissuta dal mondo antico,
richiesta dal mondo futuro, posseduta
dal mondo presente, divenne così un male.

Ora i fratelli maggiori finalmente si voltano,
smettono per un momento i loro maledetti giochi,
escono dalla loro inesorabile distrazione,
e si chiedono: «È possibile che Marilyn,
la piccola Marilyn ci abbia indicato la strada?»
Ora sei tu, la prima, tu sorella più piccola,
quella che non conta nulla, poverina, col suo sorriso,
sei tu la prima oltre le porte del mondo
abbandonato al suo destino di morte.

and gypsies, in the shopkeepers' daughters
who win beauty contests in Miami and Rome.
Like a small golden dove it vanished.

The world taught it to you,
and thus your beauty was no longer beauty.

But still you remained a little girl,
silly as antiquity, cruel as the future,
while all the stupidity and cruelty of the present
came between you and your beauty.
Passively immodest, obediently indecent,
you carried it always with you, like a smile behind the tears.
Obedience demands that you swallow many tears,
that you give yourself to others,
looking all too happy, asking for their pity.
Like a golden white shadow it vanished.

Thus surviving from the ancient world,
demanded by the future world, possessed
by the present world, your beauty became an affliction.

Now your older brothers finally turn around,
stop their dreadful games for a moment,
snap out of their inexorable distraction
and ask themselves: "Is it possible that Marilyn,
little Marilyn, has shown us the way?"
Now you're the first, little sister, you
who never mattered, poor thing, you with your smile,
you're the first outside the gates of a world
abandoned to a destiny of death.

Profezia

A Jean-Paul Sartre, che mi ha raccontato la storia di Alì dagli Occhi Azzurri.

Era nel mondo un figlio
e un giorno andò in Calabria:
era estate, ed erano
vuote le casupole,
nuove, a pandizucchero,
da fiabe di fate color
delle feci. Vuote.
Come porcili senza porci, nel centro di orti senza insalata, di campi
senza terra, di greti senza acqua. Coltivate dalla luna, le campagne.
Le spighe cresciute per bocche di scheletri. Il vento dallo Jonio
scuoteva paglia nera
come nei sogni profetici:
e la luna color delle feci
coltivava terreni
che mai l'estate amò.
Ed era nei tempi del figlio
che questo amore poteva
cominciare, e non cominciò.
Il figlio aveva degli occhi
di paglia bruciata, occhi
senza paura, e vide tutto
ciò che era male: nulla
sapeva dell'agricoltura,
delle riforme, della lotta
sindacale, degli Enti Benefattori,
lui. Ma aveva quegli occhi.

Prophecy

To Jean-Paul Sartre, who told me the story of Blue-Eyed Alì

In the world there was a son
and one day he went to Calabria.
It was summer, and
the little sugarcube houses,
new and straight from a tale
of fairies the color of feces,
were empty. Empty.
Like pigpens with no pigs, kitchen gardens with no lettuce, fields
with no earth, riverbanks with no water. Countrysides tilled by the moon.
Spikes of grain grown for the mouths of skeletons. The wind from the Ionian Sea
stirred up black straw
as in prophetic dreams:
and the moon the color of feces
tilled lands
the summer never loved.
It was in the time of the son
that this love could
begin, but it never did.
The son had eyes
of burnt straw, eyes
without fear, and saw all
that was evil: he knew
nothing about farming,
reforms, the union
struggle, Charitable Institutions.
But he had those eyes.

La tragica luna del pieno
sole, era là, a coltivare
quei cinquemila, quei ventimila
ettari sparsi di case di fate
del tempo della televisione,
porcili a pandizucchero, per
dignità imitata dal mondo padrone.
Ma non si può vivere là! Ah, per quanto ancora, l'operaio di Milano lotterà
con tanta grandezza per il suo salario? Gli occhi bruciati del figlio, nella
luna, tra gli ettari tragici, vedono ciò che non sa il lontano fratello
settentrionale. Era il tempo
quando una nuova cristianità
riduceva a penombra il mondo
del capitale: una storia finiva
in un crepuscolo in cui accadevano
i fatti, nel finire e nel nascere,
noti ed ignoti. Ma il figlio
tremava d'ira nel giorno
della sua storia: nel tempo
quando il contadino calabrese
sapeva tutto, dei concimi chimici,
della lotta sindacale, degli scherzi
degli Enti Benefattori, della
Demagogia dello Stato
e del Partito Comunista. . .

The tragic moon of the full
sun was there, tilling
those ten thousand, fifty thousand
acres dotted with fairy houses
of the television age,
sugar-cube pigpens copied
for dignity's sake from the bosses' world.
But it's unlivable there! Ah, how much longer will the Milanese worker fight
so grandly for his salary! The son's burnt eyes in the moonlight see
in those tragic acres what his distant Northern brother
does not know. It was a time
when a new Christianity
was consigning the world of capital
to the shadows: one history was ending
in a twilight in which events
known and unknown, arising and ending,
came to pass. But the son
trembled with wrath on the day
of his story—at a time
when the Calabrian peasant
knew all about chemical fertilizer,
the union struggle, the jokes
of the Charitable Institutions,
the Demagogy of the State
and of the Communist Party . . .

... e così aveva abbandonato
le sue casupole nuove
come porcili senza porci,
su radure color delle feci,
sotto montagnole rotonde
in vista dello Jonio profetico.
Tre millenni svanirono
non tre secoli, non tre anni, e si sentiva di nuovo nell'aria malarica
l'attesa dei coloni greci. Ah, per quanto ancora, operaio di Milano,
lotterai solo per il salario? Non lo vedi come questi qui ti venerano?
Quasi come un padrone.
Ti porterebbero su
dalla loro antica regione,
frutti e animali, i loro
feticci oscuri, a deporli
con l'orgoglio del rito
nelle tue stanzette novecento,
tra frigorifero e televisione,
attratti dalla tua divinità,
Tu, delle Commissioni Interne,
tu della CGIL, Divinità alleata,
nel meraviglioso sole del Nord.

. . . and so he abandoned
his new little houses
like pigpens with no pigs
in clearings the color of feces,
under round little mountains
with a view of the prophetic Ionian.
Three millennia vanished,
not three centuries, not three years, and in the malarial air one felt again
the expectations of the Greek settlers. Ah, how much longer, Milanese worker,
will you fight for your salary? Can't you see how these people worship you?
Almost like a boss.
From their ancient regions
they brought you
fruits and animals, their
obscure fetishes, and lay
them down with ritual pride
in your little twentieth-century rooms
between the refrigerator and television,
attracted by your divinity,
You of the Internal Committees,
you of the CGIL, ally and Deity
in the wondrous sun of the North.

Nella loro Terra di razze
diverse, la luna coltiva
una campagna che tu
gli hai procurata inutilmente.
Nella loro Terra di Bestie
Famigliari, la luna
è maestra d'anime che tu
hai modernizzato inutilmente. Ah, ma il figlio sa: la grazia del sapere
è un vento che cambia corso, nel cielo. Soffia ora forse dall'Africa
e tu ascolta ciò che per grazia il figlio sa. (Se egli non sorride
è perché la speranza per lui
non fu luce ma razionalità.
E la luce del sentimento
dell'Africa, che d'improvviso
spazza le Calabrie, sia un segno
senza significato, valevole
per i tempi futuri!) Ecco:
tu smetterai di lottare
per il salario e armerai
la mano dei Calabresi.

In their Land of different
races, the moon tills
a countryside you
pointlessly procured for them.
In their Land of Household
Beasts, the moon
is mistress of souls that you
have pointlessly modernized. Ah, but the son knows: the grace of knowledge
is a wind changing course in the sky. Now it blows perhaps from Africa
and you listen to what the son knows by grace. (If he doesn't smile
that is because hope for him
was not light but rationality.
And the light of the feeling
of Africa, which is suddenly
sweeping over Calabria, is a sign
without meaning, valid
for future ages!) So:
you shall stop fighting
for your salary and
arm the Calabrians.

Alì dagli Occhi Azzurri
uno dei tanti figli di figli,
scenderà da Algeri, su navi
a vela e a remi. Saranno
con lui migliaia di uomini
coi corpicini e gli occhi
di poveri cani dei padri
sulle barche varate nei Regni della Fame. Porteranno con sé i bambini,
e il pane e il formaggio, nelle carte gialle del Lunedì di Pasqua.
Porteranno le nonne e gli asini, sulle triremi rubate ai porti coloniali.
Sbarcheranno a Crotone o a Palmi,
a milioni, vestiti di stracci
asiatici, e di camice americane.
Subito i Calabresi diranno,
come maladrini a maladrini:
«Ecco i vecchi fratelli,
coi figli e il pane e formaggio!»
Da Crotone o Palmi saliranno
a Napoli, e da lì a Barcellona,
a Salonicco e a Marsiglia,
nelle Città della Malavita.
Anime e angeli, topi e pidocchi,
col germe della Storia Antica,
voleranno davanti alle willaye.

Blue-eyed Alì,
one of many sons of sons,
shall descend from Algiers
on sailboats and rowboats. With him
shall be thousands of men
with tiny bodies and the eyes
of wretched dogs of the fathers
on boats launched in the Realms of Hunger. With them they shall bring little children,
and bread and cheese wrapped in the yellow paper of Easter Monday.
They shall bring their grandmothers and donkeys, on triremes stolen in colonial ports.
They shall land at Crotone or Palmi
by the millions, dressed in Asian
rags and American shirts.
The Calabrians shall say at once,
as ruffians to ruffians:
"Here are our long-lost brothers,
with their children and bread and cheese!"
From Crotone or Palmi they'll go up
to Naples, and from there to Barcelona,
Salonika, and Marseille,
to the Cities of Crime.
Souls and angels, mice and lice
with the seed of Ancient History,
they shall fly ahead of the *willayes*.

Essi sempre umili
essi sempre deboli
essi sempre timidi
essi sempre infimi
essi sempre colpevoli
essi sempre sudditi
essi sempre piccoli,
essi che non vollero mai sapere, essi che ebbero occhi solo per implorare,
essi che vissero come assassini sotto terra, essi che vissero come banditi
in fondo al mare, essi che vissero come pazzi in mezzo al cielo,
essi che si costruirono
leggi fuori dalla legge,
essi che si adattarono
a un mondo sotto il mondo
essi che credettero
in un Dio servo di Dio,
essi che cantarono
ai massacri dei re,
essi che ballarono
alle guerre borghesi,
essi che pregarono
alle lotte operaie. . .

They forever humble
they forever weak
they forever bashful
they forever lowly
they forever guilty
they forever subjects
they forever small,
they who never wanted to know, they who only had eyes to implore,
they who lived like assassins underground, they who lived like bandits
at the bottom of the sea, they who lived like madmen in the middle of the sky,
they who created their own
laws outside the law,
they who adapted
to a world under the world,
they who believed
in a God who is God's servant,
they who sang
at the massacres of kings,
they who danced
in the bourgeois wars
they who prayed
to the workers' struggles . . .

. . . deponendo l'onestà
delle religioni contadine,
dimenticando l'onore
della malavita,
tradendo il candore
dei popoli barbari,
dietro ai loro Alì
dagli Occhi Azzurri—usciranno da sotto la terra per rapinare—
saliranno dal fondo del mare per uccidere,—scenderanno dall'alto del cielo
per espropriare—e per insegnare ai compagni operai la gioia della vita—
per insegnare ai borghesi
la gioia della libertà—
per insegnare ai cristiani
la gioia della morte
—distruggeranno Roma
e sulle sue rovine
deporranno il germe
della Storia Antica.
Poi col Papa e ogni sacramento
andranno come zingari
su verso l'Ovest e il Nord
con le bandiere rosse
di Trotzky al vento. . .

. . . casting aside the honesty
of the peasant religions,
forgetting the honor
of the underworld,
betraying the purity
of the barbarous peoples;
behind their Blue-Eyed
Alì — they shall come out from under the earth to plunder — they shall rise up
from the bottom of the sea to murder — they shall descend from the heavens above
to expropriate — to teach their worker comrades the joy of life —
to teach the bourgeois
the joy of freedom —
to teach the Christians
the joy of death
— they shall destroy Rome
and on her ruins
they shall lay the seed
of Ancient History.
Then with the Pope and all the sacraments
they shall go like gypsies
up, to the West and North
with the red banners
of Trotsky in the wind . . .

VII
Da *Trasumanar e organizzar* /
From *Transhumanize and Organize*

Richiesta di lavoro

Poesia su ordinazione è ordigno.
Il costruttore di ordigni può produrne molti
(nient'altro procurandosi che stanchezza per il lavoro manuale).
L'oggetto può essere, talvolta, ironico:
l'ordigno lo è sempre.
Sono passati i tempi in cui, vorace economizzatore,
spendevo tutto, investendo i miei soldi (molti,
perché erano il mio seme: e io ero sempre in erezione)
nell'acquisto di aree di bassissimo valore
che sarebbero state valorizzate da lì a due tre secoli.
Ero tolemaico (essendo un ragazzo)
e contavo l'eternità per l'appunto, in secoli.
Consideravo la terra il centro del mondo;
la poesia il centro della terra.
Tutto ciò era bello e logico.
Del resto, che ragioni avevo di non credere
che tutti gli uomini non fossero come me?
Poi, invece, si sono rivelati tutti di me molto migliori;
e io son risultato essere, piuttosto, uomo di razza inferiore.
Ricambiai l'apprezzamento
e capii che non volevo più scrivere poesie. Ora, però,
ora che la vocazione è vacante
—ma non la vita, non la vita—
ora che l'ispirazione, se viene, versi non ne produce—
vi prego, sappiate che son qui pronto
a fornire poesie su ordinazione: ordigni.*

Preghiera su commissione

Ti scrive un figlio che frequenta
la millesima classe delle Elementari
Caro Dio,
è venuto un certo Signor Homais a trovarci
dicendo di essere Te:
gli abbiamo creduto:

*Anche esplosivi.

Job Request

Poetry made to order is a device.
The device maker can produce many
(only tiring himself out from the manual labor).
The subject can, at times, be ironic:
the device always is.
Gone are the days when I, a voracious economizer,
would spend everything, investing my money (a lot of it,
since semen was my currency, and I always had an erection)
buying up greatly undervalued sectors
that would turn a profit some two or three centuries hence.
I was Ptolemaic (being just a kid)
and counted eternity, you guessed it, in centuries.
I considered the earth the center of the universe,
and poetry the center of the world.
This was all very fine and logical.
Besides, what reason did I have not to believe
that everyone was not like me?
Then, in fact, they all proved to be far better than me,
and I turned out to belong to an inferior race.
I returned the compliment
and realized I no longer wanted to write poetry. Now, however,
now that the vocation is gone
— but not life, not life —
now that inspiration, when it comes, does not yield any verse —
please, I want you all to know that I'm here, ready
to provide poetry made to order: devices.*

Commissioned Prayer

A boy in elementary school,
in the Thousandth Grade, writes to you:
Dear God,
a certain Mr. Homais came to see us,
saying he was You.
We believed him,

*Even explosive ones. (Author's footnote.)

ma tra noi c'era un infelice
che non faceva altro che masturbarsi,
notte e giorno; anche esibendosi
davanti a fanti e infanti; ebbene...
Il Signor Homais, caro Dio, Ti riproduceva punto per punto:
aveva un bel vestito di lana scura, col panciotto
una camicia di seta e una cravatta blu;
veniva da Lione o da Colonia, non ricordo bene
E ci parlava sempre del domani
Ma tra noi c'era quello scemo che diceva che invece Tu
avevi nome Axel...
Tutto questo al Tempo dei Tempi
Caro Dio,
liberaci dal pensiero del domani.
È del Domani che Tu ci hai parlato attraverso Ms. Homais.
Ma noi ora vogliamo vivere come lo scemo degenerato,
che seguiva il suo Axel
che era anche il Diavolo: era troppo bello per essere solo Te.
Viveva di rendita ma non era previdente.
Era povero ma non era risparmiatore.
Era puro come un angelo ma non era perbene.
Era infelice e sfruttato, ma non aveva speranza.
Caro Dio,
l'idea del potere non ci sarebbe se non ci fosse l'idea del domani;
non solo, ma senza il domani, la coscienza non avrebbe giustificazione.
Caro Dio,
facci vivere come *gli uccelli del cielo e i gigli dei campi.*

Uno dei tanti epiloghi

Ohi, Ninarieddo, ti ricordi di quel sogno...
di cui abbiamo parlato tante volte...
Io ero in macchina, e partivo solo, col sedile
vuoto accanto a me, e tu mi correvi dietro;
all'altezza dello sportello ancora semiaperto,
correndo ansioso e ostinato, mi gridavi
con un po' di pianto infantile nella voce:
«A Pa', mi porti con te? Me lo paghi il viaggio?»
Era il viaggio della vita: e solo in sogno

but with us was an unhappy boy
who did nothing but masturbate
night and day, even exposing himself
in front of children big and small. Well . . .
This Mr. Homais, dear God, imitated You in every detail:
he wore a fine dark wool suit, with waistcoat
silk shirt and blue tie;
he came from Lyon or Cologne, I forget which
And he kept telling us about tomorrow
But with us was that fool who said that in fact
Your name was Axel . . .
And all this a Long Time Ago.
Dear God,
deliver us from the thought of tomorrow.
It was Tomorrow you told us about through Mr. Homais.
But now we only want to live like the degenerate fool
who followed his Axel
who was also the Devil: he was too beautiful to be only You.
He lived on independent means but didn't plan for the future.
He was poor but didn't economize.
He was pure as an angel but wasn't respectable.
He was unhappy and exploited but had no hope.
Dear God,
the idea of power wouldn't exist without the idea of tomorrow;
on top of this, without tomorrow, conscience would have no justification.
Dear God,
let us live like *the birds in the sky and the lilies of the fields.*

One of Many Epilogues

Hey, Ninarieddo, remember that dream,
the one we talked about so many times . . . ?
I was in my car, heading off alone, the seat
beside me empty, and you were running after me;
when you reached the still half-open door,
anxious and stubbornly running, you cried out
with a childish sort of whine in your voice:
"Hey, Paolo, can you take me with you? Will you pay my way?"
It was the journey of life, and only in a dream

hai dunque osato scoprirti e chiedermi qualcosa.
Tu sai benissimo che quel sogno fa parte della realtà;
e non è un Ninetto sognato quello che ha detto quelle parole.
Tanto è vero che quando ne parliamo arrossisci.
Ieri sera, a Arezzo, nel silenzio della notte,
mentre il piantone rinchiudeva con la catena il cancello
alle tue spalle, e tu stavi per sparire,
col tuo sorriso, fulmineo e buffo, mi hai detto... «Grazie!».
«Grazie», Ninè? È la prima volta che me lo dici.
E infatti te ne accorgi, e ti correggi, senza perdere la faccia
(cosa in cui sei maestro) scherzando:
«Grazie per il passaggio». Il viaggio che tu volevi
ch'io ti pagassi era, ripeto, il viaggio della vita:
è in quel sogno di tre quattro anni fa che ho deciso
ciò a cui il mio equivoco amore per la libertà era contrario.
Se ora mi ringrazi per il passaggio... Dio mio,
mentre tu sei in gattabuia, prendo con paura
l'aereo per un luogo lontano. Della nostra vita sono insaziabile,
perché una cosa unica al mondo non può essere mai esaurita.

2 settembre 1969

Canto civile

Le loro guancie erano fresche e tenere
e forse erano baciate per la prima volta
Visti di spalle, quando le voltavano
per tornare nel tenero gruppo, erano più adulti,
coi cappotti sopra i calzoni leggeri. La loro povertà
dimentica che è il freddo inverno. Le gambe un po' arcuate
e i colletti consunti, come i fratelli maggiori,
già screditati cittadini. Essi sono ancora per qualche anno
senza prezzo: e non ci può essere niente che umilia
in chi non si può giudicare. Per quanto lo facciano
con tanta, incredibile naturalezza, essi si offrono alla vita;
e la vita a sua volta li richiede. Ne sono così pronti!
Restituiscono i baci, saggiando la novità.
Poi se ne vanno, imperturbati come sono venuti.
Ma poiché sono ancora pieni di fiducia in quella vita che li ama,
fanno sincere promesse, progettano un promettente futuro

could you drop your guard and ask me for something.
You know perfectly well that this dream belongs to reality,
and that it wasn't a dreamed Ninetto who said those words.
In fact you blush when we talk about it.
Last night in Arezzo, in the silence of the night,
when the guard was locking the gate with a chain
behind you, and you were about to disappear,
with your sudden, funny smile, you said: "Thanks!"
Thanks, Ninè? It's the first time you ever said that to me.
And in fact you realized this and corrected yourself, without losing face
(something you're a master at), saying:
"Thanks for the ride." The journey you wanted me
to pay for was, I repeat, the journey of life;
and it was in that dream some three, four years ago that I decided
what my equivocal love of freedom was opposed to.
If you now thank me for the ride, when
you're in the slammer, my God . . . In fear
I board a plane for a faraway place. My thirst for our life is unquenchable,
because something unique in all the world will never run dry.

September 2, 1969

Civic Song

Their cheeks were fresh and tender
and kissed perhaps for the first time.
Seen from behind, when they turned around
to go back to their tender group, they were more grown-up,
overcoats covering their light trousers. Their poverty
forgets that it's winter and cold. Their legs slightly bowed,
collars threadbare, just like their older brothers,
already discredited citizens. For a few more years they will
remain priceless; nothing in the world can humble
those who cannot be judged. However naturally
and incredibly they do it, they offer themselves to life;
and life demands them in turn. They are so ready for it!
They return the kisses, tasting the novelty.
Then they leave, as unruffled as they had come.
But since they are still trustful of the life that loves them,
they make sincere promises, planning a promising future

di abbracci e anche baci. Chi farebbe la rivoluzione —
se mai la si dovesse fare — se non loro? Diteglielo: sono pronti,
tutti allo stesso modo, così come abbracciano e baciano
e con lo stesso odore nelle guancie.
Ma non sarà la loro fiducia nel mondo a trionfare.
Essa deve essere trascurata dal mondo.

dicembre 1969

La strada delle puttane

Un Dio Ragazzo, che conosce il Ma-mul,* cantando
sui gioghi vicini alle nuvole basse e calde
Esso ti troverà in un luogo dove si radunano
i clienti delle puttane sopravvissute ai padroni
radi fuochi e nuvole basse ma lontane nell'orizzonte
cosparso di luci domestiche
anche le puttane in quel momento stanno quiete e ferme
come meditando o chissà per quale atavica malinconia
accanto a una luce accesa tra la carta da parato rossa
e il letto disfatto che biancheggia in quell'interno
alle cui soglie arriva il miserabile buio
I clienti parlano piano, e se qualcuno ride, o grida,
tutti lo guardano, come assorti al canto dei grilli
che gremiscono il vicino orizzonte al di là della periferia
chissà in quale notte del 1962 o '63: e chi canta a Dio
la sua canzone paterna, nata nel cuore del Ma-mul
sugli altopiani perduti sopra le foreste
dove non passano strade, fa giungere fin qui
un segno del cosmo: il Dio Ragazzo venuto dalla baracca
si stacca dai compagni, non è nulla, ha solo dei ricci.
Ma nei millenni — prima della morte —
ciò segna una data nel corso dell'essere
anche se nessuno la festeggia, o se ne accorge.
Perché un Dio Ragazzo ti può incontrare
per le strade del cosmo che passano tra le baracche
di un villaggio di puttane, sotto muraglioni antichi?
È semplice: egli viene per farti da madre.

*Tradizione sacra orale della popolazione indiana dei Kota. Ma potrebbe essere qualsiasi altra tradizione sacra.

of embraces and even kisses. If the revolution were ever
to come, who but they would bring it? Tell them so: they are
ready, all in the same way, just as they kiss and embrace
and have the same smell in their cheeks.
But their trust in the world shall not be what triumphs.
It must remain shunned by the world.

December 1969

The Whores' Road

A Boy God who knows the Ma-mul* sings
on the mountaintops near low, warm clouds
He shall find you in a place where gather
the clients of whores who've survived their owners
Scattered fires, clouds low but distant on a horizon
dotted with the lights of houses
At that moment even the whores keep quiet and still
as though meditating or from who knows what atavistic melancholy
beside a lighted lamp between red wallpaper
and an unmade bed gleaming white in a room
with the miserable darkness lapping in the doorway
The clients speak softly, and if one of them laughs or shouts,
everyone looks at him as though rapt in the song of the crickets
teeming on the nearby horizon beyond the periphery
on who knows what night in 1962 or '63; and whoever sings to God
his paternal song, born in the heart of the Ma-mul
on the lost plateaus above the forests
where no roads pass, brings a sign of the cosmos
all the way to this place: the Boy God comes out of a shack,
breaks away from his companions; he is nothing, he has only curls.
But across the millennia—before death—
this marks a date in the course of being
even if nobody celebrates or notices it.
Why would a Boy God meet you
along the roads of the cosmos that pass between the shacks
of a village of whores under great ancient walls?
Easy: he comes to be as a mother to you.

*A sacred oral tradition of the Kota population of India. But it could also be any
other sacred tradition. (Author's note.)

Versi del testamento

La solitudine: bisogna essere molto forti
per amare la solitudine; bisogna avere buone gambe
e una resistenza fuori del comune; non si deve rischiare
raffreddore, influenza o mal di gola; non si devono temere
rapinatori o assassini; se tocca camminare
per tutto il pomeriggio o magari per tutta la sera
bisogna saperlo fare senza accorgersene; da sedersi non c'è;
specie d'inverno; col vento che tira sull'erba bagnata,
e coi pietroni tra l'immondizia umidi e fangosi;
non c'è proprio nessun conforto, su ciò non c'è dubbio,
oltre a quello di avere davanti tutto un giorno e una notte
senza doveri o limiti di qualsiasi genere.
Il sesso è un pretesto. Per quanti siano gli incontri
—e anche d'inverno, per le strade abbandonate al vento,
tra le distese d'immondizia contro i palazzi lontani,
essi sono molti—non sono che momenti della solitudine;
più caldo e vivo è il corpo gentile
che unge di seme e se ne va,
più freddo e mortale è intorno il diletto deserto;
è esso che riempie di gioia, come un vento miracoloso,
non il sorriso innocente o la torbida prepotenza
di chi poi se ne va; egli si porta dietro una giovinezza
enormemente giovane; e in questo è disumano,
perché non lascia tracce, o meglio, lascia una sola traccia
che è sempre la stessa in tutte le stagioni.
Un ragazzo ai suoi primi amori
altro non è che la fecondità del mondo.
È il mondo che così arriva con lui; appare e scompare,
come una forma che muta. Restano intatte tutte le cose,
e tu potrai percorrere mezza città, non lo ritroverai più;
l'atto è compiuto, la sua ripetizione è un rito. Dunque
la solitudine è ancora più grande se una folla intera
attende il suo turno: cresce infatti il numero delle sparizioni—
l'andarsene è fuggire—e il seguente incombe sul presente
come un dovere, un sacrificio da compiere alla voglia di morte.
Invecchiando, però, la stanchezza comincia a farsi sentire,
specie nel momento in cui è appena passata l'ora di cena,

Lines from the Testament

You have to be very strong
to love solitude; you need good legs
and uncommon stamina; you can't easily
catch cold, flu, or sore throat; you can't be afraid
of muggers or murderers; if you have to walk
all afternoon or even all evening
you must know how to do this without noticing; there's nowhere to sit,
especially in winter; the wind blows over the wet grass
and there are big rocks, wet and muddy, amidst the garbage;
there's really no comfort at all, no doubt about that,
except in the fact that you've got a whole day and a night ahead of you,
with no obligations or constraints of any sort.
Sex is a pretext. No matter how many encounters you may have
— and even in winter, in the windswept streets,
between garbage heaps against a background of buildings,
there are many — they are only moments of loneliness;
the warmer, more alive the gentle body
that anoints you with semen and then leaves,
the colder and deadlier the beloved desert around you;
this is what fills you with joy like a miraculous wind,
not the innocent smile or troubled arrogance
of the one who leaves when it's over; he takes his outrageously youthful
youth away with him, and there's something inhuman in this,
for he leaves no trace, or rather, he leaves only one trace,
always the same trace, no matter the season.
A boy at the time of his first loves
is nothing if not the world's fertility.
The world arrives with him, appears and disappears
like a changing form. Things remain whole,
and you can comb half the city, but you won't find him again;
the act is over, its repetition a rite. Thus
the loneliness is all the greater if there is a whole crowd,
each awaiting his turn; this increases the number of disappearances —
when they leave, they flee — and each next encounter hangs over
    the present one
like an obligation, a sacrifice to perform to the death wish.
As you grow older, however, fatigue begins to set in,
especially right after suppertime, though nothing

e per te non è mutato niente; allora per un soffio non urli o piangi;
e ciò sarebbe enorme se non fosse appunto solo stanchezza,
e forse un po' di fame. Enorme, perché vorrebbe dire
che il tuo desiderio di solitudine non potrebbe esser più soddisfatto,
e allora cosa ti aspetta, se ciò che non è considerato solitudine
è la solitudine vera, quella che non puoi accettare?
Non c'è cena o pranzo o soddisfazione del mondo,
che valga una camminata senza fine per le strade povere,
dove bisogna essere disgraziati e forti, fratelli dei cani.

La poesia della tradizione

Oh generazione sfortunata!
Cosa succederà domani, se tale classe dirigente—
quando furono alle prime armi
non conobbero la poesia della tradizione
ne fecero un'esperienza infelice perché senza
sorriso realistico gli fu inaccessibile
e anche per quel poco che la conobbero, dovevano dimostrare
di voler conoscerla sì ma con distacco, fuori dal gioco.
Oh generazione sfortunata!
che nell'inverno del '70 usasti cappotti e scialli fantasiosi
e fosti viziata
chi ti insegnò a non sentirti inferiore—
rimuovesti le tue incertezze divinamente infantili—
chi non è aggressivo è nemico del popolo! Ah!
I libri, i vecchi libri passarono sotto i tuoi occhi
come oggetti di un vecchio nemico
sentisti l'obbligo di non cedere
davanti alla bellezza nata da ingiustizie dimenticate
fosti in fondo votata ai buoni sentimenti
da cui ti difendevi come dalla bellezza
con l'odio razziale contro la passione;
venisti al mondo, che è grande eppure così semplice,
e vi trovasti chi rideva della tradizione,
e tu prendesti alla lettera tale ironia fintamente ribalda,
erigendo barriere giovanili contro la classe dominante del passato
la gioventù passa presto; oh generazione sfortunata,
arriverai alla mezza età e poi alla vecchiaia

has changed for you; you very nearly cry out or weep at the slightest thing,
which would be terrible if it wasn't just fatigue
and perhaps a little hunger. Terrible because it would mean
that your desire for solitude could no longer be satisfied,
and what would await you then, if what is not considered solitude
is the real solitude, the kind you cannot accept?
No supper or lunch or worldly satisfaction
can compare to an endless walk down impoverished streets,
where you need to be wretched and strong, a brother to dogs.

The Poetry of Tradition

O unlucky generation!
What will happen tomorrow, if this ruling class —
when first learning the ropes
they didn't know the poetry of tradition
it was an unhappy experience for them, because without
a realistic smile, it remained inaccessible to them
and even with what little they did know about it, they had to show
that yes, they wanted to know it, but from a distance, from the sidelines.
O unlucky generation!
In the winter of '70 you wore outlandish overcoats and shawls
and you became spoiled —
who taught you not to feel inferior? —
you repressed your divinely childish uncertainties —
he who is not aggressive is an enemy of the people! Ah!
Books, old books, passed before your eyes
like the possessions of an old enemy;
you felt obliged not to give in
to a beauty born of forgotten injustices;
deep down you were devoted to the same fine feelings
you fought off just as you fought off beauty
with a racial hatred of anything passionate;
you came into the world, which is big and yet so simple,
and you found people who laughed at tradition,
and you took that falsely ribald irony literally,
erecting youthful barriers against the dominant class of the past . . .
Youth passes quickly; O unlucky generation,
you shall reach your middle years and then old age

senza aver goduto ciò che avevi diritto di godere
e che non si gode senza ansia e umiltà
e così capirai di aver servito il mondo
contro cui con zelo «portasti avanti la lotta»:
era esso che voleva gettar discredito sopra la storia—la sua;
era esso che voleva far piazza pulita del passato—il suo;
oh generazione sfortunata, e tu obbedisti disobbedendo!
Era quel mondo a chiedere ai suoi nuovi figli di aiutarlo
a contraddirsi, per continuare;
vi troverete vecchi senza l'amore per i libri e la vita:
perfetti abitanti di quel mondo rinnovato
attraverso le sue reazioni e repressioni, sì, sì, è vero,
ma soprattutto attraverso voi, che vi siete ribellati
proprio come esso voleva, Automa in quanto Tutto;
non vi si riempirono gli occhi di lacrime
contro un Battistero con caporioni e garzoni
intenti di stagione in stagione
né lacrime aveste per un'ottava del Cinquecento,
né lacrime (intellettuali, dovute alla pura ragione)
non conosceste o non riconosceste i tabernacoli degli antenati
né le sedi dei padri padroni, dipinte da
—e tutte le altre sublimi cose
non vi farà trasalire (con quelle lacrime brucianti)
il verso di un anonimo poeta simbolista morto nel
la lotta di classe vi cullò e vi impedì di piangere:
irrigiditi contro tutto ciò che non sapesse di buoni sentimenti
e di aggressività disperata
passaste una giovinezza
e, se eravate intellettuali,
non voleste dunque esserlo fino in fondo,
mentre questo era poi fra i tanti il vostro vero dovere,
e perché compiste questo tradimento?
per amore dell'operaio: ma nessuno chiede a un operaio
di non essere operaio fino in fondo
gli operai non piansero davanti ai capolavori
ma non perpetrarono tradimenti che portano al ricatto
e quindi all'infelicità
oh sfortunata generazione
piangerai, ma di lacrime senza vita
perché forse non saprai neanche riandare

without having enjoyed what you had a right to enjoy,
which cannot be enjoyed without anguish and humility,
and thus you shall realize that you served the very world
against which you "carried on the struggle":
for it was they who wanted to discredit history—their own;
it was they who wanted to make a clean sweep of the past—their own;
and you obeyed by disobeying! O unlucky generation!
That world asked its new children to help it
contradict itself, in order to go on;
and one day you shall wake up old, without any love of books or life,
perfect inhabitants of a world renewed
by its reactions and repressions—yes, yes, it's true—
but renewed especially by you, you who rebelled
just as it, the Automaton as All, wanted you to do;
your eyes didn't fill with tears
over a Baptistry with *caporioni* and apprentices
toiling from season to season,
you had no tears for Cinquecento octaves,
no tears (intellectual tears, springing from pure reason)
you didn't know or recognize the tabernacles of your forebears,
nor the abodes of the fathers and masters, as painted by . . .
—and all those other sublime things—
you don't give a start (or shed hot tears) at the sound
of a line by an anonymous Symbolist poet born in . . .
The class struggle nurtured you and forbade you to cry:
you spent your youth
resisting everything that wasn't about fine feelings
and hopeless ferocity,
and if you were intellectuals,
you didn't want to be through and through,
whereas that was your true task, among so many others.
Why this betrayal?
For love of the worker . . . But nobody asks the worker
not to be a worker through and through.
The workers didn't cry in front of old masterpieces
but they also didn't commit treachery leading to blackmail
and thus to unhappiness
O unlucky generation
you shall weep but shed only lifeless tears
because you may not even know how to go back

a ciò che non avendo avuto non hai neanche perduto;
povera generazione calvinista come alle origini della borghesia
fanciullescamente pragmatica, puerilmente attiva
tu hai cercato salvezza nell'organizzazione
(che non può altro produrre che altra organizzazione)
e hai passato i giorni della gioventù
parlando il linguaggio della democrazia burocratica
non uscendo mai dalla ripetizione delle formule,
ché organizzar significar per verba non si poria,
ma per formule sì,
ti troverai a usare l'autorità paterna in balia del potere
imparlabile che ti ha voluta contro il potere,
generazione sfortunata!
Io invecchiando vidi le vostre teste piene di dolore
dove vorticava un'idea confusa, un'assoluta certezza,
una presunzione di eroi destinati a non morire—
oh ragazzi sfortunati, che avete visto a portata di mano
una meravigliosa vittoria che non esisteva!

Atene

Ai tempi di Atene
le ragazze ridevano, alle porte di casette basse tutte uguali
(come nei quartieri poveri di Rio);
queste casette erano disposte lungo viali
che a quei tempi profumavano (non ricordavi il nome) di tigli
Le sere, come suole, erano eterne
perché c'era da concludere tutta una cerimonia
(salire per le scale polverose alle camere da letto;
che era un'ascensione; e faceva ridere ancor di più le ragazze)
fuori si continuava a vegliare
perché gli ateniesi sono chiacchieroni, soprattutto i maschi
E, soprattutto, restava quell'odore di tigli per i vialoni;
le ore che le ragazze non conoscono,
ma esse non piangono per questo, anzi ridono, ridono fra loro
Perché tutta la vita è loro e le attende, quasi eterna
Le luci tardano a spegnersi,
c'è da litigare con la sorella
che si disprezza da tutta la vita, per ragioni che non si dicono

to what you never lost, since you never had it;
poor generation, as Calvinist as at the birth of the bourgeoisie,
pettily pragmatic, childishly active
you sought salvation in organization
(which can only produce more organization)
and spent the days of your youth
speaking the language of democratic bureaucracy
never once abandoning the repetition of formulas,
for the meaning of organizing cannot be put into words,
but into formulas, yes,
you'll find yourselves wielding paternal authority, at the mercy
of the unspeakable power that wanted you to fight power,
unlucky generation!
In growing old I saw your heads fill with sorrow;
inside them swirled a muddled idea, an absolute certainty,
the presumption of heroes destined never to die—
O unfortunate children, you had within reach
a wondrous victory that didn't exist!

Athens

In the time of Athens
the girls would laugh in the doorways of squat little houses all the same
(as in the poor quarters of Rio);
houses along avenues filled, at the time,
with the fragrance (you couldn't remember the name) of lindens.
Evenings, as usual, were eternal
because one had to perform a whole ceremony
(go up dusty stairs to the bedrooms,
which was an ascension, and this made the girls laugh even more).
Outside, people were still up
because Athenians are great talkers, especially the men.
Mostly there was the lingering smell of linden along the broad avenues;
the girls don't know this time of the night,
but they don't cry over it; in fact, they laugh, laugh among themselves
Because all of life is theirs and awaits them, almost eternal
It's a while before the lights go out;
you have a bone to pick with your sister
—disdained from birth for reasons unstated

e si tengono misteriosamente in cuore;
e la madre
Ogni famiglia sa la sua; e sa com'è quella delle altre;
di vicinato in vicinato tutta Atene
è compresa nella notte di una ragazza,
che sarà grassa, ed ora è florida, di gran guancia,
e capelli degni delle antiche nonne venute dall'interno
Ma nessuno sa ciò che accadrà,
se non forse qualche vecchio mendico a cui non importa nulla;
chi non ha famiglia o vicinato
o si illude di averli
Magari in regioni lontane, legate da un entroterra
che resterà sempre sconosciuto,
o legate dal mare, l'Adriatico che si fa sempre più diafano
Comunque qui è notte d'estate,
c'è l'eternità della giovinezza,
le schermaglie sono state portate a termine vittoriosamente —
il mancato bacio,
vittoria dell'aridità della vergine;
lui se n'è andato, «alto e biondo», sprofondato nell'odore dei tigli
Si rientra a casa,
le voci si continuano ad alzare dalle altre case;
il vicinato parla, con voci insonni,
forse si sentono raganelle lontane,
e certo viene un leggero vento dal mare
C'è la guerra; e se le ragazze ridono è perché sono sante —

Timor di me?

Oh, un terribile timore;
La lietezza esplode
contro quei vetri sul buio
Ma tale lietezza, che ti fa cantare *in voce*
è un ritorno dalla morte: e chi può mai ridere —
Dietro, sotto il riquadro del cielo annerito
Riapparizione ctonia!
Non scherzo: ché tu hai esperienza
di un luogo che non ho mai esplorato, UN VUOTO
NEL COSMO

but kept mysteriously deep in your heart—
and mother.
Every family has its own story, knows the others' stories, too;
from neighborhood to neighborhood, all of Athens
is contained in the night of one girl,
who will one day get fat, but is now in bloom, chubby-cheeked
and with hair worthy of ancient grandmothers come from inland
But nobody knows what will be,
except, perhaps, for some old beggar who doesn't care;
or anyone who has no family or neighborhood
or is under the illusion that he does
Perhaps in distant regions connected by a hinterland
which will remain forever unknown,
or connected by the sea, the ever more diaphanous Adriatic . . .
Whatever the case, here it is a summer night,
youth is eternal,
and the skirmishes have been brought to a victorious conclusion—
the unrealized kiss,
victory of the virgin's aridity;
he has departed, "tall and blond," deep into the scent of the lindens.
It is time to go home,
voices continue to rise from other houses,
the neighborhood speaks with sleepless voices;
perhaps they hear frogs in the distance,
and of course a light wind blows in from the sea
It's wartime; and if the girls laugh, it's because they are holy—

Timor di me?

Oh, so terribly afraid;
Happiness explodes
against the windows over the darkness
But this happiness, which makes you sing *in voce*,
is a return from death, and who could ever laugh—
Behind, beneath the frame of blackened sky,
Chthonian apparition!
I'm not joking: for you have experienced
a place I've never explored, A VOID
IN THE COSMOS

È vero che la mia terra è piccola
Ma ho sempre affabulato sui luoghi inesplorati
con una certa lietezza, quasicché non fosse vero
Ma tu ci sei, qui, *in voce*
La luna è risorta;
le acque scorrono;
il mondo non sa di essere nuovo e la sua nuova giornata
finisce contro gli alti cornicioni e il nero del cielo
Chi c'è, in quel VUOTO DEL COSMO,
che tu porti nei tuoi desideri e conosci?
C'è il padre, sì, lui!
Tu credi che io lo conosca? Oh, come ti sbagli;
come ingenuamente dài per certo ciò che non lo è affatto;
fondi tutto il discorso, ripreso qui, cantando,
su questa presunzione che per te è umile
e non sai invece quanto sia superba
essa porta in sé i segni della volontà mortale della maggioranza—
L'occhio ilare di me mai disceso agli Inferi,
ombra infernale vagolante
nasconde
E tu ci caschi
Tu conosci di ciò che è realtà solo quell'Uomo Adulto
ossia ciò che si deve conoscere;
lei, la Donna Adulta, stia all'Inferno
o nell'Ombra che precede la vita
e di là operi pure i suoi malefizi, i suoi incantesimi;
odiala, odiala, odiala;
e se tu canti e nessuno ti sente, sorridi
semplicemente perché, per ora, intanto, sei vittoriosa—
in voce come una giovane figlia avida
che però ha sperimentato la dolcezza;
Parigi calca dietro alle tue spalle un cielo basso
con la trama dei rami neri; ormai classici;
questa è la storia—
Tu sorridi al Padre—
quella persona di cui io non ho alcuna informazione,
che ho frequentato in un sogno che evidentemente non ricordo—
strano, è da quel mostro di autorità
che proviene anche la dolcezza
se non altro come rassegnazione e breve vittoria;

It's true that my earth is small
But I've always been happy to spin yarns
about unexplored places, as if none of it were real
But you're actually in it, here, *in voce*
The moon has risen again;
the waters flow;
the world doesn't know that it's new, and the new day
ends against high cornices and the sky's blackness—
Who is there, in that VOID IN THE COSMOS,
that you know and carry around in your desires?
The father is there, yes, him!
Do you think I know him? Oh, you're so wrong;
you so naively take for granted what is not granted at all;
you base your whole argument, resumed here in song,
on this presumption, which you take for humble,
when you have no idea how proud it is
It bears the signs of the deadly will of the majority—
My cheerful eye—and I've never gone down to the Underworld—
conceals
a trembling shadow of Hell
And you fall into it
All you know about reality is the Adult Man,
that is, what one is supposed to know;
the Adult Woman, let her stay in Hell
or in the Shadow that precedes life;
let her work her witchcraft there, let her cast her spells;
hate her, hate her, hate her;
and if you sing and nobody hears you, you smile
simply because, for the moment, you are victorious—
in voce like an avid young girl
who has yet known sweetness;
Paris sketches a low sky behind you
with a weave of black branches; a classic image;
this is the story—
You smile at the Father—
a person on whom I have no information,
whom I frequented in a dream I clearly don't remember—
strangely, from that monster of authority
also comes sweetness
if only as a form of resignation and brief victory;

accidenti, come l'ho ignorato; così ignorato da non saperne niente —
cosa fare?
Tu doni, spargi doni, hai bisogno di donare,
ma il tuo dono te l'ha dato Lui, come tutto;
ed è un Nulla il dono di Nessuno;
io fingo di ricevere;
ti ringrazio, sinceramente grato;
Ma il debole sorriso sfuggente
non è di timidezza;
è lo sgomento, più terribile, ben più terribile
di avere un corpo separato, nei regni dell'essere —
se è una colpa
se non è che un incidente: ma al posto dell'Altro
per me c'è un vuoto nel cosmo
un vuoto nel cosmo
e da là tu canti.

La presenza

Ciò ch'era perduto era celeste
e l'anima malata, santa.
Il nulla era un vento che cambiava inspiegabilmente
direzione, ma ben consapevole, sempre, delle sue mete.
Nel nulla che si muoveva
ispirato in alto
capriccioso come un ruscello in basso
ciò che importava era sempre una storia
che in qualche modo era incominciata
e doveva continuare: la tua.
Chi mi aveva chiamato lì?
Ogni mattina ricominciava la tragedia dell'essere,
dietro i balconi prima chiusi e poi aperti, come in una Chiesa.
Che il vento divino soffiasse inutilmente
o solo per dei testimoni —
Poi le abitudini, queste sorelle della tragedia —
Il mare e il suo vento ebbero tutti i nostri sviscerati elogi —
Il tuo «esse est percipi» incontrava tremendi ostacoli
da superare, e ogni vittoria era una povera vittoria,

damn, I really overlooked him, so overlooked him that I know nothing
    about him—
what to do?
You give generously, you bestow gifts, you need to give,
but it was He that gave you your gift, like everything else;
and the gift of Nobody is Nothing;
I pretend to accept it;
thank you, I'm truly grateful;
But that weak, fleeting smile
is not shyness;
it's the dismay—which is worse, much worse—
of having a separate body in the realms of being—
it may be a fault
if it's not an accident: but in the place of the Other,
for me, there's a void in the cosmos
a void in the cosmos
and from there you sing.

Presence

What was lost was celestial
and the sick soul, holy.
Nothingness was a wind that changed direction
inexplicably, but always knew where it was going.
In the nothingness adrift
inspired above
capricious as a stream below
what mattered was always a story
that had somehow begun
and had to continue: your own.
Who called me there?
Every morning the tragedy of being began anew,
behind balconies first closed and then opened, as in a Church.
Whether the divine wind blew without purpose
or only for the sake of witnesses—
Then the habits, those sisters of tragedy—
The sea and its wind won all our most gushing praises—
Your "*esse est percipi*" encountered tremendous obstacles
it had to overcome, and every victory was minor,

e dovevi ricominciare subito
come una pianta che ha continuamente bisogno d'acqua.
Io però, Maria, non sono un fratello;
adempio altre funzioni, che non so;
non quella della fraternità,
almeno di quella complice
così vicina all'obbedienza e all'eroica inconsapevolezza
degli uomini, tuoi fratelli malgrado tutto, non miei.
E tu, atterrita dal sospetto di non essere più,
sai anche questo
e ti arrangi a farti da madre.
Concedi alla bambina di essere regina
di aprire e chiudere le finestre come in un rito
rispettato da ospiti, servitù, spettatori lontani.
Eppure lei, lei, la bambina,
basta che per un solo istante sia trascurata,
si sente perduta per sempre;
ah, non su isole immobili
ma sul terrore di non essere, il vento scorre
il vento divino
che non guarisce, anzi, ammala sempre più;
e tu cerchi di fermarla, quella che voleva tornare indietro,
non c'è un giorno, un'ora, un istante
in cui lo sforzo disperato possa cessare;
ti aggrappi a qualunque cosa
facendo venir voglia di baciarti.

23 agosto 1970

Ossessione soteriologica

Era quasi grigia l'erba di quella gobba, contornata dal tufo
mozzato di una cava; grigio il tufo; grigio il cielo;
c'era solo sui profili della campagna un contorno turchese.
Perché poco prima m'era successo di trovarmi con gli occhi bagnati
di lacrime improvvise, di vecchio, in un luogo qualsiasi
sull'autostrada, da dove si vedevano grandi distese
di prati, verdi d'un verde disperatamente folto: era aprile!
era la fine d'aprile! e l'avida erba trionfava rinata, presente,
forte, fitta (al sole che per un momento usciva a illuminarla).

and you had to start over again at once
like a plant that continually needs water.
But I, Maria, am not a brother;
I fulfill other functions, of which I'm not aware;
not that of brotherhood,
at least not the complicitous brotherhood
so like the obedience and heroic oblivousness
of men, your brothers in spite of everything, not mine.
And, terrified by the suspicion you no longer exist,
you know this, too,
and do your best to be your own mother.
You allow the little girl to be queen
to open and close the windows as in a ritual
respected by guests, servants, and a faraway audience.
And yet she, that little girl,
neglect her for only a moment
and she'll feel lost forever—
ah, the wind blows not over motionless islands,
but over the terror of non-being,
the divine wind
that does not heal, but indeed makes one sicker and sicker;
and you try to stop her, the girl who wanted to turn back,
and there's never a day, an hour, a moment
when the effort might cease;
you grab onto anything you can
and it makes one want to kiss you.

August 23, 1970

Soteriological Obsession

The grass on the hummock was almost gray, surrounded by a quarry's
shivered tufa; gray the tufa; gray the sky;
only the shapes of the landscape were outlined in turquoise.
What happened was that, a moment earlier, my eyes had filled
suddenly with tears, an old man's tears, at a random spot
along the motorway, from where one could see great expanses
of meadows green with a desperately lush green. It was April!
The end of April! And the avid grass was reborn in triumph, present,
strong, dense (in the sunlight that managed for a moment to illuminate it).

Ch'io abbia pianto come un vecchio, che, dopo aver tanto posseduto
il mondo, lo ritrova come una cosa che non gli spetta più,
ma, libero dagli obblighi di questo possesso, finalmente lo vede
per la sua bellezza, soltanto per la sua riapparsa bellezza...
Delle pecore pascolavano; ma, come sempre, il loro mangiare
era solo in apparenza una povera e idiota necessità.
Che cosa sanno, nel loro stato, queste grige bestie
che non possono tralasciare il loro pascolo sconsolato?
Ne vedo il muso: incapace di avere altre espressioni
se non quell'unica, di sospetto, paura e umiltà,
che gli è rimasta impressa per sempre dalle loro origini:
quel muso non mi rivela nulla. No, quel muso mi rivela tutto.
Umido e secco, con le grosse narici di un nero mostruoso,
la pelle sui denti, senza labbra, che si tira in un ghigno
timidamente avido, l'occhio così ben disegnato nel suo
nerume lucente: è uno scrigno che contiene certo un sapere;
sapere che fu interrogato a lungo dai miei fetidi padri.
Essi lo divinavano, e vi attribuivano una realtà
che era poi proprio reale! C'era addirittura uno scambio
di sapere tra bestie e uomini. E quegli uomini erano certi
che (come infatti era) superiore fosse il sapere delle bestie.
Anche le bestie ne erano conscie: e niente affatto benigne,
si occupavano, a testa bassa, del loro pascolo—solo a tratti
alzando quella loro testa che conteneva il mondo
come era, ed era conosciuto, quando lo abitavano soltanto esse—
per lanciare sugli uomini uno sguardo. La loro attualità
è durata così molti millenni. Ora qui, nei dintorni di Roma,
esse non sono più attuali. Superate e sole, la loro superbia
è una maschera: vivono aspettando la loro definitiva scomparsa.
C'è solo ancora qualcuno che si sofferma a interrogarle
(l'uomo anziano che piange alla vista di quattro prati
perché non è più certo di possederli anche in un lungo futuro).
La fine del sapere delle pecore è unita alla fine
del significato del giorno: ormai non ci saranno più
giorni—anni, Natali, Pasque: il tempo non avrà più forma d'uovo,
mentre il sapere delle pecore era proprio il sapere del ritorno.
Furono costruiti su quel sapere milioni di tabernacoli
e di recinti; milioni di templi e chiese; intere città;

There I was, weeping like an old man who, after having so possessed
the world, now rediscovers it as something to which he has no more claim
and yet, freed of the obligations of this possession, finally sees it
in all its beauty, only because its beauty has reappeared . . .
Some sheep were grazing; but, as usual, their eating
was only apparently a miserable and idiotic necessity.
What, in their condition, do they know, these gray beasts
who can never abandon their joyless pasturage?
I see that muzzle—incapable of any other expression
than the air of suspicion, fear, and humility
forever stamped on them since their beginnings.
That muzzle tells me nothing. No, that muzzle tells me everything.
Damp and dry, with broad nostrils a monstrous black,
skin over the teeth, no lips, mouth tensed in a timidly
avid grimace, eye sharply drawn in shiny
blackness—a package that surely contains knowledge,
a knowledge examined in depth by my smelly forbears.
They divined it, and the reality they ascribed to it
was truly real! There was actually an exchange
of knowledge between beast and man. And those men were certain
that the knowledge of beasts was superior (as indeed it was).
And the beasts were also aware of this, and, not the least bit benign,
they busied themselves, head down, with their grazing, only occasionally
raising their heads—which contained the world
the way it was and was known to be when they alone inhabited it—
to cast a glance at the men. Their relevance
thus lasted many thousands of years. Now, however, here on the outskirts
of Rome, they are no longer relevant. Left behind and alone, their pride
is a mask: they live only waiting to vanish for good.
All that's left is the man who sometimes stops to examine them
(the old man who weeps at the sight of a few meadows
because he's no longer sure he'll ever possess them again, even in a
        distant future).
The end of the knowledge of sheep is connected to the end
of the meaning of the day: henceforth there shall be no more
days—no more years, Christmases, or Easters. Time shall no longer be
        shaped like an egg.
For the knowledge of sheep was the knowledge of recurrence.
Upon that knowledge millions of shrines and fortifications
were built; millions of temples and churches; whole cities;

imperi di campi coltivati: e le pecore vegliavano
come vecchi muti che sanno la forma prima del tempo. Ora d'improvviso
sono tornate bambine: la loro inspiegabile vecchiezza
appare come un fenomeno passeggero, un episodio remoto:
dalla prima di esse che pascolò accanto a una capanna
a queste ultime che pascolano in una periferia,
si è compiuta un'esperienza che ha ormai perduto ogni valore.
Eppure, distratte bestie, pare che sappiano anche questo:
«Abbiamo tanto significato per voi, e ora non significhiamo
più nulla. Pazienza. Moriamo. Ma cosa incomincia
per voi, non più ossessionati dalla vostra salvezza?
Dove andate, usciti dal cerchio, per questa linea retta?»

aprile 1969

Appunto

Perché esiste la poesia lirica? Perché solo io,
e nessun altro per me, sa quali lunghe tradizioni
ha il dolore nascente dalla tinta dell'aria che si oscura;
la sera e le nuvole annunciano, insieme, notte e inverno.
Che occhi si riempiono di questa triste luce se non i miei?

Gli ultimi sogni prima di morire

Caro amico mio, tutte le notti,
si stanno facendo lavori presso la mia casa
ci son grandi arnesi, stecconate, ci son garritte
poca roba per la verità, son lavori di comune amministrazione
Caro amico mio, rincasando, tutte le notti, o quasi,
davanti ai macchinari fermi, gialli al leggero vento
Spesso, davanti alla mia casa—è più alba che notte
Caro amico mio, quasi mi spavento, vedendo
camminare senza rumore, nella strada davanti a casa mia,
quando rincaso, che è più alba ormai che notte,
un'ombra che par vada senza piedi, o con pantofole,
col viso tutto coperto
Essa avanza grigia lungo il marciapiede
(o dall'altra parte della strada, lungo la stecconata

empires of tilled fields. And the sheep kept watch
like silent elders who know the primal form of time. Now they're suddenly
children again. Their inexplicable old age
seems like a passing phenomenon, a distant episode:
from the first one that grazed beside a hut
to these last ones grazing on the outskirts of a city,
an experience that has lost all meaning has come to an end.
And yet the distracted beasts seem to know this too:
"We used to mean so much to you, and now we no longer
mean anything. Oh, well. We're dying. But what is beginning
for you, who are no longer obsessed with your salvation?
Where are you going, outside the circle, along that straight line?"

April 1969

Note

Why does lyric poetry exist? Because I alone,
and nobody else in my place, know what long traditions
lie behind the sorrow born of the hue of the darkening air.
The evening and the clouds together herald night and winter.
What eyes will fill with this sad light if not mine?

Last Dreams before Dying

My dear friend, every night —
lately there's work being done near my home
there are big contraptions, fences, sentry boxes
no big deal, really, normal administrative projects
My dear friend, when going home every night, or almost,
before the motionless machines, yellow in the gentle wind,
often, in front of my building — it's more dawn than night
My dear friend, I almost get scared when I see
walking noiselessly in the street in front of my building
when I'm returning home and by then it's more dawn than night,
a shadow that looks like it's moving without feet, or in slippers,
face entirely covered
It advances gray along the sidewalk
(or across the street, along the fence

che protegge i lavori in corso, nel silenzio)
Caro amico, a cui scrivo perché sei lontano,
non son cose che si dicono a lettore
perduto nei suoi sogni
sono i nulla della vita cui solo gli amici sanno credere
Egli, l'ombra, coperta fino agli occhi, viene,
mi passa accanto, cammina senza rumore lungo la strada
ciò che lo copre non son veli di fantasma,
è soltanto lana che lo avvolge,
il povero custode delle macchine brancolanti nel silenzio.
E qui finisce l'introduzione.
. . . .

O miei occhi
Immensa è questa immagine, perché è una delle ultime
prima che io muoia—
sono il solo a vedere il malinconico deserto
cosparso, si sa, di misere forme
sono il solo a vedere poi la luce
che altro non è che azzurro notturno che sbiadisce
accendendosi di una sua speranza;
la stessa mia, che vago avanti e indietro
per vincere il sonno
è la pietà che mi veste di povera lana grigia
fino agli occhi, come un motociclista
o uno sciatore povero. Non sembro uno spettro, lo sono.
Il silenzio misterioso che è, nel mio aspetto
è anche dentro di me
ho solo le gambe vive, che mi portano su e giù
e gli occhi che vedono le ultime immagini della vita,
quelle che porterò con me nel giorno già deciso
La famiglia mi sa qui; contribuisco al nostro pane
la pietà dei famigliari e la mia mi segue
su e giù per questa strada, oh
miei occhi dove l'immensa immagine d'una piccola strada
su cui può soffiare il vento, qualche notte,
e qualche notte non c'è che il silenzio.
. . . .

protecting the work site, in silence)
Dear friend, to whom I'm writing because you're far away,
these are not the kinds of things one tells a reader
lost in his dreams
they're the nothings of life only friends can believe
Covered up to his eyes, he, the shadow, comes forward,
passes beside me, walks noiselessly down the street
it's not a ghost's sheets covering him
he's wrapped only in wool
poor guardian of the machines groping in the silence.
Here ends the introduction.

... ...

O eyes of mine
This image is immense, because it's one of the last
before I die—
I alone see the melancholy desert
strewn, as we know, with miserable forms
I alone then see the light
which is nothing more than the blue of night fading
as it kindles with a hope of its own;
the same as mine, as I wander back and forth
to fight off sleep
it's pity that dresses me in poor gray wool
up to the eyes, like a motorcyclist
or an impoverished skier. I don't look like a specter, I *am* one.
The mysterious silence in my appearance
is also inside me
only my legs are alive, taking me up and down
and my eyes, which see life's final images,
the ones I shall take with me on the already determined day
The family knows I'm here; I help put bread on the table
their pity and my own follow me
up and down the street, oh
eyes of mine that see the vast image of a little street
where the wind may blow on some nights
and on some nights there is only silence.

... ...

O miei occhi,
forse perché ai vecchi si danno incarichi di ragazzi,
star svegli tutta la notte solo per sorvegliare,
voi che foste tutta la vita incapaci di vedere
ora per l'umiliazione rivelatrice, vedete
Di quante notti, io, guardiano, feci esperienza,
non desiderandolo, cercando di non vedere
andando su e giù come un fantasma,
negato all'aspetto come dentro di me a ogni rapporto,
che non fosse, s'intende, quella pietà
che mi vestiva e mi aveva dato il grado di custode
con la conscienza mia e della mia famiglia
Negandomi, dunque, passeggiavo
o miei occhi, che intanto guardavate
quelle notti. . . poco prima o poco dopo Pasqua,
ancora fredde che io affrontavo ben coperto
da una palandrana che mi arrivava fino ai piedi
e un passamontagna grigio
Inerte passavo davanti ai radi vivi
che rincasavano con la loro macchina
e mi perdevo senza voltarmi per il marciapiede,
o lungo il recinto sulla scarpata, verso il cantiere
Poi tornavo indietro, di nuovo solo,
cercando di non esistere (e ci sarei riuscito
se non ci fosse stata la pietà dei miei padroni
e quella dei miei famigliari):
mi appariva, allora, l'altra metà del firmamento.

Introduzione

Il futuro è davanti a me:*
lì dove dovrei procedere *completamente libero.*
Libero cioè da:
primo, Religione
secondo, Utopia—
Una tale libertà per la prima volta nella storia.
Non c'è modello di questa mia figura libera

*L'io che parla non è l'autore.

408 *

O eyes of mine,
perhaps because the old are given the tasks of youth,
staying awake all night just to keep watch,
you who all my life were unable to see
now, by revelatory humiliation, you can see —
How many nights have I, as guardian, experienced
without wanting to, trying not to see
walking up and down like a ghost,
denied in my appearance the way all rapport is denied me inside
except, of course, for the pity
that dressed me and gave me the rank of guardian
with my conscience and that of my family
Thus denying myself I used to stroll about
O eyes of mine, that meanwhile watched
those nights . . . shortly before or shortly after Easter,
nights still cold which I braved by covering up
in a housecoat that hung all the way down to my feet
and a gray ski mask
Lifeless I would pass in front of the few living souls
returning home in their cars
and wander off without turning round down the sidewalk
or along the fencing that ringed the slope, towards the work site
Then I would turn back, alone again,
trying not to exist (and I would have succeeded
if not for the pity of my bosses
and my family):
and at that moment, I would see the other half of the firmament.

Introduction

The future lies before me*
where I should proceed *totally free.*
Free, that is, from:
first, Religion
second, Utopia —
A freedom never before seen in history
There is no model for this free image of me

*The "I" speaking is not the author. (Author's note.)

né in proiezioni in cielo né in proiezioni in terra
(che usano appunto venir fatte nel futuro)
Non si prevedono ascensioni.
Ricerca del successo e dei beni superflui.
La dissociazione si presenta così potente
che non ha bisogno nemmeno di operare
riduzioni al terrestre.
È vero che io sono laico e ateo:
ma la mia nuova libertà
è laica e atea a tal punto
che non prende più nemmeno in considerazione
tali resti negativi della religione.
Brutta, triste, piatta libertà
eppure in tutta la storia umana non ce ne fu mai
di più grande.
Che farmene? Godermela
(con quell'anima cattiva che non ama nemmeno godere perché non sa)
Su un tavolato piatto di nubole bianche
appena appena arruffate qua e là,
come una graggia accalcata fino alla fine dell'orizzonte,
sporge come uno scoglio, una scaglia,
nevosa, la cima del monte Olimpo.
Magra, con ombre bluastre, ossute, dure,
ha lacerato il coltre, e sporge tagliente al sole.
Unghia, involucro duro d'insetto morto,
umile giganteggia tra le nubole.
L'ultima ierofania in ordine di tempo,
cacio sui maccheroni,
eh, è quella linguistica: credo che mai linguaggio*
sia stato assunto a luogo divino
e come tale divenuto oggetto di rito e preghiera.
Ultimo sussulto, anzi,
è stata l'interpretazione dell'intera realtà
come *ierosemia*, meglio ancora che
come *ierofania totale*. Esaurita
anche quest'ultima consacrazione
a umiliazione dei filosofi
più non esiste luogo o persona dove *ci sia* il Signore.

*Come stile, non come lessico, beninteso.

not in projections in heaven nor in projections on earth
(which are normally made in the future)
No ascensions are expected.
Pursuit of success and superfluous possessions.
Dissociation looms so powerful
that it doesn't even need to reduce
things to earthly matters.
It's true that I'm a layman and atheist:
but my new freedom
is so lay and atheistic
that it no longer even takes into consideration
such negative remains of religion.
Horrid, sad, dull freedom
and yet never before in human history has there been
any greater.
What should I do with it? Enjoy it
(with a wicked soul that doesn't even like to enjoy, because it has no
    knowledge)
Like a rock, a splinter
high above a flat expanse of white cloudes
ever so lightly ruffled here and there
like a flocke thronging all the way to the horizon,
soars the snowy peak of Mount Olympus.
Slender with its bluish, hard and bony shadows
it has shredded the blanket, jutting sharply in sunlight.
Fingernail, hard shell of dead insect,
it towers humbly among the cloudes.
The final hierophany in the order of time,
cheese on macaroni,
is, ah, linguistic: I don't believe language*
has ever been assumed to a godly sphere
and become as such an object of ritual and prayer.
The final spasm, in fact,
has been the interpretation of all reality
as *hierosemy*, which is even better than
as *total hierophany*. Once this last
consecration is also exhausted,
there is no place or person left where the Lord *might be*.

*As style, of course, not as vocabulary. (Author's note.)

Non c'è più morte mitica.
Rivolgo al monte Olimpo
il mio sguardo religioso:
è un addio.

. . . .

Allora nel futuro tabernacoli non ne avrò più.
Tutti i riti della *cultura di massa* dunque
saranno privi di unità (almeno pare, se l'unità è santa).
Vado nel futuro sapendo anche
che la mia storia non mi servirà a conoscermi.
Di ciò sarei schiavo.
So solo che la storia è un campo aperto e in espansione
(è ciò che mi rende sorprendentemente libero).
Ah, che libertà in un uomo
che non sia più affatto «portatore di valori»,
ma solo e unicamente «iniziatore di nuovi valori»!
(per i quali, naturalmente, non ha interesse né amore).
Non avrò più di conseguenza considerazioni nostalgiche
per il mondo del passato
(mettiamo la biunità del sole).
Come Cristo o Medea, è il tecnico americano. . .
Come Cristo o Medea, è la Guardia Rossa. . .
si tuffa nell'orizzonte ardente, il Ponente delle popolazioni
australiane—fa esperienza del regno dei morti—
lo dimentica—
risorge a Oriente.
Non esalterò i farmers:
«L'agricoltura è opera di peccato. Se mi ci dedico
patirò i dolori dell'inferno»*
La lamentela della religione agricola cesserà.
E così quella della realtà.†
È disumanizzandomi che sarò libero non ribelle
e fischietterò.
Bisogna aggiungere che sarà la fine anche dell'ambiguità:

*Milarepa.
†Il Caravaggio di Longhi? o almeno un muretto borbonico; o insomma tutto ciò che
è umano.

Death is no longer mythic.
My religious eyes
gaze up at Mount Olympus:
to say goodbye.

. . . .

So in the future I shall have no more tabernacles.
All the rites of my *mass culture*
will thus be deprived of unity (or so it seems, if unity is sacred).
I go into the future also knowing
that my history will not help me know myself.
And I shall be a slave to this.
I know only that history is an open field expanding
(this is what makes me so astonishingly free).
Oh what freedom for a man
no longer in any way a "bearer of values"
but only and exclusively a "founder of new values"!
(for which, naturally, he feels no interest or love).
I therefore shall no longer have any nostalgic views
of the world of the past
(say, the twofold unity of the sun).
Like Christ or Medea, it's the American technician . . .
Like Christ or Medea, it's the Red Guard . . .
diving into the fiery horizon, the West of the populations
of Australia — he experiences the realm of the dead —
forgets it —
then rises again in the East.
I shall not glorify *farmers*:
"Agriculture is the work of sin. If I devote myself to it
I shall suffer the torments of hell"*
The agricultural religion's whining shall end.
Reality's too.†
In dehumanizing myself I shall be free, unrebellious,
and whistle all the while.
I should add that it will also be the end of ambiguity:

*Milarepa. (Author's note.)
†Longhi's Caravaggio? Or at least a little wall from Bourbon times; or, in short,
everything human. (Author's note.)

solo *dentro*, completamente *dentro* l'entropia
avvengono i mutamenti di valore!
non metà dentro e metà fuori!
Sarò molto volgare, ma storicamente.
Inolre: l'unica continuità, pare,
tra il mondo di Varuna e il mondo di Nessuno,
sarà la fisicità: e, quindi, tetis.
Cosa, anche questa, destinata poi a dissolversi.
Là dove un giorno sorgeva Venezia. . .

Materiali per l'introduzione

Con la caduta del Padre e della Madre
non più Genitori, cadranno tutti gli altri Princìpi.
Siccome poi l'altra faccia del credere è il fare,
chi non crede non fa, e chi fa crede.
Ma le cose cambieranno: ci sarà *solo il fare*,
e il mutamento non avrà altro senso che il mutamento.
Là dove un tempo sorgeva Venezia. . .
Riprendiamo il discorso sul sole.

***

Il sole batteva su terre coltivate
non so se fosse su Cesarea, o Cerveteri o Ceuta

***

Il sole batteva su Spello

***

Giovane obbediente alla religione dei padri
seguii il sole nel regno dei morti.

Viaggio nella Necropoli. Sincretismo etnologico.
Giustapposizione di stili sepolcrali; ma non sia detto
che si tratti solo di costruzioni funerarie;
tutte le gerarchie degli Antenati dei Tallensi (per esempio);
civiltà ammassata su civiltà, senza prospettive; tutto frontale
(le prospettive sono superfici interne, poetiche): il caos
dell'intero Mondo dei Morti, può avere vari capitoli;

only *inside*, completely *inside* entropy
do changes of value take place!
not half inside and half outside!
I shall be very vulgar, but historically so.
Moreover: the sole continuity, apparently,
between the world of Varuna and the world of Nobody
will be physicality; and therefore thetys.
This, too, destined in time to dissolve.
In the place where Venice once stood . . .

Materials for the Introduction

With the fall of the Father and Mother
no longer Parents, all other Principles shall fall.
Since, moreover, the other side of believing is making,
he who does not believe does not make, and he who makes believes.
But things will change: there shall be *only the making*,
and change shall have no other meaning than change.
In the place where Venice once stood . . .
Let us resume the discussion of the sun.

***

The sun beat down on tilled fields
I don't know whether it was Caesarea, Cerveteri, or Ceuta

***

The sun beat down on Spello

***

A youth obedient to the religion of the fathers
I followed the sun into the realm of the dead.

Journey to the Necropolis. Ethnological syncretism.
Juxtaposition of tomb styles; but let it not be said
that this is only about funerary constructions;
all the hierarchies of the Tallensi Ancestors (for example);
civilization heaped upon civilization, no perspective; all frontal;
(the perspectives are inner, poetic surfaces): the chaos
of the entire World of the Dead; it can have various chapters;

o quelli generali (storie di popoli);
o quelli specifici; meglio direi monografici

L'ordine non prospettico
potrebbe esser dato da un'ipotesi (cui credo
da professionista anche se, in tal campo,
non sono un ricercatore impostato sul field-work... se
non...
in avventure di conoscenze...bibliche...
col buon tallensi, appunto, o col bruno indiano di Madras e dintorni
    ecc.

L'ipotesi è la seguente: la religione è sempre una proiezione
del rapporto del lattante col padre e la madre (sic). Poiché di ciò
esperienza ha il fantolino, che nulla sa, nulla sapendo,
non supera tale esperienza ma in sé la serba, intatta (seppur
    dimenticata)
e le altre che fa vi aggiunge, che appunto non l'annullano affatto,
ma altrettanto intatte le si affiancano; finché formano
quella visione puramente frontale ch'è la vera storia.

Dicevo dunque che, in quel rapporto, padre e madre
sono un'unità indistinta: la Grazia.
Il luogo della loro onnipresenza e onniveggenza
è il Terzo Cielo.

Poche sere fa a Ürgüp ebbi un sogno rivelatore.
Ero forse nei luoghi delle mie origini?
Alla presenza di mia madre (che condivideva, conscia, la mia
    infelicità)
io riprovai, accanto a un grande tavolo,
la beatitudine provata da neonato,
quando per la prima volta ho dormito e ho mangiato.

Fu probabilmente a quel punto, allorché il neonato
come nel mio sogno, con beatitudine, per la prima volta
si accorge di dormire e di mangiare,
che i due genitori da separati divengono presenti.
Non più unico Dio, ma un toro e una vacca.
Tale esperienza si aggiunge alla precedente senza superarla
convivendo nel Pantheon

either the general (histories of peoples);
or the specific; or, to put it better, the monographic

Non-perspective order
could be presented by a hypothesis (in which I believe
as a professional, even though, in this field,
I'm not a researcher with any basis in fieldwork . . . other
than . . .
adventures in biblical . . . knowledge . . .
with good Tallensi, of course, or with the Indian brown of Madras and
     environs, etc.

The hypothesis is the following: religion is always a projection
of the relationship between the suckling child and the father and mother
     (sic). Since this is experienced
by the baby, who knows nothing, he, not knowing anything,
does not overcome the experience but harbors it within, whole (even if
     forgotten),
and adds to it his other experiences, which in no way annul it
but rather line up beside it, equally whole, until they form
the purely frontal view that is true history.

As I was saying, then, in this relationship, father and mother
are an undifferentiated unit: Grace.
The place of their omnipresence and all-seeingness
is the Third Heaven.

A few evenings ago at Ürgüp I had a revealing dream.
Was I perhaps in the place of my origins?
In the presence of my mother (who shared, consciously, my unhappiness),
beside a great table, I felt again
the bliss I'd known as a newborn
when for the first time I slept and ate.

It was probably at that point, when the newborn,
as in my dream, blissfully realizes, for the first time,
that he sleeps and eats,
that the two parents, previously separate, become present.
No longer a single God, but a bull and a cow.
This experience is added to the previous one, without superseding it,
and they coexist in the Pantheon

Sicché io discesi con quel vecchio sole, da *iniziato*,
nel Regno dei Morti; comunicai
la mia esperienza attraverso l'orgia, la bestemmia,
lo scandalo per lo scandalo, però su un fondo di assoluta obbedienza.

Poi, ecco, venne il momento in cui il sole risorse;
e io ebbi l'esperienza della resurrezione.

Giovinastro carico della mia cultura,
e molto male intenzionato verso i padri della mia patria
(ma non tanto contro quelli delle patrie altrui):
come Pound giovane, negli anni dieci, che scendeva in Europa

Solo che lui ci stette, in Europa (nel Regno dei Morti),
io invece risorgerò per la seconda volta.

Accetterò Kayseri neocapitalista, e Arezzo industrializzata

Non come Pound, ma neanche come una Guardia Rossa,
non vorrò affatto distruggere per mia decisione
né la tradizione recente né *tutta* la tradizione:
sarò un giovinastro che non conoscerà la storia
e ne avrà accettata la fine — dopo la sua resurrezione.

Non c'entrerà, intendo dire, la volontà
di non voler più sapere; né la nostalgia.

Certo, si tratterà di un fenomeno a lunga scadenza;
almeno quanto è stato lungo quel tramonto a Cerveteri o Ceuta,
    quell'agonia.

Ci vorrà molto tempo prima che ci sia il nulla
dove ora c'è il tutto, in disfacimento e in rinnovamento;
non trionferò come una Guardia Cinese per aver distrutto tutto.

Quando il sole risorgerà
me ne andrò completamente immemore con la mia specializzazione
là dove un giorno sorgeva Venezia . . .

And so I went down with that ancient sun, as an *initiate*,
into the Realm of the Dead. I communicated
my experience through orgies, blasphemies,
scandal for scandal's sake, yet against a background of total obedience.

Then came the moment when the sun rose again;
and I experienced resurrection.

A young lout full of my culture
and harboring much ill will towards the fathers of my country
(but not so much against the fathers of other countries)
like the young Pound when he came over to Europe in the 1910s

Except that he remained there, in Europe (the Realm of the Dead),
whereas I shall rise again a second time.

I will accept a neocapitalist Kayseri, an industrialized Arezzo

Unlike Pound, but neither like a Red Guard;
in no way do I want my decision to destroy
either recent tradition or *all* tradition:
I'll be a young lout who doesn't know history
but will have accepted its end—after his resurrection.

What I mean is that the will to know no more
shall have nothing to do with it; nor shall nostalgia.

Of course it will be a long-term phenomenon;
at least as long as the sunset, the agony, in Cerveteri or Ceuta.

It will take a long time before there is nothingness
where today there is everything, decomposing and self-renewing:
I shall not triumph like a Chinese Red Guard for having destroyed
    everything.

When the sun rises again
I shall go away, unremembering, with my specialization
in the place where Venice once stood . . .

Altri materiali c.s.

L'OMOGENEITÀ del mondo (senza sacralità né bellezza)
sarà la mia libertà, dove mi addentro teppista.
E la mia vita sarà una serie di conquiste senza spiritualità.

***

IL POTERE INDUSTRIALE sarà solo provvisoriamente potere.
Poi, per la mia mente solo presente, dovrà dissolversi;
crollerà anch'esso sugli archetipi crollati.

***

L'INTERRELAZIONE tra società e persona
sarà così perfetta... che non ci sarà!
E il mio vivere, ripeto, sarà pura libertà.

***

PER INCULTURAZIONE sarò membro di una società
cosi unica da essere praticamente infinita.
L'unicità della cultura significa
che identificandomi con essa
non mi distiguerò da *altre culture*,
e non proverò mai più, dunque, il rimpianto atroce
di non essere altrove.

***

La nostalgia della storia (rispetto alla storia futura)
di non appartenere ad altro: uh, quanto ne ho sofferto!

***

La predizione del Paradiso
è giusta, come sempre, quando predire il Paradiso
non ha più senso. Ma l'uso del futuro (ahi)
non è ancora caduto da questa grammatica.

***

Ah, fare liberato dal credere!
Liberazione che avviene in una città panterrestre di cemento!
Il passato visto—visitato—come un sacrario,
o meglio un Pantheon, perché la rozza fede

Other Materials (as Above)

THE WORLD'S HOMOGENEITY (with nothing sacred or beautiful)
will be my freedom, which I shall enter as a hooligan.
And my life will be a series of unspiritual conquests.

***

INDUSTRIAL POWER will only temporarily be power.
Then, for my merely present mind, it will have to dissolve;
it too shall collpase, on top of the collapsed archetypes.

***

THE INTERRELATION between society and the individual
will be so perfect . . . that it will not exist!
And my life, I repeat, will be pure freedom.

***

BY ACCULTURATION I shall be a member of a society
so unique as to be practically infinite.
The uniqueness of culture means
that by identifying with it
I shall not distinguish myself from *other cultures*,
and will therefore never again feel the terrible regret
at not being somewhere else.

***

History's nostalgia (compared to future history)
over not being part of something else: oh, how I've suffered it!

***

The prediction of Paradise
is correct, as always, when predicting Paradise
ceases to mean anything. But the use of the future (alas)
has not yet been dropped from this grammar.

***

Ah, the making, free of belief!
A liberation occurring in a worldwide city of cement!
The past seen—revisited—as a sacrarium
or better yet a Pantheon, for crude faith

non supera gli Dei ma li allinea frontalmente:
le esperienze restano compresenti, anche se le più antiche
son fossili. Ora tutta nel Tempio è fossile, e tutto
è dunque allineato: nulla è superato, e neanche *dimenticato*.

***

Là dove un giorno sorgeva Venezia. . .

***

Libero dall'ossessione della religione
(di cui è prodotto il presente canto)
me ne andrò

***

Carico della mia cultura come un buon Tallensi della sua,
ligio al mio field-work, ma carico di wakan
nel bombardamento della manna-type e del mana
visito quel Santuario (in quanto io che scrivo qui)
lasciando i pezzi del mio corpo (capro?) ai vari tabernacoli
in compresenza, senza *superare* le mie successive adorazioni
ma elencandole

***

Siccome solo nella coscienza le esperienze si superano,
mentre nell'inconscio esse si allineano
così nascono insieme le sintesi della coscienza
e gli ammassi;
si ammassano le varie esperienze del Padre (sic)
come l'ho conosciuto a Bologna nel '22, onnipotente—celeste,
poi a Parma nel '23—otiosus
indi dal '24 al '27 drammatico, taurino, equino, col suo lingam
nei calzoni alla cavallerizza di sottotenente del Regio Esercito—
formato da oscuri momenti separati e insuperati
ha tuttavia, insieme, il suo fondamento e la sua unità
nella continuità del tempo, lungo cui egli ha fatto le sue apparizioni.

***

Dentro questa unità
una parte rimpiange l'altra,
da un tabernacolo rivolgo lo sguardo disperato

does not transcend the Gods but aligns them frontally:
experiences remain simultaneously present, even if the most ancient
are fossils. Now the whole Temple is a fossil, and thus
everything is aligned: nothing is transcended, or *forgotten*.

***

In the place where Venice once stood . . .

***

Free of the obsession with religion
(of which the present canto is a product)
I shall go away

***

Loaded with my culture like a good Tallensi with his own,
faithful to my fieldwork, but loaded with wakan
in the bombardment of the manna-type and mana,
I visit that Sanctuary (as myself writing here)
leaving pieces of my body (goat?) at the different tabernacles
simultaneously present, without *transcending* my successive adorations
but only cataloguing them

***

Since only in the conscious mind are experiences transcended,
while in the unconscious they line up one beside the other,
the syntheses and stockpilings of the conscious mind
thus occur together;
stockpiling the various experiences of the Father (sic)
such as I knew him in Bologna in '22, all-powerful—heavenly,
then in Parma in '23—*otiosus*
then from '24 to '27, dramatic, bullish, horselike with his lingam
in his jodhpurs as second lieutenant in the Royal Army—
Formed by separate, untranscended moments of darkness
his foundation and unity lie nevertheless
in the continuity of time, in the course of which he made his appearances.

***

Within this unity
one side regrets the other.
I look desperately away from one tabernacle

all'altro tabernacolo
non potendo essere davanti a tutti contemporaneamente,
e vendendo in ognuno la bellezza paterna del passato
la cosa peggiore del mondo
non è lo sfruttamento dell'uomo sull'uomo

∗∗∗

Là dove un tempo sorgeva Venezia. . .

∗∗∗

Libero dall'ossessione della religione
(di cui è prodotto il presente canto)
me ne andrò

Il giardino dei pesci

Vide l'orfano Caedmon—
gli scoppiava in cuore una voglia di cantare—
ed egli pensò subito a Dio Padre
Ah Caedmon, Caedmon
ti sei portato nel sarcofago la bugia;
com'erano belli gli alberelli del salmone
tra le foglie occhieggiava la carne rosa;
intorno brillavano cupi i cespi
dei frutti argentei delle aringhe—
nei grandi possessi in cui si diffondeva la Sua parola
che era così moderna, contro la vecchia barbarie
Boschetti dai rami capricciosi carichi di conchiglie,
file di pianticine d'istiofori lungo i teneri solchi
Ah Caedmon, Caedmon
che c'entra la religione?
In fondo contro la lama azzurra del cielo,
c'era un brolo di piccoli alberi di naselli,
e sotto, come piante di zucca, rampicanti,
le piante verdegrige delle triglie; lo so,
era forte la voglia di cantare,
non eri né un giardiniere né un ortolano
e tua madre ti aveva allevato sotto la lama di quel cielo
così raramente azzurro e sempre ghiacciato—

and towards the other tabernacle
unable to be before both at once
and seeing in each the fatherly beauty of the past
the worst thing in the world
is not man's exploitation of man

***

In the place where Venice once stood . . .

***

Free of the obsession with religion
(of which the present canto is a product)
I shall go away

The Garden of Fish

Caedmon saw the orphan—
a desire to sing burst forth in his heart—
and he thought at once of God the Father
Ah Caedmon, Caedmon
you bore the lie with you to the grave;
how beautiful the young salmon trees were,
the rosy flesh peering out through the leaves,
as clusters of silvery herring-fruit
shimmered all around—
in the great domains where His word, so modern,
was spreading against the old barbarism—
Thickets with whimsical boughs full of seashells,
rows of small Histiophoridae in soft furrows
Ah Caedmon, Caedmon
what's religion got to do with it?
In the distance, against the blue blade of sky,
there's an orchard of little hake trees,
and beneath them, creeping like squash vines,
some mullet plants, gray-green in color. I know
your desire to sing was great,
you were neither gardener nor farmer
and your mother raised you under a blade of sky
so seldom blue and always ice-cold—

ben lontano dal mare da cui i barbari erano giunti
a sentirsi poveri e vecchi nei confronti alle novità della Chiesa!
Le palme di ostriche godevano immobili quel solicello polare;
non un alito di vento muoveva
i graticci che reggevano le pianticine delicate
dei saraghi violetti come penne di pavone;
ah Caedmon, Caedmon
il canto ti scoppiava in petto,
non importa di cosa si canta.

far from the sea whence the barbarians had come
to feel poor and old before the Church's novelties!
Oyster-palms basked in the wan polar sun, immobile,
not a breath of wind moved
the trellises bracing the delicate sprigs
of violet sea bream like peacock plumes . . .
Ah, Caedmon, Caedmon
the song was bursting inside you,
it doesn't matter what you sing.

VIII
Last Poems

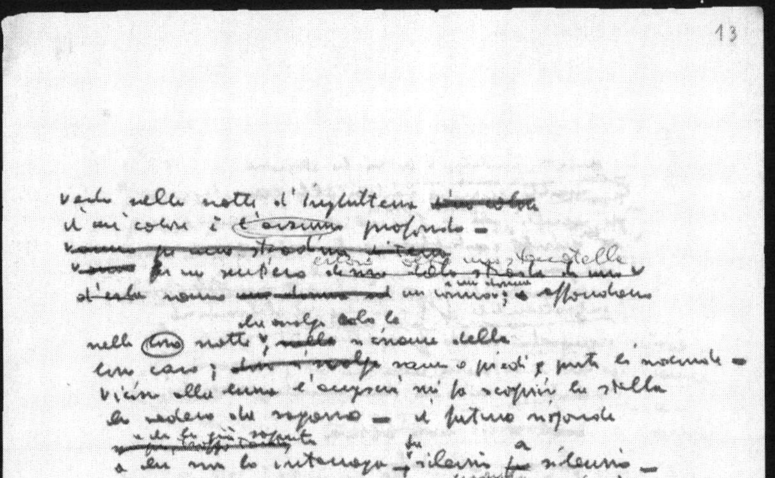

Da *L'hobby del sonetto*

[1]

Qual è l'idea felice che mi risveglia?
Questa, si sa, è l'estate più calda
che si ricordi: il sonno è un piacevole dormiveglia
specialmente se al paziente accade

di sognare di smettere di cavalcare in sella
a cavalli maschi, e saltare nella groppa sudata
di cavalle che solo scherzando mordono la briglia —
L'idea che mi ha svegliato, miracolosa come la rugiada,

è quella di come e dove potrei uccidermi:
esattamente, mio Signore, a un albero del giardino,
qui davanti, dietro la serranda: giungo quasi a ridere

della semplicità della trovata; penso perfino
di procurarmi subito una corda, da custodire, fida
e rassicurante, qui, dentro questo cassettino.

[13]

Perchè mi fermi, a un'ora in cui ci si incontra
per un triste caso, mentre sto con altri amici,
appoggiato al finestrino della loro macchina
ai bordi di un prato di puttane? Non dici

niente fermo sulla tua macchina e guardi.
Forse siamo due conoscenti che si riconoscono.
Sapere di essere stati. . . felici
non stupisce. E del resto è così tardi

che ci si lascia subito. Addio,
mio Signore al volante, visto un'ora dopo
quando ormai tutto è tornato ai tempi in cui io

non vi conoscevo; io voglio rintanarmi come un topo
nella notte sporca e illuminata, voi e il vostro Dio
siete un incidente nel cosmo senza scopo.

From *The Sonnet Hobby*

[1]

What happy thought wakes me today?
This, we know, is the hottest summer
in memory, and sleep is especially gay
if the patient happens, in his slumber,

to dream he is no longer sitting
astride stallions, but riding the sweaty rumps
of mares who pretend to chomp at the bit—
The thought that woke me, wondrous as the dew,

was how and where I might take my own life:
to wit, my Lord, from a tree in the garden,
just outside my window: I nearly laugh

at how simple this seems: I even imagine
me buying a rope, trusty and sure,
that I can hide here, in this drawer.

[13]

Why do you stop me, when by sad coincidence
we meet at an hour when I'm with other friends,
leaning into the window of their car, at the edge
of a field full of whores? You say nothing,

sitting still inside your car, watching.
Perhaps we're two acquaintances who recognize
each other. The thought we were once . . . happy
is no surprise. In any case it's very late,

and so we say goodbye. Farewell,
my Lord at the wheel, seen one hour after
everything has gone back to the time before

I knew you. I want to burrow like a mouse
into the dirty, well-lit night. You and your God
are an accident in the pointless cosmos.

[20]

Ascoltate, Signore, questa storia estiva.
Era estate, presso antichi bastioni
e una grande fontana che si apriva
come un enorme macabro fiore su ubriaconi

clienti di puttane. Ed era notte. Giuliva
si alzò una voce alle spalle di un uomo;
era la voce di un ragazzo. Lungo la riva
tra i rifiuti sparsi sotto quei torrioni

i due si presero a braccetto: e il viaggio
della vita cominciò. Più che felice
il ragazzo era festoso; e, inoltre, saggio.

Pareva che i due andassero per luoghi amici;
ma non era così; lieto il ragazzo lasciò l'uomo
presso una tomba, nel silenzio selvaggio.

[55]

Non c'era Ninetto, quando guardavo
quella piccola stella accanto alla luna,
sentendo crescere in me il sapere, da bravo
ragazzo, come una vera fortuna

che dava dolcezza al futuro. Ero avido
di bene, io! Poi finì che il futuro ebbe un unico
senso, in voi. E se io ero efficiente, e voi ignaro,
io ho fatto di tutto perché a ognuno

di noi toccasse la sua parte di capitale:
mentre voi, prodigo come un mendico,
volevate solo la vita, quella sulla quale

splendono stelle senza nome: dico
questo perché non so spossessarmi
di voi, adesso che niente più vale.

[20]

Listen, Lord, to this summer story.
In summertime near ancient ramparts
a great fountain unfolded its glory
like a huge, ghastly flower over drunkards

soliciting whores. It was night.
A playful voice called from behind a man's back;
it was a boy. Along the bank and right
through the garbage strewn under the towers,

the two walked arm in arm: and life's
journey began. More than happy,
the boy was cheerful, and also wise.

The two seemed headed for friendly places
but this was not to be; the boy left the man
near a tomb, in the barbarous silence.

[55]

Ninetto wasn't there when as a good
boy I gazed at a star beside the moon,
feeling knowledge rise up within me
like a tremendous boon that would

make the future sweet. How I avid I was
for goodness! Then it turned out the future
had only one meaning: you. And though I was
efficient and you were naive, I did

all I could do so that we would each touch
his part of this capital; whereas you, prodigal
as a beggar, wanted only life, such

as the nameless stars shine upon. I tell you
this because I am unable to divest myself
of you, now that nothing has any value.

[63]

Volevo semplicemente dire
cose dirette e dolci, d'invidia,
per dei vecchi sposi, le figure umane
che ho sempre viste come strette da un legame vile —

Volevo dire del loro amore — che dura
decenni — che quando sta per sparire
come una stella che riga il cielo —
volevo dire che di esso sopravvive

qualcosa che fu la sua illusione
non certa la sua realtà: *un semplice patto*, — che pure
era ciò che gli dava il nome —

Del mio restano invece solo le oscure
ragioni per cui è nato —
Non ebbe alcuna benedizione.

[105]

Erano quasi le due di notte — il vento
scorreva per Piazza dei Cinquecento
come in una chiesa — non c'era nemmeno immondizia,
unica vita in quell'ora — giravano

nei giardinetti gli ultimi due o tre ragazzi,
né romani né burini, in cerca
delle mille lire, ma come senza cazzi —
io parlavo in macchina con uno di loro —

un fascista, poverino, e mi affannavo
a toccargli il cuore disperato.
Tu sei giunto con la tua macchina

e hai suonato; ti era al fianco un orribile
giovane individuo; della roba rubata
pendeva al finestrino; da dove venivi e dove andavi?

[63]

I wanted simply to say
some sweet, direct things, out of envy
for old married couples, human figures
I've always seen as joined by a cowardly bond—

I wanted to say that when their love—
which lasts for decades—is about to vanish
like a star streaking the sky above—
I wanted to say that what survives this

is something like love's illusion,
certainly not its reality: *a simple pact*—which
is in fact what gave it its name—

Of mine all that's left are the cryptic
reasons for which it was born—
It never received any blessing.

[105]

It was almost two in the morning—the wind blew
through Piazza dei Cinquecento as if through
a church—and there wasn't even any garbage about,
usually the only life at that hour.

In the small parks two or three young guys
were hanging around, neither Romans nor hicks,
looking for a little cash, but as if they didn't have dicks—
I was talking with one of them in my car—

a Fascist, poor kid—and I was trying hard
to touch his desperate heart.
You pulled up in your car and honked;

beside you sat a horrendous young fellow;
some stolen goods hung out the car window.
Where had you come from, and where did you go?

C'era nel mondo—nessuno lo sapeva—
qualcosa che non aveva prezzo,
ed era unico: non c'era codice né Chiesa
che lo classificasse. Era nel mezzo

della vita e, per confrontarsi, non aveva
che se stesso. Non ebbe, per un pezzo
nemmeno senso: poi riempì l'intera
mia realtà. Era la tua gaiezza.

Quel bene hai voluto distruggerlo;
piano piano, con le tue stesse mani;
gaiamente: te n'è rimasto

un fondo, inalienabile: mi sfugge
il perché di tanta furia nel tuo animo
contro quel nostro amore così casto.

Benevento, 3 febbraio 1973

Castalia

Entro in un piccolo palcoscenico, dove c'è
un tavolo, che l'occupa quasi completamente,
con delle sedie, e, sull'angolo un microfono.
Si tratta di un teatro antico.
C'è già della gente, intorno al tavolo, e io vado a sedermi
sul lato accanto al microfono (a destra se visto dalla platea).
La mia è una presenza ufficiale, ho i vestiti del caso.
Anche gli altri (tutte faccie che conosco ma non ricordo)
hanno l'aria di essersi preparati con cura per la cerimonia.
Al microfono Graziella legge dei versi. Ma la sua voce
va persa in mezzo alla confusione dei preparativi, nel palcoscenico,
e all'enorme vuoto della platea. Dove ha imparato, Graziella,
a leggere così bene dei versi? Con voce profondamente sincera,
ingenua e apprensiva, essa legge quelle poesie
le cui strofe si ripetono uguali con brevi varianti.

[110]

There was, in the world—though nobody knew it—
something that had no price; and it was
unique. No law or Church in existence
could classify it. It came in the middle

of life, and its sole point of reference
was itself. For a while it meant
nothing; then it filled my whole
reality. It was your gayness.

You chose to destroy this boon,
ever so slowly, with your own hands,
gaily; an inalterable base

is all you have left of it. And I still
cannot understand why all the rage
in your soul against a love so chaste.
Benevento, February 3, 1973

Castalia

I walk onto a small stage, where there is
a table taking up most of the space,
some chairs, and a microphone in the corner.
I'm in an ancient theater.
There are people already gathered round the table, and I go and sit down
on the side near the microphone (to the right, if seen from the floor).
My presence there is official, and I'm dressed for the occasion.
The others, too (all faces I know but cannot remember),
seem to have carefully prepared for the ceremony.
Graziella, at the microphone, reads some verse. But her voice
gets lost amidst the confusion of the preparations on stage
and in the great void of the audience. Where did Graziella learn
to read verse so well? In a profoundly sincere voice,
naive and expressive, she reads poems
whose stanzas repeat identically with slight variants.

Sono di argomento politico, e Graziella
se ne fa umilmente paladina.
Il palcoscenico è altissimo; talmente alto che
oltre il suo bordo si vede il vuoto. Mi
alzo sulla sedia, tirando un po' il collo, e vedo che
la platea semivuota è come in fondo a un abisso. Provo le vertigini,
e comincio a sentirmi male. Del resto anche Graziella è interrotta dal-
l'arrivo di alcune persone affaccendate, che invadono la nicchia
del palcoscenico; dal loro fervore di organizzatori, vengo
così a sapere qual è la ragione per cui io sono lì. Devo consegnare un dono
a uno studente ateniese, e la cerimonia sarà ripresa dalla televisione.
Mi trovo in mano una ciotola, dove dovrà essere contenuto il dono.
Il microfono è lì, accanto a me. È allora che mi prende
una isterica, infantile, sadica collera. Col cuore che mi scoppia,
grido che mai io accetterò di fare una cosa simile, e
(benché qualcosa — contro cui specialmente si esercita, appunto,
il mio sadismo — mi trattenga) esco, ripetendo,
le mie disperate parole di rifiuto. Mi trovo così
in una grande stanza, dove altre persone stanno ad aspettare.
Il teatro deve certamente trovarsi in cima a un'altura,
nel cuore della città con dietro il mare. La grande stanza
attigua al palcoscenico è infatti invasa da una luce marina.
La gente che è lì radunata in attesa della cerimonia è
quieta, serena, luminosa. In mezzo agli altri c'è un giovane,
dalla faccia a me conosciuta. È però trasfigurato da quella
pace rituale. Sulla pelle ha come un radioso cerone, e, i capelli,
li ha freschi, ariosi, profumati. Sono lunghi, secondo l'abbietta moda:
ma molto corti, però, per quanto vaporosi, sopra la fronte: e,
in mezzo, vi splende, come una goccia ardente, una pietra
preziosa, ora azzurra ora sanguigna. Lo guardo
soffocato di rabbia, delusione e dolore, e, già volto
per uscirmene anche da lì, faccio qualche passo verso di lui.
Il suo modo di essere mi offende; quella sua
bellissima ridicola testa — a cui ho dichiarato
altre volte e tanto spesso il mio odio — e lui lo sa —
mi fa scoppiare il cuore d'amarezza e pazza voglia di vendetta.
«Davanti a tutti questi testimoni — urlo — te lo giuro:
non lavorerò mai più con te! È finita!» Non spero
di ottenere nulla con questa mia disperata minaccia: ma
non mi aspetto nemmeno tanta indifferenza, mista a un disprezzo

They are political in subject, and Graziella
humbly champions the cause.
The stage is extremely high, so high that
past its edge one sees only the void. I
get up from my chair, crane my neck a little, and see that
the half-empty pit is as though at the bottom of an abyss. My head spins
and I begin to feel ill. Graziella, meanwhile, is interrupted by
the arrival of some rather busy people, who invade the stage area;
from their organizational fervor I come
to learn the reason why I'm there. I am to give an award
to an Athenian student, and the ceremony will be broadcast on television.
There is a bowl in my hand, which is supposed to contain the award.
The microphone is there beside me. And at that moment an hysterical
rage, infantile and sadistic, comes over me. With my heart bursting
I scream that I will never agree to do such a thing, and
(although something — against which my sadism is in fact particularly
directed — holds me back) I leave, repeating
my desperate words of refusal. Then I find myself
in a big room, where other people are waiting.
The theater must surely be situated at the top of an elevation
in the heart of the city, with the sea in the distance. And in fact
the big room adjacent to the stage is invaded by a marine light.
The people assembled there awaiting the ceremony are
calm, serene, luminous. Among the crowd there is a youth
whose face I know. He is transfigured, however, by the
ritual peace. He has a radiant sort of makeup on his skin, and his hair
is fresh, airy, fragrant. He wears it long, in keeping with the vile fashion,
but very short and gauzy over his forehead,
at the center of which shines, like a drop of hot liquid, a precious
stone, blue one minute, blood-red the next. Choking
with rage, disappointment and sorrow, and already turning around
to leave that place, too, I take a few steps toward him.
His way of being offends me; that beautiful,
ridiculous head of his — of which I've expressed
my hatred on other occasions and often — and he knows this —
makes my heart burst with bitterness and mad desire for revenge.
"With all these people as my witnesses," I yell, "I swear to you,
I will never work with you again! It's over!" I don't hope
to gain anything from my desperate threat; but neither
did I expect such indifference, mixed with a disdain

ch'è quasi odio e ingratitudine, in lui, il festeggiato, che
non si scompone, aspettando che il rito incominci.
Io mi volto per uscire anche da lì, con lo sguardo nemico
di quelle pupille confitto nel cuore. Intanto,
vengo a sapere
che non molto lontano
da lì, oltre dei
monti azzurri, su dei prati
verdi che sono quelli dell'Ade,
gli altri studenti
ateniesi morti come
colui che era festeggiato
alla televisione se ne stanno immobili
a guardare le acque della
fonte Castalia, al loro fianco
non lontani ci sono i colonnelli anch'essi
certo morti in un
silenzio che non è né di venerazione né di rispetto
né di ufficiale raccoglimento, e neanche di reale pietà umana.
Sulle poche acque della fonte, tra ciuffi secchi
di erba e pietre, c'è uno sciame di api che immobili e brulicanti,
si abbeverano; e sono l'unico segno di vita.

Saluto e augurio

A è quasi sigùr che chista
a è la me ultima poesia par furlàn;
e i vuèj parlàighi a un fassista
prima di essi (o ch'al sedi) massa lontàn.

Al è un fassista zòvin,
al varà vincia un, vincia doi àins:
al è nassùt ta un pais,
e al è zut a scuela in sitàt.

Al è alt, cui ociàj, il vistìt
gris, i ciavièj curs:
quand ch'al scumìnsia a parlàmi
i crot ch'a no'l savedi nuja di politica

that is almost hatred and ingratitude, in him, the guest of honor, who
doesn't lose his composure and merely waits for the ceremony to begin.
I turn around to leave that place, too, with the inimical stare
of those eyes piercing my heart. Meanwhile
I learn
that not far
from there, beyond
the blue mountains, in green
meadows that are those of Hades,
other Athenian
students, dead
like the guest of honor
on television, stand motionless
watching the waters of the
spring of Castalia; beside them,
not far away, are the colonels, also
dead, of course, in a
silence that is not one of veneration or respect,
or official contemplation, or even of real human pity.
Over the scant waters of the spring, between dry clumps
of grass and rocks, there is a swarm of bees, teeming motionless
and drinking; they are the only sign of life.

Goodbye and Best Wishes

This will almost certainly be
my last poem in Friulian;
I want to speak to a Fascist
before I, or he, get too far away.

He's a young Fascist, maybe
twenty-one, twenty-two years old,
was born in a village,
and went to school in the city.

He's tall, wears glasses
and a gray suit, has short hair;
and when he starts talking to me,
I think he knows nothing about politics

e ch'al serci doma di difindi il latìn
e il grec, cuntra di me; no savìnt
se ch'i ami il latin, il grec — e i ciavièj curs.
Lu vuardi, al è alt e gris coma un alpìn.

«Ven cà, ven cà, Fedro.
Scolta. I vuèj fati un discors
ch'al somèa a un testamìnt.
Ma recuàrditi, i no mi fai ilusiòns

su di te: jo i sai ben, i lu sai,
ch'i no ti às, e no ti vòus vèilu,
un còur libar, e i no ti pos essi sinsèir:
ma encia si ti sos un muàrt, ti parlaràì.

Difìnt i palès di moràr o aunàr,
in nomp dai Dius, grecs o sinèis.
Mòur di amòur par li vignis.
E i fics tai ors. I socs, i stecs.

Il ciaf dai to cunpàins, tosàt.
Difìnt i ciamps tra il paìs
e la campagna, cu li so panolis,
il vas'cis dal ledàn. Difìnt il prat

tra l'ultima ciasa dal paìs e la roja.
I ciasàj a somèjn a Glìsiis:
giolt di chista idea, tènla tal còur.
La confidensa cu'l soreli e cu' la ploja,

ti lu sas, a è sapiensa santa.
Difìnt, conserva, prea! La Repùblica
a è drenti, tal cuàrp da la mari.
I paris a àn serciàt, e tornàt a sercià

di cà e di là, nassìnt, murìnt,
cambiànt: ma son dutis robis dal passàt.
Vuei: difìnd, conservà, preà. Tas:
la to ciamesa ch'a no sedi

and is trying only to defend Latin
and Greek from me, unaware
how much I love Latin and Greek—and short hair.
I look at him: he's tall and gray, like an *Alpino*.

"Come here, come here, Phaedrus.
Listen. I want to tell you something
that will sound like a testament.
But remember, I have no illusions

about you. I know, know all too well,
that your heart is not free, nor do you
wish it to be, and you cannot be sincere;
but I will speak to you, even if you are dead.

You defend the fenceposts of mulberry and alder,
in the name of the Gods, Greek or Chinese.
You're dying of love for the vineyards.
For the fig trees in gardens. For the tree stumps and sticks.

For your companions' close-cropped heads.
You defend the fields between village
and countryside, with their corncobs
and vats of manure. You defend the meadow

between the last house in the village and the canal.
The farmhouses look like Churches:
rejoice in this idea, keep it in your heart.
Intimacy with the sun and the rain,

you know, is sacred wisdom.
Defend, preserve, pray! The Republic
is within, inside the mother's body.
The fathers have searched and searched again

here and there, being born, dying,
changing: but all these are things in the past.
Today, defend, preserve, pray. Hush!
May your shirt be not black

nera, e nencia bruna. Tas! Ch'a sedi
'na ciamesa grisa. La ciamesa dal siun.
Odia chej ch'a volin dismòvisi
e dismintiàssi da li Paschis . . .

Duncia, fantàt dai cialsìns di muàrt,
i ti ài dita se ch'a volin i Dius
dai ciamps. Là ch'i ti sos nassùt.
Là che da frut i ti às imparàt

i so Comandamìns. Ma in Sitàt?
Scolta. Là Crist a no'l basta.
A coventa la Glìsia: ma ch'a sedi
moderna. E a coventin i puòrs.

Tu difint, conserva, prea:
ma ama i puòrs: ama la so diversitàt.
Ama la so voja di vivi bessòj
tal so mond, tra pras e palàs

là ch'a no rivi la peràula
dal nustri mond; ama il cunfin
ch'a àn segnàt tra nu e lòur;
ama il so dialèt inventàt ogni matina,

par no fassi capì; par no spartì
cun nissùn la so ligria.
Ama il soreli di sitàt e la miseria
dai laris; ama la ciar da la mama tal fì.

Drenti dal nustri mond, dis
di no essi borghèis, ma un sant
o un soldàt: un sant sensa ignoransa,
un soldàt sensa violensa.

Puarta cun mans di sant o soldàt
l'intimitàt cu'l Re, Destra divina
ch'a è drenti di nu, tal siùn.
Crot tal borghèis vuàrb di onestàt,

or even brown. Hush! Let it be
a gray shirt. The shirt of sleep.
Hate those who want to wake up
and forget about Easter . . .

Well, young man in a dead man's socks,
I've told you what the Gods of the fields
want from you. The Gods of where
you were born. Where you learned

their Commandments. And in the City?
Listen. There, Christ is not enough.
The Church is needed, but let her be
modern. And the poor are needed, too.

As for you: defend, preserve, pray;
but love the poor: love their difference.
Love their wish to live alone
in their world, between meadows and buildings

where word of our world
never reaches; love the boundary
they have drawn between us and them;
love the dialect they invent every morning

so no one will understand them;
so they won't have to share their joy.
Love the sun of the city and the poverty
of thieves; love the mother's flesh in the son.

And in our world, say
you are not bourgeois but a saint
or a soldier—a soldier without ignorance,
a soldier without violence.

Carry in a saint's or soldier's hands
your closeness with the King, the divine Right
that lies within us, in sleep.
Believe in the bourgeois's blind virtue,

encia s'a è 'na ilusiòn: parsè
che encia i parons, a àn
i so paròns, e son fis di paris
ch'a stan da qualchi banda dal mond.

Basta che doma il sintimìnt
da la vita al sedi par duciu cunpàin:
il rest a no impuàrta, fantàt cun in man
il Libri sensa la Peràula.

Hic desinit cantus. Ciàpiti
tu, su li spalis, chistu zèit plen.
Jo i no pos, nissun no capirès
il scàndul. Un veciu al à rispièt

dal judissi dal mond; encia
s'a no ghi impuarta nuja. E al à rispièt
di se che lui al è tal mond. A ghi tocia
difindi i so sgnerfs indebulìs,

e stà al zòuc ch'a no'l à mai vulùt.
Ciàpiti tu chistu pèis, fantàt ch'i ti mi odiis:
puàrtilu tu. Al lus tal còur. E jo i ciaminarai
lizèir, zint avant, sielzìnt par sempri

la vita, la zoventùt.»

even if this is an illusion — for
the bosses, too, have their bosses,
and are sons of fathers
somewhere in the world.

It's enough that the feeling
for life be the same for all:
the rest doesn't matter, boy with
the Book with no Word in your hand.

Hic desinit cantus. Take this
burden onto your shoulders.
I cannot: nobody would understand
the scandal. An old man must respect

the world's judgment, even if
he doesn't give a damn about it.
And he must respect what he is to the world.
He must defend his enfeebled nerves

and play the game he has never played.
Take this weight, boy, though you hate me.
Carry it yourself. It shines bright in the heart.
And I shall walk lightly on, always choosing

life, and youth."

NOTES

Of the many sources for these notes, the generous apparatus of annotations in Walter Siti's edition of *Tutte le poesie* (2003) was by far the most indispensable. References to Siti's body of commentary in those two volumes of Pasolini's poetry will be abbreviated here to Siti I and Siti II, accordingly. Similarly, references to Nico Naldini's invaluable *Pasolini, Una vita* will be abbreviated, as in the introduction, to Naldini VP.

Being deeply rooted at once in literary-artistic tradition and lived experience, Pasolini's poetry is highly allusive and requires extensive annotation for readers unfamiliar with his frames of reference. In this respect, he is a kind of modern-day Dante. The verse also contains an elaborate system of internal reference within his poetic corpus and his artistic-critical-theoretical oeuvre as a whole. My intention in compiling these annotations, beyond the primary purpose of explication, was also to give a sense of the overriding integrality of all of Pasolini's work as the vast echo chamber of a single, highly creative mind. Indeed, all of Pasolini's production — diaries, letters, and of course poetry, films, novels, and essays — is involved in a kind of endless dialogue with itself, even as it engages society and the outside world in a manner that few poets do. It is my hope that these notes will help the reader to see how the poems serve as the lifeblood of Pasolini's vast artistic and intellectual project.

I. *La meglio gioventù / The Best of Youth* (The Friulian Poems)

The volume of Pasolini's Friulian poetry that appeared in 1954 under the title of *La meglio gioventù* (here translated as "The Best of Youth") — published by the Florentine publishing house Sansoni under an imprint, the Biblioteca di Paragone, that featured authors associated with the literary-cultural review *Paragone*, edited by art historian Roberto Longhi and his wife, novelist Anna Banti — brought together in somewhat expanded form the work of three prior, smaller volumes of verse and constituted the poet's first publication by a major publisher. The earlier volumes included in this collection were *Poesie a Casarsa* (Bologna: Libreria Antiquaria Mario Landi, 1942), *Dov'è la mia patria* (Casarsa: Edizioni dell'Academiuta, 1949), and *Tal* coùr d'un frut (Tricesimo: Edizioni di Lingua Friulana, 1953), though it also featured previously uncollected work that Pasolini had published in periodicals and reviews, among them Longhi and Banti's *Paragone*. A lot of Pasolini's early Friulian production, both published and unpublished, was left out of *La meglio gioventù*, though it was republished in large part in 2003 in *Tutte le poesie*, edited by Walter Siti. Pasolini's writing in Italian from this period was also excluded, though a good deal of it would later be recuperated in the 1958 volume, *L'usignolo della Chiesa Cattolica* (see below).

La meglio gioventù won Pasolini national attention for the first time when it shared the Premio Carducci for 1954 with Paolo Volponi. By this time, of course, Pasolini was already living in Rome and writing the poetry and fiction that would catapult him to literary fame.

Page 62 "Il nini muàrt" / "Dead Boy"
According to Nico Naldini, Pasolini's cousin, friend, collaborator, and biographer, "Il nini muàrt" was composed in late July 1941 and was the second poem Pier Paolo "wrote directly in Friulian." The first such poem, inspired by the word *rosada* (see the introduction to this volume), appeared in the chapbook *I confini* and later "disappeared from the collections." (P. P. Pasolini, *Lettere 1940-1954*, ed. N. Naldini, quoted in Siti I, 1466.) Before that, Pasolini's dialect compositions were translations from Italian (Naldini, VP, 34). The Friulian title echoes Garcia Lorca's "Gacela del niño muerto," in *Divan del Tamarit* (Siti I, ibid.).

Page 62 "David"
An earlier version of this poem bore the title "Per il 'David' di Manzù" (For Manzù's 'David'), an indication that it was inspired by an eponymous sculpture by Giacomo Manzù (1908–91). Walter Siti (I, p. 1468) cites the 1938 version of Manzù's piece as the source, though the sculptor made two other similar works with the same title, dated 1936 and 1940 respectively.

Page 66 "La domènia uliva" / "Olive Sunday"
In certain regions of Italy, such as Pasolini's Friuli, the last Sunday of Lent, known most commonly as Palm Sunday, is called *La Domenica delle Olive*, or "Olive Sunday," and involves the ritual distribution of olive branches instead of palms. Just as the palms are meant to recall Christ's entry into Jerusalem—in addition to being archaic symbols of victory, regeneration, and immortality—the olive branches, traditionally symbols of peace, victory and protection, likewise commemorate Christ's triumphal entry, especially as the relevant passages in the synoptic gospels (Matthew, Mark, and Luke) do not specify the kind of tree whose branches were laid at the Lord's feet before his passing. Only John 12:13 refers specifically to palms. Similarly, the iconography of Christ's entry, especially in Italian medieval and early Renaissance art, variously finds both palm fronds and olive branches being used for this purpose. The olive branch also anticipates Christ's prayers in the Garden of Olives and prefigures his Passion, when "his sweat became like drops of blood falling down upon the ground" (Luke 22:24).

Giovanni Pascoli (1855–1912) wrote a similarly titled poem, "La domenica dell'ulivo," in *Myricae*, but the tone and style, if certainly not the content, of Pasolini's "Olive Sunday" are more reminiscent of the vernacular poems of Jacopone da Todi (1228?–1306), an early Italian poet and Franciscan monk, later beatified, perhaps best known for his Latin composition on the Virgin Mary's grief, the *Stabat Mater Dolorosa*, set to music by a host of composers over the centuries. Jacopone's vernacular *laudi* and canticles, which dramatized scriptural and legendary Christian subjects, were an important early phase in the tradition of Christian mystery and miracle plays.

Another echo of Pascoli, on the other hand, can be found in line 48, "e chistu muàrt sunsùr," a near transcription of Pascoli's "a quel morto sussurro" in "A Giorgio navarco ellenico," in *Odi e inni*, I, 22 (A. Arveda, "Premessa, Note e Apparato," in P. P. Pasolini, *La Meglio Gioventù*, A. Arveda ed., Salerno Roma 1998, quoted in Siti I, p. 1473). Interestingly, however, Pasolini's transposition of Pascoli's words into Friulian dialect changes the meaning, since *sunsùr*, while obviously having the same root as *sussurro*, means not "whisper" or "murmur," but "rumble" or "drone."

In "Gli adorati toponimi" ("Cherished Toponyms"), in *I Parlanti* (1951), Pasolini interestingly comments on lines 77–78 of "Olive Sunday," "pai vecius murs / e pai pras scurs" ("over ancient walls / and darkened fields"):

> Beyond the confine of memory, there's this obsessive image of a spot of dampness. Already in '42, when I'd just turned twenty, in my little collection of Casarsese verse I wrote the following words (which, in my mind, were faintly distinguished by the *damp* feeling that suggested them to me): *pai vecius murs / e pai pras scurs* ("over ancient walls / and darkened fields")—an expression that insistently returned, in more or less varied form, throughout the chapbook, as if setting the tone for the music of the landscape of *my days as a boy* (quoted in Siti I, p. 1473).

One finds the same image, in another evocation of youth, toward the end of chapter I of the 1949 poem "L'Italia":

> In a village of Friuli his soul was born
> confused with a damp wall
> and a patch of grass black with water[.]

An echo of this same image occurs fifteen years later in "Poem in the Shape of a Rose": "the taxi sideswipes an embankment, / the grass sharp and black from the heart / of nights swampy and mysterious from birth." The image of "black grass" also dates back to the early Friulian poetry, as in "Suite furlana": "my life / was alive as grass on a black bank."

In the first lines of the second stanza on pp. 70–71, "Li cròus a si cujèrzin / di zemis" ("The crosses are covered / with buds"), the Friulian term *zemi*, like the Italian *gemma*, can mean both "bud" and "gem."

Page 76 "Dansa di Narcìs" / "Narcissus Dancing"
According to Furio Brugnolo (quoted in Siti I, p. 1479), the metrical model for this poem is the pastorela-dansa *Per amor soi gai*, attributed to Guiraut d'Espanha, "which Pasolini reproduces, actually paraphrasing it at a few points."

Page 76 "Pastorela di Narcìs" / "Narcissus Pastourelle"
Brugnolo (ref. in Siti I, p. 1480) points out that in this poem Pasolini faithfully reproduces the meter of twelfth-century troubadour Gui d'Uissel's pastourelle "L'autrier cavalcava."

The use of the Occitan form is consistent with Pasolini's "Felibrist" wish, during his Friulian period, to create a literature directly linked to other lost Romance traditions (Provençal, Catalan, etc.). According to Siti, however, "the explicit Provençal schema is here echoed and overturned: the young man leaves for the countryside and, in accordance with the canon, encounters a girl; but this girl turns out to be himself, with his mother's dark eyes. It is almost as though Pasolini, under the influence of his early readings in psychoanalysis, wants to explain his homosexuality as an autoerotic, narcissistic obsession" (Siti I, p. 1480).

The poem also features Pasolini's recurrent theme of the doubling of his own character (cf., in this volume, "My Former Life," "The Ballad of Delirium," and "Last Dreams Before Dying").

Page 78 "Il dì da la mi muàrt" / "The Day of My Death"
Brugnolo (Siti I, 1481) points out that the nine-line stanzas, with their *ababcccbb* rhyme scheme, reproduce those of twelfth-century troubadour Cadenet's pastourelle *L'autrier lonc un bosc folhos.*

For Siti the "crystal lap" (*grin di cristàl*) in the final line may be derived from Rimbaud's "crystal arm" (*bras de cristal*) in "Being beauteous, I." If so, it is another instance of Pasolini's borrowing a trope in order to make it entirely his own. Indeed, his use of term *grin* (and later *grembo* in Italian), which normally means "lap" or "womb," to indicate the male groin is completely original and recurs in this usage throughout his poetic corpus. In so doing he eroticizes the term for "lap" when referred to the male body. The image also recurs repeatedly in his films, perhaps most notably in *Teorema*, where the camera lingers on the bulge in Terence Stamp's trousers as he reads a volume of none other than Rimbaud.

When the term *grin/grembo* appears in poems in this volume, I have translated it variously as "lap," "loins," and "groin."

Page 80 "Conzèit" / "Envoi"
Pasolini uses the traditional troubadour *envoi* (*congedo* in Italian, *conzèit* in Friulian) to close out Volume I of the 1954 edition of *La meglio gioventù*. For aesthetic reasons I have taken a slight liberty in placing the poem "Laris" before "Conzèit," even though it was not part of the original cycle of which "Conzèit" constituted the endpiece. The chronology of my selection, however, remains intact, as "Laris" dates from a 1949 cycle and was thus written before "Conzèit." According to Furio

Brugnolo (Siti I, p. 1487), Pasolini's model for this poem is the anonymous Provençal cobla *Quan lo rossinhols*.

II. *L'usignolo della Chiesa Cattolica* /
The Nightingale of the Catholic Church

Like *La meglio gioventù*, *L'usignolo della Chiesa Cattolica* was published well after most of the poems were written, and some fifteen years after Pasolini composed the sequence that gives the collection its name. Its publication in 1958 followed not only Pasolini's first novel, *Ragazzi di Vita* (1955), but also *Le ceneri di Gramsci* (1957), whose poems were written well after those of *L'usignolo*. I thus present it before *Le ceneri di Gramsci* to convey as accurately as possible the chronological sequence of the work itself. The reader should, in fact, consider the book, and the present brief selection, as the Italian-language counterpart to the Friulian compositions of *La meglio gioventù*, since their respective chronologies run more or less parallel. A few of the poems in *L'usignolo*, like the first one featured here, "Dawns," were actually translated into Italian by the author from Friulian originals.

As *L'usignolo* bounced around from publisher to publisher before finding a home, Pasolini kept adding new cycles to it. When it was finally published in 1958, the volume spanned the years 1943 to 1949, ending with the poem "La scoperta di Marx" ("Discovering Marx"), which already displays some characteristics of the poet's more mature style. The last text featured in the present selection, the "Poesiole notturne" ("Little Night Poems"), is from uncollected work from the years 1950 to 1953 that Pasolini had thought to include as an "appendix" to the 1958 Longanesi edition before suddenly changing his mind when turning in the manuscript. It is duly included in an appendix to *L'usignolo* in W. Siti's edition of *Tutte le poesie*.

In a January 26, 1947, letter to Gianfranco Contini, Pasolini indirectly explains the title of *The Nightingale of the Catholic Church*, writing that the "still-virgin twenty-one year old" he was when he wrote the title sequence had been "moved by a sort of peasant Christianity," which he'd discovered in the agrarian communities of the Friuli, "finding sweet and equivocal fonts of heresy in its exasperated Eros" (Siti I, p. 1537).

A few years later, in an unpublished "Note to *The Nightingale of the Catholic Church*" from 1951, which presumably he had hoped at the time to append to the text upon publication, Pasolini gave a somewhat different explanation:

> My encounter with my mother's hometown had allowed my adolescent goodness to take the form the Church requires of its most pious sons, the catechumens. I didn't believe in God, but I loved, or rather, I *wanted to* love the Church. I knew well that Pascal had written in one of his *Pensées*—which that year had been, along with Tommaseo's *Songs of the Greek People*, my *livre de chevet*—that one can get artificially close to God by the experience of going to Church. The Church I'd found was that of a poor Friulian village.
> —From "Nota all'Usignolo della Chiesa Cattolica," in *Saggi sulla letteratura e sull'arte*, vol. I, p. 365.

It is not clear whether Pasolini's claim to have been at the time an unbeliever is true or merely an attitude assumed a posteriori. In the 1943 cycle called "The Nightingale of the Catholic Church," which lent its title to the entire 1958 collection, he seems more wracked by doubt and tempted by blasphemy and heresy than convinced of unbelief. In fact it seems not so much "the Church" per se that fascinates him—since the poems of the "Nightingale" cycle actually subvert traditional dogma—but rather the specifically "peasant" version of Christianity he mentions to Contini in his letter. It is only in the second, 1946 cycle included in the 1958 volume, entitled "Il pianto della rosa" ("The Lament of the Rose"), the second section of which is entitled "Il non credo" (The non-Credo), that a position of unbelief emerges more clearly, though here, too, it stands against a background rife with religious imagery and neo-Baudelairean blasphemy and gnosticism. Upon openly embracing Marxism around 1947, Pasolini took a more unambiguous position and generally maintained his claim to atheism for the rest of his life, all the while charging his works with a transcendent mystical aura and a nostalgia for the primitive religions of the past, including Christianity. In his 1963 film *La ricotta*—a thirty-five-minute short about an extra playing the "good thief," who dies of overeating during the shooting of a scene of Christ's passion—the character of the filmmaker (played by Orson Welles as a sort of stand-in for Pasolini) claims that his work expresses a "profound, archaic Catholicism."

Of the poems selected here for this group, the first four come from the original cycle and chapbook *L'usignolo della Chiesa Cattolica*, from 1943, while the rest are from the years 1947–50.

Page 84 "Le albe" / "Dawns"
A longer, original version of this poem was written in Friulian ("Li albis") and published in Pasolini's self-founded review, *Stroligut di cà da l'Aga*, in April 1944 (Siti, p. 1543).

Page 84 "La Passione" / "The Passion"
This poem also appears to derive from a longer Friulian text entitled *Parafrasi della messa* (Paraphrasis of the Mass), which was broken down into lines for a priest and lines for Christ. This was later revised under the title of *Il Sacrificio*, with Christ's lines now cast into verse. These lines formed the basis for the Italian text here presented (Siti, p. 1544).

Page 92 "In Memoriam"
Again we see a doubling of the speaker, here with the dead spirit. All the lines of the poem are centered as in an epitaph (see also part VIII of "A Desperate Vitality," pp. 354–57).

Page 94 "Litania" / "Litany"
An earlier form of the poem was written in Friulian under the title "The Names of the Rosary" (Siti I, p. 1551).

The Latin epithets invoked in this litany mean, as follows: Janua Coeli, "Door to the Heavens"; Speculum Justitiae, "Mirror of Justice"; Mater Purissima, "Mother Most Pure"; Mater Castissima, "Mother Most Chaste"; Mater Inviolata, "Inviolate Mother"; Turris Eburnea, "Ivory Tower"; Stella Matutina, "Morning Star"; Regina Pacis, "Queen of Peace."

Page 98 "Lingua" / "Language"
It is important to note that Pasolini here is treating the term *lingua* (language, tongue) specifically in opposition to the term *dialetto* (dialect; see introduction, pp. 17–19). Indeed, all the cycles of *The Nightingale of the Catholic Church*—those preceding the cycle "Tragiques" (1948–49)—were written when the poet was torn, as it were, between *dialetto* (in this case Friulian) and *lingua* (Italian) as possible mediums of poetic expression.

It is also worth noting that with the Italian *lingua* comes the significant baggage, for Pasolini, of a rich and classicized literary tradition, here symbolized by the statues, the classical topoi ("waters of Arcadia"), the "ivory hendecasyllable" (the hendecasyllable being the traditional verse line of "high" and epic poetry in Italian), and the museum. Perhaps more than any other poem written at this crucial juncture, "Lingua" captures the poet's ambivalence towards the medium he will eventually choose for his mature poetry. For Pasolini, the great Italian tradition— his love of which is eloquently evinced in such poems as "L'Appennino" and the use of such painters as Piero della Francesca, Mantegna, and Pontormo as models for the imagery in his films (*The Gospel According to Matthew*, *Mamma Roma*, *La Ricotta*)— is also the matrix of the culture whose decadence and authoritarianism gave rise to Fascism. The poem's form, in the original, well captures the poet's ambivalence. Pasolini's "heretical" passions are captured in finely honed, eleven-line stanzas with an unusual rhyme scheme of *abbcddeffgg*, with slight exceptions for the third and sixth strophes.

Stanza 4, lines 2, 4 and 5: The Po, Livenza, and Idria are northern Italian rivers by whose banks Pasolini spent different periods of his childhood and youth.

Page 112 L'ex-vita / My Former Life
Stanza 1, lines 9–10: "O Individual, O Double, you find yourself / fashioned from me . . . ." This is a further instance of the doubling of character one finds in Pasolini's poetry from the start (cf. also "Narcissus Pastourelle," "The Ballad of Delirium," and "Last Dreams Before Dying"). In a 1941 letter to his friend Franco Farolfi, the young Pasolini sheds some light on the "other" self that he appears to want to exorcise in this poem. In it he writes: "I want to kill a hypersensitive, sickly adolescent who is trying to pollute my life as a man; though he is already moribund, I shall be cruel to him; even though, deep down, I love him, since he was my life up to the threshold of the present day" (Naldini, VP, p. 73).

III. *I Diari* / *The Diaries*

An important vein of Pasolini's poetry from the start, the diaristic mode was a natural one for this prolific author of thousands of pages of diaries in prose which often provided the subject matter for these and other poems. The texts included in this selection are drawn only from the cycles written during the poet's first few years in Rome. Some of these come from the two small volumes published in 1960 by the small Milanese publisher Vanni Scheiwiller: *Roma 1950. Diario*, and *Sonnetto primaverile* (1953). The others are from two cycles unpublished during the author's lifetime and collected in *Tutte le poesie*, vol. 1: *Ritmo Romano* (1951) and *Poesia con letteratura* (1951–52).

Page 140 *"Pieno di confidenza e di tepore"* / *"Full of intimacy and warmth"*
Line 7: Sacile and Idria were places in northeast Italy where Pasolini lived in early childhood. Sacile is a town on the Livenza river, repeatedly evoked in his poetry. Idria is the region surrounding the river of the same name; it became part of Slovenia after World War II.

Page 142 *"Chiusa la festa . . ."* / *"The Holiday Over . . ."*
Lines 17–18: *". . . from Testaccio / to Monteverde . . ."* Testaccio and Monteverde are districts (*rioni*) of Rome, both situated on hills not included in the famous seven. Testaccio's hill dates back to Roman times and is artificial; its population is traditionally working-class (though currently being gentrified); Monteverde, at least Monteverde Vecchio, is more bourgeois and upper-class, housing, among other things, the splendid Villa Doria-Pamphili and its large park. Monteverde Nuovo is generally working-class. For more on Testaccio, see the notes to "Gramsci's Ashes."

Page 142 *"La pioggia ha verniciato la terra"* / *"Rain has varnished the earth"*
Line 2: The Aniene is a tributary of the Tiber river, which it joins outside of Rome. Pasolini's first encounters with the Roman underclasses occurred on the banks of this torrent, where he met, among others, Sergio Citti, who went on to become a good friend and a filmmaker in his own right. Citti served, among other things, as Pasolini's guide to the subproletarian world and his linguistic advisor in his use of the Roman dialect, *il romanesco*, in the novels *Ragazzi di vita* and *Una vita violenta* and in Pasolini's first two films, *Accattone* and *Mamma Roma*. Sergio Citti also introduced Pasolini to his younger brother Franco, who went on to star in several of the poet's films, including *Accattone*, *Mamma Roma*, and *Oedipus Rex*.

IV. *Le ceneri di Gramsci* / *Gramsci's Ashes*

When it was published in 1957, *Le ceneri di Gramsci* brought Pasolini's poetry to the attention of a broad public for the first time. Particularly striking was his use of the traditional terza rima form to discuss social and political issues, and thereby to bend the form to include levels of language not normally considered "poetic." Concomitant with this tension between form and content, Pasolini sometimes used the form loosely, allowing line lengths to vary beyond the norm (the traditional hendecasyllable is already somewhat variable) and letting the characteristically interlocking rhyme scheme disappear sometimes or be carried by off-rhymes and apocopated rhymes, a strategy that became a sort of trademark of his. Nevertheless, at moments the near-perfect conjunction of rigorous form and innovative content gives the poems of this collection (all but two of which are in terza rima) a crystalline quality that belies the apparent "prosaicness" of some of the subjects. Though Pasolini would continue to use terza rima in parts of his next two volumes of verse, there is a gradual further loosening of the form over time. *Le ceneri di Gramsci* won the Premio Viareggio for 1957.

Page 152 "L'Appennino" / "The Apennines"
Part I, stanza 3, line 3: The Lucchesia is the countryside around the medieval-Renaissance town of Lucca in western Tuscany.

Part I, stanza 2, line 2: Versilia is a region along the northwestern coast of Tuscany. Traditionally consisting only of the towns of Seravezza, Stazzema, Pietrasanta, and Forte dei Marmi, Versilia is now considered to include the whole area from Marina di Carrara down to Livorno. The poet Gabriele D'Annunzio (1863–1938) celebrated Versilia in a poem of the same name in the collection *Alcyone*.

Part I, stanza 3, line 3: The Argentario is a promontory, once an island, off the coast of southwest Tuscany, opposite the isle of Elba.

Part II, stanza 2, line 3: "Pienza / or Tarquinia." Founded in the fifteenth century by the humanist Pope Pius II (Enea Silvio Piccolomini) on the site of the medieval Tuscan village of Corsignano, Pienza is a rare example of an "ideal city" built in the Renaissance according to architectural and urbanistic principles inspired by Neoplatonic philosophy. Tarquinia was an Etruscan city in northern Latium that reblossomed in the Middle Ages before its pristine ancient beauty was marred by excessive modern building after World War II.

Part II, stanza 7, line 2: "a bust of Boniface / about to turn to dust." This is probably the thirteenth-century statue of Pope Boniface VIII in a niche at the Porta della Rocca in Orvieto (Siti I, p. 1630). Boniface (1235–1303) served as pontiff from 1294 until his death.

Part III, stanza 1, line 1: "absent from his gesture." The gesture, that is, of benediction.

Part III, stanza 1, line 3: Ilaria del Carretto (d. 1405) was a young noblewoman married at age seventeen to Paolo Guinigi, lord of Lucca in the late fourteenth and early fifteenth centuries. After dying prematurely while giving birth to their second child, she was immortalized in the funerary *gisant* statue and sarcophagus by Sienese sculptor Jacopo della Quercia (ca. 1367–1438). While owing much to French Gothic models such as the royal tombs in the Basilica of Saint-Denis, Jacopo's sculpture (executed between 1406 and 1413), with its combination of personalized realism and ideal forms and its ennoblement of a person of much humbler stature than a king or queen of France, embodies the nascent Italian Renaissance and its humanist values. The effigy's eyes seem closed more in sleep than in death. Formerly in the left transept of Lucca Cathedral (as indicated by Pasolini in this poem), it is currently in the cathedral sacristy. The image of Ilaria's closed eyes hovers over the entire poem, symbolizing the mystical sleep of a nation not yet awakened to spiritual fulfillment.

Part III, stanza 6, line 1: "Jacopo." Sienese sculptor Jacopo della Quercia (ca. 1367–1438). See previous note.

Part IV, stanza 2, line 3: Ciampino is the site of Rome's second airport, which serves military as well as commercial aircraft.

Part IV, stanza 4, line 3: "from San Paolo to San Giovanni." Pasolini is referring to two of the great early Christian churches of Rome: San Paolo Fuori le Mura (Saint-Paul Outside the Walls, located outside the ancient city walls) and Saint John Lateran. Almost entirely destroyed by fire in 1823, Saint Paul's was rebuilt in the fifteen years that followed. Saint John Lateran has had many additions built onto it over the centuries, including the monumental eighteenth-century facade, but it still features much of the original structure, including the early Christian mosaics along the nave walls. In the modern age, the great square in front of Saint John's has been a popular site for political rallies, particularly of the parties of the left.

Part IV, stanza 17, line 1: "the Soratte's heights." The Monte Soratte is a mountain ridge some twenty-seven miles north of Rome. It is visible from some of the higher points in the city.

Part V, stanza 1, line 2: "ancient Luni." An ancient Etruscan city ("city of the moon") from which the Lunigiana, the surrounding region spanning northwest Tuscany and southeast Liguria, derives its name.

Part V, stanza 4, line 2: "the Serchio's and Ombrone's veins." The Serchio and Ombrone are rivers in central Italy.

Part V, stanza 7, lines 1–2: "From the Pincio / to the Aventine." The Pincio is an eminence overlooking Rome, and the Aventine one of the city's original seven hills.

Page 166 "Le ceneri di Gramsci" / "Gramsci's Ashes"
Perhaps Pasolini's most famous single poem, "Le ceneri di Gramsci" is a meditation over the grave of Antonio Gramsci (1891–1937), the leading Italian Marxist thinker of the twentieth century and a founding member of the Italian Communist Party. In it Pasolini examines his yearning for and ambivalence towards the socialist ideal, using the setting and circumstance of Gramsci's gravesite as the vehicle of an exploration into the self and its relation to society. Shortly after his release from ten years of imprisonment by the Fascist regime, Gramsci died from the harsh conditions he had endured, a fact alluded to in part III of the poem. Gramsci was of particular interest to Pasolini because a great deal of his social critique is based on an analysis of culture—in particular, the use of culture by the ruling capitalist class as a way to maintain its hegemony over society. Many of Pasolini's political and cultural positions owed a great deal to Gramsci's influence, particularly his pessimism concerning the difficulty of overcoming the powerful influence exerted by the moneyed classes in the age of mass communications. The title of the poem is a translation of the Latin inscription on the marble coffer holding the philosopher's ashes: CINERA ANTONII GRAMSCII. For more on the poem see the introduction to this volume, pp. 30–32.

Part I, stanza 1, line 2: "the darkness of the foreign garden." The poet is speaking from the Protestant cemetery (also called the "English cemetery") of Rome, where many foreigners, particularly Englishmen, including Percy Bysshe Shelley, are buried. Gramsci's ashes are interred there because the Marxist thinker was not granted a Catholic burial.

Part I, stanza 11, line 1: "the mills / of Testaccio." The Protestant cemetery is in the Roman district of Testaccio, a generally working-class area (now changing) on the Monte Testaccio. (See note to "Chiusa la festa" above, and also the first note to part VI of this poem, below.)

Part II, stanza 15, line 1: "And O ye fountains . . . ." A direct quotation from William Wordsworth's "Ode: Intimations of Immortality from Recollections of Early Childhood."

Part III, stanza 7, line 2: "during the days of your murder." Gramsci died six days after his release from prison, effectively murdered by the harsh conditions under which he had long been held.

Part III, stanza 16, line 1: "I live by not wanting" ("Vivo nel non volere"). An apparent echo of the final lines of Montale's famous poem from *Ossi di seppia* (1925), "Non chiederci la parola . . .": "Codesto solo oggi possiamo dirti, / ciò che *non* siamo, ciò che *non* vogliamo ("All we can tell you today is this: / what we are *not*, what we do *not* want"). With this echo Pasolini, despite his aesthetic opposition to Hermetic poetry at this stage of his career, seems to situate himself within the same moral dilemma as that articulated by Montale in the early 1920s, at the very start of the Fascist era.

Part V, stanza 5, lines 1–2: "burial / at Verano." The Campo Verano is a vast plot of land, originally the estate of Lucius Verus in antiquity, which in the early nineteenth century was designated by the short-lived Napoleonic administration to become the principal cemetery of Rome. Finally opened in 1836, its main entrance is in the working-class quarter of San Lorenzo, near the early Christian church of San Lorenzo Fuori le Mura. Although Pasolini invokes Verano as a burial ground for people humbler than those buried at the Protestant cemetery, Verano's land houses the mortal remains of people of all classes, high and low.

Part V, stanza 13, lines 1–2: "that swallowed him up / in the blind Tyrrhenian blue." Shelley died when his three-master sank in a storm in the Tyrrhenian sea.

Part V, stanza 16, line 1: "a young / Ciociaro sleeps." A Ciociaro is a native of the Ciociaria, a region to the southeast of Rome comprising southeastern Latium and western Abbruzzo.

Part V, stanza 16, line 3: Maremma is a marshy coastal area in southwestern Tuscany.

Part V, stanza 19, line 1: "vivid stuccoes and soft inlays." Through a suggestive image, the poet is invoking the white, marble-rich mountains ("vivid stuccoes") of the Apuan Alps and the alternating areas of greenery ("soft inlays") on their slopes.

Part V, stanza 19, line 3: The Cinquale is the area between the seashore and the Apuan Alps, the outer edge of the lower Lunigiana. It is a popular seaside resort, famed for its long beaches near Massa and Forte dei Marmi.

Part VI stanza 12, line 3: "Testaccio, naked from its great mountain / of refuse . . . ." The Monte Testaccio (Mons Testaceus in Latin), on which the Roman Testaccio district lies, is an artifical hill built in antiquity out of refuse, almost exclusively pottery shards (*testae* in Latin). It is also known as Monte dei Cocci, or

"Pottery Mountain." The great accumulation of shards took place predominantly in the second and third centuries AD, and most of the fragments came from amphorae containing olive oil. During the Middle Ages the Monte Testaccio, because of its resemblance to Mount Calvary, was used for reenactments of Christ's Passion, and over the centuries it has consistently been site of popular celebrations and rites, including Carnival games and wine-harvest rituals. In the sixteenth century it was discovered that wine cellars dug into its slopes were particularly well suited for the storage of wine because of their cool temperatures, but this practice was gradually abandoned after the hill began to be urbanized in the late nineteenth century. In Roman times Testaccio was a river port.

Pasolini's invocation of a "mountain of refuse" should nevertheless be read as a *doppio senso*, a double meaning. The image no doubt also recalls the piles of modern-day garbage he repeatedly evokes here and in other parts of Rome.

Part VI, stanza 13, line 1: *Lungoteveri* are the inner-city, heavily trafficked avenues that run along the river Tiber (Tevere, in Italian).

Part VI, stanza 13, line 3: Monteverde. See note to "Chiusa la festa . . ." / "At holiday's end . . . ."

Part VI, stanza 21, line 3: *Cappellaccio* is the external, more porous and friable part of tufa deposits, a stone commonly used in Italian construction since early Roman times. It can also refer to the surface mineral of any shallow stone deposit.

Part VI, stanza 22, line 1: "the Slaughterhouse." Founded in 1868, along with the new working-class quarters of Testaccio, and shut down in 1975, the Mattatoio (Slaughterhouse), with its neoclassical facade, is in the heart of Testaccio and is a symbol of the quarter.

Part VI, stanza 25, line 3: ". . . our history has ended." This is the first instance where Pasolini invokes "the end of history," which will become a major theme in *Poesia in forma di rosa* (1964) and in most of his subsequent works. See notes to *June 10, 1962*, as well as the introductory essay to this volume, pp. 38–39, and especially 43–44.

Page 188 "Il pianto della scavatrice" / "The Cry of the Excavator"
Part I, stanza 1, line 1: "Only loving, only knowing matter . . ." Siti (I, p. 1636) points out the similarity between this opening ("Solo l'amare, solo il conoscere / conta") and the first line of Elsa Morante's *Albi*: "Solo chi ama conosce."

Part II, stanza 1, line 1: "Poor as a cat in the Colosseum." Siti (I, p. 1636) notes another echo of Morante from *Albi*, where she writes: "Poor as a cat in the alleys of Naples . . . ."

Part II, stanza 13, line 1: "Fiumicino or the *agro*." Fiumicino is the seaside town, built on a tidal river (its name means "little river"), near which the Leonardo Da Vinci International Airport of Rome is located. The *agro romano* is the countryside around Rome, particularly that lying to the west of the city, between Rome and the sea.

Part II, stanza 14, line 2: The "Pentitentiary" is a reference to the notorious prison of Rebibbia, which was not far from Pasolini's home in Ponte Mammolo, where he lived shortly after first moving to Rome. Rebibbia is a *borgata*, one of the outlying suburbs of the city, of the sort we see featured in Pasolini's first two films, *Accattone* and *Mamma Roma*.

Part III, stanza 16, line 2: "Oh, the days of Rebbbia." That is, the time when Pasolini lived at Ponte Mammolo (see previous note).

Part III, stanza 23, line 2: "Marx and Gobetti, Gramsci and Croce." Piero Gobetti (1901–26) was a left-wing journalist, activist, author, and publisher. Despite his young age he was a pivotal figure in the early anti-Fascist movement, and the magazines he founded—such as *La Rivoluzione Liberale* and *Il Baretti*—featured writings by some of the most important philosophical, political, and literary figures of the day, including Benedetto Croce, Eugenio Montale, Antonio Gramsci, and Luigi Sturzo. Under the imprint of Piero Gobetti Editore, he also published Montale's first, groundbreaking volume of poetry, *Ossi di seppia* (Cuttlefish Bones), as well as a translation of John Stuart Mill's *On Liberty*. Having been, like Gramsci, a victim of Fascism, and sharing Gramsci's keen concern for literary and cultural issues as fundamental to the struggle against fascism and capitalism, Gobetti had a natural appeal for Pasolini, who for much of his creative life sought to reconcile the demands of artistic creativity and political engagment. After being severely beaten by Fascist thugs, Gobetti fled to Paris and eventually died there from complications ensuing from the attack. He was twenty-five.

On Antonio Gramsci, please see the note at the start of this section.

Benedetto Croce (1866–1952) was perhaps the most important Italian philosopher of the first half of the twentieth century, as well as a prominent literary critic and aesthetician. Writing in the Idealist tradition, and strongly influenced by Rousseau, Hegel, and Marx, Croce's presence and thought strongly marked Italian political thinkers (especially Gramsci) of the early and mid-twentieth century before, during and after Fascism. His extensive writings on poetry, literature, and art also had considerable influence on Italian culture during the early and mid-century. Initially a supporter of Fascism, he quickly became a firm opponent and lived in isolation during the twenty-year reign of Mussolini.

Part IV, stanza 16, line 1: ". . . But the Corso continues." The Corso is normally the main street of an Italian city or town.

V. *La religione del mio tempo* / *The Religion of My Time*

The longer poems of *La religione del mio tempo* continue some of the thematics of those of the previous collection, with the difference that the ambivalence and doubt expressed in *Gramsci* as to the poet's role in society here turn into pessimism and alienation. The temporal overlap between the earlier versions of the long poems in *La religione* and the later poems in *Gramsci* affords a glimpse into this evolution. The conjunction with history to which the poet had been aspiring since "Discovering Marx," and which he had begun to doubt in *Gramsci*, here becomes a clash with history, especially in the later poems of the volume. Formally, there are some echoes of terza rima in the long sequence entitled "La Ricchezza"; but only in the title piece, "La religione del mio tempo," and in the "Appendice alla 'Religione'" does it clearly emerge, however approximatively.

The title of the collection, and of the eponymous poem, is taken from a sonnet by the late-nineteenth-century Roman dialect poet Giuseppe Gioacchino Belli (1791–1863) (G. Jori, *Pasolini*, p. 66).

Page 220 La ricchezza / Riches
Part 1. The frescoes painted by Piero della Francesca (ca. 1412–92) in the church of Saint Francis in Arezzo represent perhaps the most ambitious cycle among the works of Piero that have come down to us over the centuries. They depict *The Legend of the True Cross*, inspired by the story of the same name recounted in *The Golden Legend* by Jacopo da Varazze (Jacobus de Voragine), and they were probably executed between 1453 and 1464. The scenes described here are among those in the church's choir: *Heraclios's victory over Cosroes*, the *Annunciation*, and the *Dream of Constantine* (Siti I, p. 1654).

Part 1, section 2, stanza 2, line 2: ". . . San Francesco's / bricks already black." That is, the bricks of the church of Saint Francis with the frescoes described in the previous secion.

Part 1, scction 2, stanza 2, line 19: "Palio." Pasolini is most likely not referring here to the Palio of Siena, the traditional horse race pitting different districts of that city against one another, but to one of several similar events held at Arezzo or in nearby towns, such as the Giostra del Saraceno (the Joust of the Saracen), the Palio dei Rioni (a race similar to the Sienese one, held annually at Castiglion Fiorentino in Arezzo province), or the Palio della Balestra (an annual competition among crossbowmen in nearby Sansepolcro, a town that features two other famous paintings of Piero's, the *Polyptych of the Misericordia*, or *Madonna of Mercy*, and a *Resurrection*). In all of the above events, participants dress in traditional medieval costumes.

Part 2, section 1, lines 8–9: "and you, behind / the wheel." These lines, according to a 1959 letter from Pasolini to Giancarlo Ferretti, are addressed to Giorgio Bassani, author, among other things, of the novel *The Garden of the Finzi-Continis*, who had accompanied Pasolini on a trip through Umbria. Bassani was a good friend of Pasolini and served as his "voice" in the dubbing for the character of the filmmaker-poet in *La ricotta* (played by Orson Welles) and in the newsreel-collage film *La rabbia* (see note to "Marilyn," p. 472).

Part 2, section 2, stanza 4, line 10: "the long Tiburtina." That is, the Via Tiburtina, an ancient Roman road originally built from Rome to Tivoli and later extended all the way to Pescara on the Adriatic coast. The modern Tiburtina follows the same path and passes through several working-class quarters in Rome.

Part 2, section 3, stanza 2, lines 8–9: "the frescoes of San / Sepolcro and Monterchi." The Tuscan towns Sansepolcro and Monterchi feature frescoes by Piero della Francesca. The painting in Monterchi is of an unusual pregnant Virgin, the *Madonna del Parto*; for Sansepolcro, see note above.

Part 2, section 3, stanza 2, line 12: "Longhi, Contini." Pasolini studied with the eminent art historian Roberto Longhi (1890–1970) at the University of Bologna and remained forever marked by his scholarly rigor and great love of Italian painting. Gianfranco Contini (1912–90), perhaps the foremost Italian literary critic (especially of poetry) and philologist of the twentieth century, wrote a positive review of Pasolini's first book of poetry, *Poesie a Casarsa*, and supported his work throughout his career. Pasolini continued to correspond with Contini for the rest of his life. Like Longhi, Contini and many aspects of his philological methodology (see introduction) had a lasting influence on Pasolini.

Part 2, section 3, stanza 5, line 1: Portonaccio is a working-class quarter of Rome clustered around the Via Tiburtina, not to be confused in this reference with the other Portonaccio near the ruins of Veio, the ancient Etruscan city.

Part 2, section 3, stanza 5, line 2: "Campo Verano." See note to "Gramsci's Ashes," Part V, stanza 5, lines 1–2, above.

Part 2, section 3, stanza 1, line 5: Piazza Vittorio is a broad, porticoed square with a park in the middle, formerly the site of a huge, lively open-air market. It is not far from Termini Station.

Part 2, section 3, stanza 3, line 3: "From San Lorenzo to Le Capannelle." San Lorenzo is an old working-class quarter of Rome that includes the early Christian church of the same name and the entrance to the Campo Verano. Le Capannelle is a former village that became absorbed into the suburban structure of Rome through the ambitious urbanization projects begun in 1945.

Part 3, line 8: ". . . between Vetralla and the Circeo." Vetralla is a town in northwest Lazio with a number of important medieval monuments. Il Circeo is a mountain by the sea in southwest Lazio that has since given its name to a protected national park, the Parco Nazionale del Circeo. According to legend, the Circeo, which is dotted with many caves, was where the sorceress Circe lived after attempting to turn Odysseus and his men into pigs. The mountain looks a bit like a reclining woman, which is probably what gave rise to the name and the legend.

Part 3, line 15: "the hazy Agro . . . ." See note to "The Cry of the Excavator" (part II, stanza 13, line 1).

Part 4, section 1, stanza 2, line 1: The Ponte Garibaldi is a modern bridge (built 1888, renovated 1953–58) leading from the Trastevere quarter into the center of town.

Part 4, section 1, stanza 3, line 4: "from the Ponte Sublicio as far as the Janiculum." The Ponte Sublicio was the oldest bridge in ancient Rome, attributed by Livy to King Ancus Martius (seventh century BC), then repeatedly renovated and rebuilt in later antiquity. Pasolini is almost certainly referring to the Ponte Aventino (also called Ponte di Testaccio), built in 1919 from plans by Marcello Piacentini. The Janiculum is the second tallest hill in Rome, though not one of the famed seven, since it lies west of the Tiber, behind the Trastevere district.

Part 4, section 1, stanza 3, lines 7–8: "old drunkards / of Ponte." "Ponte" here refers to the Roman quarter (*rione*) of Ponte, near the Ponte Sant'Angelo, from which it gets its name. A large part of old Ponte was lost in the nineteenth century when new bridges and retaining walls were built to contain the Tiber.

Part 4, section 2, stanza 1, line 1: The Baths of Caracalla are an imposing complex of well-preserved ruins of public baths built in the early third century AD by the emperor Caracalla. At the time of the poem's writing, the baths were easily accessible to the public and frequented by prostitutes and hustlers. Now one must pay to visit them, and they serve as backdrop for the Rome Opera's summer season productions.

Part 4, section 3, stanza 3, line 8: "Their pity lies in having no pity" ("la loro pietà è nell'essere spietati") echoes a line from Dante (*Paradiso* IV, 105): "per non perder pietà si fè più spietato" (so as not to lose pity, he became more pitiless).

Part 4, section 4, stanza 2, lines 26–28: ". . . Zigaina . . . Morandi . . . Mafai . . . De Pisis . . . Rosai . . . Guttuso." All twentieth-century Italian painters, each with a particular connection—personal, philosophical, or aesthetic—to Pasolini. Giuseppe Zigaina (b. 1924) was a good friend of Pasolini's from 1946, having been part of the Academiuta de Lenga Furlana, the private school Pasolini had set up to teach the Friulian dialect; Zigaina has also written extensively on Pasolini (see bibliography). Giorgio Morandi (1890–1964), an internationally renowned painter and printmaker, is famous for his contemplative still-lifes; he was born and died in Pasolini's native Bologna. Mario Mafai (1902–65) was a painter of the "Roman school," known primarily for his landscapes, still lifes, and intense colors. Filippo Tibertelli De Pisis (1896–1956) was associated early on with the Metaphysical School of Italian painters (De Chirico, Savinio) as well as the French avant-garde, but he developed a style of his own that featured still lifes, cityscapes, and sensual male nudes; he was also a devoted writer and poet and an avowed homosexual. An aristocrat by birth, he was, like Pasolini, particularly fascinated by the young men of the lower classes he would meet on the street. Ottone Rosai (1895–1957), after early associations with the Futurist and other avant-garde movements that would mark his style throughout his career, became known for his portrayals of humble, simple people. Like De Pisis and Pasolini, he was also a writer. Renato Guttuso (1911–87) was a Sicilian-born painter whose bold, vivid style with expressionist tendencies became the vehicle for a socially engaged painting, especially after World War II.

Part 4, section 5, line 25: "their Circle of Cain." The Circle of Cain is the first section of the ninth circle of Hell and houses souls who have betrayed those closest to them (Dante, *Inferno*, V,1. 107 and XXXII,1. 58).

Part 5, section 2, lines 8–11: "vital fluids steeped in deep gloom, / Belli's papal jaundice, / not purple but spent peperino, / bilious brick . . ." [nei loro succhi / vitali, è distreso un tenebrore intenso, / la papale itterizia del Belli, / non propora, ma spento peperino, / bilioso cotto . . .]. In this highly complex play on words, Pasolini creates a multilayered metaphor representing the "physical"—one might almost say "mineral"—makeup of the men who constitute the new Romans. Speaking the same Roman dialect (*romanesco*) as G. G. Belli (1791–1863)—the prolific author of sonnets in *romanesco*, many of them satirizing the papacy and the Roman clergy in general—these men have his "jaundice" in their very fluids. Moreover, in qualifying this jaundice as "papal" (*papale*), the poet is referring not only to the jaded anticlericalism shared by Belli and the new Romans, but also to the succinct, pithy nature of the language in which it is expressed, since *papale* in romanesco means "blunt, succinct." Thus their "papality" is not "purple" (the color of royalty, empire, and papal vestments at certain times of year) but "spent peperino"—that is, the color of the light-brown tufa stone (peperino) used in many Roman buildings—or "bilious brick," the yellowish, hot-fired brick used in so much Roman construction since the earliest days. It is as if the men were made of the same materials as the city itself, their humors the mortar of the urban fabric.

Part 5, section 3, line 16: "*l'intermittence du coeur.*" Proust's famous phrase is actually in the plural—"*les* intermittences du coeur" (*Du côté de Guermantes*, p. 52, M. Proust, *A la recherche du temps perdu* [Paris: Gallimard, 1954])—and it refers to the whimsical lacunae to which the affective memory is subject.

Part 5, section 3, line 21: "the Casilina." That is, the Via Casilina, the once ancient, now modern road linking Rome and Capua (which in antiquity was called Casilinum). The Casilina begins at the Porta Maggiore in Rome, the "gates of Rossellini's city" (line 22) evoked here by Pasolini. Roberto Rossellini (1906–77) was of course one of the great Neorealist filmmakers of wartime and postwar Italy, rising to prominence literally on the rubble of war-torn Rome and Berlin in such films as *Open City*, here described, and *Germany Year Zero*. *Open City* starred Anna Magnani (line 29), among others.

Part 6, section 2, line 10: "all around me was only the Language." Again, Pasolini is referring not to "language" (*linguaggio*) in the abstract sense, but specifically to the Italian language (*lingua*) as opposed to dialect. Born in 1922, the year in which Fascism came to power, he grew up in an age when speaking dialect was frowned upon, and later all but banned, by the Mussolini government. Pasolini's father, moreover, a career military man descended from the upper classes, had little tolerance for dialect and preferred that his family speak proper Italian. (See introduction, as well as the note to the poem "Lingua." The autobiographical poem "Poeta delle ceneri," in P. P. Pasolini, *Tutte le poesie*, vol. II, p. 1261, also deals with this question.)

Part 6, section 3, lines 6–9: "With our furniture on a cart, we fled / Casarsa for a remote village lost between / canals and vineyards . . . ." Pasolini is alluding to his flight with his mother to the village of Versuta after the Allies started bombing Casarsa. They escaped in time, though the ancestral home of the Colussi, Pasolini's mother's family, was nearly reduced to rubble in the bombardment. It was later rebuilt.

Part 6, section 3, lines 10–12: "One quiet morning in March, / my brother left, on a train, in secret, his pistol inside a book." This is an allusion to the departure of Guido, the poet's brother, to go fight with the partisans in the hills. Guido would eventually be killed by rival partisan factions (see note 31 to the introduction in this volume), an event to which Pasolini alludes in the next line as "the day of death and freedom."

Page 270 Da "La religione del mio tempo" / From "The Religion of My Time"
Section 1, line 1: "Two days of fever! . . ." For this poem, I have chosen to use the version that Pasolini himself published in his self-edited 1970 selection of *Poesie*, which omits the first two tercets and the first two lines of the third tercet of the text originally published in the 1961 edition (and subsequent editions) of *La religione del mio tempo*.

Section 2, stanza 16, line 3: ". . . Tommaseo, Carducci": Niccolò Tommaseo (1802–1872) was a poet in the Italian tradition of *poeti civili*, as well as a noted scholar of the Italian language. Pasolini is probably referring to Tommaseo's compilation of *I canti del popolo greco*, an anthology of Greek songs and poetry to which the young Pasolini was particularly attached (see introductory note to *The Religion of*

My Time, above). Giosuè Carducci (1835–1907), also a *poeta civile,* was one of Italy's major poets of the second half of the nineteenth century and, like Tommaseo, a patriot in the struggle for Italian unification.

Section 3, stanza 17, lines 1–2: ". . . down the distant trail / to the Fonde." The *fonde* are small ponds in the Friuli. In "Poet of Ashes," Pasolini explains:

> I would write on the banks of the little ponds
> —which down there, in my mother's village, are called by one
> of those untranslatable names, *fonde*—

The capital *F* in the present context would appear to indicate merely an idealization of the phenomenon.

Page 286 Appendice alla "Religione": Una luce / Appendix to "The Religion of My Time": A Light
This is another poem to Pasolini's mother (see also "Memories," p. 105, and "Plea to My Mother," p. 315).

Stanza 17, line 1: ". . . the bones of the other son." That is, Guido Pasolini, Pier Paolo's brother, killed in 1945 by fellow resistance fighters from rival factions (see note 31 to the introduction).

Page 292 "A Bertolucci" / "To Bertolucci"
The Bertolucci of the poem's dedication is Attilio Bertolucci (1911–2000), father of the renowned filmmaker. He was a major Italian poet of his time and a friend of Pasolini. His son, Bernardo, broke into cinema as assistant director for Pasolini's first two films, *Accattone* and *Mamma Roma.*

Page 294 "Frammento alla morte" / "To Death: A Fragment"
The poem is dedicated to Franco Fortini (1917–44), as stated by the author in an endnote in Italian editions of this poem.

Page 298 "La Rabbia" / "Rage"
Stanza 1, line 4: "since the days of Mameli." Goffredo Mameli (1827–1849) wrote the words to what has since become the Italian national anthem, "Il Canto degli Italiani" (The Song of the Italians).

Stanza 1, line 14, "where Mameli died.": At this time Pasolini and his mother were living in a house that looked onto the yard and cottage where Mameli had lived and died.

Stanza 6, lines 7–8: ". . . prevents my heart / reacting to a fragrance": Cf. excerpt from the poem "The Religion of My Time," pp. 270–85 in this volume.

VI. *Poesia in forma di rosa / Poem in the Shape of a Rose*

Poesia in forma di rosa is the first collection of Pasolini's poems to deal globally with the profound changes affecting his worldview as the fabled "economic miracle" of Italian society in the late 1950s and early '60s began to alter the aspirations of working people and the outlook of leftist intellectuals. In "Marxism and Christianity," an essay published in 1964, the same year as this volume of poems, Pasolini briefly touched upon this turning point for himself and the culture he lived in:

> The reality is that something is changing, profoundly, within the structures of our society. In culture and literature, it is projected as a crisis. At the moment when one kind of civilization, one kind of Italian society, ends and another begins, there is apparently, between the ending and the new beginning, an ideal moment of vacuum, an ideal zero moment. At this zero moment, the culture spins around itself in a whirl, as though mad, because the writers no longer have a concrete reference point in the society they have come from — because that society is finished, practically speaking, in the reality of history — nor do they any longer have prospects in the future society, because the future society is suddenly different from the one that all of us, at the moment of our political engagement, during the Fifties, had presumed or hoped for.
> [. . .]
> Like all my colleagues, like all writers, I, too, have experienced this crisis profoundly. My ideas are no longer so clear; everything I thought with great faith and energy in the Fifties seems to have been utterly emptied of meaning. And this is very dire for a writer, especially a writer of my kind. For a bourgeois writer, who has remained ideologically bourgeois, this means almost nothing, because he can continue to mull his interiorities, his own psychological and vaguely social motivations, and thus carry on in his inner world, his "ivory tower," as the cliché has it. But for an *engaged* writer, the disappearance of the deepest reasons for his engagement is a disastrous, total, and disruptive crisis.
> This cultural crisis, which involves all of Italian culture, has coincided, as I mentioned above, with my own private crisis. This was why I wrote a volume of poetry called *Poem in the shape of a rose*. It is the diaristic, expressive recording of this crisis ("Marxism and Christianity," in *Saggi sulla politica e sulla società*, W. Siti and S. De Laude, eds. [Milan: Meridiani Mondadori, 1999], pp. 792–93).

This crisis was already felt in the latter part — the "Epigrams" and "Uncivil Poems" — of the previous collection of poems, *La religione del mio tempo*; but in *Poesia in forma di rosa* it manifests itself on all levels of the poetry — form, content, frame of reference.

On a formal level, the collection features the last examples of the terza rima mode that characterized the "civic-themed" poetry, above all *Le ceneri di Gramsci*, which had won the author so much acclaim in the 1950s. But here the terza rima is even more partial than before, and in some cases is dispersed amidst free-verse and experimental forms within the body of a single poem, as in "A Desperate Vitality." Moreover, just as Pasolini brought his literary and specifically poetic sensibility to bear in the films he was beginning to make at this time, he immediately brought his cinematic experience to bear in the poems, such as the "Worldly Poems," and again in "A Desperate Vitality," where he "translates," as it were, certain techniques typical of the French *nouvelle vague* — jump cuts, visual non sequiturs, jarring shifts in viewpoint, etc. — into words and lines of poetry (see also the introduction to this volume, for the influence of film on the poetry).

The title of the collection, *Poesia in forma di rosa*, may be an echo of the opening line of Canto XXXI of the *Paradiso*, "In forma dunque di candida rosa," where Dante describes the celestial host (*milizia*) as gathered "thus in the shape of a pristine rose" (cf. G. Jori, *Pasolini*, Einaudi 2001, p. 74); but the rose—in all its senses, mystical, symbolic, and literal—is a recurrent image in Pasolini's verse.

Page 306 "Poesie mondane" / "Worldly Poems"
April 23, 1962
This poem was among the five included in the section entitled "The Poems of Mamma Roma" in *Mamma Roma* (Milan: Rizzoli, 1962). They were written while Pasolini was working on the film of the same name.

   Lines 2–5: ". . . come on, come on, Tonino, / use the fifty, don't worry about the light / burning through." Pasolini is addressing Tonino Delli Colli, the cameraman for many of his films, and telling him what lens to use, alluding to the fact that many of Pasolini's early cinematic methods were considered unorthodox.

   Line 7: ". . . over Aqua Santa." This was the name of the site (Acquasanta) on the Roman periphery where Pasolini shot his short film *La Ricotta*, starring Orson Welles in the lead role as a filmmaker directing a scene of Christ's Passion. By using the definite article when naming the place ("sull'Aqua Santa") and by separating the two words, Pasolini is playing heavily on their literal meaning as "holy water."

   Lines 11–12: ". . . A heretical Saint / (called Curse . . . ." Pasolini would later flesh out this idea in a 158-page film treatment in verse entitled *Bestemmia* (Curse), left not quite finished at the time of his death.

   Line 14: ". . . long-suffering Leonetti." Francesco Leonetti (b. 1924), a friend of Pasolini since late adolescence, became a close collaborator when in 1955 he, Pasolini, and Roberto Roversi, another longtime friend, cofounded *Officina*, which would become an influential literary magazine. (See introduction, p. 6, note 11, and p. 33.)

   Lines 18–19: ". . . asking about her son / in Umbrian, singing her torment in Umbrian." This is likely another nod to Jacopone da Todi, the vernacular medieval poet from the Umbrian town of Todi, whose influence is particularly visible in some of Pasolini's early work. See note to "Olive Sunday," above.

   Line 39–40: ". . . my furious love / of Aqua Santa in the sun." See note to line 7 of this poem, above.

Page 308 April 25, 1962
This poem was included in the section entitled "The Poems of Mamma Roma" in *Mamma Roma* (Milan: Rizzoli, 1962).

Page 310 June 10, 1962
This poem was also included in the section entitled "The Poems of Mamma Roma" in *Mamma Roma* (Milan: Rizzoli, 1962). The text of the poem here reprinted and translated, with the first eight lines of the original version excised, is from Pasolini's self-edited selection of his poetry, *Poesie* (Milan: Garzanti, 1970).

   Line 1: "Take a few steps and you're on the Appia / or Tuscolana." That is, the Via Appia and the Via Tuscolana. In all probability, given the modern imagery of the sequence, the poet is referring not to the old Appian Way (the "Appia Antica") but to the Via Appia Nuova, which runs parallel to the old road and through a number of working-class neighborhoods. Also running parallel to the Via Appia, the Via Tuscolana was a medieval road leading from the Porta di San Giovanni (the Lateran Gate) to the city of Tuscolo (Tusculum in Latin), now known as Frascati. Again, Pasolini is no doubt referring to the modern Tuscolana, which leads through vast urban housing projects built after World War II and runs past Cinecittà, the complex of film studios just outside Rome. The evocation of the two roads nevertheless implies the juxtaposition of ancient and modern, in keeping with the poet's own self-evocation as living at once in the past and present.

Line 14: "I am a force of the Past." The rest of the poem, starting from this line, is recited by Orson Welles (dubbed with the voice of novelist Giorgio Bassani), playing the part of the director, in Pasolini's film *La ricotta*.

Line 10: ". . . the first acts of Posthistory." This notion, with its variants as "the end of History" and the "new Prehistory," is one of the central themes of *Poesia in forma di rosa*. See the introduction to this volume, pp. 38–39 and 43–44.

Page 312 June 12, 1962
Line 9: ". . . The radiant Appia." That is, the modern Via Appia Nuova. See note to line 1 of *June 10, 1962*, above.

Line 13: "then Testaccio appears . . . ." On Testaccio, see in particular the note to part VI of "Le ceneri di Gramsci" / "Gramsci's Ashes," above.

Line 20: "A shadow works the camera in this age." Pasolini here works the technical language of film to highly metaphorical effect. The original text — "Ombra, chi opera in quest'era" — is splendidly ambiguous in its multiple meanings, with its play on the verb *operare*, which in the most immediate context refers to operating the movie camera (*operatore* means "cameraman," as in line 23 ("Il Pontormo con un operatore / meticoloso"). But it also plays on the philosophical, Latinate meaning of *operare* as creation and *poiesis*, thus semantically consolidating the equation of filmmaker with poet and demiurge in an image where the artist/demiurge/cameraman is, like the solid objects that become his subjects against the light of projection/creation, a "shadow" (*ombra*).

Page 316 "La persecuzione" / "Persecution"
Stanza 1, lines 2–3: "Other people's / celebration" (festa / degli altri). The poet is referring to the Roman working-class festival called, in Roman dialect, *La festa di noantri* (literally, the "festival of us others"). It is held during the mid-August high holiday when the majority of Romans from the lower middle classes on up vacate the city, and it celebrates the "others" of less means who are left behind. Pasolini's invocation of this festival as the time setting for a poem about his alienation from the lower classes is of considerable significance. It was "never for me," he says.

Stanza 41, line 3: "The Parocchietta alone against the fire." The Parrocchietta is an area on the outskirts of Rome, part of the Portuense suburb. In Pasolini's time and to a lesser degree today, it was home to many subproletarian families who had emigrated from the Italian south to the capital's periphery. It derives its name from the parish church (Parrocchia) of Santa Maria del Carmine e San Giuseppe al Casaletto.

Stanza 42, line 1: The Trullo, like the neighboring Parrocchietta, forms part of the larger Portuense district. It draws its name from the presence of a nearby first-century Roman sepulcher along the Tiber, some five meters high and in a shape recalling the traditional conical Apulian house known as a *trullo*.

Stanza 46, line 1: "their murderous national cigarette. . ." ["la loro nazionale assassina"]. "Nazionale" was an Italian government-issue low-cost brand of unfiltered cigarette known for its harshness. It was nevertheless popular because of its affordable price and the sort of "macho" cachet it conferred on its smokers because of its roughness.

Page 330 "Una disperata vitalità" / "A Desperate Vitality"
Pasolini took the title of this poem from a statement by his first intellectual mentor, the great art historian Roberto Longhi. In *Ricordo dei manieristi* (1953), Longhi wrote: "The task of twentieth-century critics is to delve into the desperate vitality of a crisis" (Siti, vol. I, p. 1732). The term "desperate vitality" was here meant to characterize the Italian Mannerists. Since Pasolini considered himself and was considered by some a "mannerist" in the general sense, the phrase is particularly apt.

Part I, parenthetical camera directions: The cursus, in classical prose, is the regular varying of clause endings, in periodic sentences with multiple clauses, to create a harmoniously ornate effect. In medieval Latin it was particularly favored in the cadencing of prayers, and many of the Catholic prayers still used today, such as the Angelus, feature this rhetorical device. In the Middle Ages the cursus worked its way back into secular language as well, as a fundamental tool of the *ars dictaminis*, the art of prose writing, and by extension of poetry writing as well. In the present context it is one of several devices whereby Pasolini confers, at times ironically, a "sacred" character on his poem.

Part II, stanza 1, line 5: "then a homegrown Italian MS ["in più domestica-italica M.F."]. MS is shorthand for "medium shot" ("media figura" in the Italian, hence the abbreviation M.F.).

Part III, stanza 13, lines 9–10: "those precious family blankets / on which I nursed the flowers of my youth." This is a cryptic reference to an early poem in Friulian, "Suspir di me mari ta na rosa" ("My Mother's Sighs over a Rose"), in which the poet's mother discovers a "white rose" (i.e., a semen stain) he has left on the sheet in the night.

Part V, stanza 3, line 2: ". . . the Appias and Centocelles of the world." For the Via Appia, see note to line 1 of *June 10, 1962*. Centocelle is an area of Rome between the Via Casilina and the Via Prenestina, to the east of the historic center. The name (Centum Cellae in Latin), which means "one hundred rooms," derives from the fact that a great barracks for the finest one hundred Roman cavalrymen of Emperor Constantine I, the *Equites Singulares*, once stood there along with its stables. The area also had an ancient Campus Martius, or drill ground, much vaster than the more famous central one on the banks of the Tiber, as well as numerous sumptuous villas of the Roman aristocracy. Since World War II the Centocelle district has been increasingly developed, but it still retains some of its antique authenticity.

Part V, stanza 5, line 4: ". . . the domains of the Caetani and Torlonia." The Caetani were a powerful family of the Roman nobility from the Middle Ages onwards, one of whose villas, opposite the tomb of Cecilia Metella, incorporates part of an ancient Roman fortification on the Via Appia Antica. The Torlonia were another princely Roman family, with numerous villas including the vast Villa Torlonia at Frascati, various aspects of which were designed by such celebrated architects as Girolamo Fontana (1668–1701) and Carlo Maderna (1556–1629).

Part V, stanza 5, line 4: ". . . the Tuscolanas and Capannnelles of the world." For the Tuscolana, see note to *June 10, 1962*; for Le Capannnelle, see note to "La Ricchezza" / "Riches," part 2, section 3, stanza 3, line 3.

Part V, stanza 11, line 3: For Casilina, see note to "La Ricchezza," part 5, section 3, line 21.

Part VI, stanza 5, lines 3–4: "With my bones, a shy, frightened / mother . . . [Con le mie ossa, una timida madre / spaventata]." An echo of Pasolini's earlier poem, "Appendix to 'The Religion of My Time': a Light" (see pp. 288–89), where he describes his mother as "poor, sweet little bones of mine [poveri, dolci ossicini miei]."

Part VIII: The lines of this section of the poem are centered to resemble the words of an epitaph (as is also the case in "In Memoriam," page 92, and in a few other poems not included here). According to the poet's lifelong friend and colleague, the painter and author Giuseppe Zigaina (*Pasolini e la morte*, 2005, pp. 82–89), Pasolini considered this section the "key" to understanding at once the poem, the volume *Poesia in forma di rosa*, and his entire oeuvre.

Part VIII, stanza 2, lines 10–11: "That is how / I can write Themes and Threnodies." The Italian *Treni* (from the Greek *threnoi*, plural of *threnos*, "funeral lament"), though also wryly punning on the image of the train in part V, should here be read principally as "Threnodies." This becomes clear in the light of the jacket copy, written by Pasolini himself, that appeared on both 1964 editions of *Poesia in forma di rosa*. That text begins: "It is certain that this whole book of short and long poems [*poesie e poemi*]—of Themes, Threnodies, and Prophecies [*Temi, Treni e Profezie*], of Diaries and Interviews and Reportages and Projects in verse—moves toward the idea that arises on the final page: that is: (a) the negation of all possible officialdom or ideological stabilization; (b) the vocation for a 'pure opposition,' like one who, because he loves too much, in reality can 'love no one or be loved by anyone'; (c) the discovery that by this point, 'the Revolution is now nothing more than a feeling.'" Giuseppe Zigaina, moreover, points out that one should read "Themes" [*Temi*] in the archaic sense of "examples" (cf. G. Zigaina, *Temi e treni di Pier Paolo Pasolini*, San Polo d'Enza: Edizioni La Scaletta, 2000).

Part VIII, lines 1–2: ". . . the age / of Analogics." Pasolini is probably referring to the post-Symbolist analogical style typical of Italian Hermetic poetry and, below (line 15), to its persistence (". . . Analogics survive").

Part VIII, stanza 3, line 3: "the worlds of the New Prehistory." See notes to *June 10, 1962*, and the introduction to this volume, pp. 38–39 and 43–44.

Part VIII, stanza 3, line 6: "as one who dreams his own downfall." A direct quote from Dante (*Inferno* XXX, 136), "qual è colui che suo dannaggio sogna." There has been a minor controversy over what Pasolini intended as the definitive version of this line. In the first edition of *Poesia in forma di rosa*, the line was as it stands here. In a second edition that immediately followed the first, which was full of printer's errors, the line was changed to "come colui che," with the rest of the line omitted. When the poem was included several years later in Pasolini's self-edited edition of selected *Poesie* (1970), the line read, "come colui che suo dannaggio sogna," a slightly corrupted version of the original Dantean hendecasyllable. The editors of the last two "complete works" editions of Pasolini's poems—*Bestemmia* (G. Chiarcossi and W. Siti, eds.; Milan: Garzanti, 1993) and *Tutte le poesie* (Walter Siti, ed.; Milan: Mondadori Meridiani, 2003)—have concluded that the truest intention was the original one, that is, the direct quote from Dante; that the second version was a gross printer's error, and the third an oversight on Pasolini's part, as it retains the "come" from the second version. On the other hand, Giuseppe Zigaina, the painter, writer, and lifelong friend of and commentator on Pasolini, claims that the truncated line from the second edition was an intentional coded "message" from the author, who in this and many other texts was alluding to the circumstances of his own eventual death, which Zigaina believes was staged as the final act in a long-prepared public self-sacrifice (see G. Zigaina, *Pasolini e la morte*, Venice: Marsilio, 2005).

I have chosen to present the line as Chiarcossi and Siti have judged it should be: that is, as an unadulterated quote from Dante.

Page 358 "Marilyn"
The poem is not from any specific collection or cycle, but is included by Walter Siti among the "Poems for Music" in the Meridiani *Tutte le poesie* edition. It made its first appearance when sung by actress Laura Betti in the recital *Giro a vuoto no. 3*, which premiered at the Teatro Gerolamo in Milan on November 12, 1962. Written on the occasion of Marilyn Monroe's death, the poem also figures, with some slight variants, in the soundtrack to the 1963 film *La Rabbia* (Rage), a fifty-minute distillation of more than ninety thousand meters of newsreel of sundry subjects of the day, including the actress, against a background of music and poetry. After making *La Rabbia*, Pasolini said: "My ambition was to invent a new genre: film as ideological-poetical essay." The film shares a title with the poem "La Rabbia," written some two years earlier (see p. 298).

Page 362 "Profezia" / "Prophecy"
From an unfinished cycle, "The Book of Crosses," included in the "Appendices" to *Poem in the Shape of a Rose*, "Prophecy" was written in 1964. The alternation of short verse lines and prosaic composition without line breaks is supposed to the give the text on each page of the poem the appearance of a cross.

Dedication: "To Jean-Paul Sartre, who told me the story of Blue-Eyed Alì." Pasolini met Sartre in 1962 in Paris, when the French translation of his novel *Una vita violenta* was published (Siti I, p. 1751).

Stanza 3, line 21: ". . . the CGIL." Acronym for Confederazione generale italiana del lavoro, one of the principal labor unions of Italy.

Stanza 5, line 11: Crotone and Palmi are towns on the Calabrian coast.

Stanza 4, line 24: "they shall fly ahead of the willayes." In the Maghreb, *willayes* are administrative territorial divisions. The word can also mean the buildings in which such administrations are based (Siti, I, p. 1751).

VII. *Trasumanar e organizzar* / *Transhumanize and Organize*

Trasumanar e organizzar gave new breath to Pasolini's poetic voice and represented a major turning point in his compositional approach. Among other things, there is almost no trace of the formalism of his earlier work, and indeed the poet's language has come to resemble more than ever his sinuous prose style. On the other hand, in more than a few cases Pasolini deliberately leaves sentences unfinished, omits or misuses punctuation, begins new sentences without punctuation, and blatantly fragments the syntax, leaving the jagged-edged poems to resonate in all their syntactical and grammatical ambiguity. In those poems where this is the case, I have tried as much as possible to preserve this "unfinished" quality, while making allowances, however, for comprehensibility. At any rate the reader should bear in mind that those instances of thoughts left hanging and of jarring shifts in tone or subject are deliberate.

The poems here included from the "Appendix" to *Trasumanar e organizzar* were not published in the original edition of the book, but were included by Walter Siti in his own appendix, which is based on Pasolini's prior models of same (for example, the original edition of *Trasumanar* contains Pasolini's own "Appendix to Book I"). Siti's appendix features poems once considered by Pasolini as part of the volume or written around the same time. Some of the poems included here from Siti's appendix were published in periodicals in the late Sixties and early Seventies and would probably have constituted the basis of another volume had Pasolini not been killed.

The "trasumanar" of the title is a Dantean coinage: "Trasumanar significar per verba / non si poria" (Going beyond the human cannot / be said in words), *Paradiso* I, 70–71. Pasolini's evocation of Dante's expression of the ineffability of his ascent into the heavenly realm at the start of the *Paradiso* well fits his desire to wed social and transcendent ideals at this stage of his life, and points as well to the fragmentation and difficulty of his own self-expression in these poems. Also curious is the fact that in this passage of the *Paradiso*, Dante likens the transhumanization he must undergo in order to enter Paradise to the metamorphosis of the mythological fisherman Glaucus, who is turned into a fish before entering the sea and becoming deified (see, inter alia, Ovid, *Metamorphoses*, XIII–XIV)—a reference which also appears to be echoed by Pasolini in "The Garden of Fish," a poem from the appendix to *Trasumanar e organizzar* (see page 424), in which the fruits borne by the plants in the archaic England of Caedmon, the first Anglo-Saxon poet and a very early Christian convert of that people, are fish. See also introduction, p. 49.

Page 378 "Preghiera su commissione" / "Commissioned Prayer"
From the cycle "Poesie su commissione" ("Commissioned Poems"), this poem was commissioned by a German Catholic publishing house, according to Pasolini's own footnote in the original edition.

Line 4: "a certain Mr. Homais." Homais is the self-important pharmacist in Flaubert's *Madame Bovary* who unwittingly gives the heroine the poison with which she kills herself. As a quintessential symbol of petit-bourgeois materialism and rationalist positivism, Homais represents the "wave of the future" that so dismayed the refined Flaubert.

Line 17: "Your name was Axel." Axel is the chief protagonist of the eponymous Symbolist play by Villiers de L'Isle-Adam and represents late Romantic, world-denying purism and absolutism. Pasolini's citations of Homais and now Axel are filtered through the interpretation given to both by Enzo Siciliano in an essay on Elsa Morante in his *Autobiografia letteraria* (Milan: Garzanti, 1970), in which he writes: "What the Romantic, and later the Symbolist, felt to be transcendent to himself (and which he implicitly designates as 'God') is what he abhors: mediocrity and the sclerotization of reality. God is Monsieur Homais" (quoted in Siti II, p. 1526). Commenting on Edmund Wilson's study of Symbolist literature, *Axel's Castle*, Siciliano goes on to write: "Villiers implies that 'God,' for him, is nothingness, the void. Destiny, to which Axel lends meaning, is the destruction and refutation of the human, because the human is Homais."

Lines 19–20: "Dear God, / deliver us from the thought of tomorrow." These lines ("Caro dio / liberaci dal pensiero del domani"), and the closing line, "let us live like *the birds in the sky and the lilies of the fields*" ("facci vivere come *gli uccelli del cielo e i gigli dei campi*"), with their echo of Matthew 6: 26–28, are a re-elaboration of the poetic monologue to Emilia in the novel *Teorema*, where the mysterious Guest says to the housekeeper, who will return to her peasant roots and become a saint: "You live entirely in the present. / Like the birds in the sky and the lilies of the fields, / you never think of tomorrow" (Appendix to Part I of *Teorema*, subchapter "Complicità tra il sottoproletariato e Dio" (The Complicity between the Underclass and God), Garzanti 1968, 1999 ed., p. 106)

Page 380 "Uno dei tanti epiloghi" / "One of Many Epilogues"
From the cycle "Piccoli poemi politici e personali" ("Little Political and Personal Poems"), in the "Appendix" to Book I of *Trasumanar e organizzar*. The poem is printed in italics because Pasolini wished it to be read as if it had been written *con la man che trema* (with trembling hand). Indeed all the poems of the "Appendix" to Book I are in italics, and the first of these is actually titled *La man che trema*. The quotation is from Dante, *Paradiso*, 13, 75–78:

> ma la natura la dà sempre scema,
> similemente operando a l'artista
> ch'a l'abito de l'arte ha man che trema.

> [but Nature always works defectively-
> she passes on that light much like an artist
> who knows his craft but has a hand that trembles.]
> —(trans. A. Mandelbaum)

Line 1: "Ninarieddo." The poem is addressed to Ninetto Davoli, a longtime companion of Pasolini. The son of Calabrian peasants who had moved to the Prenestino slum of Rome, Davoli met Pasolini during the filming of *La ricotta* in 1962. Though utterly untrained and uneducated, he went on to star in a number of Pasolini's films, including *Uccellacci e uccellini* (*Sparrows and Hawks*) and *The Arabian Nights*, as well as making briefer appearances in *Decameron*, *Teorema*, and others, often embodying the concept of angelic innocence. "Ninarieddo," the name that Pasolini calls him at the start of this poem, is a diminutive form of the already diminutive "Nino" in Calabrian dialect.

Page 382 *"Canto civile"* / *"Civic Song"*
From the cycle "Piccoli poemi politici e personali" ("Little Political and Personal Poems"), "Canto civile" is also printed in italics, for the same reasons as the preceding poem.

Page 384 *"La strada delle puttane"* / *"The Whores' Road"*
From the cycle "Charta (sporca)," this is one of the poems from this period in which Pasolini leaves some sentences unfinished and begins new independent clauses without capitalization or prior punctuation.
   Line 1: "the Ma-mul." Walter Siti writes:

> In the anthology edited by C. Leslie, *Uomo e mito nelle società primitive* [Florence: Sansoni, 1965], Pasolini may have read an essay by David G. Mandelbaum on Kota culture entitled [in the Italian translation] "Inclinazioni sociali e passioni personali." The Kota are an ethnic group of the Nilgiri region of southern India, and around 1920, following a plague epidemic and other social stresses, they experienced a "change of religion"; that is, alongside their ancient trinity of gods, they began to worship a new trinity clearly inspired by the Hinduism practiced in much of the rest of India. The "ma:mu:l," in Mandelbaum's article, is the aggregate of the ancient rules, as opposed to the "pudmu:l," the aggregate of the new rules.

Siti also mentions that the poem evokes Pasolini's first meeting with Ninetto Davoli, presenting this encounter as the "founding myth" of their relationship (Siti II, pp. 1535–36). See also sonnet 20 among the "Last Poems," p. 433 in this volume.

Page 388 *"La poesia della tradizione"* / *"The Poetry of Tradition"*
From the cycle "Poemi zoppicanti" ("Limping Poems"), this is one of the compositions in *Trasumanar e organizzar* where Pasolini leaves certain sentences hanging uncompleted at the end of a verse line, and sometimes begins a new sentence in the following line with no punctuation or capitalization. Apparently he considered this the most important poem in this collection (Gianni D'Elia, *L'eresia di Pasolini*, p. 13).
   Line 42: ". . . a Baptistry with *caporioni* and apprentices." *Caporione* was an old administrative title given to the head of a *rione*—that is, a quarter or district of a town or city. It is not clear which of the many medieval Italian baptistries Pasolini is referring to here, if any in particular, but he nevertheless invokes an image not uncommon in medieval art wherein patrons, administrators, and craftsmen might be represented on a facade, in a fresco, or in a stained-glass window.

Line 44: ". . . Cinquecento octaves." Pasolini is referring to the ottava rima verse form, made popular in the sixteenth century (the Cinquecento, in Italian terms) by Ludovico Ariosto in the *Orlando furioso*, which was a continuation of sorts of the *Orlando innamorato* by Matteo Maria Boiardo, written in the fifteenth century also in ottava rima.

Line 75: ". . . the meaning of organizing cannot be put into words." In this line ("organizzar significar per verba non si poria") Pasolini invokes the words of Dante (*Paradiso*, I, 70–71), "trasumanar significar per verba / non si poria" ("going beyond the human cannot be put into words"). And by transposing the verb *organizzar* for *trasumanar*, he not only alludes to the title of his collection, *Trasumanar e organizzar*, but institutes a sort of mutual necessity between political organization and spiritual transcendence. See introduction, p. 49, and the opening comment to this chapter, p. 473.

Page 392 "Atene" / "Athens"

This poem is from the cycle "Sineciosi della diaspora" ("Synecioses of the Diaspora"). Concerning the term "syneciosis," poet Franco Fortini wrote of Pasolini that "antithesis is found at every level of the writing [. . .] up to the most frequent figure of language, that subspecies of oxymoron that ancient rhetoric used to call syneciosis, whereby two opposites are asserted through a single subject" (F. Fortini, "La contraddizione," in *Attraverso Pasolini* [Torino: Einaudi, 1993], p. 21, quoted in "Pasolini si rilegge" by Giona Tuccini, *Romanic Review*, 1/1/05). Walter Siti further points out that this particular essay by Fortini was originally published in 1959 in the review *Il Menabò*, under the title "La poesia italiana di questi anni" ("The Italian Poetry of These Years"), after which Pasolini made the term his own and liked to define himself as a "poet of syneciosis" (Siti, II, p. 1543). Of his own tendency to deal in opposites, Pasolini wrote in his *autorecensione* or "self-review" of *Trasumanar e Organizzar*: "Inferring, however schematically, the life from the style, one may assert that Pasolini lives historically by accumulation, and that he owes his knowledge, which is not dialectical, to the eternal coexistence of opposites."

This poem is yet another in *Trasumanar e organizzar* to use fragmented, sometimes incomplete sentences and misleading punctuation.

Line 5: "(you couldn't remember the name)." The "you" to whom the poem speaks is Maria Callas, the "girl / who will one day get fat" (Siti, II, p. 1544).

Page 394 "Timor di me?"

This poem is from the cycle "La città santa" ("The Holy City"), which Pasolini described as a *canzoniere* (songbook) to opera diva Maria Callas, with whom he became very close after she starred in his film *Medea*.

Title: "Timor di me?" means "afraid of me?" and is from Leonora's recitativo in act IV of Giuseppe Verdi's *Il Trovatore*: "Timor di me? . . . Sicura, / presta è la mia difesa." As Callas had often interpreted the role of Leonora, Pasolini here is likely putting these words in her mouth, thus implying that it is *he* who is afraid of her.

Line 4: "which makes you sing *in voce*": To be *in voce* is to have one's best singing voice, in the classical operatic style, for interpreting the piece in question.

Page 398 "La presenza" / "Presence"
From the cycle "Manifestar," the poem is addressed to Maria Callas. According to Walter Siti (vol. II, p. 1551), the title alludes to a concept formulated by anthropologist Ernesto De Martino, that of the "loss of presence" first discussed in his 1948 book *Il mondo magico*.

Line 18: "esse est percipi." "To be is to be perceived," in Latin. In the philosophy of George Berkeley, *esse est percipi* is the fundamental feature of all sensible objects. *Esse est percipere* ("to be is to perceive"), on the other hand, is the fundamental quality of spirits.

Page 404 "Appunto" / "Note"
The word "appunto," if taken as a noun, means "note"; but if taken as an adverb, it means "precisely."

Page 404 "Gli ultimi sogni prima di morire" / "Last Dreams before Dying"
From Walter Siti's "Appendix" to *Trasumanar e organizzar*, this is another of the poems of this period in which Pasolini glaringly flouts conventions of capitalization and punctuation and leaves sentences unfinished. Unpublished during Pasolini's lifetime, it is likely an unfinished poem.

Page 408 "Introduzione" / "Introduction"
From Siti's "Appendix" to *Trasumanar e organizzar*, this poem is written somewhat like an outline for a broader project. But since other work in *Trasumanar* is similarly schematic, it's not clear that Pasolini necessarily intended to fill out the skeleton in a more finished work. Ever since *Poesia in forma di rosa* (1964), in fact, his poems had gradually been gaining the appearance of "works in progress" (such as the "Progetto di opere future" from that volume, or the unfinished autobiographical poem "Poeta delle ceneri," from 1965), and certainly the creative writing of the last ten or so years of Pasolini's life became increasingly concerned with "process" (e.g., *La Divina Mimesis*, *Petrolio*, or the "novel" version of *Teorema*).

Line 26: "cloudes." Pasolini deliberately miswrites *nuvole* as *nubole*.

Line 28: "flocke." Again, Pasolini purposely misspells *greggia* (flock) as *graggia*.

Line 31: "blanket." In the original, Pasolini makes the word *coltre* (blanket) masculine, when it is normally feminine.

Line 70: "I shall not glorify *farmers*." Pasolini's use of the English term in the original may be inaccurate. By this point in his career, his idealization of the peasant class had become a point of irony with his detractors and a cause for disillusionment in himself, and I think he is speaking to these circumstances in making this statement. Thus, since it is safe to assume that he meant *contadini* where he says "farmers," he should have said "peasants."

Line 72 and author's note: Milarepa (ca. 1052–ca. 1135) was a Tibetan Buddhist holy man, yogi, and poet. A major figure of the Kagyu branch of Tibetan Buddhism, he left behind a body of songs and poems, as well as many disciples who carried on his tradition.

Line 83: One of the most important gods in Vedic mythology, Varuna, in pre-

Vedic times, was in fact the omnipotent, omniscient lord of the cosmos, with a role somewhat akin to that of Zeus and God the Father. With the advent of the Vedic era, Varuna was supplanted by Indra as the supreme god, but he retained a prominent role, among his many aspects, as god of oceans and rivers and as keeper of the souls of the drowned. In this role he is also a god of the dead, with the power to grant immortality. The invocation of Varuna may be a prolepsis to the allusion to a *deus otiosus* in line 48 of the poem "Other Materials" (see below).

Line 84: For Pasolini, "thetis" (*tetis*, in the Italian spelling) meant not the silver-footed sea nymph of Greek mythology — or not *only* her — but simply "sex, both male and female," in "ancient Greek," and he attributed this definition to Gianfranco Contini, the prominent literary critic and long-distance mentor of Pasolini. He recounts his "discovery" of this meaning, and its emergence in a very early experience of sexual longing, in a 1966 essay entitled "Dal laboratorio," later grouped among the essays republished in the volume *Empirismo eretico* and now in *Saggi sulla letteratura e sull'arte* (pp. 1330–31):

> At that time in Belluno, when I was about three or three and a half years old, I felt the first twinges of sexual love, identical to what I would later feel up to the present day (which were terribly acute between the ages of sixteen and thirty): that terrible, anxious sweetness that grabs the entrails and consumes them, burns them, twisting them up like a hot, agonizing blast of wind when one stands before the object of one's love. All I remember of that object of love, I think, was the legs — and, more precisely, the hollow behind the knee, with hamstrings tensed [. . .] One day I went to look for this tender, terrible object of my longing at his home, going up some stairs in a house in Belluno — which I still have before my eyes — knocking on the door, and asking for him. I can still hear the negative reply, saying he wasn't home. I, of course, had no idea what this was about. I only felt the physical presence of that sensation, which was so hot and dense that it wrung my entrails. And so I found myself confronted with the need to "name" that sensation, and in my condition as a purely oral speaker, with no experience of writing, I invented a term. And this term, I remember perfectly, was: *teta veleta*.
>
> One day I recounted this anecdote to Gianfranco Contini, who found that it was an example of a *reminder* [in English in the original]: a linguistic phenomenon typical of prehistoric man. The *reminder* of a word from ancient Greek, *Thetis* (sex, both male and female, as everyone knows) . . .

A few years later, in an interview with Dacia Maraini, Pasolini says he also experienced the feeling of *teta veleta* for his mother's breast. In another related connection, he repeatedly evokes, in his poetry and prose, the nape of a boy's or young man's neck — which could be seen to resemble the back of the knee — as an image charged with sexual desire and tenderness.

The term *tetis* and its concomitant themes recur repeatedly in Pasolini's work. A few examples: There is the 1973 essay entitled "Thetis" (Tetis), in which he declares that, in making the three films that make up what is commonly known as the "Trilogy of Life" (*Trilogia della vita*) — *The Decameron*, *The Canterbury Tales*, and *The*

Arabian Nights—he had used sex as a "liberating force" before realizing, after the fact and to his regret, that he was contributing to consumer society's "false tolerance" of sex as a means to further its venal and despotic ends; there is the unfinished, posthumously published novel *Petrolio*, in which the main character splits, as it were, in two—into Carlo di Polis and Carlo di Tetis—effectively embodying the divide between rational civility and irrational sexuality; and there is sonnet 21 in the posthumously published sequence to Ninetto Davoli (see notes to "One of Many Epilogues," above, and to *The Sonnet Hobby*, below), where the term attains perhaps its fullest meaning as sex male and female, primal yearning, love, and the great formless mass of the sea (Thetis the Nereid), eternal symbol of unconscious drives. It opens with the lines:

> Not love, but thetis, no, no, not sex,
> but thetis, lost in the sea, not cock, thetis,
> not ass, thetis, or maybe extreme
> affection once born of tender foetus
>
> anxious for its mother, thetis, from breast
> to womb, thetis lost in joyful eyes
> and with a thousand forms, social, human, madman,
> madwoman thetis, thetis, over and over
>
> always the same, like the sea . . .

Page 414 "Materiali per l'Introduzione" / "Materials for the Introduction"
From Walter Siti's "Appendix" to *Trasumanar e organizzar*. See previous note regarding the formally unfinished character of the poem.

Line 10: "Caesarea, Cerveteri, or Ceuta." Three ancient cities, respectively in Turkey, Italy, and north Africa, which Pasolini evokes as living specimens of bygone eras that represent a continuity with the distant past that has been otherwise lost in contemporary culture.

Line 11: Like the cities mentioned in the previous note, Spello (Hispellum in antiquity), in the region of Umbria north-northeast of Rome, retains many features of its former glory. In many ways Spello embodies the timeless beauty of old Italy invoked by Pasolini in such earlier poems as "L'Italia" and "L'Appennino" (see p. 152).

Line 17: ". . . the Tallensi Ancestors." The Tallensi are a small tribal people of northern Ghana who practice a form of ancestor worship. Pasolini probably encountered the Tallensi on one or several of his many trips to Africa, and in any case he had read the writings of South African anthropologist Meyer Fortes on the tribe. Walter Siti (II, p. 1571) writes: "One characteristic of their social organization must have particularly struck Pasolini: no individual of the male sex has any juridical independence, and does not become ritually adult, until his own father dies."

Line 41: Ürgüp is a town in the area of Cappadocia known for its ancient cave dwellings and lunar landscapes, some of which served as settings in Pasolini's film *Medea*.

Page 420 "Altri materiali" / "Other Materials"
From W. Siti's "Appendix" to *Trasumanar e organizzar.*
Line 36: ". . . loaded with wakan." To a variety of American Indian groups, *wakan* means, roughly speaking, "spiritual or holy power or energy," and metaphysically transcends man's temporal and bodily existence. To the Lakota people, Wakan Tanka is "the Great Spirit." For the Maya, *wakan* means "heart of the sky."

Line 37: "mana." In Oceanic cultures, *mana*, somewhat like *wakan* (see previous note), refers to a transcendent spiritual force in animate beings and inanimate objects alike, though its signification varies according to the specific culture. In Polynesian cultures, and specifically in Hawaiian, *mana* has a rather broad meaning, encompassing at once religion and social authority. To the Melanesians, its sense comes closer to what the rational Western mind would consider a superstitious sense of luck. Its modern use as an anthropological term originates with the seminal study by Robert Henry Codrington (1830–1922), *The Melanesians* (1891). Pasolini's sense of the term appears filtered through his readings of Claude Lévi-Strauss, who discussed the concept in detail in his *Introduction à l'oeuvre de Marcel Mauss* (1950).

Line 39: "leaving pieces of my body (goat?) at the different tabernacles." This image is reminiscent of two different scenes in Pasolini's film *Medea*. In the first, a boy in Medea's native, barbaric Colchis is sacrificed, his body scattered in propitiation to the gods for a ripe harvest; in the second, Medea scatters the body of her brother, whom she has just murdered, along the road of her escape with the Argonauts, to confound her former subjects who are pursuing her. Pasolini's parenthetical invocation of the "goat" refers to the replacement of human sacrifice (here a Christic *self*-sacrifice) with animal sacrifice in primordial human society.

Line 46: "such as I knew him in Bologna in '22." That is, at the time of his (Pasolini's) birth. Pasolini was born in Bologna in 1922.

Line 48: "otiosus." Literally, "lazy." Siti (II, p. 1585) writes: "For historians of ancient religions, the *deus otiosus* is a god that has lost his prerogatives and been replaced by more recent gods." Pasolini's source was probably Mircea Eliade. Here the poet invokes his own father (lines 46–50) as the *deus otiosus*, even while conflating him with a suggestion of God the Father.

Line 49: The word "lingam" has a variety of meanings in Sanskrit — most fundamentally, "divine symbol," which includes the Shiva Lingam, a stylized stone phallus representing the Hindu God Shiva, and, most simply, "phallus." Pasolini here intends it in the latter sense, using it to refer to his father's penis, which he mythifies through his word choice.

Page 424 "Il giardino dei pesci" / "The Garden of Fish"
Line 1: Caedmon is the earliest known Anglo-Saxon poet. Believed to have died between 670 and 680 AD, he was later canonized. The only source of original information on him is the Venerable Bede's *Historia Ecclesiastica gentis Anglorum*, or *The Ecclesiastical History of the English People*, completed in the first half of the eighth century. As Bede tells it, Caedmon, a layman for much of his life, could not write or sing songs until the night he became divinely inspired by the Christian God and,

while dreaming, wrote the hymn by which he is known. With its central reference to Caedmon, Pasolini's poem seems to question, a posteriori, some of the religious motives inspiring his own initial urge to write poetry.

See the opening comment to this section (page 473) for a possible echo of Dante and, by extension Ovid et alia, in the imagery of this poem.

VIII. *Last Poems*

Page 430 "L'hobby del sonetto" / "The Sonnet Hobby"
This cycle of 112 sonnets, some unfinished, was written from 1971 to 1973 and not published until after Pasolini's death. Though a few of the poems were published in the 1993 "complete poems" edition entitled *Bestemmia* (W. Siti and G. Chiarcossi, eds., [Milan: Garzanti]), and Enzo Siciliano cited sonnet no. 105 in his 1978 biography *Vita di Pasolini*, the cycle was not printed in its entirety until the publication in 2003 of *Tutte le poesie* (Walter Siti, ed.) in the Mondadori Meridiani series.

Firmly situated in the tradition of sonnets addressed to a beloved who is either unaware of or unresponsive to the poet's love — an ancient lineage that begins with Dante and Petrarch and passes through Spenser, Sidney, and of course Shakespeare — the poems are addressed to Ninetto Davoli, Pasolini's young lover, soul mate, and fellow traveler, who in 1971 fell in love with a girl and decided to marry her (for other poems to Davoli, see "One of Many Epilogues" and "The Whores' Road"). While provoking a profound crisis in Pasolini, the break with Ninetto did not in any way sap his inspiration. The sonnet cycle is yet another element in the surprising creative output of Pasolini's last four years of life.

Sonnet [105]: Enzo Siciliano (in *Vita di Pasolini*) and René de Ceccaty (in *Pasolini*) both point out that this poem evokes circumstances similar to those of Pasolini's last night.

Page 436 "Castalia"
This poem is from those collected by Walter Siti (in *Tutte le poesie*) under the rubric of "Versi 1972–1974," which features work written too long after the texts in Siti's "Appendix" to *Trasumanar e organizzar* to be included among them, and not figuring among the new poems included in *La Nuova gioventù*. Siti (II, p. 1769), situates the writing of the poem around late 1973 or early 1974. The poem is the transcription of a dream. The title "Castalia" refers to the spring near the oracle at Delphi at the foot of Mount Parnassus. According to the myth, the font was formed when Apollo transformed the nymph Castalia. The god consecrated the spring to the Muses, and it was believed that one could draw poetic inspiration by drinking its waters or listening to its placid sound.

Line 10: "Graziella" is Pasolini's cousin, Graziella Chiarcossi, who lived with the poet and his mother in Rome during the last several years of his life.

Page 440 "Saluto e augurio" / "Goodbye and Best Wishes"
This is the last poem in the last book published in Pasolini's lifetime, *La Nuova gioventù* (1975), which includes both the reprinting and rewriting of the first phase

of his Friulian work. The poem is from the only section of that book featuring new work, both in Italian and Friulian: a series entitled "Tetro entusiasmo," or "Dark Enthusiasm" (on *La Nuova gioventù*, see the introduction to this volume, pp. 52–53).

Stanza 4, line 4: ". . . tall and gray, like an *Alpino*." The Alpini are a branch of the infantry of the Italian army, specialized in mountain combat. Their uniforms are gray.

Stanza 5, line 1: Phaedrus is Socrates's interlocutor in a number of Platonic dialogues, particularly the *Phaedrus*, in which they discuss love and rhetoric, among other subjects. The most immediate referent for Pasolini's calling his interlocutor Phaedrus in this context is a line in another of the poems of "Tetro entusiasmo," entitled "Versi sottili come righe di pioggia" ("Lines as thin as streaks of rain"), in which he refers to himself as a "wretched, impotent Socrates." But more generally the reference alludes to Pasolini's pedagogical vocation, which, as we see in a number of other poems, he brought to bear even upon his relationships with young hustlers on the street.

Stanza 19, line 2: "the King, the divine Right." The original text says, of course, "Destra divina"—referring, that is, to the political "right" as opposed to the "left," and not to the doctrine of political absolutism known as the "divine right of kings." It is not entirely clear, however, that Pasolini isn't making a veiled English pun here, since part of the poem draws inspiration from Ezra Pound (see below).

Stanza 22, line 1: "*Hic desinit cantus*." In Latin, "Here ends the song"—an echo of Pound's "Hic Explicit Cantus" ("Here unfolds the canto") at the end of canto XXXI. A number of elements in "Saluto e augurio," especially the ending, are reworkings of Fragment IV—itself a reworking of a number of the themes from Pound's *Cantos*—of Pasolini's play *Bestia da stile*. See Pasolini, *Teatro*, W. Siti and S. de Laude, eds. (Milan: Mondadori "Meridiani," 2001), pp. 849–53; and especially Walter Siti's comments in "Note e notizie sui testi" in the same volume, where he lists in detail the borrowings in Fragment IV from Pound, pp. 1207–9.

SELECTED BIBLIOGRAPHY
AND FILMOGRAPHY

PRINCIPAL WORKS BY PIER PAOLO PASOLINI

Poetry

Bestemmia: Tutte le poesie. Edited by Graziella Chiarcossi and Walter Siti, preface by
   Giovanni Giudici. Milan: Garzanti, 2 vols., 1993.
Il canto popolare. Milan: Edizioni della Meridiana, 1954.
Le ceneri di Gramsci. Milan: Garzanti, 1957. (New edition, with critical introduction
   by Walter Siti, Turin: Einaudi, 1981.)
Dal diario (1945-47). Caltanissetta: Sciascia, 1954. (New edition, with an introduc-
   tion by Leonardo Sciascia and illustrations by G. Mazzullo, 1979.)
Diarii. Casarsa: Pubblicazioni dell'Academiuta, 1945.
Dov'è la mia patria (with thirteen drawings by Giuseppe Zigaina). Casarsa: Edizioni
   dell'Academiuta, 1949.
La meglio gioventù. Florence: Sansoni (Biblioteca di *Paragone*), 1954.
La nuova gioventù: Poesie friulane 1941-1974. Turin: Einaudi, 1975.
I pianti. Casarsa: Pubblicazioni dell'Academiuta, 1946.
Poesia a Casarsa. Bologna: Libreria Antiquaria Mario Landi, 1942.
Poesia in forma di rosa. Milan: Garzanti, 1964.
Poesie. San Vito al Tagliamento: Stamperia Primon, 1945.
Poesie. Edited by Pier Paolo Pasolini. Milan: Garzanti, 1970.
*Le poesie: Le ceneri di Gramsci, La religione del mio tempo, Poesia in forma di rosa,
   Trasumanar e organizzar*. Milan: Garzanti, 1975.
Poesie dimenticate. Edited by L. Ciceri. Udine: Società filologica friulana, 1965.
Poesie scelte. Edited by Nico Naldini and Francesco Zambon. Milan: TEA, 1997.
La religione del mio tempo. Milan: Garzanti, 1961. (New edition, Turin: Einaudi, 1982.)
Roma 1950: Diario. Milan: Scheiwiller, 1960.
Sonetto primaverile (1953). Milan: Scheiwiller, 1960.
Tal còur d'un frut. Tricesimo: Edizioni di Lingua Friulana, 1953.
Trasumanar e organizzar. Milan: Garzanti, 1971.
Tutte le poesie. Edited by Walter Siti. Milan: Mondadori Meridiani, 2 vols., 2003.
L'usignolo della chiesa cattolica. Milan: Longanesi, 1958. (New edition, Turin: Einaudi,
   1976.)

Novels and Short Fiction

Alì dagli occhi azzurri. Milan: Garzanti, 1965.

Amado mio preceduto da *Atti impuri*. Edited by C. D'Angeli. Milan: Garzanti, 1982.

La Divina Mimesis. Turin: Einaudi, 1975. (New edition, with an introduction by Walter Siti, 1993.)

Un paese di temporali e di primule. Edited by Nico Naldini. Parma: Guanda, 1993.

Petrolio. Edited by M. Careri and Graziella Chiarcossi. Turin: Einaudi, 1992.

Ragazzi di vita. Milan: Garzanti, 1955. (New edition, Turin: Einaudi, 1979.)

Romàns, seguito da *Un articolo per il "Progresso"* e *Operetta marina*. Edited by Nico Naldini. Parma: Guanda, 1994.

Romanzi e racconti. Edited by Walter Siti and Silvia De Laude. Milan: Mondadori Meridiani, 2 vols., 1998.

Il sogno di una cosa. Milan: Garzanti, 1962.

Storie della città di Dio: Racconti e cronache romane (1950-1966). Edited by Walter Siti. Turin: Einaudi, 1995.

Teorema. Milan: Garzanti, 1968.

Una vita violenta. Milan: Garzanti, 1959. (New edition, Turin: Einaudi, 1979.)

Drama

Affabulazione. With a note by G. Davico Bonino. Turin: Einaudi, 1992.

Affabulazione-Pilade. Presented by Attilio Bertolucci. Milan: Garzanti, 1977.

Calderón. Milan: Garzanti, 1973.

Italie Magique, in *Potentissima Signora*. Songs and dialogues written for Laura Betti. Milan: Longanesi, 1965.

Porcile, Orgia, Bestia da stile. With a note by Arturo Roncaglia. Milan: Garzanti, 1979.

Teatro. Edited by Walter Siti and Silvia De Laude. Milan: Mondadori, 2001.

Teatro (Calderón, Affabulazione, Pilade, Porcile, Orgia, Bestia da stile). Preface by G. Davico Bonino. Milan: Garzanti, 1988.

I Turcs tal Friul (I Turchi in Friuli). Edited by Luigi Ciceri. Udine: Forum Julii, 1976. (New edition edited by A. Noferi Ciceri, Udine: Società filologica friuliana, 1995.)

Essays

Descrizioni di descrizioni. Edited by Graziella Chiarcossi. Turin: Einaudi, 1979. (New edition with a preface by G. Dossena, Milan: Garzanti, 1996.)

Empirismo eretico. Milan: Garzanti, 1972.

I film degli altri. Edited by Tullio Kezich. Parma: Guanda, 1996.

Lettere luterane. Turin: Einaudi, 1976.

Passione e ideologia (1948-1958). Milan: Garzanti, 1960. (New edition with an introduction by Cesare Segre, Turin: Einaudi, 1985. New edition with a preface by Alberto Asor Rosa, Milan: Garzanti, 1994.)

Il Portico della Morte. Edited by Cesare Segre. Milan: Garzanti, 1988.

Saggi sulla letteratura e sull'arte. Edited by Walter Siti and Silvia De Laude, 2 vols. Milan: Mondadori, 1999.

Saggi sulla politica e sulla società. Edited by Walter Siti and Silvia De Laude, 2 vols. Milan: Mondadori, 1999.

Scritti corsari. Milan: Garzanti, 1975. (New edition with a preface by Alfonso Bernardinelli, 1990.)

Interviews

Duflot, Jean. *Entretiens avec Pier Paolo Pasolini* (1969). Paris: Belfond, 1970. Second edition, expanded, *P. P. Pasolini, les dernières paroles d'un impie* (1969–1975). Edited by Jean Duflot. Paris: Belfond, 1981.

Gulinucci, M., ed. *Interviste corsare sulla politica e sulla vita 1955–1975*. Rome: Liberal Atlantide Editorial, 1995.

Magrelli, E., ed. *Con Pier Paolo Pasolini*. ("Quaderni di film critica.") Rome: Bulzoni, 1977.

Stack, Oswald. *Pasolini on Pasolini* (1968). London: Thames and Hudson, 1969.

Correspondence

Lettere 1940–1954. With a chronology of the life and works. Edited by Nico Naldini. Turin: Einaudi, 1986.

Lettere 1955–1975. Edited by Nico Naldini. Turin: Einaudi, 1988.

Pier Paolo Pasolini, Vita attraverso le lettere. Edited by Nico Naldini, with an appendix of unpublished letters. Turin: Einaudi, 1994.

Correspondence with Readers

Le belle bandiere: Dialoghi 1960–65. Edited by GianCarlo Ferretti. Rome: Editori Riuniti, 1977.

Il Caos. Edited by GianCarlo Ferretti. Rome: Editori Riuniti, 1979.

I dialoghi. Edited by G. Falaschi, with a preface by GianCarlo Ferretti. Rome: Editori Riuniti, 1992.

CRITICAL STUDIES AND BIOGRAPHIES OF PASOLINI

Allen, Barbara. *Pier Paolo Pasolini: The Poetics of Heresy*. Saratoga, CA: Anma Libri, 1982.

Annovi, Gian Maria, ed. *Fratello selvaggio: Pier Paolo Pasolini tra gioventù e nuova gioventù*. Massa: Transeuropa, 2013.

Baranski, Zygmunt G., ed. *Pasolini Old and New*. Dublin: Four Courts Press, 1999.

Bazzocchi, Marco Antonio. *I burattini filosofi: Pasolini dalla letteratura al cinema*. Milan: Bruno Mondadori, 2007.

———. *Pier Paolo Pasolini*. Milan: Bruno Mondadori, 1998.

Bellezza, Dario. *Morte di Pasolini*. Milan: Mondadori, 1981.

———. *Il poeta assassinato: Una riflessione, un'ipotesi, una sfida sulla morte di Pier Paolo Pasolini.* Venice: Marsilio, 1996.

Berardinelli, Alfonso. *La poesia verso la prosa: Controversie sulla lirica moderna.* Turin: Bollati Berlinghieri, 1994.

Betti, Laura, ed. *Pasolini: Cronaca giudiziaria, persecuzione, morte.* Milan: Garzanti, 1977.

Borgello, Giampaolo. *Il simbolo e la passione: Aspetti della linea Pascoli-Pasolini.* Milan: Mursia, 1986.

Brevini, Franco. *Per conoscere Pasolini.* Milan: Mondadori, 1981.

Brugnolo, Furio. "Il sogno di una forma." Essay in Pier Paolo Pasolini, *La nuova gioventù: Poesie friulane 1941–1974.* Turin: Einaudi, 2002.

Cadel, Francesca. *La lingua dei desideri: Il dialetto secondo Pier Paolo Pasolini.* Lecce: Manni, 2002.

Camporeale, Cosimo. *Pier Paolo Pasolini: Testimone problematico del nostro tempo; il poeta, il narratore, il regista, il giornalista.* Bari: Ladisa, 1994.

Carotenuto, Aldo. *L'autunno della coscienza: Ricerche psicologiche su Pier Paolo Pasolini.* Turin: Boringhieri, 1985.

Casi, Stefano. *Desiderio di Pasolini: Omosessualità, arte, e impegno intellettuale.* Turin: Sonda, 1990.

Conti Calabrese, Giuseppe. *Pasolini e il sacro.* Milan: Jaca Book, 1994.

Contini, Gianfranco, *Schedario di scrittori italiani moderni e contemporanei.* With the essay "Pasolini Pier Paolo." Florence: Sansoni, 1978.

———. *Ultimi esercizi ed elzeviri.* With the essay "Testimonianza per Pier Paolo Pasolini." Turin: Einaudi, 1989.

De Ceccatty, René. *Pasolini.* Paris: Gallimard, 2005.

———. *Sur Pier Paolo Pasolini.* Monaco: Editions du Rocher, 2005.

D'Elia, Gianni. *L'eresia di Pasolini.* Milan: Effigie, 2005.

———. *Il Petrolio delle Stragi.* Milan: Effigie, 2006.

———. "Verso la poesia incivile." Preface to Pier Paolo Pasolini, *La religione del mio tempo.* Milan: Garzanti, 2001.

De Santi, Gualtiero, Maria Lenti, and Roberto Rossini, eds. *Perché Pasolini.* Florence: Guaraldi, 1978.

Di Meo, Philippe, postface to *Pier Paolo Pasolini, La nouvelle jeunesse: Poèmes Frioulans. 1941–1974,* translated by Philippe di Meo. Paris: Gallimard, 2003.

Duflot, Jean. *Pasolini.* Paris: Editions Albatros, 1977.

Ferretti, GianCarlo. *La letteratura del rifiuto e altri scritti sulla crisi e sulla trasformazione dei ruoli intellettuali.* See chapters "La 'disperata vitalità' di Pasolini" and "Pasolini e l'autopunizione borghese." Milan: Mursia, 1981.

———. *Pasolini, l'universo orrendo.* Rome: Editori Riuniti, 1976.

Fortini, Franco. *Attraverso Pasolini.* Turin: Einaudi, 1993.

Gardair, Jean-Michel. *Narciso e il suo doppio: Saggio su "La nuova gioventù" di Pasolini.* Rome: Bulzoni, 1996.

Giordana, Marco Tullio. *Pasolini: Un delitto italiano.* Milan: Mondadori, 1994. (New edition, Milan: Piccola Biblioteca Oscar, Mondadori, 2005.)

Golino, Enzo. *Pasolini, il sogno di una cosa: Pedagogia, eros, letteratura dal mito del popolo alla società di massa.* Bologna: Il Mulino, 1985. (New edition, Milan: Bompiani, 1992.)

———. *Tra lucciole e palazzo: Il mito Pasolini dentro la realtà*. Palermo: Sellerio, 1995.

Gordon, Robert S. C. *Pasolini: Forms of Subjectivity*. Oxford: Clarendon Press, 1996.

Greene, Naomi. *Pier Paolo Pasolini: Cinema as Heresy*. Princeton, NJ: Princeton University Press, 1990.

Jori, Giacomo. *Pasolini*. Turin: Einaudi, 2001.

Joubert-Laurencin, Hervé. *Le dernier poète expressioniste: Ecrits sur Pasolini*. Besançon: Les Solitaires Intempestifs, 2005.

———. *Pasolini: Portrait du poète en cinéaste*. Paris: Editions de l'étoile-Cahiers du Cinéma, 1995.

La Porta, Stefano. *Pasolini: Uno gnostico innamorato della realtà*. Florence: Le Lettere, 2002.

Levergeois, Bertrand. *Pasolini: L'alphabet du refus*. Paris: Editions du Félin, 2005.

Maggi, Armando. *The Resurrection of the Body: Pier Paolo Pasolini from Saint Paul to Sade*. Chicago: University of Chicago Press, 2009.

Martellini, Luigi. *Introduzione a Pier Paolo Pasolini*. Rome: Laterza, 1989.

———. *Pier Paolo Pasolini: Introduzione e guida allo studio dell'opera pasoliniana: Storia e antologia della critica*. Florence: Le Monnier, 1983.

———. *Ritratto di Pasolini*. Rome: Laterza, 2006.

Mengaldo, Pier Vincenzo. *Profili di critici del Novecento*. Turin: Bollati Boringhieri, 1998.

Miconi, Andrea. *Pier Paolo Pasolini: La poesia, il corpo, il linguaggio*. Genoa: Costa & Nolan, 1998.

Naldini, Nico. *Breve vita di Pasolini*. Parma: Guanda, 2009.

———. *Come non si difende dai ricordi*. Rome: Cargo, 2005.

———. *Mio cugino Pasolini*. Milano: Bietti, 2000.

———. *Nei campi del Friuli (La giovinezza di Pasolini)*. Milan: Scheiwiller, 1984.

———. *Pasolini, una vita*. Turin: Einaudi, 1989.

Panzeri, Fulvio. *Guida alla lettura di Pasolini*. Milan: Mondadori, 1988.

Peterson, Thomas E. *The Paraphrase of an Imaginary Dialogue: The Poetics and Poetry of Pier Paolo Pasolini*. New York: P. Lang, 1994.

Rohdie, Sam. *The Passion of Pier Paolo Pasolini*. Bloomington: Indiana University Press, 1996.

Rumble, Patrick, and Bart Testa, eds. *Pier Paolo Pasolini: Contemporary Perspectives*. Toronto: University of Toronto Press, 1994.

Santato, Guido, ed. *Pier Paolo Pasolini: L'opera e il suo tempo*. Padua: Cleup, 1983. This book contains, among other things, the important essay by F. Brugnolo, "La metrica delle poesie friulane di Pasolini," which was published in revised and updated form under the title of "Il sogno di una forma" in the 2002 Einaudi edition of Pasolini's *La nuova gioventù*.

Schwartz, Barth David. *Pasolini Requiem*. New York: Pantheon, 1992.

Siciliano, Enzo. *Autobiografia letteraria*. Milan: Garzanti, 1970.

———. *Campo de' Fiori*. Milan: Rizzoli, 1993.

———. *Vita di Pasolini*. Milan: Mondadori, 2005. (First edition, Milan: Rizzoli, 1978.)

Snyder, Stephen. *Pier Paolo Pasolini*. Boston: Twayne, 1980.

Spagnoletti, Giacinto. *L'"impura" giovinezza di Pasolini*. Caltanisetta: Sciascia, 1998.

Stack, Oswald, and Pier Paolo Pasolini. *Pasolini on Pasolini: Interviews with Oswald Stack*. Bloomington: Indiana University Press, 1969.

Titone, Maria Sabrina. *Cantiche del novecento: Dante nell'opera di Luzi e Pasolini*. Florence: L. S. Olschki, 2001.

Tricomi, Antonio. *Pasolini: Gesto e maniera*. Soveria Mannelli: Rubbettino, 2005.

———. *Sull'opera mancata di Pasolini*. Rome: Carocci, 2005.

Vannucci, Stefania. *Pier Paolo Pasolini: Il colore della poesia*. Rome: Associazione Fondo Pier Paolo Pasolini, 1985.

Viano, Maurizio. *A Certain Realism: Making Use of Pasolini's Film Theory and Practice*. Berkeley: University of California Press, 1993.

Voza, Pasquale. *Tra continuità e diversità. Pasolini e la critica: Storia e antologia*. Naples: Liguori Editore, 1990.

Ward, David. *A Poetics of Resistance: Narrative and the Writings of Pier Paolo Pasolini*. Madison, NJ: Fairleigh Dickinson University Press, 1995. London: Associated University Presses, 1995.

Zanzotto, Andrea. *Aure e disincanti del Novecento letterario*. Milan: Mondadori, 1994. Contains the essay "Pasolini Poeta."

Zigaina, Giuseppe. *Organizzar il trasumanar: Pier Paolo Pasolini cristiano delle origini o gnostico moderno*, Venice: Marsilio, 2011.

———. *Pasolini e l'abiura: Il segno vivente e il poeta morto*. Venice: Marsilio, 1993.

———. *Pasolini e la morte: Mito, alchimia e semantica nel nulla lucente*, Venice: Marsilio, 1987. (Revised edition, *Pasolini e la morte: Un giallo puramente intellettuale*. Venice: Marsilio, 2005.)

———. *Pasolini tra enigma e profezia*. Venice: Marsilio, 1989.

———. *Tremi e treni di Pier Paolo Pasolini: un giallo puramente intellettuale*, San Polo d'Enza: Edizioni La Scaletta, 2000.

Zingari, Guido. *Il pensiero in fumo. Giordano Bruno e Pasolini: Gli eretici totali*. Genoa: Costa & Nolan, 1999.

FILMOGRAPHY

1961	*Accattone*
1962	*Mamma Roma*
1963	*La ricotta*
	Ostia
	La rabbia
1964	*Comizi d'amore*
	Sopraluoghi in Palestina
	Il Vangelo secondo Matteo
1966	*Uccellacci e uccellini*
1967	*La terra vista dalla luna*
	Edipo re
1968	*Che cosa sono le nuvole*
	Teorema

1969	*La sequenza del fiore di carta*
	Porcile
	Medea
1970	*Appunti per un'orestiade africana*
1971	*Il decamerone*
1972	*I racconti di Canterbury*
1974	*Il fiore delle mille e una notte*
	Le mura di San'a
1975	*Salò o le 120 giornate di Sodoma*

ENGLISH TRANSLATIONS

Poetry

A Desperate Vitality. Translated by Pasquale Verdicchio. La Jolla, CA: Parenthesis Writing Series, 1996.

In Danger: A Pasolini Anthology. Edited by Jack Hirschman. San Francisco: City Lights, 2010.

Pier Paolo Pasolini: Poet of Ashes. Edited by Roberto Chiesi and Andrea Mancini. Corazzano (Pisa): Titivillus, 2007. San Francisco: City Lights, 2007.

Poetry. Translated by Antonio Mazza. Toronto: Exile Editions, 1991.

Roman Poems. Pocket Poets Series, no. 41. Translated by Lawrence Ferlighetti and Francesca Valente. San Francisco: City Lights, 1986.

Selected Poems. Translated by Norman MacAfee and Luciano Martinengo. New York: Random House, 1982. (New edition, New York: Farrar, Straus & Giroux, 1996.)

Fiction

The Divine Mimesis. Translated by Thomas Erling Petersen. Berkeley, CA: Double Dance Press, 1980.

A Dream of Something. Translated by Stuart Hood. London: Quartet Books, 1988.

Petrolio. Translated by Ann Goldstein. New York: Pantheon, 1997.

The Ragazzi. Translated by Emile Capouya. New York: Grove Press, 1968. (New editions, Manchester and New York: Carcanet, 1986. London: Paladin, 1989. New edition, 2007)

Roman Nights and Other Stories. Translated by John Shepley. Marlboro, VT: Marlboro Press, 1986.

Stories from the City of God: Sketches and Chronicles of Rome, 1950–1966. Translated by Marina Harss. New York: Other Press, 2003.

Theorem. Translated by Stuart Hood. London: Quartet Books, 1992.

A Violent Life. Translated by William Weaver. London: Jonathan Cape, 1968. (Subsequent editions in 1973, 1978, 1985, 1992, and 1996. Most recent edition, Manchester: Carcanet, 2007.)

Drama, Essays, and Correspondence

Heretical Empiricism. Translated by Louise K. Barnett. Bloomington: Indiana University Press, 1988. (New edition, Washington: New Academia Publishing, 2005.)

The Letters of Pier Paolo Pasolini, 1940-1954. Edited by Nico Naldini and translated by Stuart Hood. London: Quartet, 1992.

Lutheran Letters. Translated by Stuart Hood. Manchester: Carcanet Press, 1983. Dublin: Raven Arts Press, 1983. (Second edition, New York: Carcanet Press, 1987.)

Manifesto for a New Theater, Followed by Infabulations. Translated by Thomas Simpson. Toronto: Guernica Editions, 2008.

The Massacre Game. Terminal film, text, words. 1974-75. Edited by Stephen Barber, translated by Anna Battista. Forest Hills: Sun Vision Press, 2013.

The Scent of India. Translated by David Clive Price. London: Olive Hill House 1984 (1985).

CREDITS

Italian poems are reprinted from the following editions:

INDEX OF TITLES
AND FIRST LINES